Cities and Society
in Colonial Latin
America

Cities & Society in Colonial Latin America

Edited by

Louisa Schell Hoberman

and

Susan Migden Socolow

Albuquerque
UNIVERSITY OF NEW MEXICO PRESS

Library of Congress Cataloging-in-Publication Data
Main entry under title:

Cities & society in colonial Latin America.

Includes bibliographies and index.
1. Social classes—Latin America—History—Addresses,
essays, lectures. 2. Elites—Latin America—History,
Addresses, essays, lectures. 3. Latin America—Economic
conditions—Addresses, essays, lectures. 3. Latin
America—Economic conditions—Addresses, essays,
lectures. 4. Cities and towns—Latin America—
Addresses, essays, lectures. 5. Spain—Colonies—
History—Addresses, essays, lectures. I. Hoberman,
Louisa Schell, 1942–   .II. Socolow, Susan Migden,
1941–   .III. Title: Cities and society in colonial
Latin America.
HN110.5.C58   1986   306'.098   85-20855
ISBN 0-8263-0844-9
ISBN 0-8263-0845-7 (pbk.)

FOR
John and Stevie Hoberman
Daniel, Ari, and Joshua Socolow

Contents

viii / Contents

Illustrations

x / Illustrations

Tables

Preface

This book grew out of a conversation the editors had after a thought-provoking session on Latin American social history at the American Historical Association meeting of 1979. The panel led us to consider, on the one hand, the invigorating effect of the new social history on the more traditional field of urban history and, on the other hand, the unfortunate fact that research on either subject was not easily accessible to students, since it usually appeared in monographs or scholarly articles too detailed for undergraduate course assignments. The time seemed ripe for a volume designed for undergraduates and graduates that would introduce them to urban and social history and provide sufficient information to be assigned as a text in college level courses.

We asked each contributor for an original essay combining the results of primary research with a survey of secondary literature on the topic. Consequently, each chapter is written specifically for the volume with the needs of its audience in mind. Many of the chapters have chronological subdivisions, allowing the instructor to select sections appropriate to the organization of the course. All essays in the book address common themes, but since we wanted students to appreciate the diverse approaches and styles historians can adopt, we have retained the emphasis and style of each author.

We would like to thank the contributors for their promptness, cooperation, and enthusiastic interest in the volume thoughout the stages of its preparation. They made the editing process a far less tedious task than we were assured it would be. One of the interesting aspects of the project has been a continuing dialogue with the contributors and, indirectly, with other scholars whom the contributors consulted about their essays. We also wish to express our appreciation to Mary Karasch, Asunción Lavrin, Catherine Lugar, and Susan Ramírez, for the illustrations which have greatly enriched the volume. The faculty and staff at CLADS, Boston University, and at Emory University provided indispensable assistance. A special acknowledgment of thanks is due our spouses, John Hoberman and Daniel Socolow, for their moral support, keen critical reading of our chapters, and longstanding encouragement of our scholarly pursuits.

Cities and Society
in Colonial Latin
America

ONE

Introduction

SUSAN M. SOCOLOW

The civilization that the Iberian nations implanted in the New World was profoundly urban in character. From the early days of sixteenth-century settlement, through the Baroque grandeur of the seventeenth century, to the more restrained classicism of the eighteenth-century Enlightenment, the Spanish (and, to a lesser degree, the Portuguese) world in the Americas centered on cities. Paradoxically in a civilization built on agrarian and mining economic bases, the city represented the epitome of culture, the preferred arena for social and economic exchange, and the stage for political conflict and accommodation.

From the early days of conquest and colonization through the period of Latin American independence, the cities of Latin America underwent constant changes in number, population, function, and primacy. The first city in colonial Latin America, the ill-fated settlement of Navidad established by Christopher Columbus on his first voyage to the Caribbean, failed, like many other early settlements, because of poor planning, the hostility of the Indians, and natural disasters. But the failure of one settlement or a group of settlements did not daunt the Spaniards, for they could not conceive of civilization, conquest, and colonization outside an urban setting. First in the Caribbean, and then in New Spain, Central America, and Peru, the Spaniards continued to plant their settlements, not necessarily large or populous, but certainly omnipresent. Through the course of the sixteenth century, peaking in the decades of 1530–40 and 1550–60, hundreds of towns and cities were founded in Spanish America. By 1580, there were 225 populated cities within the Spanish domains, a number that grew to 331 by 1630. In addition, by

3

1600, virtually all the major urban centers of Spanish America (and Bahia, Pernambuco and Rio de Janeiro in Portuguese America) had been founded, although not all were necessarily prospering.

Twenty-seven years earlier the Spanish crown had codified previous edicts on town planning and town founding in the *Ordenanzas de Descubrimiento y Población*. These ordinances, which postdate the founding of most colonial cities, distilled the advice that had proved most practical to town founders in the years since the conquest.

In addition to advice concerning the selection of sites ("the spot where the town is founded . . . must be in an elevated place, where healthy conditions, fertile soil, and abundance of land for farming and pasturage, fuel and wood for building, material, fresh water, a native people, comfortable surroundings, supplies, and a main road open to the north wind can be found"), detailed information on the size and location of the central plaza and the setting out of streets was contained in the *Ordenanzas*. The crown also regulated the positioning of the major buildings of the city—viceregal palace, town council hall, customshouse, arsenal, hospitals, and churches, as well as arcades for the sale of merchandise. Sanitation, defense, beauty, and convenience were also important considerations in Spanish town planning. The crown even attempted to legislate rudimentary waste disposal; "the site and building lots for slaughterhouses, fisheries, tanneries, and other things productive of filth shall be so placed that the filth can be easily disposed of." Last, the *Ordenanzas* spelled out the manner in which housing lots were to be distributed to the initial settlers and common lands were to be assigned.

Not all cities founded by the Spanish and Portuguese were successful. Many lesser urban centers were moved to more salubrious locations, while others floundered and eventually were abandoned. The decline of the indigenous population, a demographic disaster that often followed conquest in both city and countryside, affected the fate of many urban centers well into the seventeenth century. But, in general, those cities that survived their first 30 years of existence continued for the entire colonial period. Although the Indian population suffered a dramatic decline in numbers, the white component of urban populations stabilized during the seventeenth century, while the numbers of blacks and people of mixed racial ancestry grew. The result was a slow expansion of urban populations through the seventeenth and into the eighteenth centuries. (See Table 1.1.) Although population figures vary greatly according to sources, it is clear that urban growth accelerated throughout Latin America during the eighteenth century, in part the result of increased immigration from the Iberian peninsula, in part the result of an increase in the slave trade, and perhaps in part the result of improvements in sanitation, food supply, and hygiene. Population growth stimulated both urban and rural production, which led in turn to greater urban growth. Although neither economic development nor demographic growth was limitless, given the technology and medical resources of the age, for much of Latin America the late eighteenth century was a period of marked increase in these two interrelated spheres. There were exceptions, of course, the most notable being the viceregal capital of Lima. Lima lost approximately one-tenth of her population in the disastrous earthquake of 1746, and as a result barely had recouped pre-1746 population totals by the end of the colonial period. Growth rates also differed from city to city and region to region because of economic factors. Potosí, the bustling urban metropolis of the early seventeenth century, suffered a decline in population that mirrored the decrease in the silver production of its fabled mines.

Physically, many of the cities of Spanish America conformed to a grid or chessboard design, with streets intersecting at 90-degree angles, and most blocks either square or rectangular. (See Figure 1.) Another important physical characteristic of many Spanish American cities was the use of plazas around which principal administrative, judicial, and religious buildings were placed. But not every colonial city conformed to this classic model. Indeed, although the grid was the model for a proper city, when local terrain made application of the model difficult, as in mountainous mining cities or along a rugged coast, other town plans were adopted. (See Figure 2.) The Portuguese towns and cities of the sixteenth and early seventeenth centuries seem to be more spontaneous in their organization, and indeed closer to the medieval European model of narrow, twisting lanes and unevenly shaped blocks. (See Figure 3.)

All cities had their local governments—Spanish *cabildos* or Portuguese *senados da câmara*. These municipal councils, composed of one or two magistrates and a group of town councilors (*alcaldes* and *regidores* in the Spanish world; *juizes ordinários* and *vereadores* in the Portuguese colonies), performed a variety of legal, political, fiscal, and administrative duties, including overseeing local taxation, hygiene, civic works, and law enforcement, serving as a court of first instance in local civil and criminal cases, providing adequate supplies of food and water, and licensing artisan guilds. Membership in the town council always conveyed additional prestige to those selected from the local elite, whether the seat in local government was held through election, by purchase of office, or by inheritance. Much debate has centered on the degree of independence which these town councils could exercise. In general, cabildos and senados da câmara in cities far from the seat of a viceroy or high court probably had more leeway in providing local governance. Historians also have argued as to whether the end of purchase of town office, and other eighteenth century reforms introduced by the Bourbon kings in Spanish America, strengthened or weakened the institution. While the town councils were opened to yearly internal elections, they continued to be composed of members of the local elites. The Bourbon reformers, intent upon improving the financial situation of the entire empire, reallocated both fiscal and military power from the cabildo to local intendants. Under the intendants and their delegates, town income (*propios y arbitrios*), and town expenditures came under more careful scrutiny. But the Bourbon reformers also worked to collect those taxes paid to the town council in a more effective manner. Under the aegis of Bourbon intendants and viceroys, urban lighting, sanitation, and police services were improved. By the end of the eighteenth century, most major cities had a corps of *alcaldes de barrio,* public officials charged with keeping the peace, preventing public drunkenness and rowdy conduct, reporting smugglers, and keeping a record of all neighborhood inhabitants. Royal control of the cabildos probably improved as a result of the Bourbon reforms, and so did the financial situation of these bodies.

It was never an Iberian ideal to create cities in which all inhabitants were equal; in fact, institutional and philosophical inequality were basic to the hierarchical nature of colonial Latin American society. A distinction was made between *vecinos* (citizens) and *habitantes* (residents). Only a relatively few city dwellers were vecinos, those property holders, usually of Spanish or Portuguese ancestry, who, after at least four years' residence had been certified by the local town councils to attend emergency council meetings. All others were classified as habitantes, having limited political power and legal status as city dwellers, even though they might belong to other corporations. Inhabitants of towns also were viewed as being either *gente decente* (respectable people, again usually of Iberian ancestry and engaged in honorable professions) or *gente plebea* (the masses or common people). In areas of dense Indian population, there was a clear legal and cultural distinction between the members of Hispanic society *(gente de razón)* and Indians. Both legal condition and social status governed the position of the non-Hispanic in urban society. Legal status was reflected in legislation which detailed disabilities that Indians, blacks, and *castas* (persons of mixed racial ancestry) incurred. All free persons classified as black or belonging to a caste were subject to payment of tribute, and legally barred from holding any public office or joining an artisan guild. While lighter-skinned individuals might overcome these legal impediments, moving into the lesser ranked artisan guilds or holding minor cabildo posts, they were usually successful to the degree that they could "pass" as *españoles* (persons of Spanish birth or ancestry). All racially mixed persons operated under legal disabilities and in the early colony were presumed to be illegitimate. In theory, neither blacks nor *mulatos* (persons of black and white ancestry) were to carry arms, but in times of dire emergency both groups were allowed to serve in specially recruited militia regiments. Black and mulatto slaves were, of course, subject to forced labor, and were under their masters' (and mistresses') control.

Indians, on the other hand, had both legal disabilities and legal benefits. While subject to tribute payments and forced labor exactions *(encomienda, repartimiento,* and *mita)* and prohibited from using firearms or swords, purchasing wine, riding on horseback, or entering into legal contracts, Indians were exempted from paying tithes *(diezmos)* and sales tax *(alcabala).* In the outlying Indian neighborhoods *(barrios)* that surrounded large cities, Indian populations were governed by their own authorities and by Indian cabildos established along the lines of the Spanish prototype, but Spanish administrators always supervised the actions of Indian governments. Because they were considered to be legal minors, Indians also were exempted from the jurisdiction of the Inquisition, and were not subject to military service. Race was also an important social variable, with light-skinned castas enjoying higher social status than mulatos and *zambos* (persons of Indian and black ancestry). In addition, those Spaniards fortunate enough to belong to one of the privileged corporations, primarily the church and the military, enjoyed greater social prestige than other members of their society. Race, corporate membership, occupation, and cultural identification were all important variables in determining an individual's position in urban society.

The colonial Latin Amerian ideology of hierarchy was one with strong roots in the religious and political tradition of the Iberian nations. This characteristic was also, in part, the result of the conquest itself. The military successes of the Spaniards and Portuguese imposed a two-tiered social order instrumentally defined as that of conquerors and conquered. But these categories, rooted in obvious racial and cultural characteristics, were never perfectly inclusive, and within a generation new arrivals from Spain, Portugal, and other parts of Europe sought positions of political and economic power without direct personal claim to the legacy of conquest. In general, European immigrants and local-born persons of Iberian stock (*criollos*) enjoyed positions of greater power and prestige. There were also impoverished Spaniards and Indians with royal titles of nobility. However, the colonial presumption of racial hierarchy was so powerful that any efforts by the monarchies to place Indians and whites on a more equitable legal basis were disastrous failures.

Many commentators on the colonial period have emphasized the corporatist nature of Spanish and Portuguese society and their American offshoots. These authors rightly have pointed out that functionally derived social groups were central elements in these societies. Artisan guilds were prominent among urban corporate bodies, which also included merchants, churchmen, the military, and the emerging liberal professions. All of these groups tended to have limited political and economic autonomy and exercised an important measure of independence in setting and enforcing group standards and norms. Because they were represented by separate corporate bodies, and thus fell under separate legal jurisdictions, groups such as military officers and upper clergymen never developed a common class identity. Hispanic colonial society remained divided into occupational groups without developing an explicitly class-based character.

Nevertheless, colonial urban societies reflected the social stratification that existed in the large metropolises of Europe. Most colonial cities were composed of an elite, a small middle class, and a large lower stratum comprising laborers and the urban poor. The urban elite was primarily Spanish (or Portuguese) and creole, and consisted of the great landowners, the important miners and merchants, the upper-level bureaucrats and clergy, and the titled nobility who lived in great splendor with their families and their extensive retinues in the center of the city. At some undefinable point, the urban elite merged with the upper levels of the small middle class, which was also largely Spanish and creole, but which included a number of Indians, *mestizos* (persons of Indian and white ancestry), mulatos, and other castes. On the whole, the urban middle class was composed of professionals, lower-level bureaucrats, the lower clergy, managers, shopkeepers, textile manufacturers, and master artisans employed in the higher status trades. At times, the wealth of certain individuals within this group approached that of the elite but in general their holdings were much more modest; in many instances their assets were comparable to those held by persons considered lower class. Small-time entrepreneurs, such as "José the Carpenter," "Juan the bricklayer," and "Petra the corn grinder" were among this last group. Although these individuals were employed in lower-class occupations, they were the proprietors of small houses made from adobe or brick, and they had other holdings that placed them on the borderline between the lower and middle classes.

The lower class, by contrast, was composed primarily of poor Indians, blacks, mestizos, mulatos, and other racially mixed persons, as well as a large number of poor Spaniards and creoles. By far the largest segment of the urban population, the lower class was subdivided into its own peculiar hierarchical structure based on occupational status and ethnic classification. Situated at the top of this hierarchy were the small tradesmen and stallkeepers, the master artisans employed in the lower-status trades, and the journeymen artisans employed in the higher status trades. Positioned below this group were the street peddlers, the domestic servants, the unskilled day laborers, and the journeymen artisans employed in the lower status trades. Together, these two groups represented the laboring poor of most colonial cities; however, they did not constitute all the elements of the lower strata. Situated at the bottom of the social hierarchy and closely related to the laboring poor were those persons who were economically dependent or who participated in crimes and other unsavory activities. These individuals included the unemployed, the blind, the infirm, thieves, burglars, prostitutes, beggars, and the vagrants of colonial society.

Despite the disparaging remarks of colonial officials and other influential persons, all these groups were vital parts of urban society. The artisans and other persons employed in industrial enterprises enabled cities such as Mexico City, Puebla, Querétaro, Quito, and Buenos Aires to become relatively important manufacturing centers. The domestic workers and the large number of persons who provided other essential services enabled these cities to fulfill their roles as political, financial, commercial, and/or administrative centers for the Spanish and Portuguese empires. In mining cities such as Potosí, Zacatecas, and Ouro Prêto, miners and those engaged in smelting and refining precious metals were crucial to both the local and the imperial economies. Even the unemployed, the dependent, and the criminal elements of the population were important to colonial society to the degree that they reinforced the status quo by drawing together competing elements of the population into enduring political coalitions dedicated to maintaining public order and preserving the existing social structure.

The urban centers of colonial Latin America were more than points on a map; they were vital arenas for social and economic exchange, movement, and conflict. More than in any other physical location, it was in the city that different racial, occupational, and social groups met, influenced one another, and melded. At one and the same time, the hierarchical social order was affirmed and social mobility occurred. Clerical and civil authority were centered in the city, as were the physical manifestations of power—the sumptuous buildings located on the central plaza. Public processions, with each group in its proper place and wearing clothing that symbolized its role, were an integral feature of urban life which expressed and strengthened this hierarchy. Nevertheless, it was in the city that individuals and groups interacted, sometimes in harmony, sometimes in conflict. The city was the mediating point in Iberian society, the place where local elites—landowners, merchants, bureaucrats—came into contact with artisans, beggars, and vagrants; where Spaniards and Portuguese were confronted by Indians, blacks, and the panorama of mixed races. In the urban setting no one could continue long in isolation.

Glorious colonial buildings and sumptuous churches notwithstanding, the colonial cities, with all their opulence and ostentatious display (for the city was also theater), were not lacking in shabby dwellings, tenements, and other overcrowded, rudimentary housing. The city was the scene of unrelenting competition—competition for economic and political power, for physical resources such as food and housing, for jobs or professional advancement, and ultimately for survival. Although the political model called for social harmony and stability, rivalry and flux, as well as either tacit or visible disobedience and crime, were also the urban norm. Competition occurred both between and within social groups, as individuals and the corporations that represented them pressed for regional, factional, and group interests. The most notorious and acrimonious social division, that between the native-born elite and the Iberian newcomers, reverberated from Mexico City, Lima, and Bahia, the principal cities of the empires, to lesser centers throughout the colony, and echoed through both secular and clerical life. Toward the middle of the eighteenth century, visitors to New Granada, perhaps with a slight degree of exaggeration, described the situation thus:

> Cities and towns have become theaters of disunion and continuous bickering between Spaniards and creoles, which has given rise to repeated disturbances. Factional hatred increases constantly, and both sides never miss the opportunity to take vengeance or to manifest the rancor and antagonism which has taken hold of their souls.[1]

Social and economic competition went still further, as Spaniards from the Basque regions battled their countrymen from Asturias, and slaves from Upper Guinea united against those from Mozambique.

This competition, which overflowed periodically into verbal abuse and even physical confrontation, took place in urban settings which in theory were to constitute a well-ordered, well-regulated, and integral society. But while mobility and violence in the city challenged the traditional order, this challenge usually was only partial, and was effectively curtailed most of the time.

More than arenas for public and private passions, more than the physical manifestations of civilization and a civilizing society, the colonial cities of Latin America were also the administrative centers of the empire. It was through the city, and the imperial bureaucracy located there, that governance moved from the king and his councilors to the people of his colonial empire. It was in the colonial city that justice was represented, tax collection coordinated, and the royal administration housed. The city was also the seat of the cabildo, which, in addition to its functions of providing municipal justice, governing the marketplaces, and providing police, lighting, and sanitation services, also represented the most important vested interests within the urban setting.

The cities of colonial Latin America also served a vital economic function within their respective areas as producers of goods, consumers of foodstuffs and luxuries, and transit points for the movement of precious metals, goods, and specie from America to Europe. While the great cities of the continent— Mexico City, Lima, and later Buenos Aires—combined administrative, religious, commercial, industrial, and service activities, some cities, because of their location and the nature of local production, came to specialize in one activity or another. Among the types of cities found in colonial Latin America were mining centers such as Zacatecas and Potosí, agricultural centers such as Guadalajara, plantation centers such as Bahia, commercial coastal ports such as Veracruz and Portobelo, manufacturing centers such as Quito and Puebla, military centers such as Cartagena, Havana and Rio, and frontier cities such as Concepción (see Figure 5) and seventeenth century Buenos Aires. But these cities were not dedicated exclusively to one type of activity, although people engaged in this activity tended to dominate the local social, political, and economic scene. Several colonial mining centers soon developed secondary-level administrative and regional commercial functions, as did important agricultural centers. Furthermore, a city's primary function was not necessarily static: internal and external pressures could and did affect the status and role of colonial cities. Buenos Aires, for example, moved from a frontier outpost to a commercial entrêpot and the seat of viceregal administration during the course of the eighteenth century. (See Figure 6.)

Cities were also the commercial and financial centers of colonial Latin America. Regardless of the nature of agricultural or mineral production in the hinterland, it was the city that supplied much of the capital financing that production. Often the urban church served as the primary lending institution, but urban-based merchants, bureaucrats, miners, and large landowners, also provided funds. The credit systems of the colony, lines which ultimately connected the European markets with the agricultural hinterlands, all ran through important cities, the residence of the chief wholesale import-export merchants. It was in the cities that the major institutional representatives of commerce, the *consulado* (merchant guild) and at times the cabildo, were located. Additionally, urban inhabitants often supplied the major consumers' market for goods introduced from other areas.

The production of foodstuffs for the urban population spurred agrarian production in areas adjacent to the cities. Urban consumers also utilized foods produced at relatively greater distances. Mexico City, for example, drew on the Bajío for maize and wheat, imported meat from the northern cattle ranges, and also consumed cacao from Central and South America. Trade in a variety of foodstuffs, European goods, and precious metals linked cities together over hundreds of miles. Córdoba, Salta, Tucumán, and Santiago del Estero, as well as the more distant port of Buenos Aires, were part of a network that joined in Potosí. Buenos Aires also was tied via Mendoza to another market at Santiago de Chile, and via Santa Fé to Asunción. During the eighteenth century, goods shipped from these interior cities for consumption in Buenos Aires included *yerba maté* (Paraguayan tea) from Asunción, wine and dates from Mendoza, *aguardiente* (brandy) and raisins from San Juan, cloth from Cochabamba, *ponchos* (cloaks) from Córdoba, and sugar, cacao, and almonds from Santiago de Chile. The more important colonial cities—Lima, Mexico City, Buenos Aires, Quito, Bahia, and Rio, among others—were hubs for several commercial routes, while lesser cities formed part of only one or two trading circuits. But more than trade flowed into the city. The major cities of colonial Latin America also were magnets for immigrants from Europe and for a growing number of migrants from the interior who settled on the outskirts of urban nuclei.

Cities were synonymous with civilization and culture, and the urban centers of Latin America also served as the foci of colonial intellectual and artistic activity. Architectural styles were developed in the city and radiated out to the towns and the countryside. In the nunneries and monasteries of colonial cities, in the colleges and universities, and in the tribunals, men and women wrote treatises on theology, philosophy, and the nature of government and society, as well as poetry and prose. But intellectual life did not exist exclusively within these institutional domains. *Tertulias,* those typically Iberian meetings of friends to discuss both intellectual developments and local gossip, flourished among the urban elite, and served as an effective way to disseminate information before the late eighteenth-century advent of the newspaper.

The Age of Enlightenment in Latin America also would see the institution of more formal, regular meetings of like-minded community leaders gathered together in economic societies dedicated to discussing practical innovation and reform. Urban intellectual life ran the gamut from the theoretical to the practical, from discussions on the nature of man and society to classes in surgery and medicine.

In addition to serving as the intellectual heartlands of the colonies, the cities were also the providers of social welfare to the most needy segments of the population. Hospitals, orphanages, shelters for unprotected women, and schools were all urban-based institutions, operating under the supervision of the church. Reports of endemic poverty and of bands of beggars and ruffians, ill-fed and ill-housed, demonstrate clearly that colonial charity never came close to meeting the needs of colonial society. Nonetheless, the cities far outstripped the countryside in organized provision for such services.

Both urban and rural societies still existed perilously close to the margins of subsistence. Famine and epidemic disease periodically menaced society, although the colonial town councils attempted to assure adequate grain supplies and rudimentary sanitation. At least some of the rebellions that threatened colonial authorities can be traced to food shortages, especially those caused by poor grain harvests. But more than poor harvests threatened urban stability, for the cities of colonial Latin America were often unruly places where Indians, slaves, free blacks, mulatos, mestizos, and poor whites drank in local *pulperias,* or taverns, caroused in civil and religious processions, and generally threatened to get out of control.

The creation of a network of primary and secondary cities was a far more important phenomenon in Spanish America than in the Portuguese colony. This was in part a reflection of the more diversified and complex economy of the Spanish colonies, and in part a reflection of their stronger administrative organization. Cities in Portuguese America tended to be smaller and more dominated by plantation owners, although they too served important religious, administrative, and economic functions. But the primacy of the city in the colonial Spanish American landscape should not obscure either the variety of cities or the diversity of relationships between urban centers throughout Latin America. In certain landscapes one city was clearly dominant, while in other areas two or more smaller centers were of parallel importance.

Cities such as Puebla, Quito, and the viceregal capitals clearly dominated their environs, serving as centers of both agricultural and industrial production as well as carrying out vital commercial, administrative, and religious functions. In New Spain Córdoba (an agricultural center) and Orizaba (a manufacturing city), or in Brazil Olinda (an administrative center) and Recife (a seaport), are examples of cities that developed in tandem. Still other areas, such as the Mexican Bajío (containing Guanajuato, a mining center; Querétaro, a religious and commercial center; and Zamora and Valladolid, religious and educational centers) and colonial Bolivia—northwestern Argentina, featured a diversity of interconnected and economically complementary cities.

The approximately 300 years of the colonial period were far from a static time. Both externally, in their physical layout, and internally, in their social composition, the cities of Latin America changed from the sixteenth to the eighteenth century. In general, colonial cities became more complex and more grandiose over time, with public, religious, and private buildings growing ever more elaborate and sumptuous. Those cities which survived also tended to grow, albeit slowly, during this period. Of course, local economic conditions produced some exceptions to the trend.

Physical growth was directly related to economic and social developments. Sixteenth century cities usually reflected the struggle to form an economic base large enough to support urban development. Social distinctions closely reflected the distinctions between the conqueror and the conquered, with preference, both social and economic, going to those Spaniards or Portuguese who had arrived relatively early on the scene. The seventeenth century saw the emergence of a more mature society based more on corporate membership and race, a "traditional" society with powerful urban groups affluent enough to serve as patrons of a growing number of religious establishments and to construct palatial residences. (See Figure 4.)

The eighteenth century produced further change in urban Latin American society. Because of increasingly important strategic considerations, both the Spanish and Portuguese crowns became interested in revitalizing the economies of their American possessions, and both monarchies began to experiment with economic reform. To what extent these reforms responded to preexisting changes, such as gradual population growth, and to what extent the reforms themselves produced these changes is difficult to determine, but in general both the Pombaline reforms in Brazil and the Bourbon reforms in Spanish America increased social and economic mobility, moving the cities of Latin America from corporate-based societies to societies based on both corporate membership and economically determined social class. The reforms themselves combined liberal and conservative strains—increased trade, government sponsorship of new investment, opening of new areas to colonization, revitalization of old institutions. Their effects varied greatly from city to city and region to region, but in general the eighteenth century reforms both restructured urban society and redefined the relative importance of cities and groups of cities in Latin America.

The following essays deal with the major social groups present in the colonial cities of Latin America. While some of these groups are defined by occupation (for example, artisans, merchants, bureaucrats), others reflect both occupation and corporate status (artisans, clergy, military men). The essays attempt to describe the economic, political, demographic, and social characteristics of the groups in question, and to analyze how these groups acted and interacted within the urban milieu. The essays are not tied to a specific city or a specific time period; rather, they represent a synthesis of original archival research, secondary information, and interpretation concerning the groups in question. In examining the behavior of these social groups, some authors have also looked at related issues of interaction within the existing power structure, family composition, and urban spatial patterns. The degree to which the urban environment provided opportunities for social and/or racial mobility is also considered.

Many of the examples and case studies contained in the following essays are from New Spain, Peru, or Brazil. In the case of the first two regions, this is in part a result of the importance of these regions from the sixteenth century on, and in part a reflection of the concern among present-day historians for these core areas. Although fringe areas of the Spanish Empire such as the provinces of Central America, Venezuela, Chile, and Charcas were also able to sustain urban centers, they were never as numerous nor in general as prosperous as those of the core areas. Special attention has also been given to Brazil, not because of the primacy of its cities (indeed like the fringe areas of the Spanish Empire, urban growth in Brazil is to a large extent an eighteenth century phenomenon), but because we believe it is important to include Portuguese America in any discussion of colonial Latin America.

Relatively more space has also been given in this volume to groups usually identified as belonging to the colonial elites. While this concentration reflects the greater power which the elites wielded in Latin America, these groups were always in the numerical minority. Determining the exact proportion of various elite and non-elite occupational groups is a most difficult task for several reasons: a lack of sources for all periods up to the late eighteenth century, the uneven nature of existing census material, and local variations in the status of certain occupations. (Landowning, for example, while clearly an elite occupation in most of colonial Latin America, was a low status occupation in Buenos Aires.) Nevertheless it is important to have at least an approximation of the size of these groups.

Large estate owners, the apex of colonial society, probably never represented more than 1 percent of the economically active urban population. Another group of landowners, those who owned the small plots which were usually found on the outskirts of the city, were most definitely not included in the urban elite. These landowners, along with sharecroppers and farm laborers, formed approximately 3.5 to 8 percent of the urban population. Government bureaucrats accounted for another 2 to 3 percent, but only 1 percent would have been of sufficient rank and salary to be included within the urban elite. Merchants probably accounted for ½ to 3 percent of the population, with lower-status shopkeepers and traders comprising another 3 to 11 percent. The clergy was similarly divided between those with power and status (approximately .4 percent of the population); members of religious orders (approximately 3 to 4 percent); and middle status secular priests (another 3 to 4 percent). The military group varied greatly in size from one time to another, and from place to place. While important military bastions such as Caracas or Buenos Aires might have as many as 17 percent of the population in either the officer corps or the enlisted ranks, cities such as Oaxaca or Minas Gerais had very small numbers of military. Again only officers (approximately .3 percent) could be considered members of the elite. Urban professionals, a middle group consisting of physicians, lawyers, and teachers, probably accounted for no more than 1 percent of the urban dwellers.

Artisans and skilled workers were one of the largest groups in colonial Latin American cities, totaling 20 to 45 percent of the resident population. Unskilled laborers, including slaves, and servants, were another large group accounting for 30 to 40 percent. The urban poor probably totaled 5 to 10 percent, although in times of famine their numbers increased dramatically. These figures are necessarily somewhat vague, and encompass wide variations, but they do suggest that the colonial elite never rose to more than 15 percent of the urban population, while the general populace probably were 85 percent.

Although the essays are organized around the concept of social groups, it is evident that individuals, especially those in the upper class, frequently had overlapping identifications. Thus it was not unusual for a clergyman to be a landowner or a bureaucrat, or for a bureaucrat to be a merchant. The multifaceted nature of these individuals is reflected to some extent within the essays. For example, information on town councilmen is found in both the section on large landowners and the one on merchants, for both of these groups frequently included service in the local government among their multiple occupations. Likewise, although the essay on bureaucrats contains most of the material on important urban leaders, the essays on clergymen and the landed elite also include material on these two groups' participation in local bureaucracy.

Professor Ramírez describes the leading role that estate owners played in urban society. Professor Lugar's essay concentrates on merchants, a more typically urban group, and one that often provided recruits for the local aristocracy. Three other key groups in urban society—the bureaucrats, the military, and the clergy—are treated in essays by Professors Burkholder, Archer, and Ganster, respectively. Women religious and their role in both the economic and the social dimensions of urban life are discussed by Professor Lavrin. These groups all provided the socioeconomic leadership of urban society, and it was from their members that the urban elites and subelites were formed.

Professor Johnson's essay on artisans deals with a group that although essential to the economic life of the city, failed to occupy a position of social importance. Below skilled artisans came the unskilled workers—the purveyors of services considered menial—and the slaves who are studied by Professor Karasch. Clearly at the bottom of the socioeconomic ladder were the urban poor—beggars, petty criminals, and social deviants. This group is the focus of Professor Haslip-Viera's research.

Although the following essays all look at the various socioeconomic groups within the urban context, not all aspects of urban life discussed by one author are strictly comparable with those discussed by others. This is partially the result of the uneven nature of both primary and secondary source material, partially the result of authors' preferences, and partially a reflection of the differing social roles of the groups under consideration. For example, a detailed discussion of the education of the urban elite is of interest and importance, while little space is given to a consideration of the education of the urban poor, since it was nonexistent. In addition, not every group in colonial society has been studied in the following essays. There is little on colonial lawyers, medical doctors, or university professors, not because these small groups lacked importance or influence, but because of space limitations. It should also be remembered that members of these groups were frequently also land-owners, merchants or clergymen.

With the exception of the essay on female religious, women have not been given separate treatment in the chapters that follow, but have been treated as integral members of the social groups in question. This reflects the editors' belief that women did not function in colonial society as independent actors, but rather as members of the socio-occupational group of their birth. The wife of a minister of the *audiencia* (high court) or viceroy and the wife of an artisan or slave, while sharing their female condition, did not see themselves as belonging to the same social world.

Although many of the following essays have drawn upon a wide variety of ecclesiastical, judicial, municipal, imperial, national, and private archival records for information, the dense apparatus of historical footnotes has been omitted in order to make them more approachable to nonspecialists, except where the author has included a direct quotation or quantitative material. Other secondary material is included after each chapter in a section entitled "For Further Readings." We hope that this bibliography, which stresses material available in English, will be of value to students. We suggest that those seeking more specific archival citations consult other articles and books by the contributor in question.

We hope that these articles and the related research cited in the bibliography will provide students and researchers with an appreciation of the richness of colonial Latin American urban settings and the variety of social groups whose collective and individual lives were played out in these environments. We trust that future research will provide further information on the importance of the city and of urban social groups in the new world the Iberians forged.

Notes

1. Jorge Juan and Antonio de Ulloa, *Discourse and Political Reflections on the Kingdoms of Peru* (Norman, Okla.: University of Oklahoma Press, 1978), 217.

For Further Reading

For an interesting review article of colonial urban history see Susan Migden Socolow and Lyman L. Johnson, "Urbanization in Colonial Latin America," *Journal of Urban History* 8:1 (November 1981): 27–59. Another useful essay that goes beyond the colonial period is Richard M. Morse, "Trends and Patterns of Latin American Urbanization, 1750–1930," *Comparative Studies in Society and History* 16:4 (September 1974): 416–47.

Information on the state of urbanization at the beginning of the seventeenth century is contained in Jorge E. Hardoy and Carmen Aranovich, "Escalas y funciones urbanas en América hispánica hacia el año 1600," in Jorge E. Hardoy and Richard P. Schaedel, eds., *El proceso de urbanización en América desde sus orígenes hasta nuestros días* (Buenos Aires: Instituto Torcuato Di Tella, 1969): 171–208. Urban planning is covered in Woodrow Borah, "European

Cultural Influence in the Formation of the First Plan for Urban Centers that has Lasted to Our Time," in Richard P. Schaedel et al., *Urbanización y proceso social en América* (Lima: Instituto de Estudios Peruanos, 1972): 35–54.

Many of the 1573 Ordenanzas are published in Zelia Nuttall's "Royal Ordinances concerning the Laying Out of New Towns," *Hispanic American Historical Review* 4:4 (1921): 743–53; and 5:2 (1922): 249–54.

The changing role of the cabildo in providing effective town governance is studied in John Preston Moore, *The Cabildo in Peru under the Hapsburgs: A Study in the Origins and Powers of the Town Council in the Viceroyalty of Peru, 1530–1700* (Durham, N.C.: Duke University Press, 1954); and *The Cabildo in Peru under the Bourbons: A Study in the Decline and Resurgence of Local Government in the Audiencia of Lima, 1700–1824* (Durham, N.C.: Duke University Press, 1966).

For a more complete discussion of the role of race in Spanish and Portuguese colonial society see Magnus Mörner, *Race Mixture in the History of Latin America* (Boston: Little, Brown and Company, 1967).

Louisa Hoberman, "Hispanic American Political Theory as a Distinct Tradition," *Journal of the History of Ideas* 41:2 (April–June 1980): 199–218, discusses both the political ideal and the urban reality of seventeenth century Mexico City.

The Portuguese city is covered in Stuart B. Schwartz, "Cities of Empire: Mexico and Bahia in the Sixteenth Century," *Journal of Inter–american Studies and World Affairs*, 2 (1969): 616–37; and A. J. R. Russell-Wood, "Local Government in Portuguese America: A Study in Cultural Divergence," *Comparative Studies in Society and History* 6:2 (March 1974): 187–231.

For an interesting discussion on the importance of estate, class, and race in the colonial urban world see John K. Chance and William B. Taylor, "Estate and Class in a Colonial City: Oaxaca in 1792," *Comparative Studies in Society and History* 19:4 (1977): 454–87; Robert McCaa, Stuart B. Schwartz, and Arturo Grubessich, "Race and Class in Colonial Latin America: A Critique," *Comparative Studies in Society and History* 21:3 (July 1979): 421–42; and John K. Chance, "The Colonial Latin American City: Preindustrial or Capitalist?", *Urban Anthropology* 4:3 (1975): 211–28. James Lockhart, *Spanish Peru, 1532–1560: A Colonial Society* (Madison, Wis.: University of Wisconsin Press, 1968) shows a complex urban society developing at the time of the Conquest. Examples of individuals involved in economic, social, political, or religious conflict within urban settings can be found in David Sweet and Gary Nash, eds., *Struggle and Survival in Colonial America* (Berkeley: University of California Press, 1981). Networks of colonial cities are discussed in Alejandra Moreno Toscano, "Tres ejemplos de relación entre ciudades y regiones en Nueva España a finales del siglos XVIII," in Edward E. Calnek et al., *Ensayos sobre el desarrollo urbano de México* (Mexico City: SepSetentas, 1974): 95–130.

TWO

Large Landowners

SUSAN E. RAMÍREZ

Introduction

Conspicuous in many colonial Latin American urban centers, whether large or small, were the owners of large rural estates, *hacendados* in Spanish America and *fazendeiros* in Brazil. These prominent personages, renowned for their power and prestige, played a central role in the political and economic life of the city and controlled nearly all the most productive resources in the regions where their estates were located.

Large landowners, by definition, derived part of their wealth from ranching, agriculture, and rural trade and processing activities, but the city was also a center of profit and activity for them. There the landed elite bought sugar, hides, tallow, coarse cloth, and cacao from their peers; there they contracted with ship captains and muleteers to transport their products to other American and transoceanic markets. There, too, the large landowners who specialized in supplying Mexico City, Lima, Santiago, and Bahia with grains, meat, and other foodstuffs could best monitor price trends and thus decide when to sell. Hacendados and fazendeiros embellished the city by building sumptuous townhouses, which overlooked the central plaza and the more secluded and elegant squares. Their property might well include lucrative rental houses scattered throughout the urban zone. Religious, educational and cultural activities further strengthened large landowners' ties to the urban centers.

Cities were also the foci from which estate owners wielded political power. In many colonial towns and cities they dominated the *cabildos* or *senados da câmara* (town councils), the only institution of government designed to represent the colonists in their relations with metropolitan authorities. Although most council members eventually came to represent a narrow oligarchy—some by as early as the end of the sixteenth century—they did voice the concerns at least of the top echelon of creole society. As members of the municipal councils, large landowners fixed prices of staples, apportioned water, enforced judicial sentences, licensed artisans, collected local taxes, and, in the early days of the colony, granted *estancias* (grazing lands) and *chacras* (agricultural plots) within their vast municipal jurisdictions. Informal political power, exercised by the landed elite through alliances with a variety of groups, complemented and often superseded its formal political power.

The purpose of this chapter is to discuss the rise and endurance of these landowners and their families as an elite during the colonial period. The focus is on the general patterns, ignoring, in essence, region-specific booms and busts that add temporal and geographic variation. Considered here are major economic cycles from which some persons benefited, while others suffered. After the first establishment of the estates, the acquisition of a property by one person often meant the displacement of at least one other person. Despite this flux and social mobility, the group persisted and enhanced its reputation and image over time.

But it should be understood that the large landowning group in the Spanish and Portuguese American domains was not restricted to agricultural pursuits. Because such landowners bridged rural and urban worlds, they were perhaps the most multi-faceted group in colonial society. In many areas, they occupied multiple social roles. The men might be priests, bureaucrats, professionals, miners, and merchants, at the same time that the extent of their rural holdings and influence qualified them for membership in the landowning elite. Women's choices, of course, were more limited, but they might combine religious profession or philanthropy with the ownership of farms and ranches. Whether identity as a large landowner preceded or followed the exercise of other careers depended on the family, the city, and the century.

Furthermore, the collective biographies of the estate owners on which this chapter is based show the degree to which those who lived in colonial capitals differed from those who lived in provincial centers. Mexico City, Lima, and Bahia, capitals of the viceroyalties of New Spain, Peru, and Brazil, respectively, were the urban homes of landed magnates whose estates were formed early in response to urban market demands. These families raised a variety of animals and crops and also often had significant interests in non-agricultural sectors of the economy. Many aspired to, and selectively achieved, noble status. The provincial centers included both major administrative cities of the outlying areas of the empires, such as Caracas in the province of Venezuela and Santiago in the province of Chile, and cities of regional importance, such as Saña and Arequipa in Peru and Querétaro and Oaxaca in New Spain. (See Figure 7.) In those cities the elite tended to develop later and be more homogeneous. The characteristic social types were the cacao planters in Caracas and the cattle ranchers in Santiago. Large landowners tended to have a less diversified economic base and consequently their wealth rarely matched that of the great families in the viceregal seats. The differences between estate owners in the capital cities and those in the provincial centers were not absolute, however, but tended to be one of degree—of wealth, power, and influence—and, in some areas, of timing.

Rise of the Landed Elite

The origins of the landed elite were quite diverse, reflecting the variety within the process of settlement itself. Some were descendents of the colony's first elite, the *encomenderos* (recipients of grants of Indian labor and tribute) in Spanish America and *donatarios* (holders of the first immense land allotments) in Brazil. Others, particularly in outlying regions like Saña, an important provincial town on the north coast of Peru, or Querétaro, a seventeenth century center in New Spain, were settlers who had received smaller land grants from the crown. Or the smallholders might have begun as administrators of large estates and gradually accumulated property of their own. There were also latecomers to the colony who, with viceregal patronage or other powerful connections, quickly became members of the landed elite. Finally, some members of the estate-owning group got their start in other careers, as bureaucrats, professionals, or merchants.

In Spanish America after the booty of conquest an *encomienda* (grant to an encomendero) was the coveted reward of the first few who helped Francisco Pizarro, Hernando Cortés, and the other captains win the New World realms. An encomienda grant initially set the recipient up as a glorified tax collector and judge, with unrivaled, if unofficial, authority to settle disputes and consequently with power over life and property. It gave him unlimited rights to the personal services of the Indians; in fact, their responsibility was to support the encomendero and his family. In exchange, the encomendero had to defend the Indians and provide them with religious instruction. Inherent in the grant was the encomendero's promise to the crown to settle in the district and to keep a horse and weapons ready to defend the newly won territory.

An encomienda was not a grant of fee simple property rights to the land. For the first few decades after the conquest, the encomendero was known primarily as a master of people, not as an owner of land. Agricultural land was not a particularly scarce or valuable commodity. The encomendero actually did not need land because the Indians produced food, textiles, and other tribute items on the land they themselves had been cultivating for years.

The encomienda became the economic base for the encomendero, his family, and the increasing numbers of Spaniards who joined his household as personal retainers. In addition to producing and delivering foodstuffs which the encomendero could sell in the developing urban markets, encomienda Indians were used to build cities. They constructed the encomendero's residence and served as domestics. They cultivated his suburban garden plots and orchards. Once the encomendero's personal needs were met, he used the encomienda to launch complementary economic enterprises. He put the Indians to work, for instance, in building additional houses and stores for sale or lease on lots he received from the town council. The encomendero's near monopoly of native labor also made him the major labor broker for the rest of colonial society. He regularly rented Indians to non-encomenderos for short-term tasks. As the encomendero grew older and closer to death, he supplied Indian labor and, eventually, left sizable amounts of money to build the churches, convents, and monasteries of the colonial cities.

The phase of encomendero dominance was short lived, although the lifestyle and relationships of that period were to be repeated in subsequent contexts. During the course of the first century after the conquest, epidemics in the viceroyalties of New Spain in 1520–21, 1545–48, and 1576–79, and of Peru in the 1520s, 1540s, 1550s, and late 1560s decimated the Indian population, and consequently reduced the tribute-paying labor force and, thus, the value of the encomienda grants. The encomendero group also was threatened and eventually doomed by the Spanish crown's attempts to undermine its influence. The crown had watched the uncontrolled growth of encomendero power, first in Santo Domingo, then in New Spain and Peru. Disturbed by this development and by reports of physical abuse, excessive tribute demands, and continued suffering and high mortality rates among the native population, the crown adopted a policy designed to curb the encomenderos' power and end their exploitation of the Indians. Initially, the plan called for the abolition of the encomienda. But the crown underestimated the reaction of the encomenderos and eventually settled for redefining the relationship between encomendero and community by specifying and limiting Indian obligations.

Given the controls, a growing urban population, and an effective market for agricultural products, far-sighted encomenderos invested in ancillary enterprises—prominent among which were farms and stock ranches. Production was redirected from corn and beans to wheat, wine, and olive oil to satisfy the culinary preferences of European immigrants. In the process, encomenderos and their descendants and successors became the first Spaniards to own large amounts of land, the first hacendados. Not all encomenderos made a successful transition from tribute collectors to agriculturalists or ranchers. These families saw their income diminished, and their children reduced to petitioning the crown for favors or joining the growing number of poor creoles.

Crown policy influenced the formation of the hacendado group in another respect. It encouraged settlement of frontier areas, especially by newcomers who obtained land through grant, purchase, or usurpation. Pioneers were given relatively small tracts (less than 300 acres) by royal representatives to colonize the region, foster agricultural production, and serve as an independent social group which might limit encomendero influence. Unlike the northeast coast of Brazil and the initial sites of Spanish settlement, which assumed an aristocratic flavor from the beginning, outlying provinces saw the more gradual formation of landed elites.

Possessed of little capital, these settlers led a hard existence in the early colonial years. They often had sufficient resources to work only part of their original grant. Some started as employees, *mayordomos,* or administrators in the service of another. Earnings from hard work and a yearly bonus of sheep or goats, while grazing land remained common, allowed such individuals to acquire farm land. Others, who had arrived as merchants and stayed, parlayed relatively small amounts of capital into the funds necessary to acquire rural property. Most continued to raise cattle, sell hides, and trade, while tools, seeds, carts, and additional labor gradually came within their financial reach. In Saña 40 to 60 years passed before settlers had accumulated enough capital, either individually or, more often, in partnership, to buy established sugar estates from the impoverished descendants of encomenderos. Some took even longer to buy slaves and equipment, build mills, and, finally, replace their wheat with cane, in order to go into the more lucrative and certainly more prestigious business of producing sugar. Later, as the ecclesiastical and bureaucratic hierarchies became established, clerical stipends and fees and the salaries and sometimes illicit spoils of high bureaucratic office also were invested in land.

Wheat was susceptible to blight. Entire herds of pigs, sheep, and goats could perish from disease in a single season. Sugar production was subject to sharp price fluctuations caused by changes in supply and demand. The transition, then, from small producer to large could be a difficult one. Profits from the good years had to be reinvested to maintain or increase production. For these reasons, and because few had surplus capital or access to credit, turnover in the ranks of the early farmers and ranchers was great.

Thus, until around the middle of the seventeenth century, the local landed elite in the provinces was still in the process of formation. It was not yet an established and stable class, as the hereditary encomendero group that preceded it had been. In the early colonial period the cumulative process of investment and the modest stake needed to become an hacendado kept the landowning group relatively open to the entry of monied and well-born newcomers.

Despite the relative fluidity of membership in the landed group, hacendados had power to control the affairs of their localities from the start. Being a farmer or rancher in the context of the sixteenth century implied more than a strict interpretation of these terms would suggest. The organization of production on the estates automatically made owners manufacturers of sugar, preserves, wine, soap, fine leather, and other products. In Lima and Saña in Peru, as well as in Puebla and Oaxaca in New Spain, a significant number of the hacendados pursued other occupations. In Saña, by the first half of the seventeenth century, one-fifth of the 179 landowners studied traded or were merchants, with stores or import-export businesses. Nearly 20 percent more were priests—one-half the ecclesiastics in the whole region.[1] Significant numbers were self-employed as notaries, worked for the crown as high-level bureaucrats, or worked for others as mayordomos. In areas of silver and gold production, it was not unusual for miners to own land.

In Brazil and Spanish America broad economic roles made large landowners a central, and in many cases the dominant, force in society. As animal raisers and farmers, they were the major employers of unskilled labor in the region. They hired and fired mayordomos who ran the estates on a day-to-day basis. Activities in other occupations enhanced their pivotal position by bringing them into contact with members of other groups on a daily basis and providing them with additional sources of cash.

In addition, the landed elite assumed the positions of command in the local militia, despite the fact that officers often had to buy a commission and pay their men. In Brazil and Spanish America, large landowners eagerly joined the militia as soon as it was organized because military rank had been an important index of elite membership since the days of the first settlers. More than a means of defense, the militia provided the hacendado or fazendeiro with the opportunity to don uniforms and parade at the head of the columns of men on ceremonial occasions, to the delight and awe of the spectators. The image of the large landowner was enhanced further by his convictions and by the support of the church. The voluntary position of *síndico* (a lay treasurer of an ecclesiastical body), for example, typically was filled by a prosperous landowner. Estate owners vied for the prestigious position of *familiar* (lay representative) of the Inquisition. Several widowers joined the church, taking their growing sons with them to the monasteries to reside. The elite became known for its bequests, the size of which was an index of its wealth and status.

The municipal council provided estate owners with a political forum, participation in which was also a hallmark of landed status. City affairs dominated most of the discussion of council meetings. The business of establishing the city and regulating its life occupied the collective attention of the cabildo during the early years. Members devoted entire meetings to such activities as discussing petitions from newcomers for *vecino* (citizen) status and accepting qualified individuals; planning for urban expansion; founding and running the hospital; and guaranteeing the food supply. Councilmen profited personally from participation by voting themselves additional house lots, garden plots, and allotments of irrigation water. They established prices of staples they produced and fought vagrancy in the hope of increasing the labor supply. Thus, both the encomenderos who participated in the first cabildos of Lima, Santiago and Mexico City and the planters of Recife and Bahia used the municipal councils to appropriate the rural resources and labor necessary for agricultural expansion and to control the urban market for their own benefit.

Over the years, the landed elite also established informal power through close personal relationships with key decision-makers. The extended family became the means through which to influence local events. Trusting relatives participated in business ventures together. Not solely from humanitarian motives did hacendados or fazendeiros help landless but aspiring brothers, cousins, and nephews to acquire positions in the bureaucracy, on the cabildo or senado da câmara, and in the church; such help extended their own radius of informal power. Establishing a chaplaincy to support a son or nephew as a seminary student paid rich dividends later as a source of advance information regarding available mortgage funds as well as a channel of communication with the Indians or blacks of the parishes. Having a cousin who was the lieutenant governor, sheriff, or rural constable guaranteed prompt execution of directives and quick apprehension of runaway slaves.

Because family members often proved an important reserve of influence and resources, and because affinal kinship ties typically were as strong and binding as consanguineal ones, large landowners planned marriages carefully as strategic moves which would enlarge their range of contacts. In addition to joining two individuals, marriage made all the relatives of one spouse relatives of the other. Marriages between such landowning families were frequent. In Saña, for example, Juan Rodrigues Vejete, the owner of the estancias of Pomalca and Calupe, married his daughter to Fernando de Obregón, the owner of the sugar mill of Nuestra Señora de la Candelaria. Juan Martínez Palomino, the owner of a vineyard in Sárrapo, arranged for his daughter Clara to marry Roque de Saldaña, the owner of an adjoining horse ranch. Peninsular-born newcomers, among them merchants and bureaucrats, were prime candidates for the hand of an estate owner's daughter. Diego de Vera, a provincial treasurer of Peru, married the daughter of his partner and eventually acquired sole ownership of the sugar estate of Santiago de Miraflores. In Caracas immigrants like Diego de Ovalle and Pedro de Liendo, men of considerable commercial and overseas experience, married into the propertied elite.

To maintain an amalgamation of interests and to guarantee that landless persons remained willing allies, large landowners sought opportunities to befriend unrelated persons who held positions of authority in their areas. In this respect, the contradictions within the governing system worked to their advantage. Because the salaries of crown officials from the *corregidor* (district governor) down were generally too low to allow them to live in a style commensurate with their aspirations, and because payment of their salaries was sometimes years in arrears, many royal officials, particularly those without opportunities to collect incidental fees with which to defray their daily expenses and those at lower levels of the bureaucratic hierarchy, became dependent on the landed elite for loans, credit, and subsidies. Landowners often extended credit to officials when their salaries were delayed. To the official this represented a special personal favor, but to the landowner it represented a small courtesy that implied relatively little risk or cost. The favors and help that bureaucrats accepted from landowners served to undermine their impartiality.

Large landowners also bonded professionals, such as surgeon-druggists and notaries, guaranteed nonlandowners as guardians, and named them as the executors of their estates. Such consciously-built and assiduously maintained relationships tied the professionals to the lords of the land and extended their influence beyond kinship to link them even to royal judges in the capital cities.

In Spanish America landowners' ties to the Indians usually took other forms. Elite couples became *compadres* (god-parents) to Indian children, thus establishing mutual obligations between themselves and their parents. Growing specialization of the estates, tied to an export economy, also meant an expanding local market for Indian-grown produce, the distribution of which afforded more frequent and personal contact between the two major ethnic groups in the area.

This range of personal contacts, coupled with their positions of leadership, enabled the estate owner to secure additional natural resources and labor, and, in large part, explains property consolidation and concentration. Access to Indian labor, for example, depended on good relations with the corregidor or, in his stead, the *teniente* (lieutenant) and on connections in the capital. Indian labor in many areas was in perennially short supply. The corregidor apportioned such labor to local petitioners after a brief inquiry to find out if it actually was needed and with the condition that each such grant be confirmed by the viceroy. Information forwarded by the corregidor influenced the viceroy's decision on confirmation; hence, there was a need for good relations between the corregidor and the landowners, which helps explain the willingness of the large landowners to post the corregidor's bond.

The landed elite's positions and personal contacts were also helpful in securing additional irrigation water. Where water proved insufficient, landowners often took more than their share. Hacendados might counter Indian protests against this usurpation by threatening to disembowel anyone who disturbed the flow of water to their properties. Such threats of violence became rarer over the years, as hacendados established their power and adopted more subtle means to accomplish the same ends. In Saña the hacendados, through the cabildo, elected the water commissioner until 1638, and even after that contributed to his salary. Understandably, he hesitated to take action against those he knew were cheating, despite the fact that this usurpation caused the Indians farther downstream to suffer.

The hacendados' power, position, and advantage are perhaps most evident in the records concerning land; here, once again, the landowners' formal positions of power on the town council or in the militia were of less importance to their successful acquisition of land than were their key personal contacts. The territorial growth of the estates referred to above was not as simple as an outright purchase of land. In Peru, sales of privately held Indian lands, unlike private sales of property between Spanish subjects, were allowed only with the approval of the royal Indian commissioner and the local corregidor and protector of the Indians. The sale of communal lands, once considered indivisible and inalienable, also was permitted, subject to approval from Lima, to public and prior announcement for 30 days, and to auction, if worth more than 30 pesos. If worth less, the corregidor alone had the authority to allow the sale. The law then placed the corregidor and protector in pivotal positions as far as the sale of Indian lands to Spanish hacendados was concerned. Extant records of sales between Spaniards and Indians indicate that the two officials were usually cooperative.

The relationship between encomienda and hacienda and the period in which the hacienda emerged varied tremendously by region in colonial Spanish America. Although hacendados preferred to depict themselves as proud possessors of their lands and herds from time immemorial, the growth of the hacienda, as well as the concentration of the choice properties in a given locality among a limited number of interconnected families and clerical institutions, was a phenomenon that occurred at a specific point in time.

In the viceroyalty of New Spain hacienda formation began in the first area of Spanish settlement. In the Valley of Mexico, owners acquired scattered parcels of agricultural and grazing land through royal grants, purchase, and usurpation and slowly brought them together into larger estates. Most consolidation took place between 1550 and 1625. Further south, in the rich Valley of Oaxaca, the Spanish land rush began later. Between 1570 and 1643, 41 haciendas were established. Some concentration took place in the seventeenth century, but maximum expansion did not occur until the eighteenth. Around Querétaro, Zacatecas, and other northern cities, the hacienda emerged between 1610 and 1640, and consolidation took place over the next 50 years or so.

In the viceroyalty of Peru the story was much the same. Suburban plots around Lima were cultivated within the first decade after the city's founding in the mid-1530s. Peru's encomenderos invested in stock raising and agricultural enterprises for the same reasons as their New Spain counterparts in the 1550s. To both the north and south of Lima, along the coast, the founding of towns in the 1550s and 1560s spurred Spaniards' interest in the surrounding fertile, irrigated valleys. On the central coast, full-fledged haciendas appeared as early as 1580, and the process of consolidation was accomplished by 1630. To the south, in the Cañete Valley, relatively large haciendas dotted the landscape by the early 1590s and continued to grow at least until the 1630s. On the north coast, individual properties took on their definitive form and reached their characteristic size by the last quarter of the seventeenth century.

On the periphery of the Spanish Empire, where a large, sedentary Indian population either was lacking or had died off, and where costs of transportation to distant markets were prohibitive, hacienda formation and consolidation were delayed. In the province of Central America land was a surplus, almost useless commodity and therefore was of little interest before 1650. In the kingdom of Chile land still was not considered valuable nor prized in the seventeenth century. Evidence from the Caracas area of the province of Venezuela shows that hacienda-grown wheat was being exported by 1580. Expansion of cacao cultivation was delayed until the seventeenth century, however, which meant that the hacienda did not take on its characteristic form until much later, when the frontier disappeared.

In Brazil estate formation followed the general pattern present in Spanish America, except that in Brazil the large landowner, and the plantation which produced for export, seem to have had a more prominent role in colonial society. Because the Portuguese crown deemed Brazil and the early trade in dyewood of less value than other parts of the overseas empire, it entrusted early colonization to private individuals. The crown divided Brazil into 15 parallel districts that extended inland to the imaginary line established by the Treaty of Tordesillas. These were given to 13 wealthy and well-connected Portuguese nobles, called donatarios or lord-proprietors, to colonize. These, in turn, enticed followers to settle with promises of land grants. When Martim Afonso, for example, founded the first permanent settlement at São Vicente in 1532, he distributed land in huge parcels to his followers. Most of these initial, indirect attempts to settle Brazil failed, and toward the middle of the sixteenth century the crown decided to administer Brazil directly, lest it loose its New World domains to foreign encroachment.

The crown's representative in this endeavor, the governor-general Tomé de Sousa, established his headquarters at Bahia. This city and its hinterland quickly captured European attention as a major purveyor of sugar. Sugar cane had been imported from the African island of São Tomé soon after discovery in the sixteenth century. The growing and lucrative market for sugar in Europe, improved production techniques, and favorable legislation quickly turned the rich coastal land into immense sugar plantations. By the end of the century over 50 sugar mills dotted the Bahian countryside. The *senhor de engenho* (literally, the lord of the mill) thus became the archetypal landowner of Brazil, who, at first, almost totally overshadowed the less capitalized and usually smaller scale cultivators and ranchers who lived outside the rich sugar-producing zones.

Large Landowners in Their Golden Age

By about the late sixteenth century in Brazil and central New Spain, the early seventeenth century in central and southern coastal Peru, and the mid-seventeenth century in Saña, Querétaro, Caracas and Santiago, the large landowner represented the epitome of creole success and cut a memorable figure in the major city of his or her region. The size and value of the estate varied, depending on the region. The 20 to 30 hacendados who dominated Saña owned estates averaging about 550 *fanegadas* (or almost 4,000 acres) in size in the second half of the seventeenth century. These were large compared to the holdings of local Indians and to the Spanish and creole-owned vineyards of Ica to the south. Compared to properties in New Spain, the Saña holdings were about the same size as those found in Oaxaca in the eighteenth century, but miniscule when measured against the holdings of the Marqués de Aguayo at that time in the north of the viceroyalty, or against the sixteenth century land grants of Bahia that were reckoned in square miles and hundreds of thousands of acres. When hacendados owned several estates simultaneously, their domains became even larger.

Size, proximity to water, quality of soil, and dynamism of accessible markets, all determined the value of a property. In regions without rich miners or merchants, large landowners were the wealthiest persons in society. In Saña the average value or selling price of a typical estate in the second half of the seventeenth century was 29,971 *pesos* (monetary unit).[2] The owners of several estates, however, were much wealthier. Captain Martín Núñez de Arze's estates, for example, represented a fortune of over 158,000 pesos. The value of don Francisco de Palma y Vera's landholdings was well over 175,000 pesos. João Pais Barreto, one of the pioneers in developing the sugar industry in northeast Brazil and reputed to be the richest senhor de engenho in the area, owned seven sugar plantations in 1610, worth 300 to 400,000 *cruzados* (monetary unit).

The gulf between the standard of living and personal wealth of these landowners, on the one hand, and that of the professionals, minor bureaucrats, artisans, and the masses, on the other hand, was enormous. No official in provincial Peru with an annual salary of between 200 and 1,650 pesos could live like Palma y Vera. The salary of more than 200 pesos paid to the *curaca* (Indian chieftain) of a large Indian community, like Lambayeque, made him a rich and respected individual among its inhabitants; and in smaller Indian communities, like Jayanca, Pacora, and Mórrope, salaries only one-half that size gave Indian officials similar status. Even in the Spanish sector, mayordomos, with an annual salary of 200 to 300 pesos, in addition to room, board, and the use of pastures and a plot of irrigated land, could not afford to educate a son in Lima.

This wealth enabled the "hacendados" and "fazendeiros," as they liked to be called, to establish themselves as a hereditary elite within which was concentrated the power and prestige of an area. In numerous cities of colonial Latin America nearly every aspect of the economy and of local politics continued to be influenced by a large landowner, either directly in his role as an agriculturalist or rancher, priest, lawyer or judge, or bureaucrat, from corregidor or *capitão mor* (Brazilian civil and military leader) on down, or indirectly through the network of alliances formed with persons at different levels of the social structure.

The access of these landowners to the productive resources of their regions in both countryside and city became increasingly complex and calculated. Formal political power, official corruption, marriage, and compadre alliances all played a part in furthering their objectives and adding to the luster of their names. In Spanish America despite the fact that fewer substantive municipal issues were decided in the seventeenth century, the landed elite maintained its presence on the town councils. Regulation of food supply and sanitation remained important functions and the prestige value of the posts added to their desirability. If a landowner chose not to participate, he kept the council post in his extended family. Such an office, like land, passed through the generations; and especially in the smaller cities like Saña and, to a lesser extent, Querétaro (before circa 1650), the landowners ran the council as an exclusive club. In coastal Brazil where council positions were never sold, the dearth of qualified individuals and the extended kinship patterns of the sugar oligarchy meant continued control by the senhores de engenho, despite royal legislation designed to prevent one group from dominating the senados. Thus, throughout the seventeenth century the two magistrates, three aldermen, and the city attorney of Bahia most often were elected from landed and planter families long established in the region.[3]

The municipal council was not the only branch of government in which large landowners were influential. Many continued to hold high-level bureaucratic posts. Over a tenth of the landowners in Saña who are known to have had other occupations in the second half of the seventeenth century served as treasurers, accountants, corregidores, and judges in the royal bureaucracy. In Popayán four members of the Hurtado del Aguila family and three of the Aguinaga family held the position of lieutenant governor in the seventeenth century.[4] Besides conferring on the holder wide and extraordinary powers to enforce royal decisions, these positions provided them with the social standing inherent in an appointment signed by some of the highest authorities in the realm.

The militia continued to provide many estate owners with another means of enhancing their image and fulfilling an ingrained sense of "service to the King." In Bahia before 1718, the coveted position of colonel was achieved only by landowners and planters. In Saña almost 7 out of 10 landowners eligible for such service held some position of command. They outnumbered non-hacendados in positions from sergeant major on up by as much as eight to one. Militiamen had the right to the *fuero militar* (corporate privileges granted to the military) which included trial by military courts and usually meant more lenient treatment than that accorded by the civil courts. Another important consideration was the right to use military rank as a title. Prefixing a name with a military title of sufficient rank greatly enhanced a person's prestige in the eyes of his community. Those unable to assume the title of a post on the town council used their military title to add respectability to their name. Such titles generally preceded the use of the title *don* (Spanish term for gentleman). In some cases, a father identified himself as general or captain and his son assumed the title of don.

In many parts of Spanish America we find large landowners active in several spheres of local life at once. In Popayán estate owners were also merchants and miners. For example, Alonso Hurtado del Aguila, who was one of the four members of his family to hold the position of lieutenant governor, arrived in Popayán in the early seventeenth century and became a powerful merchant. He married twice—both times to women of old and prominent local families. In so doing, he acquired control of ranches and cattle, urban real estate, and, at least, one mine. Ranchers and farmers of Querétaro could also be merchants, manufacturers, and political officials in the seventeenth century. Among the members of the noble families of Mexico City, too, the merchant, miner, financier, and landowner were sometimes the same person.

The career of Don Juan Bonifacio de Seña illustrates the range of roles that an individual could play. He was a peninsular Spaniard from Burgos who arrived on the north coast of Peru prior to 1661. Soon, he and another relative owned extensive estates in Piura. His first involvement in the Saña area appears to have been his marriage to a local woman. He then served in the militia as a captain (1670), as a governor of arms (1694), and as a general and field marshal (1697). He was appointed military reviewer in 1681, served as lieutenant governor of the province in 1684 and again in 1694, and acted as corregidor in 1696 and 1697. At the end of his term as corregidor, he purchased the estates of Pomalca and Samán and the saltpeter works known as Santa Rosa de Acarleche.

Not all the estate owners in Saña were as active or in as advantageous a position to exert pressure in so many areas of local life as was Seña. Priests, who accounted for a significant proportion of all large landowners in many areas of Peru—9 percent in Abancay in 1689—during this period, by virtue of their vows could not sit on the municipal council or join the militia. Women—16 percent in Abancay in 1689, and 17 percent in Saña during the entire colonial period—were barred from participation in public life. Yet priests and women were minorities. Over three-quarters of all male landowners in Saña had professional training, engaged in nonagricultural business activities, sat on the municipal council, commanded the militia, or accepted positions in the bureaucracy at one time or another.

In seventeenth century New Spain, New Granada, Peru, and Brazil, family remained important to the large landowners, and, because they could use kin to control the productive resources of the districts, they were willing to invest in them. Estate owners continued to maintain close contact with landless branches of their extended family that might not be as well off economically because relatives often held positions in the royal bureaucracy or municipal council, or were competent professionals who provided an important source of aid. To reciprocate for favors from their "poorer" kinsmen, such landowners made generous contributions to their daughters' dowries, invited them to social gatherings, or made them the beneficiaries of a chantry or religious trust. *Compadrazgo* (ritual co-parenthood) reinforced distant kinship relations, as did financial and legal dealings. Marriages between cousins seem to have been symptomatic of strategies designed to consolidate holdings, preserve wealth, and promote the social status of the family as well. Regardless of relative position or landowning status, the various branches considered themselves part of one large family and cooperated with one another, using kinship as a basis on which to relate and act together to enhance the position of the group.

Large landowners, of course, continued to cooperate with others outside the family. One estate owner often served as the commercial agent for one or more friends and associates. The above-mentioned Seña, for example, purchased sugar from the brothers don Juan and Licenciado don Felix Rodríguez Carrasco, the owners of the estate called La Punta, and marketed it with his own. To increase his volume, he extended credit to other sugar producers and allowed them to repay him in kind. Persons traveling to major markets, like Mexico City, Veracruz, the Portobelo fair, and Lima procured imports for those who remained at home. Transactions in which one hacendado or fazendeiro sold imported goods, and especially slaves, to another frequently appear in notarial registers of the period. Large landowners also guaranteed each other. In legal matters they gave each other power of attorney to buy and sell merchandise and land, collect debts, issue wills, and represent each other before the bench. To establish and fortify their positions in those few areas that they did not control, landowners carefully cultivated close ties with persons outside their privileged circle, especially with merchants (to the extent they were a separate group) and officials.

Marriage served to ally the family with useful outsiders. The marriages of don Bonifacio de Seña and Alonso Hurtado del Aguila linked the peninsular-born individual to well-established and wide-ranging creole family networks. This pattern held not only for Peru and New Granada but also for Brazil. Throughout the seventeenth century and into the eighteenth, the daughters of prominent agriculturalists and cattlemen frequently married successful Portuguese merchants. Such matches proved advantageous to both parties. Merchant Manual Mendes Monforte inherited one of his two sugar mills from his father-in-law. Likewise, Domingos Alvares de Araújo received land valued at 5,000 cruzados as a dowry when he married a planter's daughter. Merchants were thus introduced and accepted into established society; and they, in turn, presumably used their capital, access to credit, and commercial connections to further family interests. It is important to underscore, however, that the traditional ruling families in Brazil, whose landed interests and power dated from the sixteenth century, were never supplanted by successful merchants. They admitted the newcomers into their ranks on a very selective basis.

Equally essential to the large landowners' informal network were connections with high and influential authorities in capital cities. Studies in Lima gave provincial landowners the opportunity to mix with the members of the viceregal court. A few residents of Saña, such as Dr. don Juan de Samudio y Villalobos y Mendoza and Dr. Juan de Saavedra Cavero, qualified and served as lawyers in the capital before returning. The friendships and acquaintances made in Lima served these landowners well when they later called on these contacts to expedite settlement of lawsuits. Other landowners had relatives who were either lawyers or judges on the *audiencia* (high court). Marriages with viceregal authorities were encouraged. Doña Magdalena Estrada y Hurtado, a wealthy widow, married don Alonso de Castillo de Herrera, a judge of the audiencia in Quito. He later became the governor of Huancavelica, a highland district of Peru, and judge of the audiencia in Lima, ending his career as president of that influential body. In Bahia João Pais Barreto's son and namesake married Ana Corte Real, daughter of the capitão mor of Paraíba, and his daughter, Catarina, married dom Luis de Sousa Henriques, son of the former governor-general of Brazil and nephew of the eleventh governor-general, dom Luis de Sousa, who arrived in Pernambuco in 1617. By virtue of such connections, João Pais the younger became one of the most influential men in Brazil.

Ties to the church remained strong in the seventeenth century. Large landowners willingly served as stewards of religious brotherhoods, as lay representatives of monasteries or convents in dealings with creditors and secular courts, as trustees of special funds, and as sacristans in return for prestige and for inside information on the availability of mortgage funds. A few, like a member of the Arboleda y Ortiz family of Popayán, after years dedicated to agriculture and mining pursuits joined the church and became vicar-general of the bishop (1661), treasurer (1665), and finally cantor and archdeacon (1668). A large number of the offspring of the landed elite also joined religious orders or became secular priests. Furthermore, throughout both Spanish America and Brazil, the church itself owned land and was directly dependent upon the wealthy for contributions, gifts and subsidies.

Prosperity, now as never before, allowed estate owners to be generous. The church benefited, especially from donations from the last members of old families without direct descendants to inherit their fabulous wealth, accumulated sometimes over more than a century and a half. In New Granada Dionisia Francisca Perez Manrique was widowed twice—once of a fifth-generation scion of the important Velasco family of seventeenth and eighteenth century Popayán and the second time of a peninsular-born governor of the district. She assigned her considerable and rich possessions to the Jesuits when she outlived her children. In Peru Palma y Vera decided to leave his vast holdings to found a Jesuit school in Saña as a lasting monument to his line. Doña Leonor de Saavedra y Monroy, disillusioned after two childless marriages, one to a judge of the audiencia of Quito who squandered thousands of pesos of her money, charged the administrator of her will with founding another convent. The Licenciado Raphael Suaso y Ferrer built a church for the Indians of Callanca with his fortune. Such relationships fostered the attitude that what was good for the landed elite was also good for the church.

To appreciate the extent of these connections and the pervasive influence and central position of individual landowners and their families, one need only identify and enumerate the positions held by the members of one family and the relationship of these members to other important but landless figures in local society. The eight landowners making up the immediate family of Blas Fragoso of Saña included a lawyer, a priest, a notary, and the royal accountant and treasurer of the province. Seven of the eight held positions in the militia, ranging from second lieutenant to general and field marshal. Four were active in the municipal council, serving as alderman, magistrate, rural constable, and defender of minors, respectively. The last was commissioned by the council to retrieve the records that the last corregidor had taken with him to Lima to defend his actions against the pirate Edward David. One represented the Inquisition. They had numerous business dealings with each other and did not hesitate to give each other power of attorney. Ties with other members of the elite and with landless persons were common. They posted bond for stockmen, mayordomos, tax farmers, various corregidores, and government bureaucrats; became partners in livestock raising and tanning ventures; and lent money to, and found employment for, friends of friends. Five of the eight were godfathers of children of Indian officials, Spanish bureaucrats, or professionals. Finally, these eight persons owned estates in Piura; soap and leather tanning facilities in the nearby towns of Lambayeque, Chiclayo, Motupe and Sechura; and the estates of Íllimo, Mamape, Collús, Saltur, Luya, Sasape, La Punta, Ucupe, and San Christóbal. Similar networks could be described for each of the major families or clans, as their contacts and positions multiplied.

Throughout colonial Latin America the powerful position of the hacendados and fazendeiros was reflected in their opulent physical surroundings, their apparel, their educational attainments, and their children's marriages and careers. (See Figure 8.) Besides the estates and their appurtenances, large landowners owned townhouses, comfortably furnished with tapestries, paintings, and cushioned divans. Palma y Vera, for example, lived between the convent of La Merced and the central plaza of the district capital of Saña in a mansion filled with rugs, upholstered furniture, and gold-framed mirrors. A retinue of domestic slaves served him supper from a silver service, complete with candelabras. He took pride in his personal chapel, containing a valuable collection of oil paintings and statues and in his library. He dressed in the finest fabrics, imported from England, Naples, and France. Despite owning estancias and tanneries that produced thousands of pounds of soap per year, he preferred to wash with imported soap and dry his hands on English towels. To travel, he either mounted a mule, fitted with silver-adorned saddle and stirrups, or rode in a carriage with scarlet curtains. Depictions of the colonial Latin American elite regularly show personages bedecked with jewels, richly dressed, riding fine horses, and surrounded by liveried slaves.

Such hacendados and fazendeiros were rich enough to fulfill their dreams. They sent their sons away to the seminary or university, often with allowances equal to or higher than the annual incomes of many local bureaucrats. In contrast to the situation in Saña the first half of the seventeenth century, when some landowners could not sign their names and few could claim a complete seminary education, in the second half of the century almost all the large landowners were functionally literate (defined as being able to sign one's name) and one-quarter had advanced degrees. Since no school existed in the city of Saña at the time, an education implied years of residence in the provincial capital of Trujillo or the viceregal capital of Lima itself, which gave the recipient of the degree the added distinction of being widely traveled. For their daughters, such landowners arranged marriages to persons of rank, such as the sons of the judges of the audiencia or even the judges themselves. Rich dowries of more than 16,000 pesos, which included everything needed to set up a household and enough jewels and clothing to last a lifetime, also assured beneficial matches.

The concentration of power, prestige, and wealth in the hands of so few meant the increased exclusivity of the landed elite and fewer opportunities for upward mobility for the landless. Newcomers found it increasingly difficult to establish themselves because opportunities for advancement quickly disappeared in the second half of the seventeenth century.

In many areas the frontier was gone. The bureaucracy was staffed, and no new positions were being created. The positions that became vacant on the elite-dominated municipal council stayed within the same families. Moreover, the few old, privileged, and powerful families who controlled the largest and most valuable sugar estates and ranches and most of the productive land had established distinguished ancestry as a criterion for elite membership. The greatest prestige was accorded the families who could claim descent from the original settlers of the area, probably because such descent was rare. In Saña only one family, founded by the encomendero of Túcume, Francisco de Samudio Mendoza, could claim that six generations of descendants had owned estates. Over 100 encomenderos had lived in Cuzco in 1570, but the encomendero as a social type had almost disappeared by the late seventeenth century. More common were the families who traced their origins back to the early non-encomendero settlers of the area. The descendants of Fragoso, who established himself as a gentleman farmer by acquiring the ranch called Mamape, held land for five generations prior to 1719. Diego de Rodríguez Cavanillas' family, like most of the "old" families of the period, however, dated only from the 1630s. Most sixteenth century families had retained landed status for no more than one or two generations.

The families established in Saña in the mid-seventeenth century, however, were more stable. The Rodríguez Cavanillas, for instance, continued to own Cayaltí for four generations until the death of Licenciado don Joseph Núñez de Arze, a priest with no heirs. Other members of the same branch then maintained the landowning tradition by acquiring other estates in the area, which they held until the mid-eighteenth century. The men who did manage to enter the hacendado group in the seventeenth century had served, of necessity, in more public positions than had second and later generation landowners. Public service enhanced their prestige, reputation, and contacts, all essential for increasing an outsider's chance to join the landed elite. Even then, they tended to acquire land later in their careers than did hacendados from older families, and they acquired the least expensive properties. Sixty-five percent of the estates held by first-time landowners were worth less than the average for the period.

The Landed Elite of the Late Colony

So pervasive and enduring was the hacendados' and fazendeiros' collective reputation in what we might call the landowners' golden age that it came to cloud the memory of their past and obscure the origins of many of the rich and famous. Likewise the mystique surrounding the principal landowners in some areas hid the reality of declining fortunes and delayed bankruptcy proceedings far into the future.

Certainly by the early eighteenth century or several decades before in some areas economic conditions had begun to change. The mainland sugar industry was in disarray. As early as the second half of the seventeenth century, the sugar sector of Bahia had already entered a period of extended, if uneven, decline attributable to a combination of rising costs, overexpansion, increasing competition with Caribbean production, and the fact that northern Europe relied increasingly on its own colonial sources for tropical products. The Peruvian sugar industry already had lost its northern markets as a result of the decline in the fleet system and the end of the bustling Portobelo trade fair. In these sugar-exporting enclaves, as well as that of cacao-producing Caracas, planters complained of falling prices and of a serious labor shortage as the Atlantic slave trade was disrupted by warfare and as the province of Cuba and other Caribbean producers outbid them for black labor.

Elsewhere, agriculturalists also faced hard times. Wheat, tallow, and leather from the province of Chile began entering the Peruvian markets with serious consequences for north coastal and highland production. Estate owners of Popayán suffered from declining yields, high transport costs, high labor costs, and price regulation that allegedly favored miners over farmers. A depression in the early seventeenth century in Central America deepened progressively through the 1660s, reducing many hacendados to a semi-subsistence status. Oaxacan estates suffered from a combination of droughts, frosts, wheat blight, and a fatal epidemic among cattle and sheep in the early eighteenth century. Production declined, estate values fell, and several were mortgaged and eventually sold.

By the early eighteenth century, too, the negative effects of the testamentary system, the cumulative impact of ecclesiastical mortgages and annuities, and relatively low and uncertain returns began to be felt. Over the years many estates became so overburdened with chaplaincies and other pious works that a significant portion, if not all, of the profit in some years went for payment of interest. In Oaxaca the mean average of clerical charges was 67 percent of the total capital value of estates.[5] In Saña the average for 1720–1820 was 68 percent, up 63 percent over the previous 50-year period. Lower profit rates here and in other areas were also a function of smaller markets, as well as rising transportation and labor costs that individual owners could not control.

The improvement in the large landowners' economic position had to await the last decades of the colonial period. In the province of Venezuela the cacao industry began to recover in the 1680s. But only late in the eighteenth century did conditions show signs of becoming better in most other regions. In Brazil planters benefited from supplying the markets in Europe. Sugar prices rose, nearly doubling between 1776 and 1781, and other sectors of the economy, especially cotton and tobacco, also expanded. In New Spain cochineal production in the south experienced a boom. *Pulque,* an intoxicating drink made from fermented cactus juice, became a commercial product from which the noblemen of New Spain made fortunes. Cereal producers also found relief in expanding city markets and a reviving mining economy in the northern provinces. In the region of Guatemala foreign demand for indigo increased the value of rural property. In northern Peru the cattle industry appears to have been stimulated by an upsurge in mining in the adjacent highlands.

In Spanish America the Bourbon reforms were responsible for part of this improvement. One of the crown's economic objectives was to stimulate production. To this end, the crown sponsored foreign mining missions and encouraged the importing of European technology to expand mineral output. Clubs were founded to introduce and disseminate information on new crops and techniques of scientific farming. But what the crown gave with one hand, it took away with the other. The desire to increase revenue flow to Spain meant that the Bourbons raised the general sales tax and the taxes on rum, pulque, and sugar. Worse yet was the consolidation decree, promulgated late in 1804 in New Spain, which was equivalent to recalling all the mortgages established on the estates. The funds were to be collected in cash for shipment to Spain. In the kingdom of Chile the decree was deemed so explosive an issue that the Santiago cabildo never promulgated it. In Peru its impact in the colonial period was not very significant.

The Bourbon political reforms undercut the large landowners' political defense. Attempts to revitalize the ineffectual cabildo meant that some hereditary positions were expropriated by the crown; in other areas new positions were added to the body. In some places, like Mexico City, the old members chose the new members from among their kindred and others to whom they had close economic and compadrazgo ties. The resulting cabildo became a "faction of cousins." But, in many other areas, the new members did not necessarily represent the old hacendado interests, and thus diluted their power. Attempts to centralize power by replacing the corregidor with an *inten-*

dente (provincial governor) further impinged on the informal power exercised by the established elite. The intendente, a career bureaucrat with a higher salary and often in charge of a larger area than his predecessor, seemed less responsive to local hacendados' needs and desires.

These conditions, in varying combinations, made the eighteenth century a time of great social turmoil. In Saña inattention to business, unproductive spending, and a series of floods and other natural disasters during a period of worsening overall economic conditions initiated a cycle of debt and bankruptcy that ruined the estates and brought an end to the area's legendary group of hacendados. The estate owners lacked the foresight and capital resources to recover and rebuild their damaged properties, while price declines brought a cost/price squeeze. This squeeze made it increasingly difficult for the large landowners, especially the sugar producers, who had borrowed to rebuild after the floods of 1720 and 1728, to meet their mounting obligations. Eventually, the financial conditions of most Saña hacendados gave them no choice but to suspend payments on accumulating interest and loan payments. Despite a tolerant attitude on the part of the church and other lenders, creditors eventually foreclosed to recover what they could of their original principals. Bankruptcy meant costly disruptions of production, lengthy court cases, and poor administration. Personal influence and connections failed the old landed families when they needed them the most. Estate after estate was sold to cover debts at drastically reduced prices.

The unsettling effects of the economic turnaround allowed immigrants and locally born persons of previously landless families to acquire estates during the course of the eighteenth century. In Saña by Independence new owners constituted nearly half (48 percent) of the landowning population. Of the two-thirds of those who were immigrants to the area, more than half (55 percent) came from Spain. The rest arrived from other parts of Europe, Panama, Quito, and other provinces of the Spanish domain. Their position and income had gained them admittance to the revitalized cabildo under the Bourbons. They gradually equaled and eventually surpassed members of the old families both in numbers and in power on the council. Likewise, new owners came to outnumber the old families in the growing military, although they never matched them in rank.

Similarly, the region around Cuzco in the viceroyalty of Peru saw a significant turnover in the hacendado group. New owners seem to have acquired the estates of Calca and Lares in the eighteenth century. Not a single patronym of the landowners of the late seventeenth century still appeared on a list of the landowners of the district in 1786, although it should be remembered that patronyms are not necessarily indicative of family continuity in the landed elite. In Mexico City, the northern mining district, and the Bajío, successful miners and merchants moved into the class of "new rich" and bought social acceptance with land. Likewise, in the second half of the eighteenth century, Bahian merchants purchased sugar plantations. The offspring of these landowning merchants frequently became identified exclusively as *senhores de engenho*.

In Saña the entry of the new owners into the ranks of the large landowning class did not necessarily mean that they were then as wealthy as the old landed group they displaced once had been. While it is not possible to compare the net worth of the two groups, information about the value of their estates and the degree of property concentration suggests that the former were not of the same economic standing in many instances. In contrast to the scions of the old landed families, the new owners were not necessarily born with the resources needed to acquire land. Three out of four of those known to have exercised a profession were bureaucrats, priests, or merchants before they became hacendados. These were the professions where the aspiring and socially mobile had the best opportunity to succeed. The Bourbons had opened the bureaucracy to talent, and peninsular-born technocrats began arriving in the area in significant numbers shortly after mid-century.

Commerce, in particular, promised rewards for hardworking individuals, skilled in shrewd dealings. It is, in fact, during the late eighteenth century that merchants became conspicuous as an important group in Saña: first as modest shopkeepers, and, later, by the end of the century, as respected and wealthy importers and exporters. Though few in number, they appear more and more frequently in the public record bidding in auctions for the right to collect the tithes, for the personal effects of the deceased, or for the indebted property of the old landed elite. In the sixteenth century most merchants had been located at Trujillo, and itinerant peddlers served the area. For most of the seventeenth century the corregidor's *repartimiento de comercio* (forced sale of goods to Indians), the hacendados' preference for handling their own shipping, and their agents' willingness to supply them with goods from Panama or Lima, limited commercial activities. With the end of these practices in the eighteenth century, the merchants of Saña became locally influential personages in their own right.

Both upwardly mobile professionals and enterprising immigrants were able to acquire the estates of the old landed elite on what once might have been considered modest incomes, because the estates were being sold at giveaway prices and on very easy terms. The same situation also existed in the provincial center of Oaxaca, where new owners were not the wealthiest men in the area. Their acquisition might come with the payment of a small fraction of the appraised or market value of a heavily mortgaged estate. Although a steady income from a source other than agriculture or evidence of possession of capital often convinced creditors that a potential buyer was capable of meeting his interest obligations, these sources of income were not always adequate to cover renewal plans and continued losses. Local merchants suffered from periodic economic slumps. Priests saw donations and fees diminish as baptisms and marriages were cancelled or postponed. They also suffered from the loss of the ability of the estates to pay interest on chantries and other trusts.

The upwardly mobile wanted land because of its prestige value and because they were confident that under good administration the holdings once again would produce a profit. But few had the ability to lose money continuously while waiting for investments to pay off. Eventually, many were forced by debt to sell out. The lack of financial reserves among the new owners contributed to the high turnover rate of estates during the middle and late eighteenth century.

The degree to which the Saña pattern applies elsewhere remains to be studied. Certainly, there were exceptions. In the province of Venezuela, the oldest landowning families with property nearer the coast remained prominent until the Revolutions for Independence. There, the new owners had to settle in the interior and were ruined by high freight rates and low prices. By converting their property into non-alienable estates and by diversifying their economic base, some of the established families of Mexico City persisted as a landed elite into the nineteenth century. But the late eighteenth century appears to have been a time of considerable movement into the large landowner group in many cities of colonial Latin America.

Despite the social instability of the eighteenth century, the ideal of the landed magnate remained. New owners emulated the old in very obvious ways, so the stereotypes lived on. They participated in the town council and the militia. They represented the church and built extrafamilial bonds through compadrazgo. Life in the city remained a measure of an individual landowner's success. But while position and fortune were still associated with land, land was only part of the economic base of most of the new members of the elite. Large owners continued to be persons of very diverse social and economic backgrounds, with special allegiances to several interest groups at once. In fact, toward the end of the colonial era it appeared that, for many, their gains from other economic pursuits often subsidized the agricultural sector. Although the names and faces of the landed elite changed in most areas, the image remained and the modalities of power on the local level were largely unaltered.

Conclusions

Detailed research specifically on landed elites has just begun, but recent studies indicate that in broad outline and with the proper allowances for temporal and geographic variations the story of the large landowners in one part of colonial Latin America is very similar to that of the others. Near the Spanish viceregal centers of Mexico City and Lima, the origins of a landowning elite date back to the first encomenderos and early settlers. The former used

native labor and the capital it generated to invest in ranching and agricultural enterprises, as their encomienda income decreased. They established some
of the first farms producing wheat, grapes, and sugar cane, destined to satisfy
Spanish tastes. Some of the families founded by these individuals survived
through entail and diversification of their economic base into the seventeenth
and eighteenth centuries to become a titled nobility or aristocracy. The leaders of these families were not solely identified as ranchers or farmers, but
rather more generally as "persons of affairs." Their families remained the exceptional ones with long pedigrees and exceedingly high standards of birth and
wealth for entrance. In Brazil, the counterparts were the sugar planters and
cattle barons of the mid-sixteenth century.

Less prominent settlers in these regions acquired land and began their agricultural activities somewhat later. Some of these did well, too, achieving agricultural magnate status. Rare were the individuals that ever became the equals
of the first group, however, solely on the basis of agriculture.

Settlers on the agricultural frontiers, near such provincial cities as Querétaro and Saña, started later with smaller tracts of land. Limited by generally
smaller markets and a shortage of capital, their membership in the elite tended
to be shorter, and most never achieved the wealth and pretense of the aristocratic first families in the capitals. Nevertheless, over time, these gentleman
ranchers and farmers captured the social spotlight. It was outside the viceregal centers where the settlers and their descendants were not overshadowed
by the first families that we can see most clearly how they selectively achieved
high status, wealth, and power, and evolved into a landed elite.

Except perhaps for some of the sugar planters of early colonial Brazil and a
few large landowners in remote areas that did not produce large quantities of
goods for market, most—whether the nobles of Mexico City or Lima or their
more modest provincial counterparts—did not live on their estates continuously but chose instead to live in towns and cities. As urban residents, the
large landowners functioned as mediators between town and countryside, or,
between Europeanized and non-European society. And it is in the urban setting that the landowners' power can best be documented. No sphere of city
life was untouched by them. In many colonial urban centers they were the
dominant social group. They influenced employment and pricing; they engaged
in trade, although sometimes not conspicuously. They were from the earliest
days of settlement active in city government, the administration of justice,
and the leadership of the militia. Those who were also priests swayed public
opinion. While the formal positions of power held by the landed elite were
useful to it, its connections—the interlocking networks of family, friends,
and dependents—were crucial to its ability to manipulate local situations. In
some cities the large landowning group faced more competition. Miners in
Potosí and merchants in Buenos Aires held the power elsewhere enjoyed by
the landed elite. In Antioquia agriculture was less important as a basis for
wealth and power than either extractive or commercial activities. In these

centers other groups followed the strategies originally developed by the land-ed elite in the older cities.

With the possible exception of families with entailed estates, the landed elite was relatively open. Families which lasted more than a few generations, three being a number commonly found in the literature, were in the minori-ty. The landowning elite never was completely closed to talented, well-born, energetic newcomers. It was constantly being renewed, albeit with greater speed at some moments than others. Early in the colonial era land was the prerequisite for elite standing. Only property holders could be full-fledged residents of the city; only prosperous families could occupy poorly-paid municipal posts and establish the informal influence which was essential to the continuation of their power. Later in the colony land also appeared as a confirmation of high status achieved by other means. Thus, the acquisi-tion of large estates was both a prelude to membership in the elite and an epilogue to it, depending upon the region, the time period, and the families in question.

Finally, the *hombres nuevos,* or new rich, who advanced themselves econom-ically and socially by becoming large landowners generally did not do so with the aim of destroying the aura of their predecessors, or the *antiguos ricos.* To do so would have undermined their own social ambitions. They did not aspire to shatter the hallowed circle, but to join it. Thus, although individual fami-lies may have had relatively short histories, the opposite is true of the history of the landed elite as a whole.

Notes

1. Archivo Regional de Trujillo/Palacios, 26–II–1611; and Archivo Nac-ional del Perú/Real Audiencia, 1. 24, c. 82, 1609, 48–48v and 65; and Arch-ivo Arzobispal de Trujillo/Capellanías, 1650, and Testamentos, 1789, 114v.

2. Susan E. Ramírez, *Provincial Patriarchs: Land Tenure and the Economics of Power in Colonial Peru* (Albuquerque: University of New Mexico Press, 1985), Appendix III.

3. Stuart B. Schwartz, "Cities of Empire: Mexico and Bahia in the Six-teenth Century," *Journal of Inter-american Studies* 10 (1969), 635–36; and Schwartz, *Sovereignty and Society in Colonial Brazil* (Berkeley: University of Cal-ifornia Press, 1973), 116.

4. Héctor Llanos Vargas, "Surgimiento, permanencia y transformaciones de la elite criolla de Popayán (Siglos XVI–XIX)," *Historia y espacio, Revista de estudios históricos regionales* 1:3 (1979), 82–85.

5. William B. Taylor, "Town and Country in the Valley of Oaxaca, 1750–1812," in Ida Altman and James Lockhart, eds., *Provinces of Early Mex-ico* (Los Angeles: UCLA Latin American Center, 1976), 84.

For Further Reading

There are a growing number of studies on the large landowners as a group in the colonial era. Among the most useful published works are Rae Flory and David Grant Smith, "Bahian Merchants and Planters in the Seventeenth and Early Eighteenth Centuries," *Hispanic American Historical Review* 58:4 (1978): 571–94; Mario Góngora, *Encomenderos y estancieros* (Santiago: Universidad de Chile at Valparaiso, 1970), an excellent monograph on ranchers in colonial Chile; and Ann Twinan, *Merchants and Farmers in Colonial Colombia* (Austin, Tex.: University of Texas Press, 1983). Doris Ladd, *The Mexican Nobility at Independence, 1780–1826* (Austin, Tex.: University of Texas Press, 1976), though limited to the late colonial period, is an outstanding contribution to the study of some of the largest landowners and their families in Mexico. Herbert Klein, "Hacienda and Free Community in Eighteenth Century Alto Perú: A Demographic Study of the Aymara Population of the Districts of Chulumani and Pacajes in 1786," *Journal of Latin American Studies* 7 (1975): 193–220 discusses Bolivian hacienda owners at about the same time in an article that is useful for comparison.

References to the north coast of Peru are based on the author's research results, more fully developed in Susan E. Ramírez, *Provincial Patriarchs: The Economics of Power in Colonial Peru* (Albuquerque: University of New Mexico Press, 1985), and "Instability at the Top: A Social History of the Landed Elite in Colonial Peru," to be published in the *Proceedings* of the "Unity and Diversity in Colonial Latin America" Conference (New Orleans: Middle American Research Institute, Tulane University, 1985).

For two useful genealogical guides to Peru, see Jorge Zevallos Quiñones, "Lambayeque en el siglo XVIII," *Revista del Instituto Peruano de Investigaciones Genealógicas* 1:1 (junio 1948): 89–152, and Guillermo Lohmann Villena, "Informaciones genealógicas de peruanos seguidas ante el Santo Oficio," *Revista del Instituto Peruano de Investigaciones Genealógicas* 8:8 (dic. 1955): 7–110 and 9:9 (dic. 1956): 115–252.

Three unpublished, but very important, dissertations are also of note. The first is Madelaine Glynne Dervel Evans, "The Landed Aristocracy in Peru, 1600–1680" (Ph.D. diss., University College, London, 1972); the second is Julia Linn Bell Hirschberg, "A Social History of Puebla de los Angeles, 1531–1560" (Ph.D. diss., University of Michigan, 1976); and the third is Edith Boorstein Couturier, "Hacienda of Hueyapan: The History of a Mexican Social and Economic Institution, 1550–1940" (Ph.D. diss., Columbia University, 1965).

James Lockhart, *Spanish Peru* (Madison, Wis.: University of Wisconsin Press, 1968) and Fred Bronner, "Peruvian Encomenderos in 1630: Elite Circulation and Consolidation," *Hispanic American Historical Review* 57:4 (1977): 633–59 are two standard sources on the origins of the landowning group in that region.

All the works cited above touch on the hacendados' multiple roles. David

A. Brading, *Miners and Merchants in Bourbon Mexico, 1763–1810* (Cambridge: At the University Press, 1971) and John Fisher, *Silver Mines and Silver Miners in Colonial Peru* (Liverpool: Center for Latin American Studies, University of Liverpool, 1977); Héctor Llanos Vargas, "Surgimiento, permanencia y transformaciones de la elite criolla de Popayán (Siglos XVI–XIX)," *Historia y espacio, Revista de estudios históricos regionales* 1:3 (1979): 19–104; and Ann Twinam, "Enterprise and Elites in Eighteenth-Century Medellín," *Hispanic American Historical Review* 59:3 (1979): 444–75, and *Miners, Merchants . . .* also discuss the overlap but approach landowning as peripheral to other occupational specialties. For an idea of the place of landowners in the colonial social structure in general, see John K. Chance and William B. Taylor, "Estate and Class in a Colonial City: Oaxaca in 1792," *Comparative Studies in Society and History* 19:4 (November, 1977): 454–87.

For contrasting examples of institutional ownership, one should see Herman Konrad, *A Jesuit Hacienda in Colonial Mexico: Santa Lucia, 1576–1767* (Stanford: Stanford University Press, 1980) and Nicolas P. Cushner's three volumes on Jesuit estates. They are *Lords of the Land: Sugar, Wine, and Jesuit Estates of Coastal Peru, 1600–1767* (Albany: State University of New York Press, 1980), *Farm and Factory: The Jesuits and the Development of Agrarian Capitalism in Colonial Quito, 1600–1767* (Albany: State University of New York Press, 1982), and *Jesuit Ranches and the Agrarian Development of Colonial Argentina, 1650–1767* (Albany: State University of New York Press, 1983). Stuart B. Schwartz, "The Plantations of St. Benedict: The Benedictine Sugar Mills of Colonial Brazil," *The Americas* 39:1 (1982): 1–22 is also illuminating.

Studies on the institution of the hacienda also often contain information on their owners. The classic account is François Chevalier, *Land and Society in Colonial Mexico* (Berkeley: University of California Press, 1970). This study touched off a series of similar investigations. Regionally focused monographs on Mexico include: William B. Taylor, *Landlord and Peasant in Colonial Oaxaca* (Stanford: Stanford University Press, 1972); Charles A. Harris III, *A Mexican Family Empire: The Latifundio of the Sánchez Navarros, 1765–1867* (Austin, Tex.: University of Texas Press, 1975), and Eric Van Young, *Hacienda and Market in Eighteenth-Century Mexico* (Berkeley: University of California Press, 1981). Another contribution of note is Ida Altman and James Lockhart, eds., *Provinces of Early Mexico* (Los Angeles: UCLA Latin American Center, 1976). The authors of the contributing chapters characterize the various regional elites and discuss their economic base, that often includes landed wealth.

Analogous studies for Peru include Manuel Burga, *De la encomienda a la hacienda capitalista* (Lima: Instituto de Estudios Peruanos, 1976), and Robert G. Keith, *Conquest and Agrarian Change* (Cambridge: Harvard University Press, 1976), which characterizes landowners through 1650. Magnus Mörner has also written a useful study: *Perfil de la sociedad rural del Cuzco a fines de la colonia* (Lima: Universidad del Pacífico, 1978), that includes a chapter on haciendas and, by extension, hacendados.

For information on the sugar plantations and planters of Brazil, see Alexander Marchant, "Colonial Brazil," in H. V. Livermore and W. J. Entwistle, eds., *Portugal and Brazil: An Introduction* (Oxford: Clarendon Press, 1953); Gilberto Freyre, *The Masters and the Slaves* (New York: Knopf, 1956); and Stuart B. Schwartz, *Sovereignty and Society in Colonial Brazil* (Berkeley: University of California Press, 1973); and "Cities of Empire: Mexico and Bahia in the Sixteenth Century," *Journal of Inter-american Studies* (1969): 616–37; E. Bradford Burns, *Latin America: A Concise Interpretive History* (Englewood Cliffs, New Jersey: Prentice Hall, 1977); John N. Kennedy, "Bahia Elites, 1750–1822," *Hispanic American Historical Review* 53:3 (1973): 415–439; and Dwight E. Petersen, "Sweet Success: Some Notes on the Founding of a Brazilian Sugar Dynasty, The Pais Barreto Family of Pernambuco," *The Americas* 40:3 (1984): 325–48.

Mention also should be made of contributions on other areas of Latin America. The definitive study of Hapsburg Central America is Murdo J. MacLeod, *Spanish Central America: A Socioeconomic History, 1520–1720* (Berkeley: University of California Press, 1973). Robert J. Ferry's "Cacao and Kindred: Transformations of Economy and Society in Colonial Caracas," (Ph.D. diss., University of Minnesota, 1980), and "Encomienda, African Slavery, and Agriculture in Seventeenth-Century Caracas," *Hispanic American Historical Review* 61:4 (1981): 609–35, are extremely well-documented accounts of the cacao planter society of early colonial Venezuela. Two additional studies, Mario Góngora, "Urban Social Stratification in Colonial Chile," *Hispanic American Historical Review* 45:3 (1975), and Mario Góngora and Jean Borde, *Evolución de la propiedad rural en el Valle de Puangue* (Santiago: Editorial Universitaria, 1956), round out our knowledge of colonial Chile.

THREE

Merchants

CATHERINE LUGAR

Introduction

The close alliance among the rise of towns and trade, urban life, and commercial economy that is marked in early modern European history has its expected resonance in colonial Latin America. Mercantile classes were a central element in the urban scene, from the great merchants who lived nobly among local elites to the scores of shopkeepers minding stores in the commercial quarters of the European centers that sprung up as colonial societies sank roots in American soil. Itinerant traders and peddlers hawked assorted wares through the towns and across the countryside in extensions of commercial networks that reached back across the Atlantic through metropolitan home ports to centers of European production.

An abyss, in principle if not always in practice, separated merchants proper from common tradesmen, shopkeepers, and street vendors. The merchants discussed in this chapter are primarily those major or wholesale merchants, usually peninsular-born, who managed the long distance trades. There was some variation over time in the Spanish and Portuguese terms for the merchant elite, but in the late eighteenth century, in both Spanish and Portuguese America, *comerciante* referred to the larger import-export merchants. Their worldwide business connections, handling of European and American goods, and supervision of the most important trade routes established their preeminence and distinguished them from *mercaderes,* who sold stock over the counter, or the lowlier *tratantes,* petty dealers in regional trade. While an important business line of many great merchants in the New World, retail

47

storekeeping by itself implied a subservient attendance upon a passing clientele and was considered beneath the dignity of a well-established wholesaler. The operators, counter attendants, and storeroom clerks of general stores, *pulperías* (taverns), and hardware shops, swelled the ranks of the large bulk of the population typically engaged in urban commerce, but these lower ranks were commanded at the very top by true merchant gentlemen.

In the sixteenth and seventeenth centuries the principal destinations of the transoceanic routes of the Atlantic fleets in the Spanish trade, the *carrera de Indias,* were seaport towns on the coasts. The islands were served by ships that parted from the trans–Atlantic fleet upon entering the Caribbean. Cargo vessels destined for the mainland of South America sailed on to the Isthmus of Panama, to entrepôts created first at Nombre de Díos, and later, after 1598, at Portobelo and Cartagena de Indias. The official Atlantic port of New Spain was Veracruz, at San Juan de Ulloa on the Bay of Campeche. On the Pacific side the Manila Galleon, the authorized merchantman in Mexico-Philippine trade, sailed to and from Acapulco, New Spain, after the Eastern conquests and the rise of Spanish trade there in the 1560s and after. From Panama, on the gulf of the same name, an auxiliary fleet linked the Atlantic route to the west coast of South America through Lima's port of Callao, with its own link to Arica to serve Upper Peru. The fleets reassembled at Havana, in colonial Cuba, for the return voyage in convoy to Spain. The fortunes of minor ports that were not the designated ports of call for the Indies fleets waxed and waned in response to fluctuating economic developments in the interior regions which they served, either as subsidiaries of, or in illegal competition with, the main body of oceanic trade.

The entrepôt towns, located as they were in unsalubrious lowlands, came alive only with the celebration of the commercial fair upon the arrival of the fleets, when merchants and seamen thronged their streets and temporary lodging houses. When their harbors had cleared and the last of the pack mules and caravans of wagons had rumbled out of town, they lapsed into a tropical stupor until the next fair. The major points of consumption and distribution in Spanish America were administrative capitals, particularly the viceregal cities of Mexico City and Lima, and regional centers for mines in New Galicia and Upper Peru.

In Brazil, by contrast, the major seaports were also the principal towns of the colony, serving agricultural plantation regions in the coastal hinterland. Portuguese policy permitted direct export of Brazilian products to European ports in early years, but by the end of the sixteenth century, as defense needs mounted, convoyed sailings became necessary, were regularized under the aegis of the Brazil Company (1649–84), and continued into the eighteenth century under a *junta do comércio* or board of trade at Lisbon. The fleets served all major ports, from Belem and São Luís in the north to Olinda-Recife and Bahia in the northeast and Rio de Janeiro in the central south. No comparable system of entrepôts and fairs affected an urban network in Brazil as did the one in Spanish America.

Six basic categories of goods moved along the principal routes of Atlantic commerce: 1) familiar foodstuffs—wine, oil, biscuits, beer, cheese, sausage, salt cod, grain, pasta, garlic, and preserved fruits—some of which eventually were supplanted by colonial production; 2) traditional manufactures of the home countries—shoes, hats, hosiery, soaps, wax, roping, bagging, tools, weaponry, resins, laquers, fancy bridlery—which also in time had their imitations by local artisans; 3) reexported manufactures, made elsewhere in Europe and the east and shipped via Seville-Cádiz and Lisbon, and consisting largely of a great variety of textiles—silks, satins, velvets, damasks, linens, lace, embroidered cloths, and Indian cottons; 4) medicinal drugs and exotic spices of varied European, domestic, American, and Asian origin—lavender water, quinine, tea, cinnamon, and pepper; 5) enslaved human cargoes from West Africa; and 6) commodities of American production sent in return— gold and silver, pearls, dyewoods, sugar, tobacco, cacao, cotton, hides, timber, indigo, and cochineal.

The wholesale merchants who managed the most important segments of the major routes acted on their own accounts, or in partnership with fellow merchants, or sometimes as commission agents of the great merchants of Iberian ports, often operating in a variety of arrangements. The companies mentioned in the letters of Iberian merchants of colonial times were rarely the large shareholders' organizations conjured up by our notions of enterprise today. They were rather simple partnerships between two, or a few, individuals, established by contractual arrangement with regard to the capital invested and the distribution of responsibilities among the interested parties, and generally limited to a few years duration. Merchants might have a series of such contracts for large-scale buying, selling, and shipping pending at any one time. They also often were involved in a retail outlet as part of the larger business enterprise. This was a common practice in the colonies and contrasted with European custom, which distinguished more sharply between wholesale and retail trades. In addition, large-scale import-export merchants may have owned or had shares in one or more oceangoing vessels. Some employed their own mule teams and wagons in the inland trade. The great merchant was particularly careful to avoid overly specialized activities. There was risk enough in investment in enterprises that involved ventures which might take several years to carry to completion. Sales in overstocked or understocked markets dependent on the fleet system could be extraordinarily profitable, but not always reliable.

The great merchants under discussion here are those who had the capacity, measured in experience, credit-worthiness, knowledge, and contacts, to act also as merchant financiers, lending cash and supplying credit to lesser merchants, miners, planters, ranchers, and other entrepreneurs. They collected certain royal taxes in the colony, provisioned institutions of church and crown, and left behind impressive legacies as philanthropic bequests, assisting the stability of the state and enriching the social patrimony. Their generosity to convents, monasteries, and pious foundations permitted these institutions of the church in turn, in the absence of secular bankers, to act as major sources of credit in the colony. Of the commercial classes, only the big wholesalers enjoyed opportunities for emulating, socializing with, and even marrying into families of the local aristocracies of landowners and *encomenderos*, recipients of grants of Indian labor and tribute, heirs of early conquest treasure.

Merchants dominated the commercial life that was synonymous with the city in Spanish and Portuguese America. The more extensive the administrative, productive, and cultural activities that colonial Latin American urban centers undertook, the larger were the European and Europeanized populations in residence, and, thus, the more elaborate were the commercial headquarters that located there. Merchants orchestrated a rhythmic vitality in the urban scene, in their gatherings at the great fairs of Portobelo and Cartagena when the fleets put in, in the regularity of commercial hours and market days, in the seasonal provisioning of populous towns with the harvests of the countryside. Their commercial functions were essential to, and thoroughly integrated with, the local, regional, and imperial economy. The city was their base.

Thus, the social history of the city, a commercial arena and a hub of trade, is incomplete without an examination of the roles of colonial Latin American merchants and their compatriots. They appear as central characters from the early days of colonial society through the growth and evolution of the seventeenth century to the great period of administrative reform and economic expansion in the eighteenth century, the eve of independence.

Sixteenth Century Foundations

The conquest and settlement of the Americas by the Iberian nations of Spain and Portugal was a commercial enterprise in its conception, although mounted as a military campaign and justified as a religious mission. Columbus set out to establish a trading post in the Orient, not to discover a New World. The pithy phrase, "For God, for glory and for gold," captures very well the sentiments and enthusiasm of the participants. The first agencies of empire were Lisbon's *casa da India,* organized by 1501 and incorporating other organizations created for the African trades, and the *casa de contratación,* House of Trade, established at Seville in 1503. The commercial inspiration was pervasive and the commercial forms essential to the organization and conduct of expeditions, which were known as *compañías* or partnerships and were military in style, with a business orientation.

Professional merchants, as well as men with commercial skills and connections, provided financing and acted as supply masters and agents for the return of booty to the metropolis. Christopher Columbus availed himself of the assistance of fellow Genoese in the merchant banking house of Spinola and di Negri to guarantee loans that made his first voyage possible. The next venture was financed partially from the sale of enslaved Indians whom he had brought from the Caribbean.

Mercantile agents sat out the first years of conquest in the growing town of Santo Domingo, the capital on Hispaniola which served the Caribbean region, or dispersed in other, ruder Caribbean ports. Having disposed of an initial round of supplies to outfit expeditions, men like the Burgos merchant Hernando de Castro carried on petty trade for cash and credit while waiting impatiently for the success of the adventurers and the moment of melting down of the gold collected that would make additional sales possible. They hoped for splendid profits at this stage, but the real prize was participation in the trade of established settlements. In 1520, Hernando de Castro, writing from Santiago, Cuba, to his partner in Seville, hoped "God willing, to do business with Francisco de Garay as governor and captain [of Jamaica] so that as I have written, you and I would supply all the merchandise from Castile necessary for that island. If this is done, I promise you it will be profitable. Please God that it be for his service, amen."[1]

Essential to conquest, merchants also were instrumental to the construction of Spanish colonial society in their roles as participants and partners in two institutions upon which the social and economic order was based: the Spanish town and the Indian *encomienda*. Town founding converted spoils sharing to governance. The institution of the encomienda permitted Europeans to pursue their exploitation of the Indies with continuing rights to the tribute and labor of the native population. Encomenderos were the original *vecinos* of towns, the propertied householders who composed the body eligible for service on the *cabildo,* the municipal council, as *regidores,* or councilmen, and *alcaldes,* or magistrates. As noncombatants, merchants were excluded from holding encomiendas. As transients, or as individuals with potential conflicts of interest, they were denied positions on the cabildo which regulated matters of local trade. Yet exceptions abounded, not least because of the growing commercialization of economy and society.

Superficially, the encomienda was "feudal," a precapitalist institution akin to the medieval European fief. Its holder enjoyed tribute rights in return for his military service to the crown. In the context of the Atlantic colonial economy, however, the encomienda acquired commercial value and its owner became an entrepreneur. A valuable encomienda was not only one with great numbers of tributary Indians, but one whose owner possessed either the luck or the skill to transform tribute into marketable commodities. The encomendero might profitably exploit Indian labor in mines, in agriculture, or in textile workshops. Great encomenderos, such as Hernán Cortés, conqueror of Mexico, and the Pizarros in Peru, employed salaried managers, *mayordomos,* or administrators, who handled their business affairs. Others engaged mercantile agents, entered partnerships with merchants, or simply moved into merchant activities on their own, like Juan de Guzmán, leading encomendero of the Socunusco area of colonial Central America during the mid-sixteenth century cacao boom, who shipped his cacao to the New Spain market in his own vessels.

The early cacao phenomenon spawned the growth of Spanish towns, small ports on the Pacific for shipbuilding, and commercial settlements like the entrepôt at Huehuetlán, temporary home of middlemen or merchant expediters in the cacao trade. The large town of Sonsonate had 400 vecinos, principally merchants and traders, in the 1570s, second only to the regional capital of Santiago de Guatemala, which had some 500 Spanish householders, including an affluent elite of encomenderos and encomendero-merchants connected with cacao.

Mining, not agriculture, constituted the principal impetus for Spanish colonial expansion. Trans—Atlantic trade increased with the modest rush to exploit alluvial gold in the Caribbean. Real as well as anticipated returns from minerals underwrote further conquests and settlements by Europeans. The discovery of major silver mines at Potosí in 1545, and at Zacatecas in 1546, set the pattern for commercial interest in the Indies over the long run: colonial bullion in exchange for merchandise imported from Spain.

Mining operations were often joint ventures of encomenderos, with access to labor and preference in securing land titles to mining sites, and merchant *aviadores* or *habilitadores,* the suppliers, who contributed capital for the provisions, equipment, and wages necessary to extract and refine ore. The portion of bullion and/or minted specie that the latter received in return was forwarded to Spain in exchange for imports of Spanish and foreign goods.

Most mining camps were industrial sites with no urban pretensions, but as they mushroomed they precipitated European investment in agricultural production on large haciendas and engaged a vast commercial network of middlemen employed in provisioning the camps. Merchants and traders proliferated among the swelling populations in new towns which were regional headquarters or way-stations on supply routes. The most spectacular of the boom towns was Potosí, with a population of 120,000 to 160,000 at its height, a paradise for merchants long before the century's end. Insignificant in comparison, but important in its own right, the silver capital at Zacatecas had attracted as many as 200 traders and 50 retail shops by 1600.

The development of the colonial economy and the increase in European population was mirrored in the growth of the Indies trade. Its value quadrupled from the 1540s to the 1560s as merchants switched their cargo shipments from basic provisions, high in bulk and low in value, to more luxurious merchandise. As purveyors of goods, as well as settlers, merchants were an important part of the stream of westward migration. Between 1520 and 1539, they constituted fewer than 2 percent of passengers from Seville, but from 1540 to 1559, 1 in 20 was a merchant, and from 1560 to 1579 1 in 16 fell in this category. Throughout the colonial period commerce was the preferred occupation of immigrants, and the majority of the merchant elite in every community were peninsular-born.[2]

The merchants who came out to the colonies did so as partners or agents of Spanish merchants of Seville, the capital of Andalusia, a river port on the Guadalquivir that dominated the Indies trade through the concentration of supervisory agencies there and at the larger ocean harbor at Cádiz, south on the seacoast. The Seville merchants secured a monopoly on colonial trade and the confirmation of a corporate *fuero,* or legal privilege, with the institution of the *consulado,* a merchant guild, in their city in 1543. The consulado functioned both as a tribunal, or privileged court to resolve litigation emanating from commercial transactions, and as a guild, or representative to lobby for members' interests and undertake projects on the corporation's behalf. Seville merchants were at the apex of the multilayered, intricate network of trade, composed of innumerable partnerships of greater and lesser merchants, each involving only a few individuals and limited in time and scope. The state-ordained monopoly permitted them to command supplies of trade goods and credits for the Indies. By the end of the century the merchant elite who constituted the highest layer of this network in the colonies had petitioned for and received authorization for parallel consulados at Mexico City, in 1592–94, and Lima, in 1612–13. Although limits were placed on their autonomy by the regulation of imperial trade, the American consulado merchants reduced others to the role of middlemen, dependent on them, as they were on Seville, for goods and credit, and effectively discouraged any legal alteration of this system for 200 years.

So great was the demand for merchandise in the colonies, and so inadequate were the supply lines, that illegal channels of trade opened everywhere. Anyone who could get together a bundle of trade goods competed with professional merchants. Commerce drew even the high and mighty in its wake, for many found it a necessary and effective supplement to income from official posts. The Bishop of Cuzco dealt in coca leaf for the Potosí mines; priests traded in the cacao of colonial Central America; governors everywhere overlooked regulations for a share of commercial profits.

Commerce put its mark on Brazil's coast in 1501, when Portugal initiated exploitation with a contract for dyewood collection let to Fernão de Noronha, but Portuguese America lagged considerably behind Spanish territories as an attractive market for European goods. Transient traders first visited in ships which put in to barter for supplies with Indians and to cut and collect brazilwood, which gave the colony its name and which yielded a red dye of value to the growing European textile industry. The temporary trading stations, known as *feitorias,* were ephemeral sites. Permanent settlement originated with territorial grants and the establishment of sugar plantations, worked by Indian and, later, Negro slaves, beginning in the 1530s. By the late sixteenth century 130 sugar mills scattered along the northeast and central coast, mainly in Pernambuco and Bahia, were able to ship perhaps 7,000 tons of sugar annually to European markets, much of it transported directly in foreign, especially Dutch, vessels.[3]

Portuguese success with Brazilian sugar was due to previous experience in cultivation in the Atlantic islands; to the direct interest of Europeans, particularly the Dutch, in capital investments and shipping; and to the Portuguese access to black labor created by cultivation of slave markets on the African coast since the previous century. The procurement of slaves was sufficiently important, and the risks sufficiently great, that the colonial Latin American slave trade to American ports tended to be conducted through monopolies, granted to individual contractors and, later, to state chartered companies. The Portuguese were the principal drivers of the trade in the sixteenth century, but Genoese, Spaniards, Dutch, French, and English gradually entered to supply colonies in competition. The trade in the American markets was one of many branches of commercial enterprise which merchants pursued. They dealt in slaves, a few at a time, as they dealt in other merchandise. While the trade is presumed to have absorbed a good deal of commercial capital, it also made possible the establishment of centers of production which would have been inconceivable without a coerced labor force.

Sugar and slaves molded Brazil's urban character in disproportion to other factors. The specialization in plantation production, with its slave base, discouraged the evolution of a colonial society that was truly the microcosm of the metropolis. The crown established civil and ecclesiastical administration at Bahia in 1549. As the nominal colonial capital, the settlement attracted a large white European population, 12,000 to Pernambuco's 8,000 by 1600, even though the latter port's region produced more sugar. Trade was not centralized; no one port achieved dominance during the period, and the character of the merchant presence in Brazil remained transitory for some years.

Indeed, as the interest of the Portuguese in their Far Eastern trade began to wane, the Spanish Indies became more attractive than Brazil as markets for Portuguese merchants. With the ascension of the Spanish Philip II to the Portuguese throne after a crisis of succession in 1580, for the period of the Union of the Two Crowns or the "Babylonian Captivity," 1580–1640, Portuguese merchants surged through the Indies both legally and illegally. They opened a surreptitious trade through Buenos Aires in 1582, and gained access to Spanish markets for the award of 1595, of the slave *asiento,* or contract, which allowed them to land slaves in the Río de la Plata basin and in other designated ports, such as Cartagena.

While the historical Union of the two Crowns tended to blur the national distinctions among Iberian merchant groups, the presence of New Christians operated to divide these groups. "New Christian" was a social category created at the end of the fifteenth century by the forced conversions of Jews threatened with expulsion, first from Spain in 1492, then from Portugal in 1497. The Holy Office of the Inquisition flourished in Iberia from the 1480s and migrated to the colonies in the sixteenth century to root out "secret Jews." Given the insecurity of their positions at home, New Christian merchants, more than Old Christians, were apt to respond to the beckoning of trading opportunities in the New World. While "New Christian" was not synonymous with "merchant," as once was believed, they constituted almost half of merchants with identifiable ethnic backgrounds who were active at Bahia in the seventeenth century, for example, and were an influential sector of the elite elsewhere in the Indies.

The international character of the Atlantic trading communities, the engagement in commerce by many people who otherwise would not deign to consider themselves merchants, and the bitter antagonism engendered by the persecution of the New Christians were enormously powerful factors in creating the peculiar social position which merchants occupied in the hierarchy of colonial urban society. Ambiguous social status, less than noble but above plebeian, was the legacy of their historical situation in early modern Europe. The stigma still attached to commerce was the confused product of the earlier artisan origins of traders and of medieval Catholic church prohibitions against usury, which identified moneylending with Jews. Commercial occupations were taken up by the ambitious who did not enjoy the perquisites of office or higher birth and thus suffered the rumors of ignoble origins of New Christian background, stains on one's honor which only the acquisition of wealth might erase, and then not without the fear of later discovery. This did not prevent the rise of formidable mercantile communities in Iberia. However, the Iberian merchants did not enjoy the same degree of public acceptance as did the commercial bourgeoisie of England, and they were even less accepted than in France, also a Catholic country where intolerance prevailed.

Colonial merchants shared the background, handicaps, and advantages of the metropolitan merchants who were their kin, partners, and competitors, but these were mediated by New World conditions. The importance of trade to the development of the Indies attracted many merchants as emigrants and raised them to prominence in local societies where commerce was a principal economic activity, where men of ability were in short supply and white skin monopolized privilege, or where shades of difference between entrepreneurial encomenderos and merchants were insignificant. Merchants appeared among the elites, even as members of city councils, from Santiago de Chile, a relatively rural backwater, to Lima, the viceregal capital, by the 1580s, indicating the partial success of commercial activity in overriding traditional sanctions against it.

Seventeenth Century Transformations

> Many merchants, having a treasure of three and four hundred bars and ingots of silver, each worth about five hundred *escudos,* pile them up and then spreading mattresses on them, use them as beds for sleeping.
>
> (Carletti, Lima, 1595)

Lima's commercial activity is considerable both by land and by sea.
All manufactured products and crops of the realm come to this center,
and merchandise goes out from it overland and by water to every part of
Peru, the Kingdom of New Granada, to Tucumán, and to the Kingdom
of Chile.

(Pedro de León, Portocarrero, ca. 1615)

The streets of Christendom must not compare with those in breadth and
cleanness, but especially in the riches of the shops which do adorn them.[3]

(T. Gage, Mexico City, 1625)

Seventeenth-century travelers through Spanish and Portuguese America typically reported on regional prosperity in terms of the volume of trade, the number and appearance of commercial establishments, and the reputed size of merchants' fortunes in the principal towns and cities. This particular index was less an objective standard than the consequence of a fascination with probing the true wealth of the fabled Indies. Impressions such as these lacked the underpinnings of the statistical records which more enlightened political economists of the later eighteenth century used to construct treatises, and, with an eye to a popular readership, authors allowed the exaggerated stuff of legend to creep into their accounts. Merchants, marketplaces, and trade had roles in seventeenth-century urban development, but not always in accordance with the models predicted or desired by metropolitan administrations.

Despite many buttresses to Seville's monopoly, foreign interests permeated Indies trade at every possible point. If they did not secure special license to travel to America, they attempted covert entry. When Spanish-built and owned vessels were unavailable, foreign ships carried trade. Introduced to desirable foreign-made articles by Spanish merchants, creole customers sought superior quality at cheaper prices in illegal trade, with Brazilian contrabandists who connived with Dutch traders to send goods overland to Upper Peru via Buenos Aires, and with English and French smugglers who frequented notorious pirate havens in the Caribbean. Trade war against Spain evolved into a policy of colonial settlement, led by the Dutch. With the capture of Jamaica by the English in 1655, foreigners secured a permanent base from which to raid and trade and creoles found an entrepôt closer than Seville for their customary purchases.

Colonial demand sustained contraband and promoted competition from colonial as well as foreign traders. Merchants from Peru appeared in Seville with surplus capital ready to purchase goods independently from Spanish-based partners, to the chagrin of the consulado there. Markets in Peru absorbed illegal commerce in Asian luxuries via the New Spain-Philippine trade, their merchants defying prohibitions by calling regularly at Puerto del Marqués, just north of Acapulco, despite the formal ban on this trade to Peru which had been in effect since 1631. The result of these conditions—the fraud which the monopoly and the insatiable colonial demand for foreign goods encouraged and the effects of enemy depredations—was contraction of the registered Spanish trans-Atlantic trade, which first became serious in the 1620s and never ameliorated after 1650.

As the traditional trade lifeline with the peninsula weakened, Spanish American merchants experienced a reorientation now marked by diversified development, particularly in agriculture. They invested their profits more readily in foodstuffs, cattle, sheep, tobacco, cacao, indigo, and cochineal, and produced for internal markets and for export, leading to greater commercialization and further investment in land. Private estates aimed to market surpluses, not just to be self-sufficient. This in turn stimulated intercolonial trade, which the Seville monopoly generally had labored to restrict, and encouraged growth in areas and in industries which otherwise had been neglected. Colonial merchants contributed loans and donations for defense, but they also enriched themselves as contractors and investors in local industry. In addition to acquiring land with commercial value, they were also in a position to purchase bureaucratic posts, including municipal council offices, put up for sale as revenue measures of the crown. Thus, merchants were accumulating the prerequisites for easier acceptance and incorporation into local urban elites: longterm residency, property ownership, and sources of income that did not depend so directly on the vagaries of trade.

The municipal council, a primary institution of local influence, was a theater of conflict. Struggles could turn violent, as in the "civil wars" which erupted at Potosí between 1622 and 1625, pitting Basque mining interests, in a successful defense of their control of the cabildo, against the predatory actions of non-Basque factions. In some cases the positions of merchants were enhanced. Municipal councils that previously had maintained barriers were now opened to merchant office seekers. Merchants appeared on the cabildo of Zacatecas in 1654 and 1660. In other circumstances, as in Santiago de Guatemala, after the colonial Central American cacao boom had flagged, merchants' previous influence was eclipsed by that of a new elite of landowners and royal bureaucrats.

The rise of merchant-landowners coincided with the phenomenon of "disappearing merchants," repeated instances of the failure of successful merchants to establish commercial enterprises which were handed down from father to son. Instead, the investment of profits from trade in landed property furnished a new source of family patrimony and an opportunity for creole sons to ignore the professions of their fathers. In seventeenth-century Popayán a highland center of regional trade, "to succeed in trade was to abandon it."[5] Commerce was a ladder of mobility, a producer of wealth which created, and continually re-created, a creole urban elite.

Brazil remained a marginal region where sugar plantations dotted the coasts in the neighborhood of a few ports, and backwoodsmen roamed the interior in search of Indian slaves and elusive mineral wealth. Sugar was the great money maker, and successful merchants able and willing to invest in rural property soon acquired sugar estates and mills, as well as cattle ranches which supplied the plantation complexes. The merchant-planter appeared early in the seventeenth century as the obvious counterpart to the merchant-hacendado of Spanish America. Like their Spanish brethren, the Brazilian merchants entered trade as agents and partners of Lisbon compatriots; as principal suppliers to planters in rural districts and lesser merchants of towns, they shipped out sugar and took in European goods. The few who managed to end their careers as planters and mill owners often took the first step by marrying a planter's or mill owner's daughter.

Francisco Fernandes do Sim (1593–1664) was a Madeira-born merchant of Bahia, buying sugar and importing wine in the 1620s. He had two ships in the Lisbon trade in the 1630s, and then married the daughter of a local notable who owned a sugar mill on the island of Itaparica. He died in 1664, the owner of 3 sugar plantations, a mill, a cattle ranch, and 10 houses in the city, without, however, having abandoned his commercial business. He was able to provide well for his family, including a son who was a resident planter and a daughter who married a fellow merchant of Madeira, and also to endow the city's charity house, the *santa casa da misericórdia*, with a legacy to provide dowries for orphan girls and to tend the indigent sick in the institution's hospital. Commerce permitted him to create a niche for his heirs among the local elite by buying into the landowning circle, without which he would have remained a simple representative of merchant interests.

Seventeenth-century crises also afflicted Brazil, gradually altering the character of its economy. Brazil, along with the African and Asian trade ports of the Portuguese commercial empire, under nominal Spanish authority until the Restoration in 1640, faced intervention and territorial encroachments by Dutch, English, and French competitors. The Far East was not abandoned outright, but efforts to regain control of the Brazilian northeast sugar coast, occupied by the Dutch between the 1630s and 1654, consolidated Portuguese interests with regard to their Atlantic colonies, toward which they previously had been indifferent, and tied their imperial fortunes to the more effective exploitation of Brazilian commodities and African slaves. Instrumental in the Portuguese recovery was the organization of the Brazil Company in 1649, with merchant, largely New Christian, capital. It was charged to supply the colonies with basic foodstuffs (oil, wine, codfish, flour) at fixed prices, and to convoy merchant fleets bound to Portugal laden with sugar, tobacco, cotton, and hides. In return for these services, the company received the slave trade and brazilwood monopolies, together with many privileges as the chief crown contractor in the colony. This centralization of trade was a timely measure, as Caribbean sugar had begun to oust Brazilian produce from European markets, and was accompanied by renewed efforts to discover valuable mineral deposits in the Brazilian interior. Although depression beset the Atlantic trade in the last quarter of the seventeenth century, a certain stability prevailed. The commercial climate was promising enough to attract Portugal's allies to seek treaty rights to establish merchant representatives in Brazilian ports. At Bahia, tobacco trade took up the slack left by sugar's decline and the city experienced a round of urban improvements. Gold strikes in the interior in the 1690s in the region subsequently known as Minas Gerais, or General Mines, provided a long-awaited bonanza, and in the gold rush that followed Bahia's merchants were the first to commandeer trade in slaves from the African Mina coast and in European merchandise to the mines.

By the end of the seventeenth century, the social world which all colonial Latin American merchants inhabited was similar in the opportunities it offered and the tensions that defined it. There was also a degree of symmetry in the contributions that merchants and mercantile life made to the physical geography of the colonial city in Spanish and Portuguese America. The commercial quarter near the principal marketplace was just as much an essential element of town life as the municipal government and the cathedral. A principal thoroughfare, typically called Merchants' Street or Commerce Street, ran through this district, perhaps only a block or several blocks square. In seaport towns this street paralleled the harbor, lined with landings, docks, wharfs, and waterside warehouses. (See Figure 9.) In the entrepôt towns of regulated trade, the official customs house was an imposing edifice; at Portobelo, for example, the rare stone construction stood among insubstantial thatched roof structures. At the time of the great fair, ships' crews pitched large tents to display merchants' wares and the town's few permanent residents moved out or aside to accommodate visitors, renting rooms and houses at scandalous rates.

In Mexico City the principal market faced the viceroy's palace in the main square and drew all levels of the city's commerce to it. Food vendors, petty traders, and permanently stocked retail stores competed for space under the arcades at the *Parián*. The market's name was identical to that of the Chinese quarter of Manila, the heart of the eastern luxury trade. Artisan shops and specialty retailers tended to congregate together in streets that ran nearby.

Did Lima's merchants actually sleep upon their bullion treasure, as Carletti believed? Ties between house and shop persisted even in the upper ranks of trade. The great merchants dwelt in apartments above their stores, two-story buildings indicated town houses of the elite. The ground-level areas housed rented shops, the countinghouse, and slave and servant habitations, while the merchant and his family enjoyed greater privacy on upper floors facing rear or central courtyards. In Bahia, where the term *mercador de sobrado* (town-house merchant) identified the merchant elite, wooden jalousies cut off overhanging porches from the dirt and noise of crowded streets below. Climate, reduced urban density, and custom encouraged the merchants of Buenos Aires in the eighteenth century to enjoy more spacious lodgings, but even in the more formal single-story establishments in the city center merchants maintained corner stores and backroom shops in their homes.

The sights and smells of city commerce that surprised seventeenth-century travelers as unexpected signs of wealthy trade in the colonies became, for some observers during the eighteenth and early nineteenth centuries, visions of unadulterated hardship in tropical ports. Congestion in the commercial quarter of Bahia's Lower City, along the beach, reminiscent as the city was to some of the fine views of Lisbon, put off others, who were repelled by the sight of human merchandise on view in the doorways of slave merchants and by the pungent odor of snuff tobacco manufacture, roasting coffee, and garbage spilling into rutted streets.

Few foreigners were admitted to the private homes of members of the merchant community in Brazil; for those who were, the contrast between outside commotion and domestic seclusion, public affluence and private simplicity, was stark. Yet commerce supported a style of life that included the best of what colonial trade supplied: imported house furnishings, fine clothing, retinues of slaves, and tables laden with the staples of European cuisine. With the extension of affluence in some areas during the course of the eighteenth century, some merchants adopted refinements befitting the titles of nobility that trade had secured for them. Town houses expanded into mansions, courtyards became gardens, and slave-borne litters were exchanged for horse-drawn carriages. (See Figure 10.) But such elegance generally was seen only in the consulado cities of Mexico City and Lima and in the chief Brazilian ports, Bahia and Rio de Janeiro. In Brazil the vulgar display of the mining boom had long since subsided, and a soberer style characterized the typical merchant gentlemen of the later colonial era.

Eighteenth-Century Development

In the eighteenth century both Iberian empires faced an intensification of international rivalry in the Atlantic world which forced central authorities to undertake economic development schemes and fiscal improvements in order to secure more revenue for defense. The efforts, begun fitfully in the late seventeenth century and culminating in the great reform eras in Spanish America under the reign of Charles III (1759–88) and his ministers and in Brazil during the tenure of the Marquis of Pombal, Prime Minister of José I (1750–77), targeted colonial commercial systems as the chief sources of revenue. Reforms principally affected structures of trade, how it was carried on, and by whom. Alterations in the system of incentives under which merchants were rewarded for their economic contributions to state and society were another feature of the reforms affecting commerce in the period.

Structural changes included the creation of state-chartered commercial companies and other encouragements to increase traditional agricultural exports, including sugar, tobacco, cacao, and cochineal, and to develop new ones, such as indigo, cotton, hemp, and hides. Silver-mining production revived in response to technological and capital incentives. New and improved quality in peninsular manufactures found more satisfied customers in the colonies. With the gradual abandonment of the cumbersome fleet systems, Atlantic crossing schedules improved, freight charges fell (making peninsular goods less expensive), and more peninsular and American ports entered the network of legal trade.

Measures were introduced that strengthened the merchant profession vis-à-vis competition from foreigners, less experienced or less well capitalized nationals, privileged religious corporations, and government officers engaged in trade on the sly. Pombal revived a Portuguese Board of Trade at Lisbon on which merchants, many of them his protégées, sat. Among its supervisory activities, it registered wholesale merchants in the Brazil trade. This made it possible to crack down on the commercial travelers known as *comisarios volantes,* reputed to be fronts for foreign dealers. The expulsion of the Jesuit order from Iberia and its possessions by the 1760s struck against a corporate entity that had considerable dominion over land, labor, and commodity markets in the colonies. Another wave of protoliberal secularization of the economy occured after 1800, with the consolidation decrees, the calling in of outstanding loans held by religious houses, convents and monasteries, and pious foundations, and the establishment of civil credit and banking institutions in the peninsula and the colonies.

In Spanish America efforts were made to suppress the practice of *repartimiento de comercio* under which district governors, *corregidores,* had monopolized trade with Indian communities in collusion with the consulado merchants. The latter financed the purchase of the posts of corregidores, who, in their capacity as tribute collectors, acted as mercantile agents, buying up marketable commodities from Indian producers and compelling them to take European merchandise at grossly inflated prices. Elimination of this abusive practice ideally would restore this sector of the market to free competition. The projected reforms, part of the implementation of the Ordinance of Intendants in the 1780s, touched the nerve center of the colonial system of exploitation and thus were protested, forestalled, and ultimately made unenforceable.

This professionalization and secularization of commerce was supported by attempts to promote the status of merchants by eliminating legal barriers to their advancement. The ennoblement of the merchant occupation had been proclaimed in Spain in the early seventeenth century, but this was clearly reinforced under Charles III when even artisans as a class also were declared eligible candidates for titles. In Portugal Pombal made a belated gesture in the same direction by eliminating barriers to merchant ennoblement and by annulling discriminatory practices against New Christians.

Commercial reforms and colonial economic change in general affected urban systems in the eighteenth century. Where regional development occurred,
cities and towns flourished. The rise of Havana and Caracas can be traced to
the activity of chartered commercial companies headquartered in these cities.
With the decline of the fleets, the Isthmus fairs disappeared. Portobelo followed Nombre de Díos into an urban netherworld. Control once exercised by
the consulado cities of Mexico City and Lima eroded. The administrative reorganization that created the viceroyalty of Río de la Plata in 1776, confirmed the victory of Buenos Aires over the pretensions of the Lima consulado
to dominate the fate of the trade in the Río de la Plata basin.

With the breakdown of the Andalusian monopoly, regional centers lob-
bied to obtain relief from consulado control. Guadalajara's merchant representatives argued that "urbanism" had stagnated in that city as a result of
Mexico City's indifference to their needs. In response to longstanding claims
and as part of a general program of creating institutions to foster economic
development, new consulados were created, beginning in the 1790s, at Caracas and Guatemala City (1793), Buenos Aires and Havana (1794), and Cartagena, Guadalajara, Veracruz, Santiago, and Concepción (1795). They were
not solely mercantile bodies, as the crown, in a spirit of compromise, required agricultural interests to be represented also, and at some consulados,
such as Havana and Caracas, planter interests held sway. Charged to promote
trade and development, they took up roadworks, bridge building, and other
public works projects with enthusiasm, moving the older consulados at Mexico City and Lima to do the same. In most cases, however, the disruptions of
commerce that set in soon after the creation of the new consulados and extended through the years of independence, postponed their good intentions,
and many were casualties of liberal governments under the early national
regimes.

In Brazil efforts to establish comparable institutions, corporate merchant
bodies representing their interests, had been thwarted throughout the eighteenth century by the crown's capitulation to Lisbon merchant pressure. Nevertheless, a parallel institution did exist in the four *mesas de inspeção,* boards of
commodity inspection created in the ports of Rio, Bahia, Pernambuco, and
Maranhão and headed by a crown judge. Planters also were represented on
these boards, which set prices and supervised quality but also had particular
merchant functions, acting *in loco* for the Lisbon Board of Trade to hear commercial litigation in the first instance and generally certifying all merchant
petitions as they were forwarded to Lisbon. They also were engaged by the
colonial governors in economic development programs toward the close of
the period and initiated public works improvements very similar to those of
consulados. The mesas served as prototypes for the Chambers of Commerce
first established in 1810. (See Figure 11.)

In addition to their roles in long term development trends within the colonies during the eighteenth century, colonial merchants also shared not only similar life-styles, but networks of social relationships. These included reliance on family ties, nearly universal participation in religious-fraternal associations, and similarities in the satisfaction of military obligations, together comprising a broad range of informal experiences which contributed to a common, collective experience.

Family Organization, Domestic Life, and Business

The network of personal relationships through which business generally was conducted in the Atlantic commercial world during the colonial era dramatized the importance of family ties. The family, and the relationships which created and extended it, was unrivalled as an institution, as much for merchants as for other social groups. Kinship bonds helped immigrant youth secure a commercial situation in the colonies. They encouraged personal accountability for conducting business in otherwise distant, anonymous markets poorly served by commercial courts. Merchants needed close kin ties to achieve financial and social success.

Where possible, merchants looked to blood relatives—fathers, sons, uncles, nephews, and cousins—to handle their affairs. Family names are prominent in records of powers of attorney that permitted merchants to designate agents to act for them in commercial transactions or judicial proceedings. Affinity relationships, those of marriage, constituted an additional circle of family ties. In the eighteenth century immigrant merchants most frequently married colonial-born daughters of fellow merchants, establishing relationships that united merchant capital and extended networks of reliable commercial correspondents. In addition, ties of ritual kinship bound affinity with *compadrazgo,* ritual co-parenthood. This life-long association began with the selection of spiritual sponsors, "godparents" in Catholic practice, who witnessed the baptisms of infants and the marriages of couples. On these occasions, merchants and their wives called on merchant peers and relatives to stand up for their children. Elite merchants extended themselves as godparents for the offspring of junior partners, clerks, and clientele in a mutually satisfying expression of noblesse oblige that further reinforced the cohesiveness of mercantile society.

Marriage and family formation under these circumstances was a critical opportunity in a professional career. It was an important means by which immigrant merchants, in wave upon wave from the first days of the colony until late colonial times, attained social position. In many instances, the unmarried immigrant in his mid-thirties sought as a spouse a younger, colonial-born woman, often half his age, who could offer him entry into a local family in exchange for his merchant capital. Even if he were capital poor, his new wife's dowry in goods or cash was considered fair return for his pure European ancestry and commercial skills. For the white European-born male, marriage could be a vehicle for considerable social and economic mobility. A merchant father had an eye for suitable candidates for his daughters, drawn from his circle of associates and subordinates. A young man in his employ had several years to demonstrate his probity and worth.

Whereas economic interests and social custom promoted intermarriage and family-connected commercial enterprises at the broad base of the merchant community, at the upper levels the merchant elite could expect to reach outward to marry into other elite sectors of colonial society. By the late eighteenth century, in the viceregal capitals, in *audiencia* (high court) cities, and in commercial and administrative centers, wealthy merchants experienced no obstacles to consideration among the highest ranks of regional elites. At this level, marriages between immigrant merchants and creole women merged the diverse business interests and political influence of increasingly integrated upper strata composed of royal officials, great landowners, and mining magnates, with fortunes made from overseas trade. Depending on the city, well-to-do merchants might marry and acquire land that had some commercial value, whether prior to or as the result of a "successful" marriage. Merchants at Buenos Aires, for example, rarely invested in ranch lands in the hinterland, although they did acquire rural properties that provided garden and orchard produce, and allowed them and their families opportunities for the equivalent of a "vacation retreat." At Bahia by the late eighteenth century, the active merchant-planter was a rare phenomenon. Fewer than 10 percent of leading merchants were also mill owners, and of these a third were Brazilian-born. There were cases, nevertheless, which illustrated the principle that marriage was the primary link between rural and urban interests and economic and political elites.

The families of Antonio Cardozo dos Santos and Pedro Rodrigues Bandeira are exemplary in this respect. Bandeira, born in the northern Portuguese port of Viana do Castelo around 1710, was a successful merchant in Bahia at midcentury, active in the Africa, Lisbon, and mining supply trades, who married the widowed daughter of a prominent tobacco exporter with properties in the Reconçavo, the near Bahian hinterland. Of their four children, two of his three girls were married; the eldest to Custodio Ferreira Dias, a clerk employed by her father who later did well in trade; the second, to Francisco Vianna, the university-educated son of fellow merchant Frutuoso Vicent Vianna. The fourth child, a son, remained a bachelor, notable as a sugar mill owner and opulent merchant-entrepreneur, a supporter of the Brazilian cause at independence, and dignified as a comendador of the regime. António Cardozo dos Santos was also from northern Portugal, born around 1716, the son of farmers at Vila Nova de Gaia in the Oporto district. He was sent as a youth to an uncle in Brazil who secured him employment as an apprentice in the merchant house of the Cruz family, notable Lisbon merchants, at Bahia. He married quite late, approaching 60, to the young daughter of a family active in the African trade, who bore him two children before his death in 1786. The widow carried on trade in his name, and then married a local artillery officer, while her daughter wed a lieutenant colonel in the infantry, Feliberto Caldeira Brant Pontes, a career officer also, and the future Marqués de Barbacena. The two men joined the male heir, Pedro Antonio Cardozo dos Santos, in sugar production, trade, and entrepreneurial ventures with Bandeira, and, like the latter, were distinguished supporters and beneficiaries of Brazilian independence. Knowledge of the financial affairs of these families is admittedly superficial, but the process is sufficiently clear: alliance of commercial wealth of the late 1700s with the capital holdings of the landed aristocracy of the early empire.

Marriage and family, the primary agency for the transfer of wealth, also dictated the disposition of merchant estates. Since many merchants married and chose younger women whose child-bearing years were at their maximum, well-to-do merchants tended to have fairly large families, limited by infertility and infant mortality, both less serious among the more prosperous strata. Thus, in the best documented case, late eighteenth-century Buenos Aires, merchant couples produced an average of 7 children of whom 4.7 reached early adulthood, with more females than males among the survivors.[6] The risk inherent in colonial trade and the partible inheritance laws of the Iberian world impeded the easy transmission of mercantile wealth intact. The entailed estate, or *mayorazgo,* was limited to those with large rural properties. Without such protection, merchants' estates were divided upon death, with the surviving spouse receiving one-half and the children even portions of the remainder. Up to one-fifth of the total estate could be set aside for special bequests, charitable donations, and funeral expenses. Childless merchants were more often the notable philanthropists of their time. With a large family care had to be exercised to prevent the total dissolution of the estate.

Merchants' sons had two alternatives: to continue in trade or to abandon it. At least one son of merchants of great wealth was apt to persist in commerce, but, thanks to the parental fortune, others could abandon trade for careers in the military, church, or colonial bureaucracy, leaving the future of the business to sons-in-law. Creole sons who chose to continue in their fathers' occupation did so in circumstances closer to those in which the older generation had begun. They were sent out at an early age to apprentice and clerk for other relatives or business associates in branches of the trade, just as their fathers had done before them, although with the security represented by the father's position.

The role of women in securing the continuity of the family enterprise was surprisingly important. Most merchants' daughters married, since in the late eighteenth century convent life was a less attractive option than it previously had been. Merchant widows were also more apt to remarry than other women in their age group. Family-based commercial houses were dependent on personal contacts, a short-lived credibility, and a clientele that disappeared without close attention. Arranged marriages in which women had little say guaranteed extension of the business and created some of the remarkable mercantile clans which flourished in the eighteenth century. Women were key instruments rather than active agents in the business and social organization of the period. The prerogative of widows to contract business constituted an exceptional and limited operation, presumably carried on under close supervision by family overseers.

In the case of the successful merchant who did not marry, or who left no worthy direct heir, family strategies also included an effective mechanism for the inheritance of the business in uncle-nephew relationships. These were not necessarily the most common, but were certainly one of the more striking phenomena in merchant society. Bachelor uncles received children of siblings as apprentices and yielded the business to the most able upon their death or retirement from the colony. Married uncles drew their immigrant nephews into marriage with their daughters. The higher up the scale of merchant wealth one went, the more family ties of all varieties prevailed. Virtually 90 percent of the middle and upper level merchants in Buenos Aires were linked by some kinship tie to at least one other *porteño* merchant.

In the eighteenth century powerful merchant families, some deservingly called mercantile clans, stood out in every major center of trade. In these cities they had a share of local, urban-based power, monopolizing trade, active in civic affairs, purchasing government posts, literally buying titles of nobility, and second to none in prestige. Examples are legion, but these families included the Basavilbasos and Lezicas in Buenos Aires, the Conde de Bassoco and the Marqués de Inguanzo in Mexico City, the Septién family of Guanajuato, and the Cardozo dos Santos and Rodrigues Bandeiras of Bahia.

The Marqués de Aycinena of Guatemala City is a particularly good example of an ambitious merchant who rode the Bourbon reform era to attain high prominence for his family. Juan Fermín de Aycinena migrated to New Spain at 19, parlaying mule-trading and strategic marriages over the years into dominance of the Guatemalan indigo trade. He was among the leading merchants who pushed for transfer and rebuilding of the capital after the earthquake in the 1770s and used his millions to purchase the title of *marquesado* in 1781. He and his heirs played a leading role first on the liberal and then on the conservative side during and after independence.

The characteristic way in which the family served business and business served the family was a common feature of colonial merchant society. It created closely knit communities and corporate traditions even in centers of colonial trade which were prohibited from organizing consulados. The urban base of family networks also reinforced the city's role as a center of political and social, as well as economic, influence.

Religion and Philanthropy

Merchants were especially prominent in the religious and philanthropic life of towns. The much vaunted "piety" of the age expressed, for merchants as for other members of society, belief in the tenets of the church and acceptance of community obligations which were carried out in anticipation of recognition in this life and in the next. As the principal institution in the organization of charity, the church monopolized channels of social integration and communal activity. Although in the late eighteenth century philanthropy was partially secularized and Americans aware of Enlightenment thought were critical of ecclesiastical power, church organizations continued to be important vehicles for merchants' civic and social activity. Religious brotherhoods, or *cofradías* (*irmandades* in Portuguese), operated in parish churches or neighborhood chapels. Third Orders, the lay organizations attached to conventual establishments of mendicants and other religious orders like the Dominicans, the Franciscans, and the brotherhoods, were mechanisms for the satisfaction of pious obligations and the administration of charity.

Brotherhoods organized popular participation in the body politic in the era prior to the secularization of civic culture, when the religious calendar principally ordered the cycle of public events. Banners, elaborately decorated statues of patron saints, and special costumes of brotherhoods participating in the annual Corpus Christi processions were magnificent displays that testified to the corporate tradition of urban life. Some brotherhoods were more prestigious than others, but eighteenth-century merchants were active in the membership and the governing bodies of these societies at all levels on the social scale.

At Bahia, merchants engaged in the slave trade to Mina on the West African coast formed a brotherhood dedicated to St. Anthony and raised their own chapel in the early 1700s at the height of that trade. In town, in the principal parishes of the commercial district, Conceição and Pilar, and in the Chapel of Corpo Santo, merchants congregated in a number of active religious fraternities. Merchants had a history of entry into the Third Orders of the Carmelites and the Franciscans, institutions dominated by the planter elite, although New Christian origins in the seventeenth century once had barred admission to some. Yet another Third Order, St. Dominic, was founded in the 1730s. A brief serial record of admissions decades later, from 1817 to 1821, just prior to Independence, indicates that at least half the new members were merchants, a number of them junior clerks in the employ of officers of the order.[7] Third Order membership was clearly a step recommended for advancement in a mercantile career.

The merchant elite in the community at Buenos Aires in the late eighteenth century was much less active in the city's cofradías, which served the increasingly heterogenous lower classes, than in the more prestigious Third Orders. Forty percent of merchants were Third Order members, while only 8 percent were members of cofradías. In the latter, they typically served as principal officers of the parish level organizations. The Third Order of St. Dominic outranked the others in social prestige in Buenos Aires. Merchants' membership in this order unquestionably demonstrated acceptance into local society.

In the category of quasi-religious charitable society, both Bahia and Buenos Aires had yet another pair of comparable socially prestigious and useful institutions, the *hermandad de la caridad,* and the *santa casa da misericórdia.* The hermandad, founded at Buenos Aires in 1743, was, like Bahia's santa casa, which dated from the late sixteenth century, an association of local notables, authorized by crown and diocese to undertake large-scale projects in urban welfare. They administered funds, given as bequests or received as alms, to support hospitals, pharmacies, orphanages, and women's retreat houses, to feed prisoners, to bury paupers, to endower indigent young women, and to subsidize needy widows. They extended loans at interest from their endowments, taking urban property as collateral, and in this way as well as through specific bequests, came to own or administer city real estate. The hermandad at Buenos Aires had acquired rural ranch property which had belonged to the Jesuits in northern Argentina after the expulsion of the order in the 1760s. The business experience which made merchants attractive as trustees and financial managers of convents, or deputies of the crown in handling public revenues, was equally welcome here. Merchants requested as well as extended loans. Well-placed contacts among those in charge of these colonial "banks" were especially useful to merchant borrowers. In 1791, merchants formed 20 percent of hermandad membership, but 48 percent of its governing body. Sixty-one percent of the highest positions on the Board of Guardians of the santa casa da misericórdia were merchant-held in the period 1780 to 1800.

Many leading merchants were, as individuals, generous benefactors of local public institutions concerned for the commonweal. A substantial portion of mercantile capital found its way into church hands. Merchants readily assumed their religious obligations as they took up their civic duties, in expectation of both moral and material reward. In hallowed corridors and board rooms of the religious charitable societies which remain a presence in the old city of Bahia, oil-on-canvas portraits of black-frocked and sober merchants of the late colonial era take their place along with the representatives of the planter elite as reminders of the roles the merchants played as leaders of these institutions.

Military and Civic Obligations

As pillars in the regional and imperial economies, merchants were called upon to contribute to the defense of the kingdom. In the prosecution of widespread warfare in the seventeenth and eighteenth centuries, merchants suffered periodic levies of "voluntary contribution" solicited for defense needs. These often took the form of exactions against the community as a whole, with individual donations anted up to make the quota. The *avería* tax on colonial trade was such a defense levy, contracted until 1641 by the consulado of Seville, but later reorganized as a direct assessment upon the merchant communities through their own consulados or deputy organizations. In colonial cities merchants were accessible subscribers to such levies. Two-thirds of the contributors to an 1804 donation at Bahia were merchants. However, the returns to individuals were not negligible, for, like the sums of customs duties paid into the treasury over the years, these taxes were listed as services to the kingdom when merchants sought honorary posts and special favors from the state.

Merchants were among the urban groups called upon to form local militias in the military reforms of the mid-eighteenth century, but these companies constituted less influential forms of civic participation and not all merchants shared enthusiasm for them. The *regimento dos homens úteis do estado* (regiment of tradesmen) at Bahia, for example, was organized in the 1760s. Its principal duty was to police the increasingly populous urban center and to act as a reserve in case of foreign attack. The very idea of tradesmen as part-time soldiers, "grocers in gold braid," scandalized some elite creoles and Europeans, who interpreted this patriotic service as one more attempt to affect status by persons undeserving of the privileges of the *fuero militar* (corporate military privileges).

Militia duty may have served this ulterior purpose in earlier decades, but it had lost its cachet by 1800. Established businessmen regarded the occasional demands of reserve service as unwelcome distractions during the busy commercial season. They commonly petitioned for exemption, noting the greater contribution to the state made in the exercise of trade. In 1799, Bahian merchants were alleged to prefer to subsidize 200 regular troops rather than carry on the outmoded traditions of the úteis regiment.

About the same time, merchants in Buenos Aires resisted the compromise of a newly created *batallón de milicias urbana del cuerpo de comercio* (batallion of urban merchant militia) and struggled for total exemption from military duties. In their arguments, the merchants of both ports stressed similar themes: they had a distinctive corporate activity that merited exemption; the very practice of long distance trade itself was a contribution to the glory of the state; they did not need this honor of service to confer dignity. The Buenos

Aires merchants won their exemption in 1801. The military fuero was less important to them than previously.

Town Councils and Merchant Power

In the viceroyal capitals, in seaport cities, and in regional commercial centers of the interior, wherever trade flourished, merchants and their families constituted a vital sector of the elite, distinguished by their wealth, their prominence in kinship networks, and their many contributions to organizations and associations at the center of urban society. Despite this prominence, throughout the colonial era there were repeated instances of tension related to the presence of men from the merchant class in municipal government, a tension which reflected the generalized ambiguity about merchants' role in the social order and the ebb and flow of royal concerns about manifestations of overweening creole power.

Access to influence in supervising local commerce and tax farming attracted peninsular businessmen, but officeholders were not supposed to be active merchants and the requirements of permanent residence and property ownership disqualified transient traders. By the eighteenth century, however, early proscriptions which discouraged merchant participation were rendered immaterial, as much by the greater frequency with which big merchants invested in local properties and committed themselves to long stays in the colony as by the recognition of the political necessity of integrating the merchant elite into the local structures of power, in order to avoid or preempt conflict between creoles and *peninsulares* (persons born in Spain or Portugal). Thus, with the resurgence of peninsular commercial interests in the colonies, merchant representation in city councils tended to increase. Bastions of powerful creole families, like the cabildo of Mexico City, where the absorption of the newly rich was a traditional instrument used to strengthen creole dominance, were forced by the crown to accept peninsular merchants as honorary appointees, beginning in the 1770s, in order to increase the peninsular presence. In colonial Central America, where the economy had undergone a more radical reorientation toward the world market in the eighteenth century, the combination of commercial prosperity, Bourbon administrative reforms, and the destruction of Guatemala City by earthquake in 1773 permitted peninsular merchants, acting through the reorganized cabildo, to assume unprecedented power within the community and beyond, ultimately subjecting much of the region to their economic monopoly.

In the Brazilian seaport city of Bahia, a major center of export of plantation products such as sugar and tobacco and of the import of African slaves and European manufactures, the great families who owned sugar mill estates and cattle ranches in the nearby Reconâcavo traditionally dominated the town council. In the late seventeenth century merchants, particularly merchant-planters, infiltrated this domain to constitute a small, firm 13 percent. In the early eighteenth century, from 1700 to 1739, 23 percent of council positions went to merchants. Later in the period, from 1780 to 1808, the three aldermen (*vereador*) posts and the position of attorney (*procurador geral*), 106 openings in all, were filled by 33 merchants, constituting 32 percent of the total, a figure considerably inflated because of the regularity with which the one post of attorney went to a merchant. The real break occurred in 1808, with the opening of the ports, the de facto end of the colonial system and the increase in trade. Between 1809 and 1820, the eve of independence, merchants held 63 percent of the openings for alderman and attorney.[8]

In the transformation of the eighteenth century, sparked by commercial growth, wherever economic development was high on the agenda, merchants tended to take leading positions in municipal government. The rise of São Paulo as a commercial and distribution center of the southern interior plateau of Brazil in the second half of the eighteenth century can be traced to the cooperative roles of traditional landed families and immigrant businessmen who were active on the municipal council in creating the necessary facilities, roads, shelters, and public works projects at the port of Santos and in backing the establishment of a mint. During this period, merchants and businessmen represented at least one-third to one-half of the São Paulo council members. A more dramatic illustration is the cabildo of Buenos Aires, virtually a merchants' council after 1775. Even in the regional commercial center of Guadalajara, there is a recognizable shift toward the representation of merchant interests in the cabildo around 1800.

The notion of an eighteenth-century merchant ascendancy is, however, too facile to describe a process which had been under way since the beginning of the European colonial enterprise and which also had clear limits in colonial urban society. Individual merchants, or even merchants as a class, did not suddenly humble a once-dominant landowning elite in colonial society. It was in the eighteenth century, however, that concerns for improved commercial performance at the imperial level moved colonial administrators to offer institutional supports and incentives to merchants, groups both in the peninsula and overseas. This, in turn, promoted the success of merchants in those cities and towns which were centers of commercial exchange and distribution activities, not only in reaping the profits of an increased trade, but also in benefitting from the lapse of residual prejudices against the merchant class.

Notes

1. James Lockhart and Enrique Otte, eds., *Letters and People of the Spanish Indies: The Sixteenth Century* (Cambridge: At the University Press, 1976), 30–31.

2. For the rise of trade, see J. H. Paerry, *The Spanish Seaborne Empire* (New York: Knopf, 1969), 120–23; on emigration, see Peter Boyd-Bowman, "Patterns of Spanish Emigration to the Indies until 1600," *Hispanic American Historical Review* 56 (1976), 592–96.

3. For estimates of Brazilian sugar production, see Frédéric Mauro, *Le Portugal et l'Atlantique au XVIIe siècle, 1570–1670* (Paris: S.E.V.P.E.N., 1960), 236.

4. Irving Leonard, ed., *Colonial Travelers in Latin America* (New York: Knopf, 1972), 83, 102–03; J. Eric S. Thompson, ed., *Thomas Gage's Travels in the New World* (Norman, Okla.: University of Oklahoma Press, 1958), 67.

5. Peter Marzahl, "Creoles and Government: The Cabildo of Popayán," *Hispanic American Historical Review* 54 (1974), 648.

6. Susan Socolow, *The Merchants of Buenos Aires, 1778–1810* (Cambridge: At the University Press, 1978), 48. Socolow's careful study is the source of subsequent references in this chapter to the social activities of Buenos Aires merchants in the period.

7. Catherine Lugar, "The Merchant Community of Salvador, Bahia, 1780–1830" (Ph.D. diss., State University of New York at Stony Brook, 1980), 224.

8. Rae Flory and David Grant Smith, "Bahian Merchants and Planters in the Seventeenth and Early Eighteenth Centuries," *Hispanic American Historical Review* 58 (1978), 590–91. See also the previously cited work by Lugar.

For Further Reading

Most accounts of social and economic history in colonial Latin America treat merchants as a group to some extent, but specialized studies of merchants and their role in the early modern era form an increasingly significant body of material. Although merchants constituted an elite stratum and were relatively literate as a group, in the absence of easily accessible personal documentation, such as diaries, memoirs, and correspondence, the continuity of the merchants' presence and the extent of their contributions went largely unrecognized. With the increasing interest in social history in general and exploitation of local records in institutional and notarial archives and parish registers in particular, merchant groups, as well as individual merchant personalities, have taken their rightful place in the forefront of colonial society. The recovery and publication of sets of letter books, with all the minutiae of day-to-day transactions, have brought concrete detail and specificity to the picture of colonial commerce and of merchants' lives. Few document collections, the raw stuff of historical analysis, are available in English translation, and some fine dissertation studies have not yet been published, but selections of these are noted here, along with some useful monographs and articles to orient those who wish to read further in merchant history.

The character of the economies, the structures of international trade, and the fluctuations of commercial relations in the American empires of Spain and Portugal, essential background to understanding the role of the Iberian and Latin American merchants, are developed in Vitorino Magalhaes Godinho, *L'Economie de l'empire portugaise aux XVe et XVIe siècles* (Paris: S.E.V.-.P.E.N., 1969); Frederic Mauro, *Le Portugal et l'Atlantique au XVIIe siècle, 1570–1670* (Paris: S.E.V.P.E.N., 1960); and Huguette and Pierre Chaunu, *Seville et l'Atlantique (1504–1650)*, 8 vols. (Paris: S.E.V.P.E.N., 1955–59). For aspects of eighteenth-century changes, see Antonio García-Baquero González, *Cádiz y el Atlántico, (1717–1778)*, 2 vols. (Seville: Escuela de Estudios Hispano-Americanos, 1976), and Fernando A. Novais, *Brasil na crise do antigo sistema colonial, 1777–1808* (São Paulo: Editorial Hucitec, 1979). The worlds of the metropolitan merchants in the early years of American trade are portrayed in Ruth Pike, *Aristocrats and Traders: Sevillian Society in the Sixteenth Century* (Ithaca: Cornell University Press, 1972) and J. Gentil da Silva, *Stratégie des affairs`a Lisbonne entre 1595 et 1607* (Paris: S.E.V.P.E.N., 1956), and the origins of the institution of the consulado in Robert S. Smith, *The Spanish Guild Merchant (1250–1700): A History of the Consulado* (Durham, N.C.: Duke University Press, 1940).

Examples of business correspondence of early commercial travellers in Spanish America appear in James Lockhart and Enrique Otte, eds., *Letters and People of the Spanish Indies: The Sixteenth Century* (Cambridge: At the University Press, 1976). Merchants and entrepreneurial encomenderos are featured prominently in James Lockhart, *Spanish Peru, 1532–1560: A Colonial Society* (Madison, Wis.: University of Wisconsin Press, 1968), a model social history based on the author's pioneering efforts in notarial archives. How the mining industry multiplied the need for commercial services in its immediate vicinity and forged infrastructure development region-wide is illustrated in Peter Bakewell, *Silver Mining and Society in Colonial Mexico: Zacatecas, 1545–1700* (Cambridge: At the University Press, 1971) and Gwendolyn Cobb, "Supply and Transportation for the Potosí Mines, 1545–1640," *Hispanic American Historical Review* 29 (1949): 25–45.

Studies of merchants in the mid-colonial period are rare. In "Merchants in Seventeenth Century Mexico City: A Preliminary Portrait," *Hispanic American Historical Review* 57 (August 1977): 479–503, Louisa Hoberman emphasizes the importance of the Philippine trade to New Spain's economic development and identifies different patterns of the disposal of mercantile wealth. Rae Flory and David Grant Smith jointly offer some of the more important findings of their respective dissertations in "Bahian Merchants and Planters in the Seventeenth and Early Eighteenth Centuries," *Hispanic American Historical Review* 58 (1978): 571–94 (q.v., Flory, "Bahian Society in the Mid-Colonial Period: The Sugar Planters, Tobacco Growers, Merchants and Artisans of Salvador and the Bahian Reconcavo, 1680–1725," (Ph.D. diss., University of Texas, 1978), and Smith, "The Mercantile Class of Portugal and Brazil in the Seventeenth Century: A Socio-Economic Study of the Merchants of Lisbon and Bahia, 1620–1690," (Ph.D. diss., University of Texas, 1975). Eulalia Maria Lahmeyer Lobo, *Aspectos da influencia dos homens de negocio na politica comercial ibero-Americana, seculo XVII* (Rio de Janeiro: Biblioteca do Exército Editôra, 1962), discusses institutional channels open to merchants in the context of changing economic and political conditions in the Atlantic trade.

For merchants in the later eighteenth century, Susan M. Socolow has published several studies on Buenos Aires. See the following works by her: *The Merchants of Buenos Aires, 1778–1810* (Cambridge: At the University Press, 1978), which treats many aspects of the merchants as a social group; "Marriage, Birth, and Inheritance: The Merchants of Eighteenth Century Buenos Aires," *Hispanic American Historical Review* 60:3 (August 1980): 387–406; and "La burguesía comerciante de Buenos Aires en el siglo XVIII," *Desarrollo económico* 18:70 (julio–septiembre 1978): 205–16. Other comprehensive studies of this period are John E. Kicza, *Business and Society in Late Colonial Mexico* (Albuquerque: University of New Mexico Press, 1983); Miles Wortman, *Government and Society in Central America, 1680–1840* (New York: Columbia University Press, 1982); D. A. Brading, *Miners and Merchants in Bourbon Mexico, 1763–1810* (Cambridge: At the University Press, 1971); Brian R. Hamnett, *Politics and Trade in Southern Mexico, 1750–1821* (Cambridge: At the University Press, 1971); and Ann Twinam, *Miners, Merchants and Farmers in Colonial Columbia* (Austin, Tex.: University of Texas Press, 1983). Dauril Alden, "Vicissitudes of Trade in the Portuguese Atlantic Empire During the First Half of the Eighteenth Century: A Review Article," *The Americas* 32 (1975): 282–91, explores the breadth of topics illuminated in the records of Francisco Pinheiro, merchant at Lisbon in the heyday of the provisioning trade of Minas Gerais, chiefly through Rio de Janeiro. Pinheiro's records are published as *Negócios coloniais, uma correspondência comercial do século XVIII*, 5 vols., ed. Luis Lisanti Filho (Brasília: Ministerio da Fazenda, 1973). Important Brazilian merchant communities near the close of the colonial era are treated by Elizabeth Anne Kuznesof, "The Role of the Merchants in the Economic Development of São Paulo, 1765–1850," *Hispanic American Historical Review* 60 (1980): 571–92; Eulalia Maria Lahmeyer Lobo, "Rio de Janeiro e Charleston, South Carolina, as communidades de mercaderes no século XVIII," *Journal of Inter-American Studies and World Affairs* 12 (1970): 565–82; and Catherine Lugar, "The Merchant Community of Salvador, Bahia, 1780–1830," (Ph.D. diss., State University of New York at Stony Brook, 1980). A number of studies have utilized records of the traditional consulados at Mexico City and Lima, as well as newer ones created on the periphery, to estimate the potential influence of great merchants and the actual character of their political role at the approach of independence. These include Christiana Borchard de Moreno, "Los miembros del consulado de la ciudad de México en la época de Carlos III," *Jahrbuch für Geschichte von Staat, Wirtschaft und Gesellschaft Latein-*

amerikas 14 (1977): 134–60; John T. S. Meltzer, "Kingdom to Republic in Peru: The Consulado de Comercio of Lima and the Independence of Peru, 1809–1825," (Ph.D. diss., Tulane University, 1978); Ruben Villaseñor Bordes, *El mercantil consulado de Guadalajara* (Guadalajara: The Author, 1970); Peter J. Lampros, "Merchant Planter Cooperation and Conflict: The Havana Consulado, 1794–1832," (Ph.D. diss., Tulane University, 1980); Ralph Lee Woodward, Jr., *Class Privilege and Economic Development: The Consulado de Comercio of Guatemala, 1793–1871* (Chapel Hill, N.C.: University of North Carolina Press, 1966); and Jay Kinsbruner, "The Political Status of the Chilean Merchants at the End of the Colonial Period: The Concepción Example, 1790–1810," *The Americas* 29 (1972): 30–56.

FOUR

Bureaucrats

MARK A. BURKHOLDER

Introduction

After a protracted series of attacks, each capable of causing death, Juan Dávalos y Toledo spoke briefly with the viceroy of Peru and his colleagues on
Lima's *audiencia* (high court) on December 6, 1629. Two days later, at four
o'clock in the morning, the *alcalde del crimen* (criminal judge of the audiencia)
succumbed. His estate, seemingly little more than a few books, was so modest that in his last will and testament Dávalos had beseeched the Franciscans
to bury him out of charity. Viceroy Conde de Chinchón was so moved by the
judge's poverty that he personally provided 300 pesos to help with the funeral expenses. Following his example, the visitor general and the remaining
audiencia ministers also contributed substantial sums. With similar generosity, the judge's creditors cancelled his debts. A Lima matron magnanimously
offered the widow housing for her remaining years. On December 9, the viceroy, audiencia, tribunal of accounts, and other tribunals of Lima attended the
funeral. After escorting the bereaved family home, the Conde de Chinchón
drew from his pocket an appointment as *corregidor* (district governor) of Quis-
picanche for Pedro Dávalos y Toledo, the eldest son of the deceased, and informed Juan, a younger son, that an appointment as head of an infantry
company in Callao soon would follow.

A continent away and a half-century later, cathedral bells clanged the alarm
well before dawn on October 15, 1685. A warehouse on Calle Santo Domingo in Mexico City had burst into flames and firefighters were needed.

Stocked with sugar, olive oil, and cinnamon, the building burned for over two hours. The owner, Francisco de Rodezno, was a government auditor who had left the Old World for the New in 1677. Like many auditors in the late seventeenth century, Rodezno had purchased his appointment and subsequently devoted himself to wringing a profit from his investment. He married a woman from Puebla in the fall of 1680, and by the end of the decade had at least one son. Considered prosperous by 1689, Rodezno left a complex estate in Mexico City upon his death in the mid-1730s. By the time of his death, moreover, his American born and educated son José had been well-established for years. Undoubtedly aided by his father's cash, while still a minor José had purchased an appointment in 1710 as a supernumerary judge on the audiencia of Guatemala. Thus the immigrant auditor not only had prospered himself, but had placed his son in an even more prestigious position.

The length of Spanish rule in the Americas, the number of offices available, and the thousands of men who filled the posts make it possible to multiply such vignettes almost endlessly. Perhaps Andrés Pardo de Lago, a native of New Granada who served on the audiencias of Guadalajara and Mexico in the mid-seventeenth century, displayed even greater integrity than Dávalos. When laid to rest in his black robe of office and adorned with the distinctive hood and tassel of a doctor of civil law, Pardo was mourned by the archbishop, viceroy, audiencia, city council, tribunals, clerics, and "all the nobility of the realm" as a man renowned "for his great goodness and Christian proceeding."[1] Rodezno's use of office for personal benefit was probably modest compared to that of José Perfecto de Salas, who allegedly made over two million *pesos* during his long tenure as legal advisor to Viceroy Manuel de Amat in Peru in the late eighteenth century. Seen in broad perspective, however, the careers of Dávalos and Rodezno represent the ends of a continuum of attitude and action, stretching from those officials who perceived office as a public trust to those who viewed it as a source of private gain.

Both Dávalos and Rodezno displayed one characteristic common to officeholders in general and particularly obvious among those in high positions. For most of their adult lives, they had lived and worked, played and prayed, in cities. Officeholders' participation in urban social, economic, and political activities, as well as in administrative and judicial matters, placed them, as a group, in the mainstream of city life.

In Mexico City, Lima, Bogotá, Quito, and the other regional capitals of Spanish America, colonial bureaucracy reached full flower. Offices regularly outlasted the men who held them, and the number of posts increased over time. While family prominence might wax and wane, the recipients of the highest offices were, by virtue of their posts, members of the social and political elite of the capitals. Thus bureaucrats became an institutionalized part of the urban setting. Far more than the famous *conquistadores* (conquerors) the urban bureaucrats represented Spain's domination of the Indies; their presence was imprinted indelibly on the colonial landscape.

Founding an Imperial Bureaucracy

The discovery, exploration, and settlement of the New World presented the Spanish crown with traditional problems set in a new environment. Defense, the establishment and maintenance of royal authority, the extraction of revenue, and the provision of justice to a diverse population were just a few of the challenges that had appeared even before Christopher Columbus died. To meet them, the crown relied heavily upon bureaucrats scattered in the cities and towns that were founded in the wake of conquest. The immensity of the Indies made its division into more manageable units imperative. Within a few decades the crown had established an array of administrative entities of unequal size, shape, population, and importance.

The two major divisions from the sixteenth until well into the eighteenth century were the viceroyalties of New Spain and Peru. The northern viceroyalty encompassed land from the northern boundary of the province of Panama to what is presently the United States as well as to the Caribbean islands, and included part of the province of Venezuela. Even the Philippine islands fell under its jurisdiction. The viceroyalty of Peru included Panama and encompassed all Spanish possessions in South America, with the exception of a strip of Venezuela. When the crown created the viceroyalties of New Granada and the Río de la Plata in 1739 and 1776, respectively, it carved both from the viceroyalty of Peru.

The very size of the viceroyalties and the presence of rich mining regions in the heart of each has made them well known. However, the next largest territorial unit, the audiencia, was in many ways more important. Dating from 1511, with the establishment of a court and administrative body also called an audiencia in Santo Domingo, these territories increased in number as the empire expanded territorially, as well as in both white and *casta* (racially mixed) population. The last audiencia was created in 1787, when highland Peru became a separate administrative district with its capital in Cuzco. With this newest addition, the number of audiencias totaled thirteen. As the following list reveals, except for Cuzco and Guadalajara, each of the mainland audiencias became, with modest modifications, the geographic basis for an independent country in the nineteenth century, while its capital city became the national capital.

Audiencia District	Modern Counterpart
Mexico (and Guadalajara)	Mexico

Guatemala	Central America
Caracas	Venezuela
Bogotá	Columbia
Panama (until extinction in 1751)	Panama
Quito	Ecuador
Lima (and Cuzco)	Peru
Charcas (Chuquisaca)	Bolivia
Santiago	Chile
Buenos Aires	Argentina

The audiencias themselves were divided into smaller districts variously called *corregimientos, alcaldías mayores, gobernaciones,* and, in most of the Empire by 1790, *subdelegaciones.* Groups of the latter comprised intendencies which, from their creation in the late eighteenth century, formed intermediate-sized units within audiencias. The small districts were administered from capitals located in each. Disparate in size, population, and wealth, these provinces, especially the ones most distant from the audiencia capitals, were often subject to rapacious government by officials who were effectively beyond the reach of administrators residing in the audiencia capitals.

Cities, towns, and other municipalities of assorted names were the smallest and most numerous territorial units in the Empire. As did every other jurisdiction, these housed officials of varied titles and responsibilities. The number and importance of the officials, of course, were not the same in a viceregal capital as in a small provincial hamlet. While the latter might have only a handful of local posts, the number of royal offices alone reached over 400 in both Lima and Mexico City by the later eighteenth century.

Listing the territorial units from smaller to larger—municipalities, provinces, audiencias, viceroyalties, and Empire—suggests a pyramidal structure culminating in centralized authority in the hands of the monarch and his advisors in Spain. Reality belied this schema, however. A more accurate image is that of a group of wheels with their hubs in the audiencia capitals and their spokes extending outward to the provinces. The Spanish court, in turn, formed the hub of a wheel whose spokes were the audiencias. From this perspective, decentralization was pronounced in imperial administration.

An awareness of the principal administrative bodies in Spain is necessary in order to understand the imperial bureaucracy as a whole. The importance of the bureaucrats in the viceregal and audiencia capitals to the formulation, implementation, and modification of royal policy, however, makes it essential to focus more attention on the men who held office in the New World. What kinds of offices were there? What responsibilities did they entail? How did officials secure their appointments? Who were the officials, and from where did they come? What kinds of ties bound officials to each other and to the urban centers in which they served? These are some of the questions that will be discussed in the rest of this chapter.

Bureaucratic Organization

Viewed from a broad perspective, four major groups of officeholders provided administration and justice in the New World. Three of these four groups were resident in colonial cities. The highest ranking group was the central administration, based in the Council of the Indies and the House of Trade and located in Spain. In marked contrast to all other officials, few members of the central administration had ever been to the New World. Political administrators formed the second group. Viceroys, captains general, presidents, and provincial executives theoretically served term appointments that usually were less than six years in length. Professional bureaucrats formed the third, and in many ways the most powerful, group in the Indies. These judges, crown attorneys on audiencias, and ministers of the treasury (*caja real*) and accounting offices (*tribunales de cuentas*) held lifetime appointments, forfeited only for cause—such as a serious violation of professional ethics, flagrant abuse of office (usually for personal gain), or excessively scandalous behavior. Finally, there were numerous local and lesser royal offices ranging from chief constable to notary to inspector for weights and measures to city councilman. These were primarily fee-producing or largely honorific positions, and only a few carried even token salaries. Except for elected magistrates, or *alcaldes ordinarios,* incumbents in these posts normally held appointments for life, although many chose to leave office prior to their deaths.

Research on the men named to local and royal positions for the colonial period as a whole reveals that royal and private favors, inheritance, the crown's financial needs, and even "merit" were responsible for their appointments. The importance of each factor varied over time and depended on the office involved. In general, however, the crown's recurrent financial traumas had the greatest effect on appointments to these posts.

Maturation

The euphoria arising from conquest and treasure soon disappeared before the more mundane need to exploit the resources of the New World systematically. In the early decades of Spanish colonization, the crown normally created offices to meet specific needs. From its perspective, officials were necessary to oversee orderly expansion and settlement, provide general administration, mete out justice, collect and disburse taxes, perform ceremonial roles, and deal with local problems. As a general rule, the more responsible and central a post was to the exercise of royal authority, the more care the crown took in filling it; in other words, the crown displayed reluctance to relinquish control over a specific post in direct relation to that post's importance to administration, justice, the treasury, and defense. Financial distress, however, induced the crown to make exceptions to this general policy for immediate cash.

From the outset the crown used its undisputed power of patronage over the empire to pay for services with offices rather than money. As contemporaries expressed it, such a grant of office was a *merced*, a gift producing a source of income for its recipient that could be held until his death and, at times, passed on to his heirs. Thus, for example, Columbus, Pizarro, and Ponce de León received, among other benefits, offices as rewards for exploration, conquest, and settlement.

In Castile recipients of offices as mercedes could "renounce" them in favor of another person, an action that the crown routinely, although not necessarily, accepted and confirmed. With this precedent set, it was but a short step for persons favored with such posts in the Indies to realize immediate gain by privately selling and then publicly renouncing the office received.

Shortly after the conquest of New Spain, the crown took another step that it would repeat on countless subsequent occasions. In 1525, it gave Alonso Pérez de Valera the post of city councilman (*regidor*) for Mexico City in perpetuity. Other comparable appointments resulted both in an end to elected councilmen and, by 1529, in an excessive number of appointees. In short, even before the conquest of Peru was under way, individual purchase of office and inheritable posts existed in the New World.

The crown's view of offices for the Indies altered significantly in 1558. Again following the precedent set in Castile, it decided to sell offices for the Indies on its own account. While he continued to grant most posts as mercedes, Philip II, immediately following the crown's bankruptcy in 1557, introduced the concept of office as a *renta*, or source of income for the royal treasury. The first posts the crown sold were those of *escribano*, or notary, and *alférez*, or municipal standard bearer. The first position could be sold for life, the second in perpetuity if the price offered were sufficiently high.

The crown's alienation of offices expanded in 1581, when, in an effort to improve sales, Philip II agreed that all escribanos, both present and future, could renounce their posts once for a tax of one-third of the positions' value. Although he had sought earlier to open up more positions for sale, it was only after the defeat of the Armada in 1588 had exacerbated the crown's financial woes that, in 1591, the king approved the systematic sale of the post of regidor and related municipal positions for one lifetime.

A royal decree (*cédula*) issued in 1606 rounded out the sale of local offices, a process begun timidly in 1559. By 1606, the list of salable posts included the full range of fee-collecting, honorific, and municipal offices. The decree provided that present and future purchasers held the *oficios vendibles y renunciables,* as the group was known, in full propriety and enjoyed full rights of renunciation in perpetuity upon payment of appropriate taxes. Half of the value of a salable office was paid as a tax at the time of the first renunciation. Subsequently, the tax was one-third of the value of the post. While the decree alienated the positions from crown control, it instituted a steady source of revenue for the ever-depleted royal coffers. It also guaranteed, of course, that families could retain a given position for generation after generation. Entrenchment of local families in local office, in short, was blessed by law.

While peninsulars held the first positions of regidor and alcalde ordinario on the city councils of Mexico City and Lima, inheritance and sales soon brought a predominance of native sons. Men born in America, and probably almost exclusively in New Spain, comprised a majority of the aldermen in Mexico City from 1590 to 1699. Creole hegemony continued for the remainder of the colonial era. Indeed, faced with a virtual monopoly by native sons, in 1772, the crown created six elective positions of honorary alderman, three of which had to be filled by peninsulars. The result was that the city council elected three *radicados,* peninsulars entrenched in Mexico City society and more linked to local than to royal interests.

In Lima local families soon dominated the position of alderman for the same reasons as in Mexico City. A detailed examination of the men elected to the post of alcalde ordinario shows a shift from peninsular to native predominance as well. While only 13 of 70 alcaldes came from Peru in the years 1535 to 1599, the tables turned dramatically in the seventeenth century when peninsulars accounted for only 20 percent of the men elected and natives of Peru for 71 percent. Native son dominance continued to increase at the expense of peninsulars in the eighteenth and early nineteenth centuries, rising to 81 percent from 1700 to 1799 and to 88 percent from 1800 to 1821.

The local posts sold varied greatly in value, and thus in price. Alderman posts in Mexico City sold for amounts between 3,000 and 6,000 *pesos* in the late sixteenth century. With the provisions for inheritance set forth in 1606, however, the price quickly rose to 10,000 pesos. The value of office could decline over time as well. For example, a regimiento in Lima sold for 11,000 pesos in 1700, but only 6,000 pesos in 1760. The fee-earning capacity of some positions greatly enhanced their price. In 1737, for example, the post of chief notary (*escribano mayor*) of the Lima city council sold for 45,000 pesos. In contrast, the same post in Huancavelica in 1740 brought only 9,500 pesos. In Mexico City the post of chief constable (*alguacil mayor*) of the accounting tribunal in Mexico was highly prized. For 45,000 pesos paid in 1655, Pedro Mejía purchased the post, along with the rights to name a lieutenant to serve with him and to receive the salary of *contador mayor* (chief accountant of the tribunal of accounts). One of the highest prices paid in Lima for any position was 80,173 *pesos escudos* paid in 1702, by the Conde de San Juan de Lurigancho for the post of treasurer of the Lima mint. In 1629, a consortium of merchants had financed the purchase of the comparable post in Mexico City for 140,000 pesos.

From the year 1591, when oficios vendibles y renunciables began to appear as a separate item on the summary accounts for the central treasury in Mexico City, until 1808, the proceeds from the sales and taxes on these offices totaled over nine million pesos. While the average yearly income was some 42,000 pesos a year, the range varied from a high of 300,342 pesos in 1606–07 to a low of 826 pesos in 1614–15. As a greater proportion of income came to be generated not by the initial sale of office but by subsequent transfer, the income itself decreased. While annual revenue from the oficios vendibles y renunciables had exceeded 10,000 pesos nine times from 1591 to 1630, from 1631 to 1713 that sum was exceeded only four times, and subsequently never reached. After 1750, the mean annual yield for oficios vendibles in New Spain was under 24,000 pesos.

Excluded from the category of oficios vendibles y renunciables were precisely those positions that the crown rightly considered most central to its maintenance of authority, revenue, and security—those held by the political administrators and professional bureaucrats. Under unrelenting financial pressure, however, the crown gradually turned these offices too into a source of revenue, although it never alienated them in perpetuity.

As the Spanish crown's involvement in European wars repeatedly ravaged royal finances, the desire for offices and the crown's need for money came to coincide. Under continued financial pressure, the crown started selling appointments to treasury posts and the tribunals of accounts in 1633. Provincial administrative positions went on the block in 1677. A decade later, in late 1687, the systematic sale of audiencia appointments began. By 1700, the crown even had sold appointments for the office of viceroy.

The effect of the sale of offices and appointments on the composition of the bureaucracy and its activities cannot be overestimated. First, it determined who the bureaucrats would be. Service at home, if an appropriate position were available, was far more attractive both for peninsulars and for creoles than service in another district on either side of the Atlantic. Thus an immediate result of the sales was to increase the number of men who served in their home region (native sons) and other long-term residents in bureaucratic offices. The corollary to this was a diminution in the crown's ability to control the officeholders. In addition, the purchase of an office increased the pressure on the incumbent to emerge with not only a secure income, but a definite profit. Given the modest salaries associated with non-fee-earning positions, the temptation to resort to extralegal sources of income was irresistible for many bureaucrats. This, too, worked against the crown's interest.

Not far behind each conquistador in the New World was a royal official sent to secure and remit to Spain the crown's share of all treasure. While networks of provincial treasures were established for both New Spain and Peru, the central offices were located in Mexico City and Lima. By the seventeenth century the Lima treasury had three senior officials who collected taxes: a comptroller (*contador*) who oversaw collection and disbursement, a treasurer (*tesorero*) who actually handled the funds, and a business manager (*factor*) who was responsible for selling confiscated goods, collecting taxes paid in kind at public auction, stocking the armories in Lima and Callao, and handling any other commercial transactions associated with the treasury. Assisted by subordinates and often a supernumerary official awaiting a vacancy in a senior office, the *oficiales reales,* as the senior officials were known collectively, were responsible for the honest and efficient handling of the king's finances. In 1605, the crown ordered the establishment of tribunals of accounts in Lima, Mexico City, and Bogotá. Staffed by a small number of auditors, these tribunals were not only to serve as watchdogs for the treasury offices and accounts, but also to collect taxes in arrears from whatever source.

Treasury officials and auditors of the tribunals of accounts received lifetime appointments. While these officials almost always earned lower, and usually substantially lower, salaries than audiencia ministers, their compensation still was well above that earned by the average government employee. Because of the salary, the rank, the security, and, in some cases at least, the financial opportunities available for a person with access to government funds, there was considerable demand for appointments.

Prior to 1633, peninsulars secured far more appointments to the treasuries and tribunals of accounts than did creoles. If the case in Lima is representative, however, most of the peninsulars named were already resident in the Indies at the time of appointment. Viceregal recommendations were particularly important in the appointment of peninsulars as successive viceroys sought to secure posts for their friends and retainers. Only 2 creoles, both native sons, were among the 20 men who served on the tribunal of accounts in Lima from its opening in 1607 to 1633.

Before 1633, appointees were generally experienced public servants with prior service in local or provincial political offices, as functionaries in royal tribunals, or as treasury officers in regional sub-treasuries (*cajas*). In contrast to the background of audiencia ministers, an education at the university level was exceptional among these persons. It was experience that counted, and appointees to Lima often could boast many years of it, frequently outside the capital. For example, Bartolomé Astete de Ulloa left his native Spain for Peru at the age of twenty, arriving in 1598. Following military service and employment in minor posts, he became treasurer for the Potosí district. After working as factor and then, beginning in 1623, as *corregidor* (district governor) for Potosí, he became comptroller for the Lima treasury in 1628, a post he held until his death in 1662. Thus, three decades of service antedated his reaching the Lima treasury.

By 1633, in an effort to wring out still a few more pesos for the war-exhausted Spanish exchequer, the crown turned to the desperate expedient of systematically selling *hacienda* (royal treasury) posts, including those of treasurer and comptroller. Unlike the sale of oficios vendibles y renunciables, which was done in many cases at public auction, the sale of *hacienda* appointments was effected through private negotiation between the purchaser and the crown. The decision to sell the appointments resulted in an altered pool of candidates and a noticeable decline in the standards for appointees to the central treasury and tribunal of accounts in Lima. The Council of the Indies' fear that sales would result in the appointment of dishonest, incapable officeholders, with primary interests divorced from the crown's financial wellbeing, proved correct. The expansion of local ties that followed from sales weakened royal control of these important institutions and undermined efforts to implement increased taxation in the viceroyalty.

Appointees after 1633 were often younger and less experienced than their predecessors. This insured limited maturity and knowledge but, barring premature death, allowed for decades of service. In addition, as money replaced merit as the primary criterion for appointment, would-be purchasers sought the most coveted posts—those in Lima—with particular avidity. Native sons were especially anxious to secure the offices and, once in place, showed no desire to leave. As the previous promotion patterns fell into disuse, officials in regional subtreasuries remained in their backwaters and undoubtedly created or strengthened social, political, and economic ties to leading local families.

In the years from 1701 to 1744 alone, the crown sold at least 31 appointments of regent, auditor, and *oficial* (clerk) of the tribunal of accounts and central treasury in Mexico City. As elsewhere, native sons availed themselves of the crown's financial distress and paid cash for a lifetime post. In 1708, José Benito de Terreros Ochoa paid 5000 pesos escudos for a supernumerary position as auditor for the tribunal of accounts, with full salary and prequisites. Three years later his brother Antonio, already a *relator* (office of the court) for the audiencia of Mexico, secured an appointment as a supernumerary *oidor* (judge) on that tribunal, probably also for a cash payment. In 1740, Francisco Miguel de Berrio y Saldívar, another native son, purchased an appointment as auditor of the tribunal of accounts for 15,500 pesos fuertes.

The sales, of course, did give the crown immediate income. In the seventeenth century the price paid for appointments in the treasury office of Lima varied from 5,375 pesos to 18,750 pesos. Appointments in the tribunal of accounts cost from 2,500 to 20,000 pesos. The post of regent of the tribunal of accounts brought 26,000 pesos fuertes in 1733. Twelve years later Simón de Ontañón, Conde de las Lagunas, paid 31,200 pesos fuertes for a *futura*, or promise of succession, to the same position. The peak price for the office in Mexico City was paid in 1740, when Juan Chrisostomo de Barroeta gave 38,000 pesos fuertes for the appointment and the right to name a man to serve were he himself unable to do so.

The post of provincial administrator—variously called *alcalde mayor*, *corregidor*, and *gobernador*—was the next one sold. In the sixteenth century the crown had introduced provincial administrators who resided in the urban centers of the interior, both to provide sustenance for non-encomenderos and poor encomenderos (recipient of Indian labor and tribute) and to expand royal authority from the urban areas into the countryside and over the indigenous population. The posts were numerous—88 in Peru in 1633, and about 200 in New Spain. Although cases can be found of men serving or at least holding appointments as a provincial administrator in two or more locations, a single appointment and service of five years or less were more common. While the crown named lawyers to many corregimientos in Spain, in the New World it preferred men with military, or at least militia, backgrounds.

For about a century after the stabilization of these provincial positions in the years 1570 to 1580, most of the men named received their appointments from viceroys or other executives resident in the Indies. During the century dominated by viceregal rather than royal provision of the offices, the notorious system of *repartimiento de comercio* took root. Although located at varying distances from the viceregal capitals, provincial administrators were closely linked to them economically. Using goods advanced by merchants in Mexico City and Lima, the officials participated in the profitable repartimiento of merchandise by which Indians were forced to purchase mules, clothing, food, and other items, whether needed or not. In some regions at least, their production was subjected as well to monopolistic control by avaricious officials.

Some provincial administrators also were linked to viceregal capitals by reason of birth or residence there. In the seventeenth century, for example, some two dozen Lima-born alcaldes ordinarios of the capital served as corregidores during their careers. In New Spain and Peru, descendants of the conquistadores and early settlers were successful in gaining appointments as corregidor. The fact that viceroys enjoyed the right of patronage over the majority of the positions served to help them in their pursuit of appointment, despite the namings of viceregal retainers that occurred.

By 1677, an ever more financially desperate crown began to sell the appointments of corregidor and alcalde mayor. The result was that by 1700, nearly all of these positions had passed from viceregal to royal provision. As was the case with the treasury positions, the crown sold the appointments of corregidor and alcalde mayor on an individual basis, with the amount and terms of the agreement varying. In 1708, for example, Eugenio de Alvarado purchased an appointment to succeed Pedro de Alzamora as corregidor of the city of Trujillo in the viceroyalty of Peru for 6,000 pesos. For the price, Alvarado secured the right to name a lieutenant to serve for him and an assurance that the purchase was firm and that the crown would not renege by means of a subsequent reform. Nicolás Antonio Clerque, however, paid only 1,000 pesos for an appointment as corregidor of the Villa of Santa in Peru. The right to future possession of the much more desirable post of corregidor of Mexico City, and an accompanying rank of colonel, sold in 1731 for 16,000 pesos, while a 1735 appointment secured a futura as alcalde mayor of Tacuba for Mathías García de Gismeros for 1,000 pesos. García de Gismeros also obtained the right to name a lieutenant to serve in his place.

In contrast to the situation regarding local and treasury posts, creoles seem to have secured fewer, not more, provincial offices when the crown began to sell appointments in 1677. This may have been because wealthy and well-educated creoles, especially those who went to Spain, devoted their attention to securing either the more prestigious audiencia and treasury positions or hereditary offices. In addition, the close link between repartimiento of merchandise and provincial officials made it particularly advantageous for monopolistic merchants in Spain to loan purchase costs and travel expenses to men whom they knew personally and whom they could trust to distribute their goods—usually men born in Spain.

Term appointments meant that provincial officials rotated frequently. In contrast, audiencias displayed a notable continuity in personnel. The tribunals were the supreme courts of their districts and subject to appeal to the Council of the Indies only in cases involving major sums of money. Additionally, they had administrative and financial responsibilities. Arguably, the audiencias were the most important single civil institution in the colonies.

From the founding of the first audiencia in Santo Domingo in 1511 to 1808, just under 1,300 men were named to serve on the New World tribunals. Residing in capital cities that became the leading urban centers of the mainland American empire, these men comprised the most highly educated and professional branch of royal administration. Dressed in distinctive black robes, the ministers formed a prominent and highly visible part of urban life. In addition to performing judicial, legislative, and executive duties, they participated in parades, celebrations, funeral processions, baptisms, and other social activities. (See Figure 11.) Unlike the handful of American-born viceroys, none of whom served in the audiencia district of his birth, a number of these ministers secured audiencia appointments in their native districts.

Almost 75 years and just over 200 initial audiencia appointments had passed before the first creoles were named to New World tribunals. In 1585, Antonio Ribera Maldonado, a native of Mexico City, and Hernando de Saavedra Valderrama, a native of Lima, were selected for the courts in Manila and Mexico City, respectively. Given the still small number of creole men born prior to 1560, and thus having attained the minimum age of 25 years required for such a high appointment, these early selections demonstrated that place of birth would not prevent the American-born from receiving offices of high rank and responsibility. That Ribera and Saavedra were named to courts outside their home districts, on the other hand, accurately presaged that, regardless of general legislation calling for native-son appointments to office, the crown had little inclination to apply these requirements to the audiencias.

Only after naming two more creoles to tribunals outside their home districts did the crown appoint a native son. Alonso Bravo de Saravia secured an appointment to the audiencia of Lima, albeit to the junior position of alcalde del crimen in 1602. Alonso, the son of Melchor Bravo de Saravia, the eighth oidor or civil judge named to Lima, was born about 1570. As a boy he went to Spain with his parents, spending some years in the family home in Soria. Passing to the University of Salamanca, he secured the necessary formal education to qualify for an appointment. A Knight of Santiago since 1611, he was transferred from Lima to Mexico City in 1620 to serve as an oidor there.

Alonso Bravo's initial appointment as a native son was unique for 35 years. Indeed, prior to 1687, only six men began their audiencia careers in their home districts. Although very sparing with native son appointments, the crown nevertheless named Americans in every decade from the 1580s to the 1820s. After 1607, in fact, only twice prior to the conclusion of the War of the Spanish Succession in 1713, did more than two calendar years pass without at least one American appointment.

Table 4.1 shows three major periods of American appointments to the New World courts. Beginning with a cluster of American namings (four in 1610–11), the first period extends to the initiation of the systematic sale of audiencia appointments in late 1687. With creoles receiving nearly one of four initial appointments over most of the seventeenth century, a long and repeatedly reinforced record of American success had been established. During this period, Americans benefited from the availability of universities in the major cities of the New World, especially the University of San Marcos in Lima. Modeled on Spanish institutions, the leading universities of San Marcos and Mexico had offered the background in civil and canon law necessary for an audiencia position since the second half of the sixteenth century. As Table 4.2 indicates, South Americans in general and natives of Peru in particular dominated the ranks of American appointees during this period. The University of San Marcos provided the requisite credentials for most of these persons, as well as lobbying at court on behalf of its alumni. During this period, the practice of Americans traveling to Spain to advance their own cases was solidified. A protracted stay at court could yield valuable social, business, and even, for the American who married a peninsular woman, family ties. An audiencia appointment was an elusive goal, but the American who was well-connected at court and persistent in his efforts there had a much better chance of attaining it than did men who remained in the New World.

The appointment of *limeño* (Lima-born) Miguel Núñez de Sanabria as alcalde del crimen of the audiencia of Lima in November 1687, in return for 17,000 pesos initiated the second period, an Age of Impotence that lasted until 1750. For much of this period the crown was unable to staff the audiencias with the kind of appointees it preferred. Yielding to financial necessity, it followed a model already used for treasury posts and provincial administration positions and made individual arrangements with the purchasers. The price paid varied with the location of the office and the special conditions the buyer wanted. The highest price paid was paid by Domingo de Orrantia in 1749. Orrantia, a native of Lima, paid 47,500 pesos for an appointment as a supernumerary oidor and dispensations for being underage to serve the post, marry a native of the district, and hold property in the district. By contrast, in 1740, peninsular Juan José Martínez Patiño paid only 8,000 pesos for a supernumerary appointment as oidor for the audiencia of Guatemala.

The sales that began in 1687 enabled a record number of Americans, including unprecedented numbers of native sons, to reach New World courts.

Table 4.1 Origins of New Men Named to American Audiencias, 1610–1808

| | 1610–1687 | | 1687–1750 | | | | 1751–1808 | | Total | |
| | | | All Appointments | | Initial Appointments* | | | | | |
	No.	(%)	No.	(%)	No.	(% of all Appointments)	No.	(%)	No.	(%)
Peninsulars	108	(28.)	158	(50.5)	13	(8.2)	203	(76.)	469	(48.7)
Creoles	93	(24.2)	139	(44.4)	103	(74.1)	63	(24.)	295	(30.6)
Unknown**	184	(47.8)	16	(5.1)	5	(31.3)	—		200	(20.7)
Total	385	(100.0)	313	(100.0)	121	(38.7)	266	(100.0)	964	(100.0)

*Men who purchased their initial audiencia appointments and the percentage of purchasers. Another 12 men, all creoles, probably purchased their initial appointments.

**Nearly all ministers of unknown origin were undoubtedly peninsulars.

Table 4.2   District of Birth for Americans Named to
American Audiencias, 1610–1808

	1610–1687		1687–1750			1751–1808		Total	
	No.	N.S.*	No.	N.S.*	**	No.	N.S.	No.	N.S.
Buenos Aires	—	—	—	—		—	3	3	—
Caracas	—	—	—	—		—	4	4	—
Chile	5	—	5	2	2	9	4	19	6
Charcas	7	1	6	2		—	3	16	3
Cuzco	—	—	—	—		—	1	1	—
Guadalajara	—	—	5	2	2	1	—	6	2
Guatemala	—	—	2	—		—	3	5	—
Lima	51	3	73	27	25	10	1	134	31
Manila	—	—	—	—		—	—	—	—
Mexico	6	—	26	11	8	5	—	37	11
Panama	7	—	6	4	2	—	—	13	4
Quito	3	—	3	3	3	1	—	7	3
Bogotá	7	1	4	1	1	11	3	22	5
Santo Domingo	4	—	8	1		—	10	1	22	2
Unknown	3	—	1	—		—	2	—	6	—
	93	5 (5%)	139	53 (38%)	43	63	9 (14%)	295	67 (23%)

*Native Sons. Named to home tribunal by *initial* appointment. Men who moved to their home tribunal with a second or subsequent appointment are *not* counted as native sons in this table.
**Native sons who purchased first audiencia appointment.

Table 4.1 highlights the greatly increased representation of Americans in general and the importance of sales in their appointments. Table 4.2 reveals both the continued preeminence of natives of Peru and the unprecedented number of appointments of native sons that resulted from sales. While sales did not account for all American entry to the courts, they were responsible for a substantial majority of the appointments of creoles named during the Age of Impotence.

The termination of sales at midcentury opened an Age of Authority that extended to 1808. During these years, marked by reforms in many areas, the crown pursued a steady and at times even dramatically enforced policy of increasing peninsular representation and reducing ties between ministers and the districts they served. Tables 4.1 and 4.2 reveal the impact of this policy and the resulting decline in creole appointments in general and native-son appointments in particular. Recognizing the impact of the policy which was followed after 1750, affected parties protested. Individuals who found their careers stymied objected, at times vociferously. Complaints and calls for change also came from city councils, as they perceived the loss of employment opportunities for local men and the reduction of local influence in administration.

By 1687, the sale of appointments for offices by contract with the crown had reached immense proportions. Seventy-five posts in the Viceroyalty of Peru were sold in that year. Although fewer sales occurred in the several years that followed, the total for 1688 to 1695 was over 230. As an appointment to the Council of the Indies already had been sold in 1675 for 50,000 *doblones* the only notable position that remained unsold was that of viceroy.

The office of viceroy held the greatest concentration of authority and responsibility in the New World. Established in New Spain in 1535, in a successful effort to curb the conquistadores and to establish royal authority, the office was extended to Peru in 1543. The crown created a third viceroyalty for New Granada in 1739, and a fourth for the Río de la Plata in 1776. As the pinnacle of authority within their respective domains, the viceroys bore the responsibility for financial, administrative, military, and judicial matters.

From 1535 to 1808, the crown gave regular appointments to only 92 men for the posts of viceroy for New Spain, Peru, New Granada, and the Río de la Plata. Especially in the beginning, it took special care to name men of impeccable social standing and demonstrated ability. Three of New Spain's first four viceroys, Antonio de Mendoza (1535–50), Luis de Velasco "The Elder" (1550–64), and Martín Enríquez de Almansa (1568–80), were strong and capable executives. Luis de Velasco "The Younger" (1590–95 and 1607–11) also earned high marks, but many of his successors were undistinguished. While these four men came from noble families, they were untitled. In contrast, an examination of their successors reveals that, except for one archbishop of Mexico, all prior to Baylio Fray María de Bucareli y Ursúa (1771–79) bore the titles of *conde* (count), *marqués* (marquis), or, in six cases, *duque* (duke). Many, moreover, belonged to a military order. Similar lustre accrued to viceroys in Peru, nine of whom, in fact, previously had served the office in New Spain.

From the sixteenth century on, many viceroys could claim military qualifications. The extension of European conflicts to the New World, in fact, led the crown to emphasize New World military experience in its appointments. One consequence of the crown's emphasis upon military ability and leadership demonstrated in the New World was a decline in the social background of the viceroys. New World service was rarely seen as desirable by the Europeans, and men without noble titles frequently held officerships. In general, the greater weight given to relevant ability over birth resulted in viceroys who, as a group, served their posts satisfactorily.

Although Mendoza, Velasco "The Elder," and Enríquez de Almansa served more than a decade each, the average tenure in office for seventeenth- and eighteenth-century viceroys in both New Spain and Peru was between six and seven years. In the new viceroyalties of New Granada and the Río de la Plata, the average tenure was comparable for the first but less than four years for the second. Extremes in length of service ran from the Conde de Superunda in Peru, who served just over 16 years in the office (1745–61), to the Duque de Veragua in New Spain (1673), who died within a month of reaching Vera Cruz. With only a few exceptions, viceroys were men born and reared in Spain.

Accorded lavish receptions upon arrival and housed in a palace on the central plaza, every viceroy by definition held the ranking social as well as political position in his capital city. Viceroys routinely traveled to their posts escorted by family, friends, and retainers. They expected and often sought to use their offices to benefit these persons, regardless of legislation to the contrary. The patronage they exercised, although reduced over time, offered opportunities to favor retainers as well as to gain substantial sums through the private sale of appointments and favors. Repeatedly, viceroys named retainers to lucrative commissions, appointed them to corregidor or other posts, and smiled beneficently when their minions married local encomenderas or their wives' ladies-in-waiting made favorable matches. By using their office in this manner, they set an example that other bureaucrats tried to emulate, to the best of their ability, for their own more limited staff and families.

Special emphasis must be placed on viceroys' limited tenure, for it contrasted with the lifetime appointments associated with most royal offices. While the king might transfer audiencia ministers and treasury officials at his pleasure, an appointment guaranteed them lifetime employment, barring dismissal for cause. In practice, audiencias, the central treasuries, and the tribunals of accounts regularly had ministers who had served longer in the regional capital than had the chief executive. Given the authority, prestige, and salary associated with their positions, in addition to the normal longer tenure, these ministers found themselves desirable marriage partners and in circumstances that enabled them to benefit financially from establishing local ties. Most who were not native sons—men born in the region in which they served—developed such ties and became *radicados,* and thus were more sympathetic to at least some local interests than they had been upon their arrival as outsiders.

In the last five years of the seventeenth century, the crown finally put its most important single administrative post on the block as well. With the sale of the appointment of Viceroy of Peru to the Conde de Cañete in the mid-1690s, the crown at last had traversed the full distance begun with the authorized sale of *escribanías* (notary public offices) in 1558. While no sale of an appointment of viceroy in the eighteenth century has been uncovered, the crown did sell appointments to the Council of the Indies during the War of the Spanish Succession and, on at least one occasion, again during the War of Jenkins' Ear.

By the middle of the eighteenth century the crown's improved finances enabled it to terminate the sale of audiencia appointments, governorships, corregimientos, alcaldías mayores, and treasury positions. The legacy of the earlier sales, however, would affect the composition of the bureaucracy until late in the century. Although within every decade the king had conferred some positions without monetary payment, it was precisely the widespread reliance upon sales as a fiscal device that brought the crown to the nadir of its control over the colonies. As a corollary, sales resulted in more access to power, both direct and indirect, for the local population in urban centers than had been the case since the crown first set about establishing a full-scale bureaucracy in the New World.

The Royal Bureaucrats

Bureaucrats and local officeholders were spread throughout the empire, with major concentrations of them present only in the audiencia and viceregal capitals. Lima and Mexico City, in particular, housed prominent bureaucracies whose presence was underscored frequently through the participation of the high-ranking bureaucrats in the innumerable processions that added color, excitement, and recreation to urban life. A religious celebration, the arrival or departure of a new viceroy or archbishop, a funeral, an *auto-da-fé* (public punishment of persons convicted by the Inquisition), and other occasions called for parades that brought people of all groups in society to participate or simply to gawk. (See Figure 12.) The public reception of a viceroy of Peru in 1674 was especially magnificent. Cavalry companies, representatives of the royal *colegios* (secondary schools) in Lima, of the University of San Marcos, and of the merchant guild, treasury officials, and audiencia ministers wearing their somber black robes of office passed before the viceroy, who was seated on a reviewing stand. When they had passed, the viceroy mounted a horse led by two city magistrates dressed in red velvet and joined the procession, riding near a large canopy held by the city aldermen. A company of lancers formed the rear guard. At different times aristocrats, members of the military orders, and brilliantly arrayed lackeys and pages were present. The formally attired royal and local officeholders located in the middle of the procession emphasized the symbolic as well as the tangible centrality of royal authority and bureaucrats in urban life.

The very location of principal offices on the central plazas underscored the importance of bureaucrats in colonial cities. Those officials who received direct appointments from the king to high-ranking and managerial positions formed the core of the bureaucracy: audiencia ministers, treasury officials, senior auditors, and, as they were created, the heads of separate major offices such as the tobacco monopoly. Below them were a host of support positions whose number increased slowly until the eighteenth century. Then, especially from around mid-century on, rapid expansion of the bureaucracy took place.

Despite the variety of responsibilities, salary, and perquisites they enjoyed, members of the royal bureaucracies in the capitals had several characteristics in common. That all bureaucrats were men was so obvious to contemporaries that it elicited no comment. Equally commonly assumed, but less rigorously enforced, was that bureaucrats would have acceptable social backgrounds. Legitimate birth and freedom from Moorish or Jewish blood were required, although occasionally celebrated bastards and men of less than pure Spanish descent did hold office.

The family backgrounds of government officials varied considerably within the peninsular and creole segments of society. Although no systematic examinations of the families of large groups of bureaucrats have been made, the variation present among fathers of audiencia ministers in Lima illustrates the range of backgrounds for those men who ascended to the peak of the bureaucracy. Army and militia officers, high-ranking bureaucrats, members of military orders, titled nobles, and merchants accounted for most of the identified fathers. The lowest position or status given was public escribano in Lima. One notable characteristic of native sons named to the audiencia of Lima from 1687 to 1750 was that nearly two-thirds of them were first-generation creoles on their paternal side. A "typical" native-son appointee to Lima during these years was the son of a peninsular father from the north of Spain and a mother from Lima. The father held a military commission or a post in local government. The family had sufficient resources to see the son through a legal education in Lima, and a trip to Spain, some time at court, and, probably, to provide at least a portion of the cost of an appointment.

Bureaucrats varied widely in age. Aside from audiencia ministers and officials who had started out as merchants, bureaucrats commonly began their careers in their teens or early twenties, at times working as *entretenidos* (apprentices) with little or no salary until death or promotion opened an entry position. Since the crown offered no retirement plan and normally considered retirement only for men who had become blind, deaf, or subject to debilitating illnesses, the bureaucracy always had a geriatric flavor.

The repeated entry of boys into the lower ranks of the bureaucracy is a reminder that educational qualifications ran the gamut from minimal literacy for positions in which reading and writing were necessary to university degrees through the doctorate held by some audiencia ministers. The academic prerequisite for matriculation in a university was proficiency in Latin, associated with completion of a course in rhetoric. Since memorization was a primary requirement for ultimately receiving a baccalaureate, boys of prodigious facility could graduate in their early teens. Small wonder that the careers of bureaucrats often began early.

The location of the most famous secondary schools in regional capitals meant that the students were drawn from less populated areas into the major urban centers. The famous Jesuit colegio of San Martín in Lima, for example, attracted students from nearly 20 separate places of birth in 1618. Among others, Chile, Panama, Chuquisaca, Quito, Paita, Saña, Arequipa, Cartagena, and several areas of Spain were represented, while a numerous contingent of students came from Lima itself. One implication of this was that students absorbed the attitudes and perspectives of the capital city well before they became bureaucrats. Most students undoubtedly emerged as confirmed urbanites, with interests and expectations based upon the pleasures and opportunities of the capital.

While some cities, most notably Buenos Aires, lacked universities, by the close of the colonial period 25 had been founded in America. Although a majority of these did not have all five of the major faculties (philosophy, theology, laws, canons, and medicine), as a group they provided thousands of young men with access to higher education, degrees, and the employment opportunities that followed. As many as 150,000 youths may have received degrees during the colonial period.

Bureaucratic positions provided an income, security, and, at least in the case of higher ones, prestige. The salaries paid varied greatly. Excluding those of the viceroys, who enjoyed princely sums that reached as high as 60,500 pesos, the range was still substantial. For most of the colonial period, audiencia ministers were the highest paid bureaucrats, with salaries that ultimately reached 5,000 pesos in Lima. Senior auditors on the tribunal of accounts in Lima received 3,645 pesos in 1774. Treasury officials earned slightly less with 3,240 pesos and several other auditors earned just over 2,000 pesos. The vast majority of employees, however, earned less than 1,000 pesos a year, a sum just slightly above the salary of a regular army captain.

The crown provided some variance in salaries, depending upon the location of the bureaucrat. According to the chief auditor for the Indies in 1772, Tomás Ortiz de Landazuri, Lima was the most desirable location for an audiencia minister. Not only was it the ranking tribunal in America, but the court enjoyed a generous salary, opportunities for extra compensation, a "pleasant climate," and a ready availability of consumer goods and foodstuffs. Mexico City, in contrast, had lower salaries, fewer commissions available, higher expenses, and a heavier workload.

The value of a salary (normally paid with some regularity) deserves emphasis. To produce the 5,000 peso salary received by audiencia ministers in Lima after the salary adjustment of 1776 would have required income-producing property worth as much as 100,000 pesos. Few persons commanded that much investment capital. And, aside from mortgages such as those issued by religious bodies, few investments would offer security comparable to the receipt of a government salary. Were salary the only attractive feature of the job, high officials undoubtedly still would have been viewed as attractive marital partners.

For low-ranking government employees, salaries were often modest at best. A single official who earned 500 pesos a year in Mexico City in the early nineteenth century was hard-pressed to make ends meet. Housing, meals and beverages, a servant (paid only five pesos a month), candles, boots and shoes, clothing, and the services of a barber consumed his salary. Given the additional expense that a family entailed, many bureaucrats never married.

There are no overall figures available on the percentage of bureaucrats who married. Most viceroys were married, although some were already widowers when they assumed office. Census data in the late colonial period for Mexico City reveal that approximately one-third of the bureaucrats remained single. It appears that marriage in the thirties or later was more common than early marriage among bureaucrats, a consequence of the modest salaries that most received.

Among the advantages of a high-ranking bureaucratic position for the single man was the possibility of marrying a wife who brought a rich dowry. When Mayor Bravo de Saravia married Juan Jiménez de Montalvo, an oidor of Lima, for example, she brought a dowry of 24,000 pesos. At about the same time, Agueda de los Rios i Lisperguer wed Blas de Torres Altamirano, bringing a dowry of 50,000 pesos. At least half of the audiencia ministers named from 1687 to 1808 were married, many to women born in the New World. The benefits that royal service could bring were related directly to one's rank in the bureaucratic hierarchy. Thus an audiencia minister was in a much better position to enrich himself than was a lesser official.

The range of salaries that government employees received meant that employees did not reside in one part of a capital alone. The pattern that existed was that of a fan, with the plaza mayor, or central square, providing the pivot. Fronting on the plaza in Mexico City, for example, were the cathedral and the viceregal palace. As in Lima, the viceroy living in the splendor of a rent-free palace provided the most conspicuous example of proximity to employment and centrality within the urban setting. A small number of other officials also resided in the buildings in which they worked, but they paid rent. The superintendent of the customs office in Mexico City, for example, paid 830 pesos annually for a small apartment in the customs building in the early nineteenth century.

A residence close to the center of a city was considered desirable, and higher ranking bureaucrats generally lived within easy walking distance of their offices. A few oidores in Lima lived as close as the adjacent block. Many lived within six blocks of the royal palace where they worked. In 1613, the postmaster general (*correo mayor*), several aldermen of the city council, and the administrator of the sales tax lived just two blocks away. Housing patterns in Mexico City, and probably elsewhere as well, provided well-integrated accommodations for a spectrum of social and economic groups. While the best paid officials might have private homes, most bureaucrats resided in apartment and tenement buildings spread throughout the city.

The salaries government employees received made them important purchasers of local services and of a wide range of consumer items. The more highly paid officials were expected to maintain a style of life appropriate to their positions. In consequence, they were among the urban buyers of slaves and imported luxury items as well as the employers of domestic labor.

Domestic slaves formed part of the household retinue for the wealthy and even for many persons of lesser means. From viceroy to clerks, many bureaucrats owned slaves. Those who went to Peru from Spain in the sixteenth century received a majority of the licenses granted to individuals to import slaves. The number of slaves that could be imported varied with the official's rank, with most being allowed two or three slaves. In addition, bureaucrats were free to purchase slaves in the New World. Slaves not only performed routine household duties, but also served for many years as armed escorts for high-ranking bureaucrats. Such public display both fed the officials' vanity and stimulated private citizens to emulate them. (See Figure 13.)

While most government salaries were modest, they offered at least minimal security for the employee. Coupled with a lifetime appointment, they made the bureaucrat in any post the envy of many contemporaries. For a position among those at the top of the bureaucracy, competition was extremely keen, and officeseekers (*pretendientes*) often went to great expense and devoted years of effort to secure the coveted office.

The viceroy of Peru's appointment of 52 corregidores from some 600 candidates in around 1670, confirms the existence of competition for office, especially office that offered possibilities of substantial gain within a brief period. Competition for high-ranking offices in the capital could be even stiffer. For posts that the crown filled directly, however, the locus of competition shifted from the regional capitals to the court itself.

Men from any region of the Empire were at a particular disadvantage in the pursuit of high-ranking positions. Characteristically, they most desired an appointment within their home district. They sought, in other words, to be native sons. Named to positions within another district, they normally would enter as outsiders, without social or economic ties to the region, in the same manner as would a peninsular. Even the largest bureaucracies in America, those in Mexico City and Lima, however, had few vacancies at the top.

In both the central treasury offices and audiencias, limited opportunity existed for appointment. From 1620 to 1700, only 20 treasury officials were named for the central treasury office in Lima. During the same year the King appointed 75 men for the 8 posts of oidor of the audiencia of Lima, and, coincidentally, an equal number of men as oidores of the audiencia of Mexico. Because some of the oidor appointments went to men already serving on these courts as alcaldes del crimen or *fiscales* (crown attorneys), the actual number of positions available on the tribunals was even smaller. Moreover, since death was the primary cause of vacancies, the vagaries of individuals' health resulted in periods of several years during which there were no openings.

In specific cases, and especially when it sold appointments, the crown would name supernumerary ministers or grant futuras, promises of a future regular appointment. This benefited the recipients, but ultimately resulted in even longer periods without appointments. From 1695 to 1699, for example, no new oidores were named for the audiencia of Lima. The practice, moreover, meant additional uncertainty for office seekers in general and a potentially greater burden for American applicants in particular.

Far more attention has been devoted to the movement of peninsulars to the New World than to that of creoles to Spain. For Americans who sought high office in the viceregal and audiencia capitals, however, a voyage to Spain and a sojourn at court, while not indispensable, could prove most helpful. The practice of traveling to Spain began early. While a few Americans matriculated at Salamanca or another Spanish university, many went principally to solicit office or other signs of royal largesse. What began as a trickle had turned into a steady stream by the seventeenth century.

High-ranking bureaucrats belonged by definition to the ruling elite of the capital cities in which they served. Their ability to pass on their status to their heirs, however, varied. The opportunities were probably greatest for those men who married following their appointment to office, and thus bestowed upon any children a life begun under the aura surrounding their employment. Ministers whose children were young at the time of their appointment could benefit almost as greatly. On the other hand, a minister who had been named late in life and whose children were already grown and employed at the time of his appointment was less able to help his heirs. Timing, in short, played a part in the transmission of elite status from bureaucrat to heirs.

Some bureaucrats were able not only to pass on high status but even to establish dynastic succession in the bureaucracy. Families such as that of limeño oidor Miguel Núñez de Sanabria, his son, oidor Gregorio Núñez de Rojas, and his grandson, oidor José Antonio Villalta y Núñez, served in the same branch of bureaucracy over generations.

Marriages could create webs of family ties within the bureaucracy that extended among several major regional capitals. The above-mentioned José Antonio Villalta y Núñez, oidor in Charcas, for example, married the daughter of Lima oidor José de Santiago Concha. The marriage gave him two brothers-in-law and a nephew were were audiencia ministers. Together the relatives served on the courts of Charcas, Chile, and Lima. Nephew José de Santiago Concha Jiménez Lobatón remained on Chile's tribunal until the Wars of Independence finally ousted him.

Family connections linked branches of the bureaucracy and bureaucrats, clerics, merchants, *hacendados* (large landowners), elected city officials, and other groups of society as well. Alcaldes of the Lima city council repeatedly were sons, grandsons, or sons-in-law of audiencia ministers. Often siblings achieved prominence in different branches of the local bureaucracy. Tomás de Querejazu y Mollinedo, brother of an oidor of Lima in the eighteeth century, belonged to the city's cathedral chapter. José Borda y Echevarría was the chief auditor of the tribunal of accounts and the brother of criminal judge Manuel Antonio de Borda. While not all audiencia ministers had ties to other officials, the familiar intermingling of royal and local office deserves emphasis as an arena for elite coalescence.

Prominent bureaucrats often were tied also through marriage and kinship to the most powerful financial interests of the colony in which they served. As an oidor of Mexico, Francisco Leandro de Viana married the daughter of a marqués and gained control over prosperous estates. José de Tagle, an oidor of Lima, was the son of one of the city's richest merchants, owned a major estate, rented out urban property, and was involved in commerce. His extended family and financial interests gave him links with nearly every major part of Lima society.

An important contemporary certification of family and personal lustre for much of the colonial era was membership in a military order—Santiago, Calatrava, or Alcántara. To enter an order, the candidate had to be granted membership by the king; be of legitimate birth and proven noble lineage, free from any trace of Jewish or Moorish blood, condemnation by the Inquisition, or employment in a base occupation; and possess sufficient economic resources to maintain the honor with dignity. Dispensation from meeting one of these personal prerequisites usually could be obtained for a price.

The number of members in the New World was never large, a fact that enhanced the attractiveness of entering an order. The viceregal capitals of Mexico City and Lima boasted the largest concentrations, but even in these cities the numbers were small. Mexico City had only 33 members in 1653; Lima had 40 in 1700. Both peninsulars and creoles entered the orders, but men of American birth counted for less than 5 percent (865 members) of the total. Men coveted membership in a military order, and many considered it an ample and adequate reward for protracted or unusual service to the crown.

High-ranking public officials, notably those on the audiencias, the treasuries, and the accounting tribunals, were conspicuous recipients of memberships in both the military orders and, later, the Order of Charles III. This civil order, established in 1771, with the specific purpose of recognizing meritorious civil servants, reduced the emphasis on noble ancestry; persons who could not have met a military order's genealogical tests were admitted on the basis of their bureaucratic service. As a result of its creation, few high-ranking bureaucrats entered military orders after mid-century, being admitted instead to the Order of Charles III.

Like those who held titles of nobility, bureaucrats who entered a military or civil order were unmistakably among the most prominent persons in urban centers, and formed part of the political and social elites of each regional capital. The marriages high bureaucrats and their children contracted, the property they owned, the income they enjoyed, the residences in which they lived, the carriages in which they rode, and their prominence in public parades and celebrations revealed their status. Some miners, merchants, and hacendados, especially in Mexico City in the late colonial period, were much wealthier, but high-ranking officials in every regional capital were powerful and visible representatives of royal authority. It took the Wars of Independence in the early nineteenth century to destroy the stability, flexibility, and general tranquillity that thousands of bureaucrats, both high and low, had labored to establish and then to preserve.

Notes

1. Gregorio M. de Guijo, *Diario, 1648–64,* 2 vols. (Mexico City: Editorial Porrua, 1952), 2: 15.

For Further Reading

Historians have paid more attention to governing and administrative institutions than to bureaucrats as individuals or a group. C. H. Haring, *The Spanish Empire in America* (New York: Oxford University Press, 1947), provides the classic discussion of government and administration at all levels. John Leddy Phelan, "Authority and Flexibility in the Spanish Imperial Bureaucracy," *Administrative Science Quarterly* 5:1 (June 1960): 47–65, explains in general terms how the system actually worked. Ernesto Schäfer, *El consejo real y supremo de las Indias,* 2 vols. (Seville: Escuela de Estudios Hispano-Americanos, 1935–47), provides a wealth of material, including lists of the councilors of the Indies, viceroys, captains-general, presidents, and audiencia ministers up to 1700. The influx of councilors with American experience is considered in Mark A. Burkholder, "The Council of the Indies in the Late Eighteenth Century: A New Perspective," *Hispanic American Historical Review* 56:3 (August 1976): 404–23.

J. H. Parry, *The Sale of Public Office in the Spanish Indies under the Hapsburgs* (Berkeley: University of California Press, 1953), is a useful brief discussion of the topic. His conclusions about the impact of sales on corruption have been challenged by John Leddy Phelan, *The Kingdom of Quito in the Seventeenth Century* (Madison, Wis.: University of Wisconsin Press, 1967). Francisco Tomás y Valiente, *La venta de oficios en Indias (1492–1606)* (Madrid: Instituto de Estudios Administrativos, 1972) is valuable for understanding the progression of sales from their Castilian precedents to 1606. Kenneth J. Andrien,

"The Sale of Fiscal Offices and the Decline of Royal Authority in the Vice-royalty of Peru, 1633–1700," *Hispanic American Historical Review* 62:1 (February 1982): 49–71, describes the adverse impact of the sales on royal authority in Peru. Although Saint Augustine was scarcely urban, Amy Bushnell, *The King's Coffers: Proprietors of the Spanish Florida Treasury, 1565–1702* (Gainesville, Fla.: University Presses of Florida, 1981) is the only full examination of any treasury in the Empire. Guillermo Lohmann Villena, *El corregidor de indios en el Perú bajo los Austrias* (Madrid: Ediciones Cultura Hispánica, 1957); Alfredo Moreno Cebrián, *El corregidor de indios y la economía peruana del siglo XVIII* (Madrid: Instituto Gonzalo Fernández de Oviedo, 1977); Alberto Yalí Román, "Sobre, alcaldías, mayores y corregimientos en Indias: Un ensayo de interpretación," *Jahrbuch für Geschichte von Staat, Wirtschaft, und Geselschaft Lateinamerikas* 9 (1972), 1–39; and Brian R. Hamnett, *Politics and Trade in Southern Mexico, 1750–1821* (Cambridge: At the University Press, 1971) are useful for studying provincial administration.

Few viceroys have received scholarly biographical treatment in English. However, Lewis Hanke, *Guía de las fuentes en el Archivo General de Indias para el estudio de la administración virreinal española en México y en el Perú, 1535–1700,* 3 vols. (Cologne: Böhlan Verlag, 1977), and *Los virreyes españoles en América durante el gobierno de la casa de Austria,* 12 vols. (Madrid: Biblioteca de Autores Españoles, 1976–80) presents relevant bibliography and invaluable documentation.

J. H. Parry, *The Audiencia of New Galicia in the Sixteenth Century* (Cambridge: At the University Press, 1948), Phelan, *The Kingdom of Quito;* and Constance Ann Crowder Carter, "Law and Society in Colonial Mexico: Audiencia Judges in Mexican Society from the Tello de Sandoval Visita General, 1543–1547" (Ph.D. diss., Columbia University, 1971); and, for Brazil, Stuart B. Schwartz, *Sovereignty and Society in Colonial Brazil: The High Court of Bahia and Its Judges, 1609–1751* (Berkeley: University of California Press, 1973) are modern treatments of audiencias. José María Restrepo Sáenz, *Biografías de los mandatarios y ministros de la real audiencia (1671–1819)* (Bogotá: Editorial Cromos, 1952); Abraham de Silva i Molina, *Oidores de la real audiencia de Santiago de Chile durante el siglo XVII* (Santiago de Chile: Imprenta Barcelona, 1903); and Guillermo Lohmann Villena, *Los ministros de la audiencia de Lima en el reinado de los Borbones (1700–1821)* (Seville: Escuela de Estudios Hispano-Americanos, 1974) present biographical information on ministers in three courts. Mark A. Burkholder and D. S. Chandler, *From Impotence to Authority: The Spanish Crown and the American Audiencias, 1687–1808* (Columbia, Mo.: University of Missouri Press, 1977) examine the nearly 700 ministers named to all New World tribunals as well as changes in appointees and appointment policy, and provide lists of appointees for 135 years. Biographical sketches of the individual ministers covered in *From Impotence to Authority* are in the same authors' *Biographical Dictionary of Audiencia Ministers in America, 1687–1821* (Westport, Conn.: Greenwood Press, 1982). The saga of a Peruvian's successful pursuit of an appointment to the Audiencia of Lima is told in Mark A. Burkholder, *Politics of a Colonial Career: José Baquijano and the Audiencia of Lima* (Albuquerque: University of New Mexico Press, 1980).

John Preston Moore, *The Cabildo in Peru under the Hapsburgs* (Durham, N.C.: Duke University Press, 1954) and *The Cabildo in Peru under the Bourbons* (Durham, N.C.: Duke University Press, 1966), and Dominic Azikiwe Nwasike, "Mexico City Town Government, 1590–1650: Study in Aldermanic Background and Performance" (Ph.D. diss., University of Wisconsin, 1972) consider local government in two centers of empire. Peter Marzahl, *Town in the Empire: Government, Politics, and Society in Seventeenth Century Popayan* (Austin, Tex.: University of Texas Press, 1978) examines a provincial town. For an analysis of the cabildo's response to urban crisis, see Louisa S. Hoberman, "Bureaucracy and Disaster: Mexico City and the Flood of 1629," *Journal of Latin American Studies* 6:2 (Fall 1974): 211–30.

A general treatment of the intendant system is Luis Navarro García, *Intendencias en Indias* (Seville: Escuela de Estudios Hispano-Americanos, 1959). Regional examinations include John Lynch, *Spanish Colonial Administration, 1782–1810: The Intendant System in the Viceroyalty of the Río de la Plata* (London: University of London Press, 1958); J. R. Fisher, *Government and Society in Colonial Peru: The Intendant System, 1784–1814* (London: The Athlone Press, 1970); D. A. Brading, *Miners and Merchants in Bourbon Mexico, 1763–1810* (Cambridge: At the University Press, 1971); and Hamnett, *Politics and Trade*. The only examination of a viceregal bureaucracy as a whole is Linda J. Arnold, "Bureaucracy and Bureaucrats in Mexico City, 1742–1835," (Ph.D. diss., The University of Texas, 1982).

Interrelationships among bureaucrats and local society can be discovered in Guillermo Lohmann Villena, *Los americanos en las órdenes nobiliarias (1529–1900)*, 2 vols. (Madrid: Instituto Gonzalo Fernández Oviedo, 1947). The implications of such ties are developed in John Leddy Phelan, *The People and the King: The Comunero Revolution in Colombia, 1781* (Madison, Wis.: University of Wisconsin Press, 1978), and, as the best example of an integrated political history, Jacques A. Barbier, *Reform and Politics in Bourbon Chile, 1755–1796* (Ottawa: University of Ottawa Press, 1980).

Principal Cities of Colonial South America

Principal Cities of Colonial Mexico,

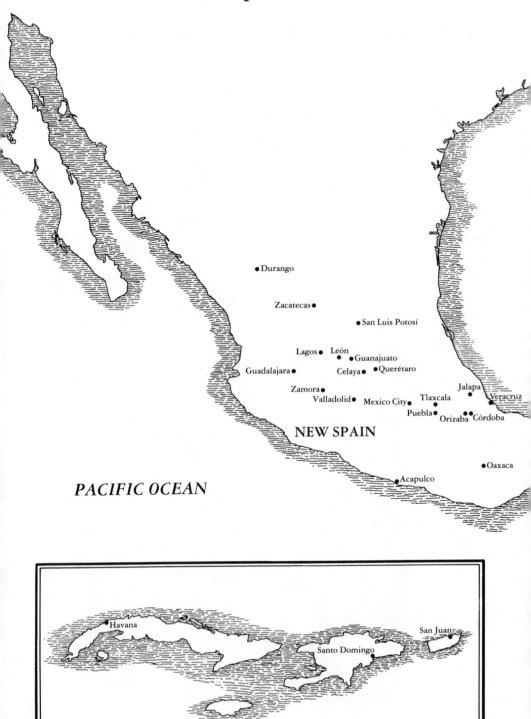

● Durango

Zacatecas ●

● San Luis Potosí

Lagos ● León
● ● Guanajuato
Guadalajara ● Celaya ● ● Querétaro

Zamora ●
Valladolid ● Mexico City ●
Jalapa ●
Tlaxcala ● Veracruz
Puebla ● Orizaba ● ● Córdoba

NEW SPAIN

● Oaxaca

● Acapulco

PACIFIC OCEAN

● Havana

San Juan ●

Santo Domingo ●

GULF OF MEXICO

●Havana

●Mérida

●Campeche

CARIBBEAN SEA

●San Cristóbal

Guatemala City ●   ●Comayagua

San Salvador ●

●León
●Granada

Nombre de Dios
Portobelo●
Panama City●

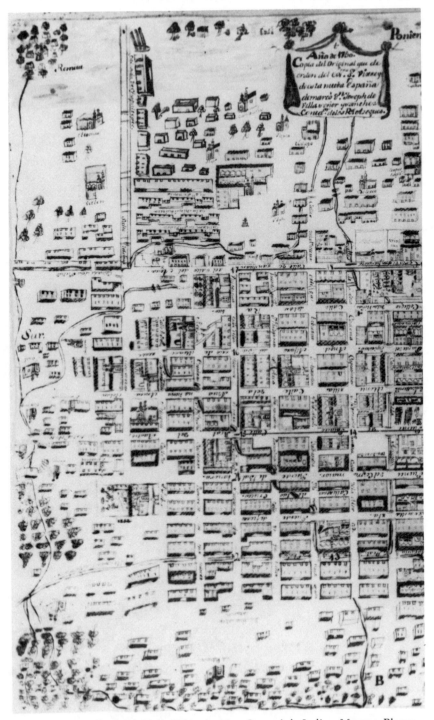

Fig. 1.   Map of Mexico City, 1751. Archivo General de Indias, Mapas y Planos, México, 178 (hereafter cited as AGI, M y P).

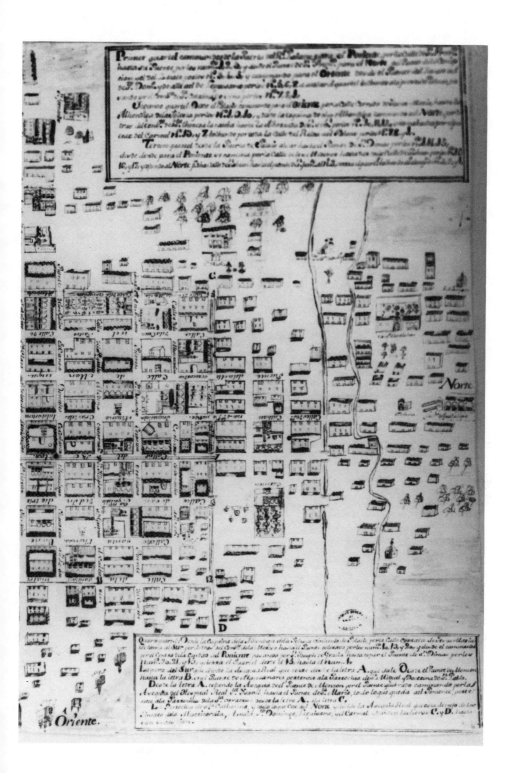

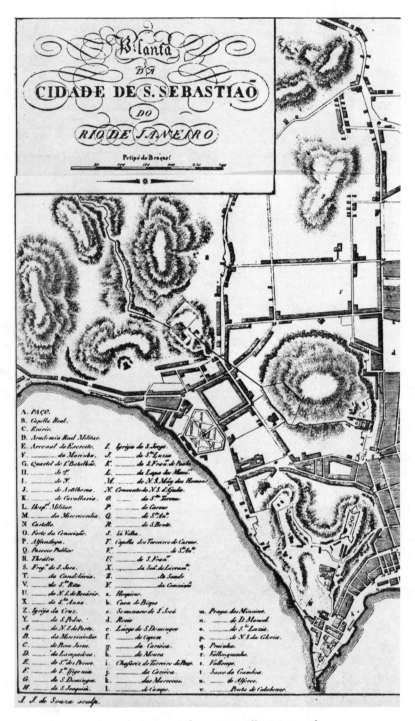

Fig. 2. Map of Rio de Janeiro, after 1818. *Album cartográfico do Rio de Janeiro (seculos XVII e XIX),* ed. Lygia da Fonseca Fernandes de Cunha (Rio de Janeiro: Ministerio da Educaçáo e Culture, 1978).

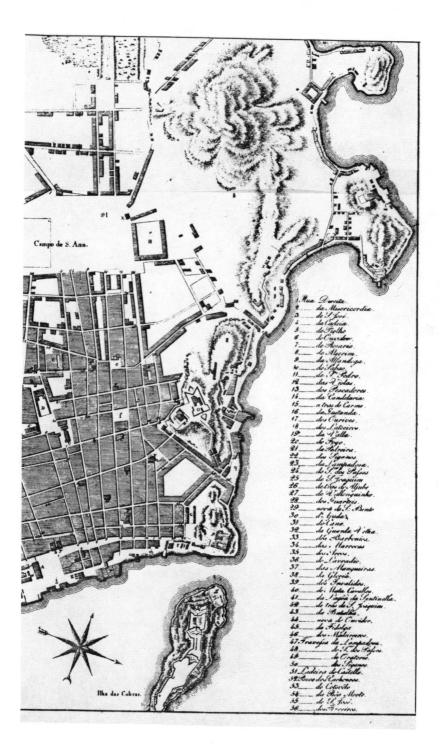

Fig. 3. Lower and Upper City, Bahia, early eighteenth century. Archivo Histórico da Câmara Municipal, Bahia (hereafter cited as AHCM, Bahia).

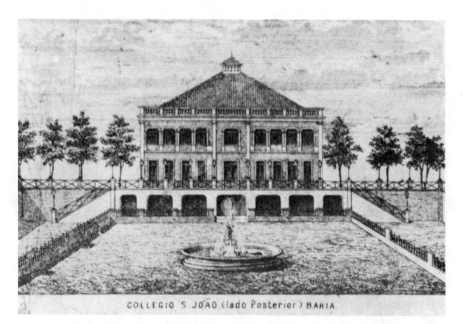

COLLEGIO S JOÃO (lado Posterior) BAHIA

Fig. 4. House built by wealthy merchant, Bahia, eighteenth century. AHCM, Bahia.

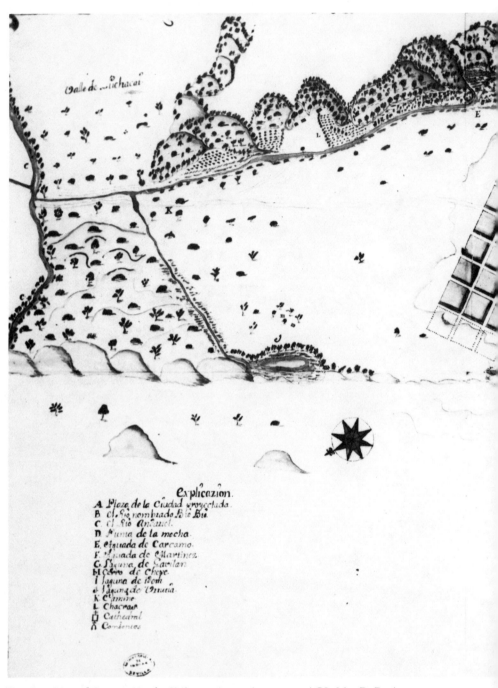

Explicazion.
A Plaza de la Ciudad proyectada.
B el Rio nombrado Bío Bío.
C el Rio Andeluel.
D Puma de la mocha.
E Aguada de Carcamo.
F Aguada de Martinez.
G Laguna de Gavilan.
H Cerro de Chepe.
I Laguna de Isom.
J Laguna de Umaia.
K Camino.
L Chacras.
☐ Cathedral.
Ñ Conbentos.

Fig. 5.   Map of Concepción de Chile, c. sixteenth century. AGI, M y P, Perú y
Chile, 35.

114

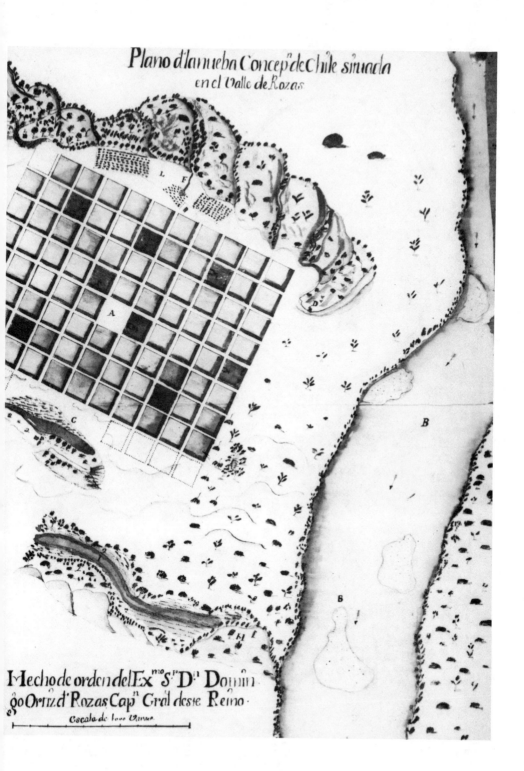

Plano d'la nueba Concep.n de Chile situada
en el Valle de Rozas

Hecho de orden del Ex.mo S.r D.n Domingo Ortiz d' Rozas Cap.n Gral deste Reino.

Escala de 1000 Uaras.

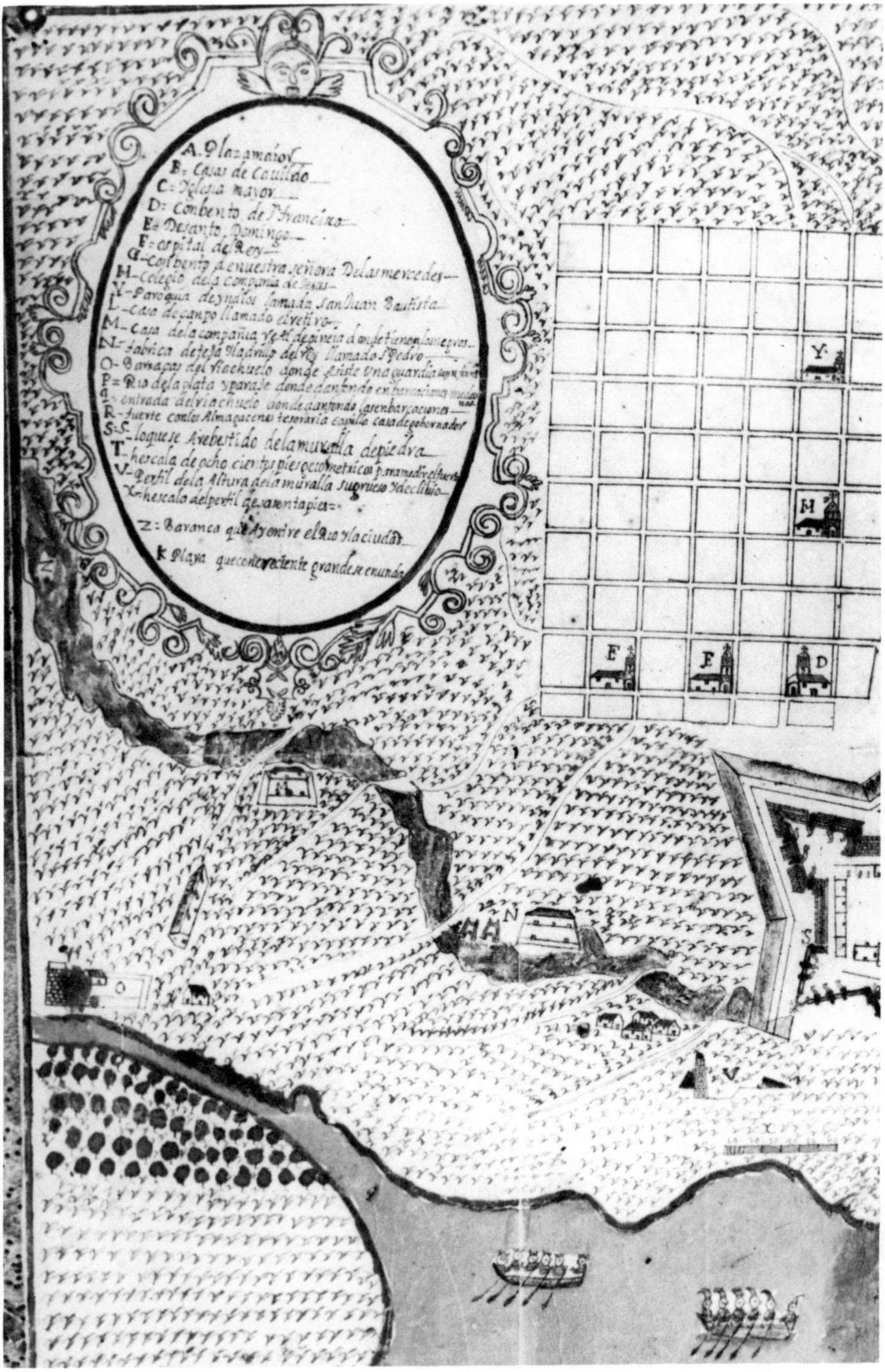

A. Plaza maior
B. Casas de Cauildo
C. Iglesia mayor
D. Conbento de S. Francisco
E. De S.to Domingo
F. ospital del Rey
G. Conbento de nuestra señora Delas mercedes
H. Colegio dela compañia de Jesus
I. Parroquia de yndios llamada San Juan Bautista
L. Casa de campo llamado el retiro
M. Casa dela compañia, y el sitio de iglesia donde tienen su negocio
N. fabrica de S.ta Iglesia de Rey llamado S. Pedro
O. Barrancas ael riachuelo donde asiste una guardia
P. Rio dela plata y parage donde dan fondo en buena clima naos
Q. entrada del riachuelo donde dan fondo y embarcan acunas
R. fuerte con los Almacenes y en el la casa de gobernador
S.S. lo que se a rebestido dela muralla de piedra
T. escala de ocho cientos pies geometricos y namedi e fuera
V. Perfil dela Altura dela muralla superior y de el llano
X. escala del perfil de la antepilea
Z. Baranca que ay en tre el Rio y la ciudad
K. Playa que con recidente grande se enunda

Fig. 6. Map of Buenos Aires, 1713. AGI, M y P, Buenos Aires, 39.

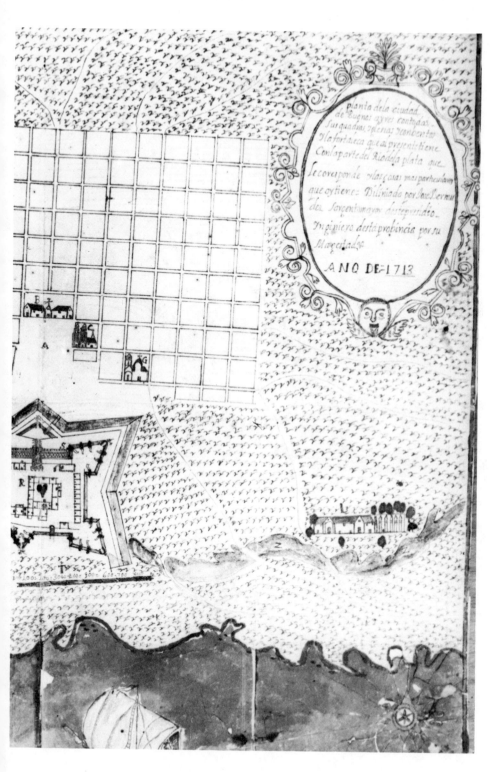

planta dela ciudad
de Buenos ayres contodas
sus quadras, plazas yconbentos
yla fortaleza que al prejenti tiene
Conlaparte del Rio dela plata que
le coresponde y las casas mas particulares
que oytiene. Dibuxada por Iose Bermudes
del Sargentomayor desteprendio
Yngipiero desta propincia por su
Magestad en
AÑO DE=1713

Fig. 7. City of Saña, early seventeenth century. Felipe Guaman Poma de Ayala, *Nueva crónica y buen gobierno* (Paris; University of Paris, 1936).

Fig. 8.　Gentlemen and ladies watching procession, Mexico City, eighteenth century. Detail, The Plaza Mayor of Mexico City, Anonymous, Museo Nacional de Historia, (hereafter cited as Plaza Mayor).

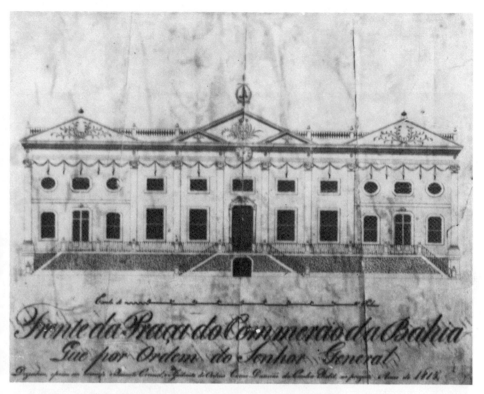

Fig. 11. *(Above)* Chamber of Commerce, Bahia, 1818. AHCM, Bahia.

Fig. 9. *(Opposite, top)* View of Bahia, early nineteenth century. AHCM, Bahia.

Fig. 10. *(Opposite, bottom)* House with courtyard built by wealthy merchant, Bahia, eighteenth century. AHCM, Bahia.

Fig. 12.   High officials in their carriage and spectators representing diverse social
          groups, Mexico City, eighteenth century, Detail, Plaza Mayor.

Fig. 13.   *(Opposite)* Francisco de Pauls Sanz, Superintendent of the Viceroyalty of
          Río de la Plata, c. 1785. Painting, Museo Histórico Nacional, Buenos
          Aires.

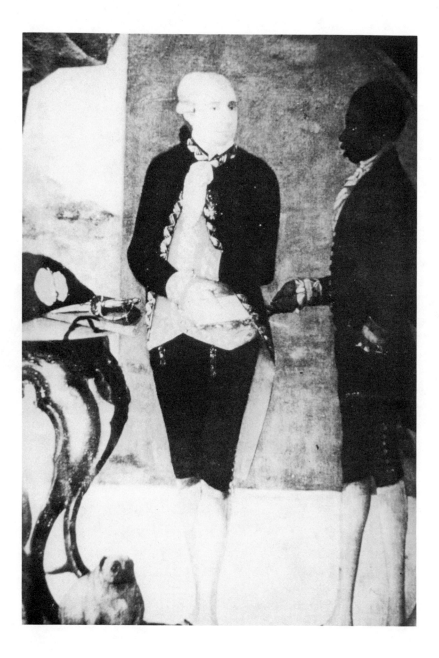

Fig. 14. Franciscan and Bishop Quiroga. Florian Baucke, S. J., *Iconografía colonial rioplatense*, 1749–1767 (Buenos Aires, 1935).

124

Fig. 15.   Jesuits and their pupils. Baucke, *Iconografía*.

TRAJES DE LAS RELIGIOSAS DE LOS CONVENTOS DE MEXICO DE LOS COLEGIOS
Y RECOGIMIENTOS

Fig. 17.   Gallegos of Spain. Baucke, *Iconografía*.

Fig. 16.   *(Opposite)* Habits of the female religious of the Viceroyalty of New Spain, eighteenth century. Anonymous, Archivo Fotográfico del Instituto Nacional de Antropología e Historia, Mexico City.

Fig. 18.   Fortification of Lima, 1687. AGI, M y P, Perú Y Chile, 13.

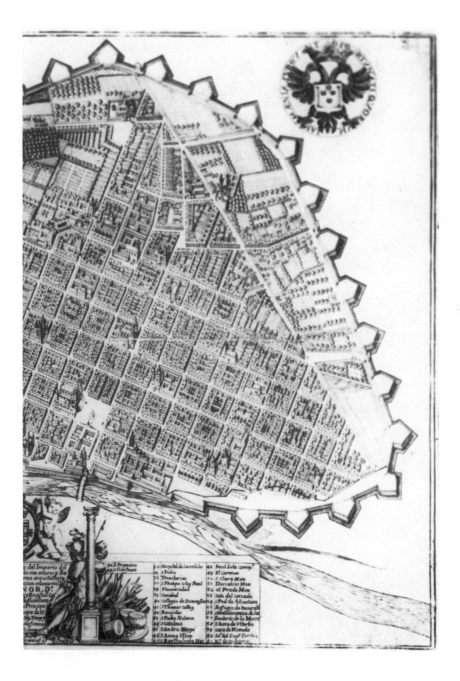

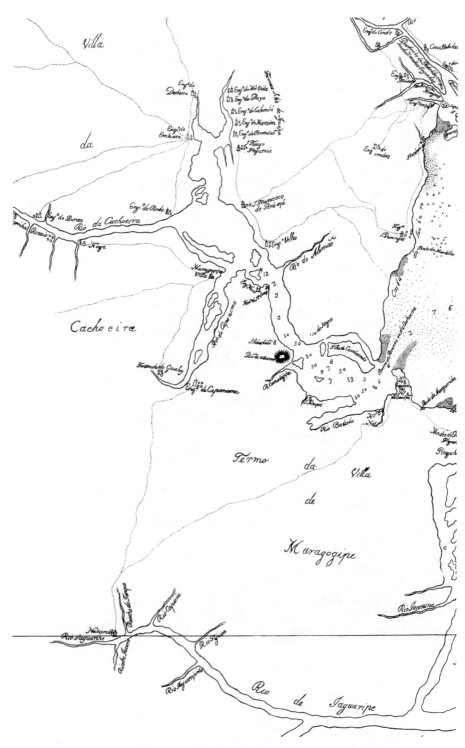

Fig. 19. A portion of the coastal Bahia and adjacent waterways. Luiz dos Santos Vilhena, Recopilação de noticias (Bahia Imprenta Oficial do Estado, 1921).

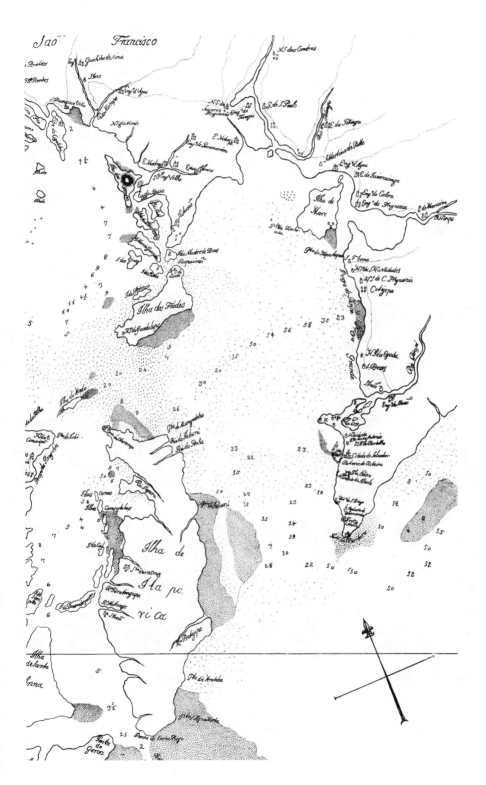

Fig. 20.   Market scene, Rio de janeiro, 1820. Unknown.

Fig. 23.   Indian women selling fruits and vegetables in their stalls, men selling
fish, Mexico City, eighteenth century. Detail, Plaza Mayor.

Fig. 21.   *(Opposite, top)* Water carrier, women selling food, and men selling
clothing, Mexico City, eighteenth century. Detail, Plaza Mayor.

Fig. 22.   *(Opposite, bottom)* Ill-clad, armed thief, attempting to flee, with
well-to-do pursuers, Mexico City, eighteenth century. Detail, Plaza
Mayor.

Plano del pizo alto.

Archivo | SALA CAPITULAR.

Corredor del pizo alto.

Fig. 24. Design for the City Council building, including layout of the upper story, Luján, Río de la Plata, 1788. AGI, M y P, Buenos Aires, 288.

FIVE

Churchmen

PAUL GANSTER

Introduction

The urban skyline of Spanish America was highlighted by the massive buildings and high towers of numerous ecclesiastical establishments. The bells of
those towers filled the cities with a sea of sound when ringing out the daily
canonical hours or proclaiming special events, such as the imposition of an
interdict by the bishop or archbishop or the birth of a new heir to the throne.
Down below the towers, on the street level, the presence of the church was
also inescapable. In the large cities of the American empire of Spain, such as
Lima and Mexico City, and in the smaller cities as well, the religious architecture usually was situated with open areas in front—the central plaza or a
smaller square on a side street. These open spaces not only provided the residents with a convenient location from which to view the wonders of the mag-
nificently carved doors, the intricate facades, and the towers of the churches,
but they also provided locations for public fountains, markets, and secular
and religious festivals. The plazas served as centers for urban life where representatives of all social and racial groups mingled, always overshadowed by
the religious edifices that were symbolic of community piety and devotion.

Among the milling throngs to be found at certain times of the day in all
urban areas were a group of men distinguished from other people by their
distinctive forms of dress. Some of these men were regular clergy, members
of one of the orders of friars who followed a set of rules and lived within a
religious community. Others were secular clergy, part of the organizations
headed by bishops and archbishops, men charged with ministering to the
spiritual needs of the populace on a daily basis. Added to the numbers of

friars and secular clerics were a large group of men who had not taken formal religious vows in any order nor been ordained by a bishop, but who had donned some form of clerical garb, or habit, and worked with the friars and seculars as assistants, as aides, or in specific posts in the various ecclesiastical establishments.

The total number of churchmen in the colonial cities was not insignificant; in fact, travelers frequently commented on the large number of urban ecclesiastics. The urban areas, at least to outsiders, seem always to have been priest-ridden. It is difficult to determine how many clerics there were in the cities, for censuses are often lacking or imprecise. Nevertheless, sufficient data are available to make some general estimates.

The city of Trujillo, on the north coast of Peru, had a population of 9,289 souls in 1763. Of that population, 140, or 1.5 percent of the total, were friars and clerics. Although this does not seem to be a particularly large number, it should be pointed out that there were 3,650 slaves and *mulatos* (persons of black and white ancestry), 2,300 *mestizos* (persons of Indian and white ancestry), 289 Indians, and only 3,050 people who were acknowledged to be white, that is, persons of Spanish birth or descent (*español*). Since, as will be seen later in this essay, the vast majority of clerics in Spanish America from the español category, a more meaningful ratio would be that of clerics to the total population of European descent, which is 4.6 percent. Or, if it is assumed that half of the español population were male, then 9.2 percent of the white men in the city, or approximately 1 out of every 11, were clerics. If we then were to include men who wore religious garb but were not technically clerics, the figure would be much higher: 1 for every 7 or 8 español laymen.

The percentages of churchmen in selected segments of the population in other colonial cities are roughly comparable. In New Spain Puebla had a population of 14,500 Indians, 34,095 *castas* (persons of mixed racial ancestry), and 19,710 españoles, or whites, for a total of 67,765, in 1781. There, the ordained priests were 1.4 percent of the total population, 5.2 percent of the españoles, and 10.4 percent of the males of Spanish birth or descent. In other words, slightly more than 1 in 10 of the español men of Puebla were priests. In Mexico City, 1.4 percent of the 113,234 inhabitants in 1790 were regular and secular clergy. There, the ratio of clerics to the white population was probably similar to that in Puebla. In Mérida, the isolated capital of the Yucatán peninsula, where españoles were very much in the minority, the 133 secular and regular clergy comprised only .45 percent of the city's population in 1794. But the clerical population was 3.9 percent of the español population, or 7.8 percent of the white men—figures that were similar to those in other Spanish American cities.

As these figures suggest, the numbers of ecclesiastical establishments in the cities were large. Lima, with an eighteenth-century population of about 50,000, has a magnificent cathedral, some 6 parish churches, 11 hospitals, 15 nunneries, 19 monasteries, a retreat for divorced women, an oratorio, various novitiates and colleges, and several retreat houses. Trujillo, with a population slightly over 9,000 in the eighteenth century, had a similar ecclesiastical presence, with a cathedral, 5 parish churches, a seminary, 5 monasteries, 1 hospital, a college, and 2 nunneries. These numbers of church institutions and edifices seem to have been characteristic for other urban areas of Spanish America.

The concentration of clerics in the urban areas of the Spanish empire is not surprising, for a similar pattern may be observed in Spain during the conquest period and is evident as well from the earliest days in the Indies. In early Peru clerics arrived with the military phase of the conquest. Shortly after the establishment of each city, a church with one or more secular priests and a number of monasteries were founded. Throughout the conquest period the secular priests were more numerous than the regulars, and the tendency of both was to leave the countryside, where they were most needed, and congregate in the cities, a situation that has continued to the present day in Spanish America.

Urban concentration and high visibility both in the ordinary existence and in the social life of the urban centers characterized the group of churchmen in Spanish America. But who were these men who were so prominent in the cities and towns of the American empire? What was it that set them apart from others, or constituted the clerical state? What were the main features of the history and development of the institutional church in Spanish America? What were the requisites for admittance to the clerical union? What constituted the characteristic clerical career, and what were the range of activities in which clerics became involved in order to make a living? What were the social and family backgrounds of these men of the church? What position did clerics occupy, individually and collectively, in urban society? Drawing on information resulting from research on the clergy of New Spain and Peru in the eighteenth century and on comparative material from other periods and areas of urban Spanish America, this chapter will provide an overview of the men who staffed the church in the colonial cities of Spanish America.

Church Presence In The Indies

The presence of the church was so obvious in the great epic events of the conquests of Peru and New Spain and their aftermaths that it is often assumed that the ecclesiastical involvement was on an institutional level and that the corporate presence had been there since the earliest Spanish voyages of discovery and expansion to the Indies. This is an erroneous assumption, because for more than a decade after the discovery of the Indies the presence of the church was surprisingly small and ineffectual. Not only did the hardbitten mariners of the voyages of discovery have little need of clerics, but prior to discovery the Spanish monarchs had been engaged in a clear effort to reform the corrupt and decadent Spanish church, a policy that was implemented only through increasing royal control of the church. The Catholic monarchs were not about to permit the establishment of a permanent and strong religious structure in their new possessions until the papacy had granted to the crown the concessions necessary to ensure royal dominance of an institutionalized church in the Indies. Spain was able successfully to negotiate the concessions it desired, but not until 1508, and by then the declining indigenous populations and the shifting focus of Hispanic colonization made the development of an organized church in the Indies impractical until the 1520s.

The delay in establishing the church firmly was worth the wait, from the royal perspective, for patience and hard bargaining had resulted in the crown's obtaining full patronage rights for the church in the Indies. This royal patronage, or *patronato real,*, meant that the papacy granted to the crown the privilege of founding and organizing the church overseas and the right of naming all clergy to benefices, or church posts with attached incomes, such as those of parish priest, cathedral chapter member, or bishop. In short, the patronato assured that the church in the American colonies of Spain would be controlled almost totally by the royal government (except in areas of dogma), and that the church would function effectively as an arm of the state. The church in the Indies would serve the needs of the state.

With the movement of a significant Spanish presence into the mainland areas, beginning in the 1520s, the crown generally followed the policy of establishing a bishopric concurrent with the colonization of any new region. At times, the new bishoprics swept in with the waves of conquest, only to pull up stakes and move along as the conquests incorporated newer and richer areas. The first bishopric or diocese to be established on the mainland was that at Darien in 1513 (subsequently moved to Panama City in 1524). A diocese was created for the area around Mexico City in 1519, but was transferred to Tlaxcala in 1525, and thence to Puebla. Mexico City's bishopric was not established until 1530, and from there dioceses radiated outward to the regions or cities of Comayagua (Honduras) in 1531, León (Nicaragua) in 1531, Guatemala City in 1534, Oaxaca in 1535, Michoacán in 1536, Chiapas in 1538, Guadalajara in 1548, and Yucatán in 1561. A similar pattern was evident in South America with the founding of bishoprics in Túmbez in 1529, Cuzco in 1536, and Lima in 1539. By the end of the colonial period there were 10 archdioceses and 38 dioceses in Spanish America, all rooted firmly in the urban centers of the empire.

The ecclesiastical structure of the new foundations was similar to that of Spain, generally modeled after Seville except for the provisions of royal patronage. Each newly conquered area was divided into large territorial units, called bishoprics or archbishoprics, and headed by a bishop or an archbishop who was headquartered in the major city of the region. Each of these then was divided up into a number of smaller spatial units based on population and called parishes. This was the most basic ecclesiastical unit, for it was the parish priest who had day-to-day contact with the population and dispensed to them the sacraments necessary for salvation. Only one parish priest, or other priests with his permission, could administer sacraments within the parish boundaries. This monopoly of services guaranteed the cleric holding a benifice an adequate income and protected him from encroachments by other ordained priests, which was a potentially serious problem in the priest-filled cities.

The bishop also was aided in governing his diocese by a central bureaucracy and a number of church courts that had cognizance of matters ranging from accusations against clerics to divorces to probate of estates left by the faithful. The cathedral chapter also provided essential support in the running of the diocese. This group of men was charged with maintaining the principal church of the bishopric and seeing to the perpetual observance of the canonical hours in the cathedral. Moreover, the chapter was charged with the collection of the tithes on agricultural products, the major source of revenue for the diocesan structure. Finally, the chapter ran the diocese in the absence of a bishop, a frequent occurrence in an era of poor transportation and high mortality rates among churchmen. Given all these duties and powers, the chapter members obviously had great prestige in the cities of Spanish America.

With the conquests and church foundations came significant numbers of secular clerics, including both those carrying official appointments to the new sees and those who came using their own resources to seek positions in the newly-established hierarchies. Historians once believed that the great majority of churchmen in the Indies through a good part of the sixteenth century were regulars, but it is now clear that friars and secular clerics were present in Peru during the conquest period in roughly equal numbers. It also appears that the predominance of regulars in New Spain was not as great as once was thought. Moreover, the seculars seem to have been even more prone to concentration in the urban areas than were the regulars, so that they were an equally vital element in the cities of the Indies from the start.

The friars were present in the Caribbean from a very early date, and arrived on the mainland in force. The three mendicant orders, the Franciscans, the Dominicans, and the Augustinians, were established in New Spain not long after the conquest (in 1523, 1526, and 1533 respectively) and immediately began their work of conversion of millions of Indians. (See Figure 14.) They soon had divided the newly conquered country up among themselves, but the competition for souls was always most intense in the rich and densely populated areas around the major urban center of the colony—Mexico City. King Philip II complained of this in 1561, noting that "the religious prefer to establish themselves in the rich green lands near the city of Mexico, leaving stretches of twenty to thirty leagues untended, because the religious avoid the rough, poor, and hot regions."[1]

By the 1570s a tremendous expansion had been achieved by the regular orders in the Indies, and particularly in New Spain. At that time there were over 200 religious establishments in New Spain; most of these were in Indian towns, with 2 or 3 friars and lay brothers supervising thousands of Indian charges. At the same time, the centripetal forces of the cities had become evident, even among the highly motivated Mendicants. All the principal cities of the realm had great religious establishments with considerable populations, supported by systems of rural estates. Although the urban components were necessary as support for the primarily rural proselytizing functions, a point was quickly reached where the urban establishments took on a life of their own. After the initial burst of rural activity, the great flowering of the orders occured in the cities of New Spain. With some variations, similar patterns are visible elsewhere in the Spanish Indies, and the presence of the orders in any urban landscape was a significant one. The ratio of urban to rural friars continued to increase throughout the colonial period.

As an institution, then, the church became established quickly and permanently after the major conquests. By the last quarter of the sixteenth century, the major features of the secular hierarchy and the regular orders were in place. A bitter rivalry between the regulars and seculars had begun, subsiding somewhat late in the colonial period with increased state control over both branches of the church. Both the regulars and the seculars were rooted firmly in the urban areas. Both drained off wealth from the countryside in the form of produce from rural estates or through the collection of tithes. By the end of the sixteenth century, most of the men in both secular and regular branches of the church spent most of their time in the cities.

The Urban Churchmen

The churchmen encountered in the urban landscape were of diverse regional and social origins, and played varied roles within the church. At the same time, they were different from other men in the world and enjoyed their own corporate identity. The Catholic and Spanish world was divided into two population groups: the clergy and the laity. Since the clerical state was considered to be divinely ordained, the distinction between men of the cloth and other men was of divine origin and therefore unquestionable. Hence, the considerable prestige enjoyed by all religious men in colonial Spanish America is understandable.

The transition from the mundane to the divine was regulated by legal requirements and widely followed practices. For secular priests, the tonsure (*tonsura*), a sacred ceremony in which hair was clipped so as to leave a bald circle near the back of the head, marked entry into the clerical union in a probationary status. For regular clergy, entry was signaled by joining a religious community and living according to the rules of the order and in obedience to a superior.

At the time that a man joined the regular or secular branch of the church, he also was required to don the distinctive garb appropriate to his new status. For the seculars, this was a long black habit that reached to the heels; for the regulars, it was roughly the same, but with variations in color and detail according to the practice of the individual order. The civil and church authorities made a great fuss over this requirement, and expended a great deal of energy throughout the colonial period to see that it was followed. The gap between the clergy and the laity was enormous, and the outward signs of this difference were considered to be of paramount importance. As the Council of Trent declared, "although the habit does not make the monk, it is necessary that the ecclesiastics always wear garb convenient to their own state in order that they manifest the interior honesty of their customs through the exterior decency of their clothes."[2] It was this different dress that made the churchmen so noticeable in the urban throngs and made them appear to constitute so large a part of the cities' population. (Figure 13.)

The first tonsure, or joining with a religious order, accorded a man the protection of the *fuero eclesiástico*, or the corporate privileges enjoyed by churchmen. Most important, these privileges usually removed the ecclesiastic from the jurisdiction of the civil courts and assured that his case would be heard by the church tribunals. At the same time, as part of his incorporation into the ecclesiastical union, each man was put under the supervision of a particular ecclesiastical authority, whether secular or regular. This assured that each urban churchman was directly accountable to a superior in the geographical area of his residence.

Holy Orders

The tonsure and simple affiliation with a religious order brought men into the clerical union, and both of these were accomplished with relative ease. However, these were not irrevocable steps, for the regular could leave his community and cast off his habit. The secular could lose the tonsure by refusal to wear the habit or by various legal and moral transgressions. Admittance to the clerical union at this level had the advantage of nonpermanence. However, full participation in the church was only attained, for the secular, through the process of ordination, which was, in practice, requisite for those seeking the most important posts in the secular church—those of parish priest, cathedral chapter member, bishop, or archbishop. For the regular, going through a training and probationary period, the novitiate, and then professing the solemn vows of poverty, chastity, and obedience were necessary in order to become a full-fledged friar in one of the orders. The regular also could pass through the ordination process and become a priest able to dispense the sacraments and function as a parish priest in those Indian parishes reserved to the care of the regulars.

Priesthood traditionally has been defined as a sacrament through which a man receives the authority to pardon sins, offer the sacrifice of the mass, and administer other sacraments of the church, with the exception of ordination and confirmation, which are reserved for bishops. In this position as mediator between God and man, the parish priest was involved with the faithful both in routine matters and in the critical events of their lives, including baptism, marriage, and death. He was also an indispensable element in the continual round of festivals that marked the religious calendar of each parish.

The sacrament of holy orders was received in successive steps, or grades, broadly grouped into the minor orders and the major orders. The minor orders were revocable, but those who received major orders were dedicated and consecrated irrevocably to the church and were required to observe perpetual chastity. Not advancing beyond minor orders kept options open. Often a young man would take the minor orders in order to obtain the rents from a chaplaincy or because of parental pressure, only later to discover that he had no real vocation for a career as a priest. Then, too, there is little doubt that many individuals received the tonsure or minor orders merely to gain the protection offered by the fuero eclesiástico. The tonsure and minor orders did afford a young man a modicum of social prestige, as well as a certain amount of institutional support as a member of the clerical union, and as such were considered worthwhile. Thus, although many men went through all of the steps of the ordination process, others took the tonsure and/or minor orders and then went on with their lives very much as did laymen. The process of ordination was sufficiently flexible to accommodate the needs of individuals, their families, and society.

The legal and customary requirements for ordination were numerous, and greatly restricted the number of men who were able to become priests. All candidates were supposed to be persons of good demeanor and were required to produce witnesses attesting to their character and general circumstances. A candidate was also to be of legitimate birth and from an old Christian lineage, free of the taint of Moorish, Jewish, Indian, or Black blood (*limpieza de sangre*). Also, the family was to be free of individuals who had been prosecuted by the Inquisition. It is true that there were a few cases of racially mixed clergy, but these occurred primarily in the provincial towns, on the fringes of empire, or later in the colonial period when there was a relaxing of the requirements. Occasionally a man of illegitimate birth did receive a dispensation and was ordained. Generally, however, all of these rules were enforced, particularly in the major cities.

A certain level of education was necessary for acceptance into the priesthood, and in practice the trend was toward increasingly higher educational levels for ordained men throughout the colonial period. In New Spain, the educational levels of clerics improved from the last part of the sixteenth century on. Twenty-three percent of the 95 priests in the archdiocese of Mexico in 1569 had university degrees, primarily bachelor's degrees. Six years later, the number of parish priests had increased to 115 and the percentage of men with university degrees had grown to 29 percent. A similar trend is to be seen in the neighboring diocese of Puebla during the same period. By the eighteenth century the majority of men ordained in Lima and Mexico City had graduated from one of the colleges and had received university degrees. A few of the parish priests in those dioceses held only the bachelor's degree, the licenciate, or the master's, but the vast majority of them held the doctorate in theology or in canon and civil laws. In the more isolated province of Yucatán in the second half of the eighteenth century the educational attainments of the priests were much more modest. A study of a group of 288 priests revealed that 234 claimed to have studied philosophy, theology, or arts but that only some 44 indicated that they had obtained a bachelor's degree. Thus, only a small proportion of the priests in Yucatán had a bachelor's degree and those holding a licenciate or a doctorate were quite rare, usually residing in Mérida, the most important city of the peninsula.

A clear pattern is evident for much of the colonial period. The most highly educated priests were concentrated in the urban areas and particularly in the most important cities of the viceroyalties, such as Lima and Mexico City. The provincial cities and the rural areas had much lower levels of formal education among the clergy. This is entirely logical, for the major cities were much more desirable places to live and work. Thus, the competition for posts was more intense and the most highly qualified candidates had a distinct advantage. At the same time, these metropolitan capitals had the best educational infrastructures, and it was thus more convenient for their residents to attain higher educational goals.

The primary education of prospective clerics was handled by private tutors, by informal schools established by churchmen, or by schools located in some of the convents that one could attend as early as the age of four. (See Figure 15.) Secondary education was provided in the larger cities by the diocesan seminaries and by schools (colegios) run by the various religious orders. Generally, the best education was offered in the Jesuit colleges. Although all of these institutions provided scholarships for needy students, the recipients were inevitably sons of noble families or families of high social rank. Students without scholarships had to pay tuition as well as room and board. Consequently, providing a secondary education for male offspring would have been extremely burdensome for families of humble origin and modest means. Similarly, financing university education would have been difficult for the members of the lower strata of society. In essence, the costs of meeting the educational requirements limited the secular priesthood to the sons of the relatively successful families of colonial society. At the lowest levels, this might include petty merchants, prosperous artisans, and others of similar social standing and wealth.

Another crucial requirement for ordination as a priest was that the interested individual demonstrate his possession of a guaranteed, lifelong means of support, called the *congrua*. This rule, designed to prevent the development of a class of indigent clerics, generally was enforced by the bishops, In Lima and Mexico City in the late colonial period, this income amounted to 200 pesos annually, a sum which would maintain a priest at a minimum level of decency. There were several ways in which the requirement of a congrua could be met. The individual could obtain a benefice, such as a parish post or a position on the ecclesiastical chapter, but this was unusual. Occasionally, a man met the congrua requirements by simply pointing out that he came from a wealthy family and was assured of lifelong support. Infrequently, great intellectual talents were accepted as proof that the person in question always would be gainfully employed. A more usual source for the congrua income was *capellanías,* or endowed chantry funds. Basically, a capellanía was a foundation, or endowment, wherein the recipient priest had the obligation of saying a certain number of masses annually for the benefit of the souls of the founder and his relatives. The income for the chantry almost invariably was derived from the annual interest paid on a *censo,* or mortgage on urban and rural real property.

There were several different types of capellanías with distinct legal structures. Some were under direct church control; others constituted, in effect, a part of a family's resources and functioned as small entails to retain a certain amount of wealth within the lineage. The importance of the capellanías as part of the colonial structure should not be underestimated. By the end of the colonial period, a significant proportion of urban and rural property was encumbered with censos that provided the income for the capellanías. These served to channel rural wealth into the cities and to support a large group of urban churchmen. It seems probable that the majority of ordained priests depended upon the different forms of capellanías for their livings. Many priests held a number of chantries and thus enjoyed a comfortable income, while others put together a respectable material lifestyle by combining the capellanía with other employments.

Another way in which to comply with the congrua requirements was to seek ordination on the basis of knowledge of an Indian language, termed a *título de suficiencia de lengua.* There was a chronic shortage of priests for the rural Indian parishes, since urban life was far preferable to most men, and usually anyone with a sufficient understanding of an Indian language could obtain a benefice easily. But a shortage of priests who knew Indian languages persisted throughout the colonial period. Often a capable man would learn an Indian language for ordination, serve an Indian parish briefly, and escape to an urban post at the first opportunity. While there was a surplus of priests in the cities, there were vacant parish benefices in the rural areas, but many preferred urban employment or underemployment to banishment to a rural area.

The Council of Trent set no specific age requirements for the tonsura and minor orders; rather, the level of education determined when these titles could be conferred. This meant that the tonsura and minor orders could be obtained at an early age. At times, the tonsure was received as early as age 10, but more often the first steps towards priesthood were not taken until the young man was in his mid to late teens and engaged in his studies at one of the colonial colleges. Many did wait until as late as their mid-twenties, and then obtained both minor and major orders in rapid succession. Occasionally, an older man whose wife had died and whose children were established in careers or married would seek ordination. In the final analysis, the age at which an individual received his minor orders depended upon the age at which he formulated, or had formulated for him, career goals. Some obviously were selected by their parents for clerical careers at an early age. Such men obtained capellanías and were granted minor orders while still quite young. Others delayed the decision and kept their options open until a more advanced age. Specific age requirements were established for the major orders. The first steps of major orders could not be taken until age 21 and the final step of full ordination required that a man be 25 years old.

The overall result of many of these requirements was to have a profound effect on the social and racial composition of the group of ordained men in the colonial cities. The racial qualifications assured that the priests would be almost entirely of European, or what passed as European descent. The congrua and education norms generally could be met only by men whose families were prosperous. Therefore, the urban priests were white and came from the upper levels of colonial society. The few ordained men from humble origins or of obvious mixed heritage were the exceptions, and tended to be found in the peripheral areas of the empire.

Regional Origins Of The Clergy

A basic characteristic of churchmen that was of considerable import to the people of the colonial cities and that also has received attention from present-day scholars is their regional origins. Initially, of course, all churchmen in the Indies were Spanish- or foreign-born, and either arrived in the New World as members of the church or joined it after immigration. Within a short time after the conquest, creoles began appearing in considerable numbers within the ranks of the churchmen, so that by some time in the last quarter of the sixteenth century the creoles probably outnumbered the peninsulars within the church in most areas of the Indies.

The creole domination of the secular clergy lasted for the duration of the colonial period. The only exception was at the level of bishop or archbishop, where peninsulars made up the majority of the appointments. For example, of the 159 bishops who served in the Spanish Indies during the period 1504 to 1620, 84 percent were from Spain, 14 percent were creoles, and 2 percent were of unknown regional origins. About two-thirds of these bishops were friars and only one-third were from the secular church. Clearly, the crown had a policy of favoring peninsular-born friars in its appointments to sees in the New World, and available evidence indicates that this situation persisted for the duration of Spanish rule in America.

The best data on the regional origins of chapter members are for the Lima and Mexico City cathedrals in the eighteenth century. For the period 1700 to 1799, creoles constituted approximately 85 percent of the appointments who were seated in the Lima chapter; for the Mexico City body, the figure was about 70 percent. Most men were appointed to the lowest posts in the chapters and then ascended through a slow, orderly system of promotion called the *asenso*. Only rarely were men brought in directly to the highest and most powerful posts. Thus, since more creoles were named to the chapters, more survived to occupy leadership positions. The norm for Lima and Mexico City in the eighteenth century was a creole chapter with creole leadership.

The creole stranglehold on the chapters was so great that the anticreole policies of the Bourbon kings had little real impact. The royal decrees of 1776, restricting creoles to only one-third of the chapter posts while inviting the Americans to compete for peninsular posts, had only an insignificant effect on the Mexico City and Lima chapters, despite the tremendous uproar stirred up in the Indies by the legislation.

The ranks of the parish priests in the colonial cities were also filled primarily by local men. The urban benefices were, without a doubt, the most prized posts in the parish system, and competition for them was intense. Unlike the chapters, the parish posts were filled by contests held in the Indies, so that it was harder for a European interloper to move in. Occasionally, a peninsular fresh off the boat was able to obtain an urban parish, but almost always he was a member of the official entourage of a bishop, archbishop, viceroy, or governor. These individuals were rare exceptions and their quick success produced considerable local grumbling.

The creole control of the cathedral chapters and the parishes, when combined with long periods between bishops ("vacant sees"), meant that the American-born churchmen exercised great power within the colonial secular church. Because these men came out of the local urban societies, the creole establishment came to regard these posts as part of the patrimony owed to them by the crown for the conquest and settlement of the Indies. The secular church was not a foreign institution imposed on the Americans. Rather, it was an integral part of local society, staffed principally by local sons.

The picture of the regional origins of the friars is much more complex, given the relative autonomy of each order in establishing recruitment and governance policies. The experience of the Franciscan Holy Gospel province in New Spain seems to have been characteristic of the regular orders in Spanish American cities, with due allowance for spatial and temporal differences. During the first years of its existence, the order was composed exclusively of friars who had arrived from Spain and elsewhere in Europe for the great task at hand. Toward the middle of the sixteenth century, increasing numbers of men joined the order in New Spain, including both those born in the Indies and those who were natives of Spain but had immigrated to New Spain by themselves or as part of family groups. By the early seventeenth century, three distinct groups based on regional origins had emerged: the creoles, men who had been born in New Spain and who had take the habit there; the *hijos de provincia,* men who had been born in Spain but had taken the habit in Mexico; and the *gachupines,* natives of Spain who had joined the order there. The entire seventeenth century was marked by a struggle among these three groups for dominance of the province and control of its important offices, a contest that was evident in the internal history of most other religious orders in Spanish America. The demographics of colonial New Spain were on the side of the ever-expanding numbers of creoles. As native-born vocations increased and as Spanish immigration tapered off or remained constant, the gachupines and the hijos de provincia fought bitterly to retain control. As was the case throughout Spanish America, the higher authorities eventually were forced to intervene and to impose a rotation of office-holding among the contesting parties, a device generally known as the *alternativa.* These arrangements usually discriminated against the creoles and favored the smaller Spanish group, underlining the anticreole bias of the Spanish crown.

In the Holy Gospel province, this arrangement was instituted by the second decade of the seventeenth century and continued, with some minor adjustments, throughout the century. The creoles constituted an overwhelming majority, and at times, as in 1650, there were not even enough Spanish friars to occupy the offices allotted to their faction. By 1703, for example, there were 703 men in the province; 61 were Spaniards, 70 were hijos de provindia, and 559 were creoles.

The colonial cities at times were turbulent places, and the otherworldly image of the calm brought by the overpowering ecclesiastical presence frequently was shattered by very worldly events, including stabbings, muggings, assaults, duels, assassinations, and murders. Men of the church were not immune from these forays into the seamier side of life, either as victims or as perpetrators. This penchant for violence combined with the passions of regionalism within the walls of the monasteries to produce great tumults that scandalized the cities. In 1680 and 1681, there was an uproar in the Franciscan convent in Lima over the imposition of a new provincial according to the alternativa. Only the intervention of the viceroy, with troops supported by artillery, and the eviction of one of the warring factions restored calm to the cloisters.

Regionally based squabbles, which at times resulted in bloodshed, were most pronounced in the monasteries of the colonial cities. Although situated in the urban centers, the convents were largely isolated from the ameliorative efforts of broader societal contact and integration. The artificial societies formed by communal living arrangements forced the peninsular Spaniards into close association and alliance with each other. Generally, they had no social or family connections outside the walls to build networks of linkages to their creole colleagues. In the absence of familial bonds, regional binds predominated. Thus, the pressures and frustrations of conventual life were vented on men of the opposite party.

In contrast, there appears to have been very little of the intense creole/ peninsular animosity within the ranks of the secular church. The explanation for this rather profound difference is that the branches of the secular church continually absorbed the peninsulars, who never constituted a serious threat to the normal procedures for promotion and career advancement. Moreover, creole chapter members and parish priests were generally from local creole societies that had been accepting and incorporating Spanish immigrants for generations. Thus, each chapter member or parish priest had a father, brother-in-law, grandfather, or cousin who was a peninsular immigrant, and, given the strength of familial ties, it was difficult to be openly hostile to Spaniards.

Social Origins Of Churchmen

The importance of the church in the colonial urban life of Spanish America is obvious. It is also evident that a great many men were attached to the church in myriad positions. But who these men were and why they joined the church is less clear. The answer to these two questions involves an examination not only of the individuals involved, but of the familial and societal context from which they came.

It often had been assumed that large families were considered desireable in the late colonial period, but this is not necessarily so. Too many children could erode family resources seriously, given the considerable expense of providing dowries for daughters and financing appropriate education and careers for sons. Most families of the urban middle and elite groups needed only a son and a daughter or two to pass on their social and biological heritage. The best family strategy for dealing with children in excess of this number was to move them into careers in the church.

Other considerations were involved in deciding on church careers for male offspring. Piety was much valued in the colonial cities, and occasionally a colonial family sent all its sons into the church, thereby teminating its lineage. Family prestige and power could be enhanced through direct connections with the different corporate elements of the colonial cities, including the secular and regular branches of the church. Children who became parish priests, chapter members, or otherwise atached to the diocesan hierarchy could contribute significantly to the wealth of the family. At the very least, the church provided a suitable career for the son of an important family. At the same time, placing a son in the clergy at any level enhanced the social position of a family of more modest origins. Many colonial families regularly established sons in positions in the secular church for generation after generation, although this pattern does show significant variation regionally and over time.

The same general rationale is true for those families who encouraged their sons to become members of the regular church. There, however, the opportunities for the friar to prosper materially and aid his family economically were, in theory, non-existent. However, a vocation with an order could provide a man with a good living, and, through rising in the order, becoming a preacher of note, or winning a chair at the university, he could win public acclaim that also would accrue to his family. The ordained friar could baptize, perform marriages, and inter family members. Although he could participate in his family's religious life, he could not involve himself in the day-to-day administration of the family finances. The regulars invariably were much more removed from family and society than were the seculars.

Overall, then, the church did not prey on society, but formed a key part of the broader social structure and fulfilled important societal functions. The relationship between church and family was not antagonistic, but symbiotic, as the two constituted key subsystems of the colonial social order.

As pointed out earlier, the vast majority of ordained men encountered in the urban areas were whites or españoles. There is, however, very little information on the racial origins of the lowest levels of the secular clergy in the cities. It does appear that there was a larger representation of mixed blood here, specifically among the group of tonsured clerics of low status and of minor orders who performed menial and servile tasks around the churches and other edifices of the secular branch of the church. The desire of mestizo families to place sons in the church at any level is apparent, and no doubt a cleric son could aid in the process of upward social mobility, and acceptance as españoles.

The racial makeup of the regulars was not significantly different from that of the seculars, if the Franciscan province of the Holy Gospel in New Spain is at all representative of the other orders. A study of 1,200 individuals who were admitted to the province in the seventeenth century turned up only 50 who showed any sign of being mestizos and no more than 10 who were Indians. Racial restrictions were tightened in the eighteenth century, so that what had been an insignificant number in the seventeenth century became an infinitesimal one in the eighteenth century. Although few Indians and mestizos took the habit in the Holy Gospel province, larger numbers of these racial groups did live in the convents of the order. In the sixteenth century the Franciscans began admitting Indians and others, dressing them in a religious habit similar to that of the lay brothers associated with the order, but without binding them with religious vows. At times they were admitted as simple servants; later in the seventeenth century some were received as lay brothers, and very, very few were accepted as professed religious. Infrequently, an Indian of substance would renounce his worldly property and retire to a life of prayer in the convent, but, although he behaved as a friar, he was not granted the official status.

While the regional and racial characteristics of the urban churchmen are fairly clearcut, their social origins are a different matter. From the conquest on, there was a tendency for arriving Spanish churchmen either to obscure or to amplify their peninsular social origins. Despite the confusion this caused, it is apparent that during the conquest period, those Spanish churchmen who had university degrees, who concentrated in the cities, and who held the best posts were from the *hidalgo* sector (the large group of petty nobility) or from the substantial middle class. The rural priests and those who sometimes found low-level urban employment tended to come from families of artisans, small merchants, or petty hidalgos.

The social origins of the American-born chapter members of the late colonial period can be sketched rather precisely. Briefly, all of the eighteenth-century Lima and Mexico City chapter members whose social origins are known came from all subgroups in the upper and upper middle ranges of the social scale. At the top, they included men whose immediate family members were titled nobility, and ran downward through sons of old, aristocratic families, members of the noble and military orders, high bureaucrats such as *audiencia* judges or important treasury officials, municipal officials (*alcaldes* and *regidores*), prominent wholesale merchants, miners, owners of landed estates, career military, and some professionals. There is no evidence that any of these churchmen came from the lower levels of the urban middle groups, such as petty merchants, commercial farmers or tradesmen.

The creole establishment produced chapter members who were socially suited to occupy such important offices in the church. As chapter members, they were present at all the great public occasions in the cities along with the leaders of the civil government and other major corporate bodies, as well as men who were acknowledged purely as leaders of society—the titled nobles and the *caballeros* (members) of the military orders. Funerals, running of the bulls in one of the plazas, the theater, reception of the viceroy, military musters, celebrations of the birth of a heir to the throne, dedication of a new church—these were all public events at which the chapter members commingled with their social peers. They were occasions to which many of the chapter members had been accustomed since an early age.

The urban parish priests were cut from much the same cloth as their creole chapter colleagues, at least in the major cities of the Spanish empire. The urban parishes were benefices that were much sought after, both for their urban location and because they were stepping stones to chapter positions. Competition for them was intense. Many of the priests who were stuck in the rural parishes, however, were from much more modest origins. Their families were headed by small merchants, lower-level professionals, medium-sized farmers, minor officials, or perhaps prestigious artisans who could afford to educate their sons but not much more. Even the educational levels of these men tended to be lower, which restricted job mobility.

The social backgrounds of the seculars were much the same in the provincial dioceses as in the metropolitan centers, although the provincial social structure was a truncated version of that of the major urban centers of the empire. In the provincial cities the titled nobility, the caballeros of the military orders, the important civil bureaucrats, and the large merchants were often totally missing or much reduced in number. But the provincial elites were very much identifiable as such, and regularly sent sons into the secular church to play a dominant role in the local parishes and cathedral chapters.

Reliable information on the social origins of friars in the colonial cities is in short supply. The major exception is the seventeenth-century members of the Holy Gospel province, one of six colonial Mexican Franciscan provinces. The candidates who took the habit in the Holy Gospel novitiates of Puebla and Mexico City represent a surprising diversity of socioeconomic backgrounds. At best, only a very small number of the Franciscans could claim a direct link to the very upper levels of urban society. A few more came from middle and lower levels of the elite. These included the sons of wealthy merchants and members of the *consulado* (merchant guild), large landowners, professionals, important municipal officers, and high-level viceregal bureaucrats. But members of all of these elite or upper-level groups constituted only a small percentage of the province's friars.

What is most striking about the Holy Gospel Franciscans is that the majority of them were from the urban middle groups, and at times from the lowest ranks. Occupations represented here included petty merchants, minor local officials, and many artisans. Some of the craftsmen, including the goldsmiths and silversmiths, were men of means and prestige; others, such as the weavers, tailors, and silk spinners occupied a middle position, while the stone cutters, pavers, and carpenters were at times not much above laborers in wealth or status. However, there were very few sons of poor journeymen among the religious. Thus, although humble and not wealthy, these families were moderately comfortable, at least to the point that they were respectable and could provide a minimum of education for their sons, although the youths rarely had university degrees when they joined the province.

In sum, it is evident that the majority of the Franciscans joining New Spain's Holy Gospel province in New Spain in the seventeenth century were from the urban middle elements of society, with a small group from the various elite sectors. As there was minimal representation from the very top of the elites, the same was true of representation from the bottom end of the urban social scale. The presence of Indians and mestizos was exceptional, and Spanish men from the urban laboring and poor groups simply were not present. The Franciscans of the Holy Gospel province came predominantly from the middle and lower middle sectors of urban society. Their origins were there-

fore considerably more humble than those of their secular correligionists—
the parish priests and chapter members.

Career Patterns

Many churchmen followed definite paterns in their professional lives, from
education through ordination or taking the habit to the types of early jobs
they held through benefices and promotion from one to another. There was a
spatial component in these careers, and the cities were always the center. There
was also a temporal component, as the ecclesiastical system was erected, developed, and matured.

In sixteenth-century Peru and New Spain the goal of many secular clerics
was to win a parish or chapter post, preferably in the principal city of the
viceroyalty. Although many men served in rural parishes and at times had
strong economic connections in rural areas, most priests preferred to take lower-
ranking jobs in order to be in a city. Many served in the rural parishes only
because that service counted heavily in consideration for an appointment to a
cathedral chapter. The preference for the cathedrals of Mexico City and Lima
was also apparent, for men would refuse promotions even to the post of bishop
in a provincial city just to stay with the metropolitan ecclesiastical *cabildos*
(councils). In this formative period for the church in the Indies, there was a
considerable amount of geographic mobility, both from job to job within the
diocese and from one diocese to another.

This mobility declined markedly later in the colonial period because of
several different factors. Procedures for appointments to the upper clergy became institutionalized, as was the case with the establishment of the *oposición*
(public examination) which favored native sons. Moreover, as the creole population grew, the competition for these apointments and for the chapter posts
intensified. With respect to the chapter posts, the result was the implementation of bureaucratic procedures on the part of the Spanish government which
made it difficult for an individual to move quickly from one chapter to another. Furthermore, a system of slow, orderly promotion within each chapter, the asenso system, was developed and produced great stability among
personnel.

By the eighteenth century patterns were well established in both the education and the careers of the secular clergy. In Lima, as in Mexico City, it was
clearly a tradition for clergy to obtain an education within their own dioceses
or archdioceses. Completion of education and ordination, however, did not
automatically assure that an aspiring young cleric would move into a parish
post. Although many of the clerics of Lima and Mexico City aimed first at a
parish benefice, usually a number of years passed before this became possible.
In the interim, suitable employment was found teaching in the college or

university as a holder of a chair or as a substitute, serving as an interim, an assistant (*teniente*), or a coadjutor for the holder of a parish benefice, saying masses for the holder of a capellanía, serving in minor posts in the ecclesiastical bureaucracy, or working as a lawyer in the civil and church courts. This could cover a period of a few years, or it could stretch out over a decade or more. All the while, the young cleric would be acquiring experience, entering the oposiciones, and building his curriculum vitae. Some men, of course, never advanced their careers beyond these minor posts.

Once appointed to a parish benefice, the priest usually would attempt to change parishes a number of times, with the hope of moving closer to the metropolitan urban center. A few priests remained permanently in rural parishes by choice, and more stayed there because they lacked the qualities for promotion to urban areas. But it should be pointed out that many men who held rural benefices actually spent little time in the bucolic environs ministering to the spiritual needs of their flocks. Instead, they managed to find ways to reside in the cities. One common device was for rural priests to come to the city that was the seat of the bishop or archbishop in order to enter the public contests for vacant parishes that were held every two years or so. The contestants had to be present physically, and the proceedings could drag on for three, four, or five months or more. A wily priest usually could spend several more months in travel and another month or two in attending to urgent personal business, and then could manage to have a bout with some chronic illness that lasted for several months. Then, too, a public contest for a chair in the university might delay him for several more months. Consequently, it was not unheard of for a rural priest to spend half or more of his time in the city. The bishops and their staffs fought this battle constantly, but apparently with little lasting success. The forces drawing churchmen to the cities were too intense to be overcome by mere regulation and decree.

While the characteristic career progression was from rural parish to urban parish and then to the cathedral chapter, variance in career patterns was related quite directly to the social background of the churchmen involved. As a general rule the young man from a very important colonial family would obtain his first parish sooner, be promoted to an urban parish more quickly, join the chapter at a younger age and at a higher level, and ascend through the cathedral ranks more quickly than his peers of more modest social origins. Occasionally, a man would go directly from a minor urban post to the chapter without any parish experience, but these were the sons of exceptionally powerful families. Others, with significant resources at their disposal, would journey to Spain to pursue their pretensions at court; about 20 percent of the colonial Mexicans secured their appointments at court, while the figure was half that for Lima. This was a luxury available only to relatively few clerics. The path left open to the cleric of modest but comfortable circumstances was that of the rural parish apprenticeship and slow promotion to the city.

The post of priest of an urban parish or a position on a cathedral chapter, a prebend, were the most desirable of numerous alternatives for secular churchmen. It is clear that only a small percentage of the members of the secular clergy who were ordained ever obtained these lofty appointments, probably somewhere in the range of 5 to 10 percent. With such a small percentage of the clerics holding parish benefices or chapter posts, the question arises of what the rest of the men did to earn a living?

Most of the urban parishes employed several assistant priests to administer the sacraments to the parishioners; these individuals were paid a salary by the priest who held the benefice. These positions, known as *tenientes de cura,* could provide valuable experience for a young man early in his career. Often, the post was a cleric's mainstay for many years, and its income was supplemented by other activities. The teniente position enjoyed moderate income and prestige in the large urban centers; in the smaller cities it supported the cleric at a level barely above subsistence. Other positions for clerics at the parish churches included that of *sacristán,* a job that involved care of the physical plant of the edifice. Again, a sacristan's job provided a good living in the larger cities, but otherwise was relatively menial.

Other employment opportunities were present for clerics in the various branches of the ecclesiastical bureaucracy, particularly in the urban centers that were the seats of the bishop or archbishop. The church court system of each diocese employed a considerable number of clerics, some in full-time capacities and more in part-time positions. The main tribunals—the *juzgado de testamentos* (probate court), *capellanías y obras pías* (court of chantries and charitable foundations), and the *vicariato* (vicarship)—had a number of judges, notaries, porters, bailiffs, messengers, and other functionaries. Frequently the judges were chapter members, sometimes they were parish priests, and occasionally they were just priests with degrees and practical training in canon and civil law. The Inquisition had a similar range of jobs for clerics, although it also employed a high percentage of laymen. The same was true for the *juzgado de la cruzada,* the organization charged with the publication and sale of the bulls of the crusade in each diocese of the Spanish American empire. The courts, both ecclesiastical and civil, provided a great deal of part-time work for clerics who were also canon and civil lawyers and who were given tasks that ranged from shepherding matrimonial dispensation petitions through the courts to defending clients in civil and criminal suits.

The cathedral chapters had a number of churchmen associated with them in addition to the canons. As the chapters were charged with the important task of collecting the tithe revenues upon which the ecclesiastical edifice was constructed and the civil government partially depended, they employed accountants, treasurers, and collectors. Some dioceses maintained their own complete collection machinery for the tithes; others let the task out to the highest bidder. In either case, numbers of clerics were employed as tithe collectors and many were located permanently in the cities.

The chapters also saw to the upkeep of the cathedral and its day-to-day operation, a task that required numbers of employees that varied with the size and wealth of the city. The position of choir chaplains was a benefice in the cathedral for which appropriately qualified clerics competed. Invariably there was a large contingent of musicians, assistants for the various divine services, organ pumpers, dog catchers, bell ringers, and many other minor functionaries. Some of these jobs went only to clerics; others were open to all, but were beneath the status of a cleric.

The archbishops and bishops and their hierarchies were also charged with overseeing the convents of nuns, which abounded in the urban landscape. These could be large and complex communities, housing hundreds of people, only a fraction of whom were professed nuns. The church appointed a churchman to oversee each convent and to take care of the many duties which the cloistered nuns were unable to perform. This cleric was involved in a wide range of daily tasks, such as granting a novice permission to dispose of her worldly goods and to profess, or instituting a suit to collect a debt owed the establishment. Also, each convent needed a chaplain to say the daily mass and to take care of the other spiritual needs of the female community. These often were salaried positions, and at times constituted the main livelihood of an ordained cleric. Clerics also found employment opportunities in the urban charities, including hospitals and orphanages. Although many of these institutions were run by the orders, secular clerics frequently were involved in administrative capacities or as chaplains. The *cofradías,* or lay confraternities, that were so prominent on the urban scene often had clerics as members and as officers.

The educational system of the colonial cities also occupied considerable numbers of clerics. Many of the private tutors and teachers who ran grammar schools were clerics. The staff of the seminary was comprised largely of secular clergy and the university's faculty had a large contingent of secular churchmen. Clerics also formed the majority of relatively large official families of bishops and archbishops. When the prelate was newly arrived, most of his clerical family were Spaniards, but invariably he incorporated promising young creoles into his household as pages, assistant chaplains, secretaries, or masters of ceremonies. Churchmen also were to be found as chaplains or advisors to the city council, or even to the viceroy. Often these positions carried no salary, but the additional title and the honor were adequate compensation for the cleric involved. Churchmen might make a career of any of the activities named above and depend upon it as a primary source of support. However, the clerics were very much like other men in colonial society and rarely concentrated their energies on one single task. Instead, they typically were involved with a whole range of income-producing activities. Simultaneously, as churchman might hold a chantry, substitute in a university chair, and undertake some legal work, while pursuing any number of business ventures.

Through these multiple sources of employment, the secular clerics worked themselves permanently and deeply into the fabric of the institutional life of the colonial cities. This was not as true for the regular churchmen, who, as members of the orders, were under certain constraints. Their opportunities for participation in urban life as individuals were largely restricted to education, caring for the sick, or other charitable and social works in which their orders were engaged, although at times friars did serve in various capacities with different secular institutions. Many of the urban monasteries had schools and colleges to provide education for their own novices and for the public. Moreover, individual friars competed for and served in chairs at the universities and colleges, and leading scholars of the colonial cities were often friars. Many of the renowned preachers of the day were members of the orders and were prevailed upon to deliver sermons on festive occasions. The monasteries often held public processions, and the inauguration of a new monastic church was always an event of great public interest to all social groups. Occasionally friars were called upon to serve as advisors in differing capacities for the viceregal governments. Regulars commonly were named as the royal representatives at the public contests for parish posts or for the few chapter posts that were filled in this fashion. Some regulars also were named to bishoprics.

Through these activities, a friar could advance his career and gain considerable renown. At the same time, friars were much restrained in pursuing career interests that were not in accord with the rules of their orders. In the major urban centers the heads of the orders, the bishops, and the civil government officials seem to have been fairly successful in assuring that the regulars resided in their convents, did not become involved in business dealings, and so forth. Of course there were cases of friars who lived very much as they pleased—as described in the Quito region in the eighteenth century by Juan and Ulloa—but the general impression is that the regulars of the larger cities generally lived according to rule.

The regulars were very much a visible presence in the colonial urban landscape. Their daily movements to and from their convents to teach, preach, minister to the sick, advise government officials, or tend to the myriad details that were required to keep the various religious establishments functioning brought many of these distinctively dressed men out into the city streets. They had a profound effect on the educational, intellectual, and religious life of the cities. Like that of the seculars, their presence on the urban scene was constant and obvious to the urban populace.

Many clerics whose primary activity was in some sort of post within the ecclesiastical structure also were involved in business dealings of some kind. Others were primarily men of affairs to whom ecclesiastical duties were only a minor element in their lives. All of these types and ranges of activities were perfectly natural and accepted within Hispanic urban society. Priests and clerics were men; as such they were expected to make a living, and involvement in business ventures was a perfectly acceptable way to do so. The priest-businessman was a social and economic type who was present from the conquest period on. There were, as would be expected, both legal and informal limits and boundaries for such activities. A cathedral chapter prebend or an urban parish priest could very well own rural property, and, in fact, clerics displayed the colonial penchant for landownership to a considerable extent. However, when a beneficed man began to devote inordinate amounts of his time to private and pecuniary activities to the detriment of his clerical duties, official questions often were raised. When the situation became extreme, ecclesiastical or even civil authorities might intervene.

It is clear that, by the late colonial period, most of the economic activities of clerics were concentrated in real properties. Many had capellanías whose principal was invested in censos on urban and rural properties. Collection of the income from these censos was often a time-consuming task for the clerics involved. Many churchmen were charged with administering family estates and properties, and many invested in rural properties of all sizes. Partly, this was done in order to have a nearby place in the countryside to which to escape for vacations and weekends, is also was done for the prestige of owning land and as a business investment. At times, the cleric managed the property himself and took great interest in the daily details of its operation. Otherwise, a business partner or paid administrator was in charge of the actual business activities. Clerics also occasionally invested in urban properties, and there are even cases of clerics who were, in essence, slumlords, renting out high-density properties to many people and receiving a very high return on their investments. Inns also were frequently found in the investment portfolios of clerics.

Clerics also were much involved in lending money out at interest, including their own money, that of relatives, and that of widows and spinsters. Although it was not common for clerics to be involved directly in trade, many did invest in, and even own, tanneries, harness shops, printing presses, bakeries, and other shops.

The social prestige and respectability of clerics was certainly an advantage for those who engaged in business activities. Beneficed clergy had regular incomes that could be diverted in part to investment activities, and it appears that clerics had excellent access to the church-controlled sources of capital, principally mortgage funds. Clerics who engaged in activities such as the collection of tithes also had a particlar advantage in certain economic activities, such as trade in commodities. Also involved in this economic endeavor were the clerics who administered rural properties and often traded in the items they produced.

Life-Styles

The life-styles and wealth of the urban clerics displayed a range and diversity similar to that of the churchmen's economic activities. Some clerics lived sumptuously, in the same fashion as the wealthy nobles and merchants. They owned urban mansions (*casas principales*) that were furnished with private chapels, extensive libraries, large collections of paintings and sculpture, fine china and solid silver tableware, ornate furniture, and rare tapestries. A rural *hacienda* or country house often provided an alternative to the dust and noise of the cities. They travelled in fine coaches with matched teams of horses or mules, dressed in the richest of clothing, and had large staffs of servants. Other wealthy churchmen eschewed fine material possessions and lived quite simply, while diverting considerable sums to charitable purposes.

Most clerics did not live in luxury, but instead enjoyed adequate incomes from a variety of sources, dressed well but modestly, and had comfortable shelter and sufficient food and drink. There was, however, a group of clerics who did live an essentially hand-to-mouth existence. Although all clerics who had taken orders had the congrua, at times the property from which the censo income came was overencumbered or had deteriorated in its productive capacity, resulting in a loss in income. With a reduced congrua, with no benefice or other salaried post, and without family resources, these clerics led a very humble existence.

The creole clerics usually remained very much involved in family affairs. Not infrequently, the churchman was the oldest man in a colonial family and assumed the duties that fell to the patriarch. He managed the family's wealth, saw to the education of the young people, negotiated for marriage partners, and helped establish the younger men in appropriate careers. Many churchmen, both creoles and peninsulars, set up establishments that amounted to large families. Often a well-to-do canon would purchase a large *casa principal*; bring sisters, nephews, and nieces to live with him; have slaves and servants with their children; and sponsor distant relatives from another colony or from Spain, or younger clerics—all living together under one roof and all depending on the churchman in some fashion. Men, women, children, and infants of a variety of social and racial types all lived together in one large household, in a large patriarchal unit. In this fashion, the cleric established what amounted to the *casa poblada,* the populated house, that had been present in the Indies since the conquest period and that represented an enduring Hispanic social ideal. In many respects these units were indistinguishable from other elite households.

The range of what might be called the social activities of the urban churchmen was great. For those attached to an order of a branch of the secular church, religious activities were central. The monasteries, the parish churches, and the cathedrals all had a daily religious ritual that diverted the energies of their members. It should be emphasized that, in the colonial cities, most public religious ceremonies were also public social occasions. They provided the opportunity for all social groups to turn out, and individuals with social pretensions were able to display their status through expensive clothing, the best seats from which to view the events, or nearness to the viceroy, the archbishop, or other important personages. At these events, friends could meet, new relationships could be struck up, and old animosities could be pursued. At the religious activities the churchmen played a central role, but they also would turn out for other occasions both collectively and individually. The regulars, or course, were more limited in the sorts of diversions in which they might participate than were their secular peers.

Clerics often were to be found at the evening concourse of urban residents who gathered on the public squares or along tree-lined avenues such as the *alameda* in Lima to observe and to be seen, to chat and to exchange gossip. They attended the theater, the bullfights, and scholarly disputations in the universities. The churchmen visited friends for a cup of morning chocolate or for an afternoon discussion of the day's events. They went for picnics and excursions into the countryside. They also shared in the failings of ordinary men by gambling, drinking, and consorting with women of less than perfect reputation.

The seculars and the regulars were set apart from other people in the colonial cities by their divinely ordained ecclesiastical status. Yet, at the same time, the church was not imposed on an unwilling populace, but instead was an institution that was very much a part of the fabric of society. Those associated with the orders were restricted to some extent by their vows, but the seculars were full participants in the daily ebb and flow of urban life.

NOTES

1. Robert Ricard, *The Spiritual Conquest of Mexico* (Berkeley: University of California Press, 1966), 82.
2. Justo Donoso, *Instituciones de derecho canónico americano* (Paris: Librería de Rosa y Bouret, 1868), Vol. I, 211.

FOR FURTHER READING

Printed sources for the study of urban churchmen are widely scattered, are uneven both in their geographic and in their thematic coverage, and usually do not distinguish between the urban and rural activities of these men. Excellent general studies of the church in colonial Spanish America include Antonio Ybot León, *La iglesia y los eclesiásticos en la empresa de Indias*, 2 vols.

(Barcelona: Editores, Salvat, 1954); the chapter on the church in C.H. Haring, *The Spanish Empire in America* (New York: Oxford University Press, 1947), Antonine Tibesar, "Church in Latin Amreica," in the *New Catholic Encyclopedia*, Vol. 8 (New York: McGraw-Hill, 1967) 448–61, and Richard E. Greenleaf, ed., *The Roman Catholic Church in Colonial Latin America* (New York: Knopf, 1971). A useful source of information on the legal structure of the colonial church and on matters such as ordination requirements is Justo Donoso, *Instituciones de derecho canónico americano,* 3 vols. (Paris: Librería de Rosa y Bouret, 1868).

Churchmen and how they fit into the social structure are discussed in James Lockhart, *Spanish Peru, 1532–1560: A Colonial Society* (Madison, Wis.: University of Wisconsin Press, 1968). Documentation for this same region in the sixteenth and seventeenth centuries is to be found in Emilio Lissón Chávez, ed., *La iglesia de España en el Perú,* 5 vols. (Seville: no publisher, 1943–47). The social and institutional history of the seculars in early Mexico is treated by John Frederick Schwaller in various works, including *The Origins of Church Wealth in Mexico* (Albuquerque: University of New Mexico Press, 1985), and *The Church and Clergy in Sixteenth Century Mexico* (forthcoming, University of New Mexico Press). Richard E. Greenleaf, *The Mexican Inquisition of the Sixteenth Century* (Albuquerque: University of New Mexico Press, 1969) treats an important urban institution. The classic work on the regulars in early Mexico is Robert Ricard, *The Spiritual Conquest of Mexico* (Berkeley: University of California Press, 1966). Francisco Morales, *Ethnic and Social Background of the Franciscan Friars in Seventeenth-Century Mexico* (Washington, D.C.: Academy of American Franciscan History, 1973) provides excellent information on the social history of this order. A superb source of material on urban clerics and the role of religion in colonial Lima is Robert Ryal Miller, ed., *Chronicle of Colonial Lima The Diary of Josephe and Francisco Mugaburu, 1640–1697* (Norman, Okla.: University of Oklahoma Press, 1975).

The seculars of eighteenth-century Lima and Mexico are thoroughly discussed in the following works by Paul Ganster: "A Social History of the Secular Clergy of Lima during the Middle Decades of the Eighteenth Century" (Ph.D. diss., UCLA, 1974); "Social Origins and Career Patterns of the Upper Levels of the Secular Clergy in Eighteenth-Century Peru and Mexico," *Proceedings of the American Historical Association* (Ann Arbor: University Microfilms, 1978); Cristóbal Béquer, Wayward Prebend," in Gary Nash and David Sweet, eds., *Struggle and Survival in Colonial America* (Berkeley: University of California Press, 1981); and "La familia Gómez de Cervantes: sociedad y familia en México colonial," *Historia mexicana* 122 (octubre-diciembre 1981): 197–232. John Edward Kicza, "Business and Society in Late Colonial Mexico City" (Ph.D. diss., UCLA, 1979) includes very useful material on the range of business activities of secular clerics in late colonial Mexico City. Incidental information on the role of clerics in elite families is encountered in John Mark Tutino, "Creole Mexico: Spanish Elites, Haciendas, and Indian Towns, 1750–1810" ((Ph.D. diss., University of Texas, 1976). Also of use for this period is Susan Migden Socolow, *The Merchants of Buenos Aires, 1778–1810: Family and Commerce* (Cambridge: At the University Press, 1978). N. M. Farriss, *Crown and Clergy in Colonial Mexico, 1759–1821: The Crisis of Ecclesiastical Privilege* (London: The Athlone Press, 1968) treats the successful late colonial efforts of the crown to establish greater control over the secular church. Michael Joseph Fallon, "The Secular Clergy in the Diocese of Yucatán, 1750–1800" (Ph.D. diss., Catholic University of America, 1979) is a thorough study of the seculars in the Yucatán peninsula. Marta Espejo-Ponce Hunt, "Colonial Yucatán: Town and Region in the Seventeenth Century" (Ph.D. diss., UCLA, 1974) supplies useful material on the church and society, as does Peter Marzahl, *Town in the Empire: Government, Politics, and Society in Seventeenth-Century Popayán* (Austin, Tex.: University of Texas Press, 1978). Jorge Juan and Antonio de Ulloa, *Noticias secretas de América* (Buenos Aires: Ediciones Mar Oceano, 1953) provide a most critical first-hand account of the seculars and regulars in Quito and Peru in the first half of the eighteenth century. An abridged English version of this last work is John J. TePaske, ed., *Discourse and Political Reflections on the Kingdoms of Peru* (Norman, Okla.: University of Oklahoma Press, 1978).

SIX

Female Religious

ASUNCIÓN LAVRIN

Introduction

Nunneries were an important element in the urban landscape of Spanish American cities. Their residents were held in great reverence by the populace and by the social elites as well, as examples of selfless sacrifice whose prayers benefited the entire community. Piety apart, nunneries had strong social connections with ruling families, and their economic ties spread even further and deeper, as their loans and properties in rural and urban settings linked them to persons of both sexes and various social and ethnic backgrounds.

Nuns were the most easily identifiable female group in Spanish American cities. They lived together within the physical boundaries of an architectural unit, the convent, and were an important element in the hierarchical structure of one of the most influential institutions in colonial society, the Catholic church. The church lent them its own spiritual, social, and economic strength. No other group of women had the internal coherence, economic power, or social prestige that nuns enjoyed. Thus, despite their relatively small numbers within the total female population, they commanded both authority and respect in the cities and beyond their confines.

Unlike monasteries, which could be founded in either city or countryside, nunneries were rarely built beyond city limits. They were strictly urban institutions, as it was considered undesirable to have women living as hermits in rural areas exposed to physical risks and lacking the support services which could be provided only in an urban location, such as a supply of food, health services, and skilled craftsmen for building construction and maintenance. An urban location was also a necessity in order to remain close to the religious authorities who regulated their spiritual lives and to their most likely sources of financial support, the urban rich and poor, whose alms and endowments sustained the hundreds of women who lived within the cloisters.

The foundation of nunneries in Spanish America began in New Spain in the mid-sixteenth century, barely 30 years after the conquest, and continued through the last years of the colonial period. In 1536, Fray Juan de Zumárraga, first bishop of New Spain, requested the crown to send either *beatas* (pious lay women) or nuns to New Spain to establish the foundations of Christian life among the female Indian population. The concept of convents for Indians did not take hold, and the women who came from Spain soon joined the secular life. But despite these setbacks, the Conceptionist Order established its first convent, La Concepción, around 1550, for daughters of conquistadors and settlers. In Peru, the convent of La Encarnación, following the Rules of Saint Augustine, emerged in 1561 from a *recogimiento* (shelter) that had been established in 1558.

The appeal of religious life lasted for over 250 years, and only began to subside after independence. The immediate roots of such a consistent attraction are found in the religious spirit pervading the peninsula in the sixteenth century. Early in that century, after the political and religious unification of Spain, and prior to the Protestant Reformation, the Catholic church in Spain had initiated a process of internal reform aimed at regaining the spirit of the primitive Christian church. A new order for women, the Conceptionist, was approved by the pope in 1415, and eventually became extremely popular both in Spain and in its colonies. Equally important was the work of Santa Teresa de Jesús, who reformed the Carmelite Order, founded numerous convents in the peninsula, and through a process of stringent regulation restored respectability to female convent life.

By the sixteenth century, one of the most important spiritual forces within the Spanish church was that of recogimiento, the withdrawal of the self in order to reach God through mystical contemplation. This idea was readily accepted by religious as well as lay persons for observance in their lives. The word recogimiento was also eventually used to mean a place of shelter to which women could retreat in search of physical protection and spiritual development. Roman Catholicism after the Council of Trent (1545–63) stressed the cult of the Virgin Mary and the saints, works or "deeds" aimed toward perfection, and the acceptance of the church as an intermediary between God and humanity. A powerful religious drive prevailed in Spain and its colonies through the sixteenth and seventeenth centuries, and serves to explain the flowering of convent life among both men and women, and the strong spirituality characteristic of the age.

Religious life for women meant enclosure, a complete physical retreat from the world. This was certainly contrary to the goals of most male orders, which were mobilized for spiritual conquest. However, enclosure did not isolate these women from their world or their times. On the contrary, it helped them to become better defined as a group, perhaps elusive in presence, but with a strong and distinct character within colonial society. Bonds with the surrounding community were established through the acts of foundation and the patrons who sustained the convents; the social connections of the nuns; their relations with their ecclesiastical superiors; the economic interests of the convents as institutions, and the intellectual role the convents played in colonial cities.

Foundation and Patronage

The initial thrust in the establishment of female convents took place during the second half of the sixteenth century in the main centers of the Spanish empire, and during the first half of the seventeenth century in the outlying and more distant cities. This period witnessed a significant demographic decline in the indigenous population, but at the same time saw the beginning of the development of a property owner and merchant class which was to patronize these institutions throughout the seventeenth century. Nunneries were, nonetheless, latecomers in the expansion of the church, having been preceded by numerous monasteries and by the secular church itself. Indeed, female convents had to compete with both institutions for patronage during a period of economic transition. Such competition meant that their establishment fell under the careful scrutiny of city councils, *audiencias,* and the crown itself. As anxious as the government was to spread Christianity, it was also concerned about the financial resources of the land and the population and the deflection of these resources to pious ends rather than mercantile or industrial purposes. Thus, on many occasions city councils, audiencias, and other religious orders gave negative assessments of the proposed establishment of convents. The crown, in response, issued numerous rarely enforced orders against the spread of both male and female convents, and stalled in giving its consent to their foundation. Nevertheless, foundations continued.

Despite adverse circumstances and the temporary lack of support from other urban institutions, nunneries grew continuously in number throughout the seventeenth and eighteenth centuries. The mobilization of capital and human resources for their foundation and the subsequent support required was one of the most remarkable socio-economic processes in urban Spanish America. What moved people from all walks of life to join forces, collect money, petition the crown, and then wait, sometimes for several decades, for the completion of these institutions? The reasons given by the petitioners themselves cover a broad spectrum, and help explain how nuns and nunneries were perceived by the rest of the society.

Religious or devotional reasons appear frequently, especially for the foundation of Carmelite convents in the late sixteenth century and throughout the seventeenth century. Santa Teresa died in 1582, and was canonized in 1622. A wave of religious fervor followed both events and inspired numerous Carmelite foundations. Stricter observances of religious life, such as those practiced by the Capuchine or Carmelite orders, were created for women willing to follow a most demanding vocation. In general, petitions argued that convents were good for "public edification." The example of women who abandoned family and wordly cares for prayer, obedience, poverty, and chastity, as their vows stated, exerted a strong fascination on the minds of most lay persons. Stories of the piety, ascetic practices, and even "miraculous" deeds of some nuns never ceased to flow from behind convent walls into the city streets, creating flurries of religious excitement and resulting in further patronage.

Religious reasons were important, but the social circumstances of many women of Spanish descent, especially from the last quarter of the sixteenth century on, were also significant considerations in the promotion of convents. Many daughters or relatives of conquistadors or early settlers who did not succeed in maintaining an economically comfortable situation were forced to look at convents as desirable places for shelter or retreat from a world in which they could not compete successfully. The importance of "equal" marriages seems to have increased as differences between rich and poor, white and non-white, became better delineated. Retreat into a convent thus became an alternative for "noble but poor" maidens who could not marry well or were left as orphans without resources. Remarks about lack of social alternatives are rarely explicit, and the few direct allusions to conventual life as an alternative to marriage are found only in eighteenth-century documents. The governor of Buenos Aires, for example, in a petition supporting the foundation of the convent of Santa Catalina de Sena, mentioned the exorbitant costs of marriage for "honest citizens." Throughout colonial Latin America earlier statements make oblique comments about the unprotected situation of women "of quality," who must not fall below their social status.

The education of girls as one purpose of convent foundations is mentioned less frequently than one might expect, considering the fact that numerous girls were placed in convents for that specific purpose. Only with the establishment of the convents of La Enseñanza in the eighteenth century did education become the overriding concern of some founders and patrons.

But convents were founded not only to respond to the spiritual, educational, or socio-economic needs of the women who entered their doors. They also responded to individual and urban perceptions of prosperity and of a fitting reflection of the glory of God. Indeed, there was a relationship between the availability of private wealth, the well-being of the area or the city as a whole, the geographical location of pre-existing nunneries, and the size of the population in these convents. As cities grew in size and the number of potentially wealthy patrons increased, sponsors argued that there were enough *vecinos* (citizens) to sustain a given number of nunneries through direct donations or through the less visible, but equally important, acts of daily alms. The general wealth in agricultural or mineral products of the area was a key element in most petitions, since evidence of the capability to sustain one or more contemplative institutions had to be offered. Support of nunneries thus became an index to the wealth of a given city.

The number of nunneries already in existence also was used as an argument by prospective founders. Contrary to the reasoning of many city councils, which wished to put a stop to convent foundations, private patrons cited the overpopulation of certain convents as a good indication of the need for yet another, since many potential postulants saw their desires frustrated by the lack of a place in which to profess. Some petitioners buttressed their argument by citing the vast expanses of territory for which only a few convents were available. This reasoning was used to obtain the foundation of a Carmelite convent in Guatemala, as well as convents in cities such as Tucumán and Córdoba in colonial Argentina.

Since the crown was unwilling to extend sustained or substantial economic aid to contemplative institutions, few requests failed to mention that the new foundation would cost the Royal Exchequer nothing. Capuchine or discalced convents, following more austere rules of religious observance, stressed their willingness to receive poor girls, thus offering women without means the possibility of profession. The Capuchine convent of La Purísima Concepción of Guadalajara was founded with the inheritance of a woman of considerable means, who left all her properties on the condition that rich girls should be not be admitted unless no poor ones could be found who met the requirements. Such foundations failed to mention the fact that the convents expected to receive a great deal of financial support from the community. Conversely, orders requiring dowries stressed that they would not become a burden to the city or economic competitors with other convents precisely because the postulants would bring their own means of sustenance. Although justified by various and sometimes antagonistic reasons, convents were universally seen as a solution to the problem of unprotected women from the elite classes.

The founders and patrons of female convents were men and women with well-established fortunes derived from mining, mercantile, or agricultural enterprises who wished to satisfy their own religious and social aims. Undoubtedly, they were sincere in their belief that nunneries were desirable institutions, both for the social functions they performed and the religious goals they pursued. Patrons also achieved a great deal of social prestige by supporting a convent, and this was an important incentive in a status-conscious society. The patrons could demand and obtain special privileges from the nunneries, such as masses for their souls and those of their families, burial in the convent church, and the right to appoint members of their family or protégés as unendowed nuns.

An element of civic pride was also present in many foundations, since some patrons wished to enhance the cities or towns where they resided with the presence of a convent. The majority of the convents founded in eighteenth-century New Spain were located outside Mexico City, sometimes in relatively small towns. For example, Manual Tomás de la Canal, a knight of Calatrava who had made a fortune in business, sponsored the foundation of a Capuchine convent in his town of San Miguel el Grande. He died in 1749, before royal approval was obtained. Four years later one of his daughters proceeded with the foundation, taking the veil in the convent when it was finished.

The amount of money required to found a convent or to sustain it was substantial. Captain Diego del Castillo donated 80,000 pesos in 1686, to sustain the convent of Santa Isabel in Mexico City. In the same decade, Captain Esteban Molina Mosquera and his wife Manuela de la Barrera donated 400,000 pesos to the Carmelites of Santa Teresa la Antigua in the same city. Their only daughter, a nun in that convent, spent the rest of the family's wealth founding yet another convent, that of Santa Teresa la Nueva, only fifteen years later. Other families also involved themselves in the building or refurbishing of nunneries, spending significant sums for the sake of religion and social status. Between 1613 and 1628, two branches of the Tejeda family in the city of Córdoba founded two convents, Santa Catalina and the Carmelites of San José. Doña Leonor de Tejeda, daughter of one of the first settlers, donated all her belongings to found Santa Catalina. Juan de Tejeda gave his houses and twelve slaves. Two of his daughters, his widow, and three granddaughters eventually professed in the convent. Bishop Fernando Arias y Ugarte founded Santa Clara in Santa Fé de Bogotá in 1625, for his sister and nieces. There is no evidence that any of these professions were forced. Convents strongly patronized by some families became an extension of these families, and were regarded as the obvious places of retreat for their female members.

Women played a leading part in the acts of foundation and patronage. These women were usually widows, or, if single, felt a vocation for religious life and eventually professed in the convents they patronized or helped to found. Female patrons often expressed a feeling of sympathy for the plight of other women who wished to profess or retreat from the world. Sixteen convents in New Spain were founded or directly promoted by widows or single women between the mid-sixteenth century and the end of the eighteenth century. In addition, two other convents were founded by young heiresses who later professed in them. Nine out of thirteen convents founded in Lima between 1561 and 1732 were either inspired or promoted by women. In other cities of Spanish America, the presence of women founders is similarly confirmed. In Santa Fé de Bogotá, Doña María Caycedo, wife of an *oidor* (high court judge) donated gold mines in Ibagué, 34 slaves, and a cattle and cacao hacienda, all valued at 40,000 pesos, to found the convent of La Enseñanza. She personally took charge of supervising the construction of the building. Other convents patronized or founded by women were those of Santa Inés and the Carmelites in Bogotá, Santa Clara and Santa Teresa in Cartagena, Santa

Catarina de Seña in Quito, the Capuchines of Santísima Trinidad in Santiago, and Santa Clara and Santa Catalina in Arequipa, to cite a few.

Couples, without heirs also acted frequently as patrons. The Marquis of San Miguel de la Vega and his independently rich wife, Dionisia Pérez Manrique, joined their fortunes to found the discalced Carmelites of Popayán. Pérez Manrique contributed over 70,000 pesos of her own. Nuestra Señora de los Remedios, in Cuzco, was founded by Luisa de Padilla and Jerónimo de Pacheco, and Doña Luisa professed in it when she became a widow. Juan Solano de Herrera and his wife Francisca de Vega Monsalve, a childless couple, sent 30,000 pesos as a donation to the convent of discalced Carmelites in Guatemala City. Finally, Francisco Aguirre Caballero and his wife brought the order of Santa Brígida to Mexico City, spending over 100,000 pesos on its foundation.

Patronage of nunneries was not confined to the laity, and clerics were also strong convent supporters. Bishop Agustín de Ugarte y Sarabia (of Guatemala City, Arequipa, and Quito), contributed large amounts of money to the foundations of Santa Teresa of Quito and Lima, respectively. According to contemporary sources, the amount ranged from 140,000 to 180,000 pesos. Fray Melchor Maldonado de Saavedra, bishop of Córdoba, and Fray Juan de Arguinao, archbishop of Pamplona, New Granada, were patrons of the convents of Santa Catalina and Santa Inés de Monte Policiano, respectively. Both donated cash and properties to these institutions, and Arguinao refounded Santa Inés by repurchasing and returning to the convent the haciendas that sustained it and that had been sold as a result of a suit against it.

Because nunneries were regarded as part of the community, it is not surprising to find the general population and the city councils involved in their foundation and patronage. Popular collections were carried out in some cities to accumulate the money necessary for a given foundation; this procedure was carried out with the convent of Nuestra Señora del Carmen and San José in Santiago. Between the 1670s and 1680s, smaller donations were stored up to make a grand total of 24,000 pesos, and the convent was founded in 1684. The vecinos of La Plata and Potosí gathered 40,000 pesos to help found a Carmelite convent in Chuquisaca. Santa María la Gracia, a Franciscan foundation in Trujillo, was started by Viceroy Conde de Villa (Fernando Torres Portugal), but the inhabitants of the city collected 20,000 pesos towards the foundation. Even *cabildos* (town councils) assumed patronage under special circumstances. Members of the cabildo, the justices of the city, and members of the regiment of Oropesa, Peru, donated over 20,000 pesos in the mid-seventeenth century for the foundation of the convent of Santa Clara. In Arequipa, Santa Catalina was under the direct patronage of the cabildo, which had promoted its foundation since 1550, by collecting alms and purchasing houses for the institution. Viceroy Toledo and the Bishop of Cuzco had approved this foundation under such secular patronage, but a century later the ecclesiastical authorities, feeling uncomfortable with the situation, put pressure on the cabildo, which reluctantly relinquished its right of patronage.

The process of foundation implied spreading or branching out from a "mother" convent, from which the nuns left to form a new community elsewhere. For the nuns, branching out meant traveling long distances between cities, on horse or mule back, or by cart, coach, or ship. The original founders of all orders migrated from Spain in small groups of three or four nuns, sometimes accompanied by their servants. Most frequently, these nuns were members of the Conceptionist order, the most popular in Spanish America, or of the Carmelites or the Franciscans. At their destination they assumed the direction of the new convent and received the local postulants. Sometimes some of the founders returned to their original convents; this happened most often when they had moved from one area of the empire to another, and not when they had come from Spain.

Branching out could emanate from one main city, such as the capital of a viceroyalty, to provincial cities, as in the case of the Conceptionists of Quito, from which the convents of Loja, Cuenca, Riobamba and Pasto were founded. La Concepción of Santa Fé de Bogotá was founded by nuns of the convent of Santa Clara in Tunja, which also was the center from which the convents of San Juan Bautista and Santa Clara in the diocese of Mérida (province of Venezuela) emerged. In this instance the branching took place among provincial cities, and went from the smaller city to the capital of the *audiencia* (high court). The Clares of Havana were founded by nuns from Cartagena, while the founders of the Carmelites of Caracas came from Mexico City. Lima served as the center of departure for the Capuchines of Santiago, the Carmelites of Guatemala City, the Conceptionists of Panama, and those of Concepción and Santiago. In turn, Santiago was the origin for the nuns of La Enseñanza of Mendoza and the Carmelites of Chuquisaca.

Such traveling took place only in the case of the foundation of convents. The majority of nuns professed in their city of birth or came from nearby towns in adjacent jurisdictions. In general, women traveled long distances to profess only on unusual occasions, or in the case of very special convents, such as those reserved for Indians in New Spain, which attracted novices from a broad geographical area.

Location and Convent Life

The location of nunneries within cities and towns was often as close to the center plaza as possible, utilizing good sites within the Spanish section. Rarely were convents placed in the indigenous *barrios* (neighborhoods) or in distant areas. Reports on the locations proposed for the establishment of a nunnery had to be filed prior to its foundation and approved by the religious authorities and the cabildo. The sites had to be adequate to build the cloisters and a church, or, if an existing structure was used, it had to be capable of undergoing the necessary refurbishing. Humid, windy, or exposed sites were rejected if they were judged unsuitable, unhealthy, or uncomfortable for the nuns. Despite such precautions, mistakes were made. The convent of Santa Clara in the diocese of Mérida (province of Venezuela) was originally built in 1651, outside the city, near the confluence of two rivers. In 1686, the convent had to be moved to the center of town after a flood had damaged it severely. The growth of the internal population of the convent also could force it to move to a larger building.

There was no specific preference for new construction in the establishment of convents. Numerous convents were founded in houses donated by patrons to speed up the process of royal approval. The convent of Santa Catalina, in Quito, was established in a set of private homes adapted for enclosure. As the convent expanded, adjacent properties were purchased and adapted for convent use. The convent of Santa Teresa, in the same city, was founded in houses purchased by the audiencia in 1653. The houses proved to be humid and cold, and the community decided to move to the center of town. A captain related to Santa Teresa gave them his house, on a site capable of accommodating a church, a vegetable and flower garden, and retreat cottages for nuns living in greater austerity apart from the larger community.

Although the physical plants of nunneries varied significantly in style, they had a number of architectural elements in common. All had a church attached to the cloister, which was open to the public for devotional purposes. Nuns prayed in the *coro,* a room which was separated from the church by grills and curtains, but from which they could see the main altar and hear mass. The larger communities had an upper and a lower coro. Communion was received through an opening in the coro's grill. Special religious ceremonies for the nuns also were carried out in these rooms.

Adjacent to the church were the cloisters, separated from the street by high fences, or, if the convent were flush with the street, with few openings to the exterior, all well above ground, for it was essential that the nuns remain unseen. All convents had a *portería,* or entry room, where the daily business of receiving food and services took place. The portería was the meeting ground between the cloisters and the world outside. Vendors peddled their wares there; pious people stopped for news of the nuns; and servants, craftsmen, confessors, and *mayordomo* (manager) passed through to carry out their business in the *locutorios.* The latter were the rooms where nuns met relatives, friends, and others with whom they carried out special transactions; there confessors tended to the spiritual needs of their charges, lay borrowers came to request funds, and administrators had business talks with the nuns. In discalced or strict convents the nuns remained behind curtains during these exchanges with lay persons, so as not to break their seclusion. This practice was not followed in other orders.

In the seventeenth century locutorios became "wordly," in the opinion of religious authorities. Music was played on special occasions, religious plays were performed, refreshments were served for special visitors, and gatherings of family and friends took place in an atmosphere of joy and excitement. Several attempts were made in this and the ensuing century to put an end to such practices, but their success was uneven and was not complete at the end of the colonial period.

Behind the locutorios were the cloisters, to which few lay people had access. Convents which expanded by adding houses to their main structure were frequently rather picturesque in appearance because of the irregularity of their design. Different levels of floors were not infrequent, with staircases connecting patios, narrow halls, working rooms, and private cells. The custom of buying houses adjacent to the convent resulted, in some cases, in the incorporation of streets into the convent itself. If the convent was built from scratch, a more regular plant could be expected. Usually such convents were organized around a large patio or several smaller ones, with cells and special working rooms facing the patio and separated from it by a broad hall. The patios had gardens and fountains, for the visual enjoyment of the nuns. The convent of La Enseñanza in Mexico City, built in the mid-eighteenth century, had one of the most beautifully conceived architectural plans of its period.

In the less strict orders nuns lived in their own private cells, purchased for them by their families and used until their death, when the rooms reverted to the convent. These cells might have cooking areas, where a servant or a slave fixed the nun's meals. In more strict orders, a refectory and a communal kitchen replaced such personal arrangements. In most instances convents had a number of common rooms, such as the penitence room, the infirmary, the chapter or council room for communal meetings, the recreation room, and the clothes and laundry room. Some convents had vegetable gardens and small dwellings for retreat. In some parts of Spanish America, convents apparently kept poultry for the provision of the eggs and meat. Other convents manufactured pottery to earn some extra income; work rooms and kilns were operated by servants or slaves. Still others specialized in the manufacture of ribbons, sweets, and works of stitchery, which required special facilities within the convents where such activities could be carried out. Selling such goods implied yet another form of interrelationship with the city, which softened the theoretically rigid isolation of the encloistered women.

Religious observances had important nuances, however, which determined the degree of contact with the world. The Franciscan and Carmelite orders had discalced, or stricter, branches which demanded a higher degree of personal self-denial than did the regular observant of other convents. Members of these branches wore woolen habits, ate sparingly in a communal refectory and out of one common kitchen, observed a greater number of religious fasts, engaged in frequent personal discipline, and prayed longer hours than did their sisters in religion. The atmosphere of discalced convents was restrained and austere, demanding greater personal stamina and attracting fewer nuns. For their members, only through such tests of endurance was salvation ensured. Nuns of other orders did not feel, however, that they were less dedicated observants. They were assured by ecclesiastical authorities that there were many ways to reach God, and thus harmony was preserved within the body of the church. (See Figure 16.)

Numerical Growth

The walls of the convent separated the lay world from world with its own internal hierarchy; social, economic, and ethnic divisions; financial problems; personal quarrels among its inhabitants; and confrontations with its own superiors and with other institutions outside. Convents housed hundreds of inhabitants, of whom nuns and novices were usually a minority. The rest were slaves, servants, and lay girls and women seeking retreat or shelter. In 1700, La Concepción of Lima had a total of 1,041 inhabitants. Only 318 were nuns, novices, or lay sisters.[1] This was a very large convent, and probably not representative in terms of population numbers. However, less affluent and populated convents often housed between 50 and 100 nuns at any given time throughout the seventeenth century.

Convent populations increased significantly from the sixteenth to the seventeenth century. La Concepción of Lima, which had 80 nuns at the beginning of the seventeenth century had 247 in 1700. The population of the Augustinian convent of La Concepción in Santiago jumped from 10 nuns in 1578 to 150 in 1619. The discalced convents, because of the vows of poverty they followed, never housed as many nuns. In fact, their rules established a fixed number of nuns, 21 or 33, and they rarely allowed more nuns to profess. The Carmelites of Buenos Aires had only 18 members in 1733. Convents founded in the eighteenth century in general, did not expand as rapidly as those founded earlier in the colonial period. The Capuchines of Señor San José, of Lagos, Guadalajara, founded in 1759 with 27 nuns, had only 77 in 1781. The available data indicate that nunneries stabilized their population between 1650 and 1750, and that a decline in actual numbers had begun in certain cities by the late colonial period. Santa Clara of Mexico, founded in 1573, had 170 nuns at the end of the next three decades, in 1603. However, in the 51 years between 1696 and 1747 only 121 nuns professed, and by 1750, the convent housed 79 nuns.[2] At the end of the colonial period, there were 888 professed nuns in Mexico City. In 1814, the number remained almost the same, with 852 nuns in the city's convents. An increased spirit of secularization may explain this steady decline in professions.

The large number of secular inhabitants in the cloisters was always a source of concern for ecclesiastical authorities, who perceived their presence as disruptive to the religious atmosphere and conducive to innumerable transgressions of convent discipline. Since the mid-seventeenth century the church hierarchy had tried to restrict the number of servants and secular residents, without much success. In the 1770s, as part of a broader plan of reform in religious observance, the bishops and archbishop of New Spain adopted a plan to curtail the number of secular persons in the cloisters. Several years of confrontation followed, for most nuns were reluctant to live without their servants and protégées, but by 1790, a significant number of secular residents had abandoned the convents. In that year the 888 nuns in the convents of Mexico City had only 943 servants.

The Social Milieu

Secular individuals and servants, free or slave, blacks, mulatos (persons of black and white ancestry), Indians, and mestizos (persons of Indian and white ancestry) represented the ethnic heterogeneity of colonial urban society itself. On the other hand, the nuns, their protégées or pupils, and the upper-class women who retired to the convents belonged to the top layer of society, descendants of Spanish settlers or their creole offspring. The narrow admission policies applied to postulants ensured that the socio-ethnic background of the majority of nuns in Spanish America was very homogeneous. The only exceptions were the convents founded in New Spain for Indians and some of the convents in South America, which admitted a select but small number of mestizas.

Not until the eighteenth century was there any thought of founding convents for Indian women. Early in this century the Marqués de Valero, Viceroy of New Spain, left an endowment for the foundation of Corpus Christi, a convent for noble Indians. After some debate, it was opened in 1724, with white nuns charged with leading the first indigenous professants. A bitter controversy ensued several years later, as the white nuns attempted to increase their own numbers and reduce those of the Indians. Eventually the crown ruled in favor of the Indians, and the convent remained Indian in composition. It also remained elitist in character, since only *cacicas,* or noble Indian women, were allowed to profess. Only in 1808 was the convent of Nuestra Señora de Guadalupe, for Indian women of all social classes, founded in Mexico City, thus providing the first opportunity for non-cacicas to profess.

Patrons and founders of convents had the right to specify the ethnic group for which they were intended. Restrictive clauses, such as those inserted by the founder of the Augustinians of Chuquisaca, clearly stated that mestizas or women with admixtures of African or Moor ancestry should not be admitted as postulants. While a number of mestizas of high social ranking were admitted to some convents during the sixteenth and seventeenth centuries, it seems that social bias became more rigid during the seventeenth century and such cases became much less frequent. Professants also were required to be the legitimate offspring of Christian parents; however, as records in New Spain attest, a number of illegitimate women were allowed to profess after the bishop or archbishop had granted permission to overlook their "defect of birth."

Specific economic restrictions were never expressed in the rules of the orders or in the clauses of foundation. Nunneries were accessible to all white women who could afford the expenses incurred in profession, or who had patrons to pay for them. The cost of profession varied, depending on the conventual order and on the period; it also bore a direct relationship to the social position of the postulant. Capuchine and discalced orders did not favor expensive celebrations of profession, and were willing to receive smaller dowries. Thus, they remained poorer than other convents. On the other hand, some of the Conceptionist convents attracted women of the upper classes, in part because their observance was not so demanding, and they allowed a greater degree of personal freedom within the convent. Nondiscalced orders required dowries in all instances, and usually celebrated profession with two ceremonies: one for the entrance of the novice into the convent, and a second one for her final profession as a black-veiled nun. Parents usually bought a cell for their daughters, and among the most affluent it was also customary to allocate a sum of money, invested at five percent interest, which the nun received as a yearly allowance for her own expenses in the convent.

The amount of money required as dowry changed over time and varied from area to area. In the sixteenth and seventeenth centuries dowries ranged from 1,000 to 2,000 pesos. Inflation and the greater financial requirements of convents in the late seventeenth century resulted in an increase up to 3,000 pesos, and by the end of the colonial period some convents were demanding 4,000 pesos. Cash was preferred for dowries, but in the seventeenth century some convents allowed parents to place liens on their properties in lieu of cash, although this was not a universal practice. Women who professed as lay sisters (white-veiled nuns) paid smaller dowries, but they were required to perform physical labor in the convent. They were usually daughters of impoverished families who relied on benefactors to provide for the expenses of taking the veil. Thus, socio-economic distinctions were reflected even among the convent elite.

For poor white women desirous of entering a convent, relatives and friends were one source of patronage. Another was the annual lottery run by certain confraternities which generated funds to dower eligible girls. These dowries, which allowed women "to take state" (either the married state or the professed state), usually provided 300 pesos. Some confraternities such as Santísimo Sacramento of Mexico City, had the endowment of girls as one of their missions. At the end of the colonial period Santísimo Sacramento boasted that it had invested over one million pesos in the endowment of several thousand girls. Yet another source of patronage comprised pious men and women who provided large amounts of money to be invested in loans or liens and used the interest for annual allocations of endowments. Some convents accepted girls with special abilities, such as a good voice or the knowledge of a musical instrument, as *monjas capellanas*, or unendowed nuns, using their artistic services to the institution in lieu of a dowry.

Despite the presence of many women of limited means within the convent walls, most nuns came from more comfortable surroundings. In-depth studies of the family provenance of professed nuns are scarce. However, it is possible to make some generalizations regarding the family origins of the professants. Members of the nobility did not show much inclination to became nuns, and few women from titled families took the veil. It must be pointed out, however, that nobility titles in Spanish America did not start increasing in number until the second half of the seventeenth century, when the convent population started to taper off. Furthermore, the vows of chastity and the renunciation of worldly possessions implied in profession, although not always strictly adhered to, could not possibly meet the need for transferring wealth within elite kinship networks. Even when nuns did not renounce their inheritance portions, they used them to benefit the convent, not their families. Thus, women of titled families hardly could have been encouraged to take the veil. Nonetheless, some did. The younger daughter of the Marqués of San Miguel de Aguayo, María Ignacia Azlor y Echevers, professed in the Order of Mary and was the founder of the convent of La Enseñanza in Mexico City. The widowed Marquesa of Selvanevada retired to convent life and founded the Carmelite convent in Querétaro.

The next echelon down in the social order, that of members of leading bureaucrats, wealthy merchants and landowners, provided a substantial number of professants during the colonial period. In the sixteenth century concepts of social hierarchy were not completely crystalized. Impoverished descendants of conquistadores and settlers gained access to convents on grounds of their economic need, although these women still were perceived as members of the social elite. Some convents founded in this century to provide refuge for poor white women rapidly became associated with the "best" families. Both Santa Catalina and Santa Clara in Quito, for example, became very popular among members of the highest stratum of society. Santa Catalina was founded by the niece of Juan Martínez Siliceo, archbishop of Toledo, the richest diocese in Spain. It immediately attracted relatives of bureaucrats and conquistadores, and even a descendant of Christopher Columbus.

Throughout the colonial period, the daughters of members of military orders, captains, town councilmen, and governors, stand out in the records of convent professions. Yet the majority of women listed in these records are registered simply as daughters of *dons* or *doñas* (gentlemen or women). Since these appellations have lost much of their social meaning with time, it is difficult to ascertain the exact status of the family. However, one of the few studies of the socio-economic backgrounds of professing nuns, those of Santa Clara in Quérérato, states that only 10 percent of them came from poor families. The combination of social and ethnic selectivity, prestige attached to familial connection with the church, and the increasing economic power of convents after the second half of the seventeenth century gave the convents a social standing that benefited all of their members.

Economic Underpinnings

The social and religious needs which nunneries were perceived to fulfill had to be sustained physically by private or community patronage. The crown exercised control over the material aspects of convent foundations, and in the late colonial period it encouraged policies of spiritual reform. However, it did not provide economic aid, as it assumed that the institutions would find mechanisms to sustain themselves. Royal aid came in the form of small sums of money for annual contributions over limited periods of time, for the sustenance of the community, or for providing oil for the main altar lamps. Indian labor in the form of *repartimiento* (draft labor) was given to some convents while they were under construction, or for repairs thereafter. The crown also could authorize the transfer of the labor or tribute from Indian encomienda from a private beneficiary to a convent. The first nunnery founded in New Granada, that of Santa Clara in Tunja (1573), was endowed by conquistador Francisco de Salgüero and his wife Juana Macías Figueroa. The couple had a repartimiento and in 1580, the city of Tunja requested the crown to transfer it in perpetuity to the convent for its sustenance. In Caracas, La Concepción was founded in 1636, with nuns brought from Santo Domingo. In 1638, the Franciscans petitioned the crown for an encomienda then held by Abbess Doña Isabel de Tiedra y Carabajal to be turned over to the convent. The encomienda provided labor to tend the *haciendas* (large rural estate) and cattle owned by the nuns.

Since nunneries were part of the urban and regional economy, they partook of the economic cycles of their respective areas, and reflected the general wealth or poverty of certain regions. In backwater areas of the empire, nunneries had fewer opportunities to prosper than in such centers of trade and wealth as Mexico City or Lima. However, regardless of their location, nunneries turned to the crown in times of financial crisis, although their pleas were not always answered. For example, the first convent of Santiago, that of La Concepción, founded in 1564, requested an annual sum of 3,000 pesos from the crown in 1568, because of its lack of endowments and the instability of its income. In 1590, the Audiencia of Quito wrote to the crown on behalf of the convent of La Concepción, in Pasto, asking for the allocation of a source of income for such an "exemplary" institution.

In 1745, the Capuchine convent of Nuestra Señora del Pilar, in Buenos Aires, received royal approval for its foundation, despite the fact that it lacked both adequate housing and affluent patrons. The hope that the financial situation of the convent would improve did not materialize, and the crown had to provide 12,000 pesos to help build a new church and cloisters in 1769. Perhaps one of the best examples of the correlation between the local economy and the financial well-being of any nunnery is that of the discalced Carmelites of Puerto Rico, who received a royal license of foundation in 1646, and opened the doors of the convent in 1651. Although the vecinos had petitioned for the foundation since the first decade of the century, they were unable to support it adequately after it became a reality. As a result, the Carmelites, like the island itself, lived a life of penury throughout the seventeenth and eighteenth centuries, relieved only by unevenly allocated alms from the crown and by the charitable contributions of Bishop Fernando de Valdivia, who at the beginning of the eighteenth century helped to improve the physical plant of the convent.

In contrast, several nunneries in Mexico City, despite inauspicious financial starts in the sixteenth century and lean times in he first half of the seventeenth century, succeeded in consolidating their economic assets toward the end of the century and had become extremely wealthy institutions by the end of the colonial period. Such was the case with the Conceptionist convents of La Concepción and La Encarnación, which had assets of over a million pesos each in houses, loans to a select number of borrowers, and liens on numerous rural and urban properties. In fact, by the mid-eighteenth century, 18 nunneries in Mexico City had an estimated seven million pesos in properties, liens, and loans.[3] Such stupendous economic growth was tied to private funding. The economic development of nunneries depended, to a significant degree, on the development of an affluent group of urban patrons who could sustain not only their foundations, but also their subsequent financial needs. This class did not start to develop in many cities until the seventeenth century, and it is during this century that lay patronage of religious institutions began the sustained mobilization of important sums of money through the establishment of chantries, endowment funds, donation of properties or cash, and establishment of liens on their properties.

The convents which were founded in the sixteenth century were endowed with enough money to finish their buildings, but most convents had little capital left to sustain economic growth. Such capital was expected to be obtained from several sources, as cited above, and from the dowries of the nuns themselves. Cash was used for the purchase of properties, or given to selected individuals in the form of long-term loans, with property mortgaged on behalf of the convent as collateral. Nunneries were not necessarily interested in the return of these loans as long as the borrower paid the 5 percent interest punctually. Thus, rural and urban properties often remained mortgaged to convents for many decades, since the lien was transferred to subsequent buyers. If urban or rural property was acquired directly by the convent, it was rented for a sum equivalent to 5 percent of its value. Mayordomos managed these properties for the nuns. Being encloistered, nuns depended on the honesty of the administrators and on their own business acumen to receive a steady income. Leased properties could become unprofitable if the leaser could not make them yield enough to sustain himself and to pay the annual interest to the convent. On the other hand, rental of urban properties involved nunneries in the usual problems of arrears in payments faced by most landlords.

Yet another form of income was that derived from liens voluntarily imposed by patrons on their properties to the benefit of a convent. There was no exchange of cash in these instances, the patron notarized the lien, and from then on paid the interest of 5 percent of the total lien to the institution. If the property was sold, the purchaser either paid the assumed lien in cash to the convent or continued to pay its interest. Most of these liens could be redeemed by giving the capital to the convent in cash. Perpetual or unredeemable liens were used by some patrons during the sixteenth century, but they became very rare thereafter.

As convents prospered toward the end of the seventeenth century, some of them had enough cash in their coffers to invest in short-term loans, with a fixed date of return. Those loans were given most frequently to well-established merchants and property owners, who could post reliable collateral or obtain the backing of several bondsmen. In time, loans with a fixed return date (*depósitos*) became one of the preferred forms of investment of the wealthiest nunneries. By the end of the eighteenth century such convents as Jesús María, La Concepción, and La Encarnación, of Mexico City, had several hundred thousand pesos each in loans. The beneficiaries of such loans were the most prestigious members of the urban elites, men and women whose families were, or had been, patrons of the church, and whose own female relatives might be nuns in a convent. The majority of these borrowers paid their interest and capital punctually, and supported each other as bondsmen. Thus, a network of mutual interest was built among members of the elite and the convents.

The availability of cash from convent coffers created a credit system, centered in the city, that encompassed rural and urban borrowers ranging from large landowners to owners of small properties. Larger and more prestigious nunneries lent to the very rich in preference to others. However, smaller convents with limited capital to lend served the needs of less exalted members of the community. As lending or credit institutions, nunneries had one significant drawback that precludes comparing them to modern banks. They never paid interest to their donors or depositors. The benefits which any donor expected to receive from these institutions were purely spiritual: masses on behalf of their souls, the potential grace of God, or their eternal salvation. Thus, convents circulated cash for their own benefit, and in doing so they rendered a service to a specific socio-economic class, that of property owners. The economic benefits that less well-to-do members of society derived from convents were reduced to salaries derived from working as masons, carpenters, craftsmen, or artisans in the building or repair of cloisters and churches.

In addition to their role as urban-based financial institutions, nunneries also played a paramount role as urban landlords. Because rural properties were distant and unpredictable in terms of profit, convents slowly switched to the acquisition of urban real estate, although many retained some rural land. The proximity of urban holdings to the convents themselves made the property more manageable. Nunneries held an interesting array of urban real estate: large single houses, multiple tenant properties, baths, shops, and even shacks. Some convents owned more properties than others, but, on the whole, they controlled a considerable number of houses. In the city of Mexico, the only city for which analytical data are available, by the end of the eighteenth century, 8 of the largest nunneries owned urban property valued at over seven million pesos. The total value of all the urban property held by nineteen nunneries in Mexico City was over 10 million pesos. The church as a whole owned 47.08 percent of all urban property, and within the church no other institution controlled as much of this property as did the nunneries.

House ownership put the convents in contact with a broad spectrum of urban society. The large and more expensive houses were occupied by titled families, high-ranking bureaucrats, audiencia lawyers, and rich merchants. Urban rents tended to increase slowly throughout the colonial period. By the mid-eighteenth century such properties rented for sums between 500 and 1,000 pesos yearly. Medium-sized and small buildings were rented to artisans, lesser bureaucrats, and smaller merchants. Rents for two- or three-room houses ranged between 8 and 20 pesos monthly, based on the location and condition of the house. Convents also owned multiple tenant dwellings in which persons such as cobblers, washerwomen, bakers, food vendors, and tailors lived. In general, tenants of the Mexico City convents were many years in arrears on their rent payments, but convents were usually benevolent landlords and did not press poorer tenants very hard.

The nunneries' relations with the city extended beyond property ownership. In pursuit of their economic interests, they gathered information on properties for sale, vecinos who needed loans, the affairs of their tenants in the city or the countryside, the state of supplies of foodstuffs for the city, and the price of such commodities as cloth, wood, stone, wax, and produce. They also took note of the salaries paid to workers and artisans, from whom they commissioned everything from portraits, paintings, and altars to iron grilles and fireworks. These were all legitimate concerns for women who, despite having renounced the world spiritually, could not help remaining in touch with it to sustain the material underpinnings of their religious life.

Religious Life

Just as economic interests linked nuns to the world, so did their own religious affairs. Despite the usual submissiveness of nuns to their superiors, a result of their vow of obedience, confrontations among nuns and their prelates flared up occasionally, creating situations of tension and distress not only within the convent, but within the city itself. One of the longer lasting conflicts between a prelate and his flock took place in the Capuchine convent of Buenos Aires, where a dissident group of nuns rebelled against their bishop, alleging that he was allowing racially mixed women to enter the convent as nuns. The bishop was obliged to suspend elections and stop admitting novices for 17 years in order to prevent the continuation of internal disorders which had gone beyond the walls of the institution. The dissent started in 1768, and not until the death of the rebel leader in 1787, did the convent return to the normal pursuit of its affairs. Neither Bishop Manuel Antonio de la Torre nor his successor were able during this time to establish order within the convent.

The well-known rivalry between the secular and regular church, especially in the seventeenth century, involved nunneries as well as members of the cabildo and the audiencia. Cognizant of the contest for power between friars and clergy, some nuns sought to solve the internal problems of their institutions by appealing to members of the opposing parties, thus triggering veritable local wars of interest in their towns. Nuns' relatives, other religious institutions, and the royal government never failed to become involved. Observance was usually weakened while members of the secular and the regular church struggled for control of the nunneries. Instead of the quiet devotion usually associated with convents, religious warfare fueled by the involvement of several parties transformed the nunneries into centers of dramatic urban confrontation. These conflicts often triggered a chain of violence in which all the city took part. Among the best examples of the conflicts provoked by nuns, or inflicted upon them by their superiors, is that which took place in Santiago de Chile in the seventeenth century.

The convent of Santa Clara in Santiago traced its roots to a *beatairo* (a home for pious lay women) in Osorno, which had to be abandoned after an Indian attack. In 1604, the convent joined the order of Clare nuns and was placed under Franciscan authority by the Bishop of Santiago. In 1641, unhappy with the rule of the Franciscans, the nuns sent a secret message to Rome concerning their situation. Having received no reply by 1654, 50 black-veil nuns and 30 lay sisters requested that the bishop put them under his secular authority. The Franciscans responded to the attempted secession by physically attacking the nunnery in an effort to reimpose their authority. The case was submitted to two ecclesiastical judges, who ruled against the Franciscans. The Franciscans then appealed to the audiencia and to the viceroy in Lima, who upheld them in their case. But the order was first ignored by the audiencia of Santiago. A second order from Lima to restore the Franciscans' authority was only carried out when an oidor in the absence of the president of the Santiago audiencia. The convent was surrounded by soldiers, and a battle ensued between them and a group of male relatives of the nuns, while over 60 nuns escaped from the cloisters, taking refuge in the Augustinian nunnery of La Concepción. By then the whole town had been involved in the skirmish, which almost developed into a riot. Eventually, the nuns returned to their convent and accepted the temporal authority of the Franciscan provincial until the Pope ruled on their appeal. In 1661, the bishop was granted authority over the convent by papal resolution.

These and other disorders were attributed by some religious authorities of the period to the increasing encroachment on the nunneries by worldly interests. Far from being isolated from mundane cares, the nuns were distracted by the meddling of their families, friends, and protectors. Concern over status and power did not stop at the door of the convent. Rather, there was a link between their affairs and those of the city. Elections for positions in internal governments of the institutions often involved family rivalries and competition between opposing factions both inside and outside the nunnery. The abbesses of some wealthy convents were often the daughters of the best families in town, who tried to use their influence to determine the outcomes of such elections. This happened frequently enough in Lima to move the secular authorities to order that the convents be surrounded by soldiers until the elections had taken place. Winners of new religious elections in that city celebrated with music, feasting, and even horse races in the vicinity of the convent. Incidents such as these, along with more personal incidents, such as the wearing of ornamented habits, the reception of friends and family with displays of food, or the playing of music by city orchestras in the locutorios called forth the remonstrance of strict bishops and archbishops on numerous occasions, but their condemnation was often ignored.

In the late eighteenth century several archbishops and bishops in Lima and Mexico City undertook a series of ecclesiastical reforms to reestablish convent discipline. In New Spain, the return to what was called *vida común* or communal life, was adopted unanimously by the chief religious authorities. Vida común implied a return to simpler observance and the renunciation of personal cells, servants, slaves, and other material comforts. Inevitably, personal confrontations between nunneries and religious authorities ensued, with the involvement of lay authorities and town people. The nuns' reluctance was eventually overcome by allowing a dual system of observance, enforcing the stricter one only for the new professants.

The Cultural Dimension

Another important dimension of both nuns and nunneries in the urban context of Spanish America is their impact on colonial culture. Significant intellectual currents moved within the walls of the cloisters, sustained by the only groups of educated women found in colonial cities. The education of women had received some attention in Spain during the late fifteenth and early sixteenth centuries, but by the time that the urban centers of the New World began to develop the concept was already waning in the peninsula. Colonial cities were not propitious arenas for the development of an educated female elite. The majority of lay women remained illiterate, or partook of an education which did not go beyond the so-called feminine arts of stitchery and cooking. Only a handful of secular women were capable of reading beyond the catechism, or writing short letters in poor handwriting.

On the other hand, religious life required certain literacy skills beyond those possessed by other women. Nuns were expected to read and write well, to keep accounts, and to know some Latin for their prayers. Many excelled in their learning and mastered these skills beyond the expectations of the period. Nuns also served as teachers of young female pupils who were placed in convents to be educated until they were of age. In fact, the education imparted to young girls was not systematic, and varied considerably according to the abilities of the teacher. Even after the introduction of the convents of La Enseñanza, where nuns were specially trained to teach girls, female education remained limited in scope, suited to support the role of women as mothers and housewives.

Ironically, nuns have a place in history of colonial culture not because of their role as educators, but because they frequently were encouraged by their confessors to write about themselves as a means of understanding their personal problems, conquering their infirmities, and intensifying their inner religious experiences. The result was a considerable number of autobiographies, biographies, chronicles of religious institutions, books of spiritual exercises, and personal letters. Since these were considered not literary but religious exercises, they either remained stacked in manuscript form in the archives of convents, or lost and only remembered through references in other works. One good example is the writings of Sor Melchora de la Asunción, who was one of the first nuns to profess in the Carmelite convent of Puebla and was reputed to be "one of the best talents of Spain" in matters of religion. However, not a single piece of her writings has been discovered. Others have been more fortunate, and their works have been unearthed from convent archives after several hundred years of oblivion. Catalina de Jesús Herrera (1717–95), a native of Guayaquil who joined the Dominician convent of Santa Catalina, wrote a full-length work describing her spiritual experience, first published in 1950, under the name of *Secrets Between the Soul and God*. Sor Gertrudis de

San Ildefonso (1652–1709) a Clare nun of the audiencia of Quito, wrote an autobiography of good literary quality at the instigation of her confessor.

In Lima two figures stand out, Sor Paula de Jesús Nazareno (1687–1754) and Sor Juana María Azaña (1696–1748). Sor Paula was the daughter of a knight of Alcantara, entered the convent of Nuestra Señora de las Mercedes in 1719. She wrote an autobiography, which remains unpublished, and many poems, some of which were first published in 1955, 201 years after her death. Sor Juana was the daughter of General Don Pedro de Azaña. Born in Abancay, she professed in the Capuchine convent of Jesús María against her parents' will. She wrote numerous poems and theatrical pieces, which have been published only in part.

The genre of mystical prose had its best exponent in Sor Francisca Josefa de la Concepción de Castillo (1671–1742), a Clare nun in the city of Tunja. Sor Francisca Josefa wrote two important works, her autobiography and a diary of her spiritual life entitled *Mis afectos (My affections)*. Her autobiography was written as an act of obedience, and it is a valuable document of the inner life of the convent and the difficulties of maintaining a religious profession. Since it was first published in the nineteenth century, the *My Affections* has been considered a masterpiece of elegance and insightful spirituality, unequalled by any other piece written by a woman in this genre during the colonial period.

Among the writers of biography is Sor María Rosa de Ayala, one of the Spanish founders of the Capuchine convent of Jesús María in Lima, who wrote the life of Nicolás Ayllón, better known as Nicolás de Dios, founder of the convent. Her sister in religion, Sor María Gertrudis de Alva, wrote a very interesting and unusual diary of the trip of the founding nuns from Spain to Lima. Both works were first published in the mid-twentieth century.

In New Spain the works of Sor Sebastiana Josefa de la Trinidad, a Franciscan nun in the convent of San Juan de la Penitencia, and Sor María Marcela, a Capuchine from Querétaro, both of whom wrote narratives of their spiritual lives, remain in manuscript form. A similar fate has befallen the nuns who composed theatrical pieces for professions, with the exception of Sor María Ana Agueda de San Ignacio, author of several books of religious exercises and religious advice that display a delicate mixture of asceticism and mysticism. Sor María received recognition during her life, as the Bishop of Puebla, Pantalón Alvarez, paid for the publication of her works in 1758.

By far the best known writer of the colonial period in Spanish America was Sor Juana Inés de la Cruz (1648–95), acclaimed in her own life as the Tenth Muse. Sor Juana, born out of wedlock in a small town in New Spain, was brought to Mexico City for her education. Hardly beyond puberty, she was introduced in the viceregal court after her extraordinary learning gifts became known. She spent several years as a protégée of doting *virreinas* (viceroy's wife) and surrounded by admiring courtiers, and experienced a meteoric ascent to fame and recognition. Her youthful works in praise of life, love, and the patrons of her art did not forecast her sudden decision to take the veil. Yet, at around the age of 18, aided by two patrons, she tried out religious life in a Carmelite convent. Finding the observance too strict, she left, only to enter the convent of San Gerónimo a short time later. Having professed early in her twenties, she spent most of her productive years as the most popular and best known veiled figure in the New World. Sor Juana's own explanation for her decision to become a nun, a puzzling act for one who had attained such social success, was that she felt little inclination toward the married state, and that the convent was the most suitable place for the pursuit of her intellectual endeavors. Some have questioned Sor Juana's sincerety without realizing that, while she was a women of genius, she was also a sincere Catholic in a century of strong religious beliefs. While she could confess that she found certain aspects of religious life disagreeable, her profession was an act of her own will which she never regretted, and which, indeed allowed a life unencumbered by family obligations and devoted to learning and writing.

During most of her life as a nun, Sor Juana wrote literary works which had no direct relation to religion, as well as poetry for religious feasts, plays, philosophical treatises in poetry and prose, and theological critiques. Her mind knew no bounds, and in her learning she pursued all subjects, from mathematics to music. Innumerable visitors came to the grilles to talk to her, including some contemporary savants with whom she held many a learned conversation. Although mildly criticized for her activities by some of her superiors, she succeeded in living a life carefully balanced between the world outside and the world within the cloisters.

The challenge of theology, however, took Sor Juana along a path that eventually culminated in the final crisis of her life. Piqued by a pompous, self-serving interpretation of Christ's sacrifices by the Portuguese Jesuit theologian Antonio Vieira, Sor Juana undertook the task of rebutting his argument with hers, which later proved to be somewhat unorthodox in the ages of the established church. Her rebuttal was published by the Bishop of Puebla, Manuel Fernández de Santa Cruz, under the title of *Carta atenagórica* (letter in the style of Athena). It has been claimed that the bishop was an admirer who wished to further Sor Juana's image as a religious writer. However, in a later letter to Sor Juana, the bishop, under a religious pen name, rebuked her mildly for not devoting more of her time to religious writings and to the duties of her state. Sor Juana's response to Bishop Fernández de Santa Cruz, *Respuesta a Sor Filotea de la Cruz,* is a tour de force in Spanish American literature. It is also a magnificient autobiographical essay in which Sor Juana explains her inner drives and argues for the right of women to use their intellectual abilities, contradicting many of the church's restrictions on women's activities.

The *Respuesta* was Sor Juana's swan song. In 1698, she suffered a religious crisis as difficult to explain as is her entrance into the convent. As a result, she disposed of most of her books, recalled her long-time Jesuit confessor Antonio Núñez, and devoted her last years to a life of prayer and penitence.

In 1695, she died during an epidemic which ravaged Mexico City. The breadth of her interests, the quality of her literary production, and the challenge which she posed to seventeenth century society have made of this nun an unusual and memorable figure.

Other Female Institutions

The powerful example provided by the nunneries as institutions especially suited to satisfy the needs of some women prompted the establishment of other types of institutions for the protection of women, based on principles similar to those of the nunneries. These institutions also required living within a closed physical environment and engaging in carefully structured religious practices and manual occupations considered appropriate for women. The degree of strictness, as well as the various goals pursued by the founders of such establishments, resulted in the development of several types of shelters: beaterios, recogimientos, and orphanages. Beaterios were voluntary associations of beatas, or pious women who wished to pursue a religious life without taking the irrevocable vows demanded by convent life, especially that of perpetual enclosure. They followed the rules of Third Orders (Dominican, Franciscan, etc.), which required simple vows, and were subject to the authority of the secular church. Beatas wore habits and lived secluded lives modeled after those of nuns. Some lay women retired to beaterios for companionship, including orphans and the recently widowed.

As a rule, beaterios sheltered women coming from less affluent backgrounds than those of professed nuns, although some beaterios, such as that of Santa Rosa de Lima, in Guatemala City, housed women of the best families in the city. Thus, many beaterios were poor, and beatas had to engage in handicrafts to sustain themselves. Beaterios usually did not admit nonwhites, although this was not a fixed rule. Some were founded exclusively for Indian women, such as those of Nuestra Señora del Rosario, in Guatemala City, and Nuestra Señora de Copacabana, in Lima.

Beaterios could develop into convents if they found adequate patronage, and if they could convince both religious and lay authorities of the need for such a change. A devout Indian living in Nuestra Señora de Copacabana tried unsuccessfully for many years at the end of the seventeenth century to raise funds to transform it into a convent. On the other hand, the convent of Jesús María, in Guadalajara, made the transition from beaterio to convent with little trouble. Beaterios could take girls in to provide them an education, especially in cities without many other educational resources. As in other respects, they copied convent practices when engaging in such a task. The beaterio of San José de Gracia, in Querétaro, founded in 1739, took on teaching duties in 1768, at the suggestion of Archbishop Antonio de Lorenzana. In the last decade of the century the crown, then enthusiastically supporting the idea of educational centers for women, placed the beaterio under royal patronage.

Recogimientos were places where women of all ages and economic backgrounds, lacking family resources or male protection, could retreat, temporarily or for many years, in search of the security which they did not possess in the world. Most of these women were regarded as reputable members of society, but acknowledged to be in difficult circumstances. The recogimiento offered them a shelter where they could preserve their honor and good social standing despite adverse personal experiences. Recogimientos appeared very early after the conquest, as towns faced the growth of an unexpected number of unattached women, whites or mestizas, who were in need of temporary protection until they could "take state." The main concern was to prevent their falling into the temptation of concubinage or "dishonest" actions.

Recogimientos, however, were also institutions where "fallen" women were sent for punishment and re-education. Women who had committed adultery or bigamy, had engaged in prostitution, or were in the process of separating from their husbands landed in certain recogimientos founded for such purposes. In many instances there was a certain ambiguity in the character of both beaterios and recogimientos, stemming from their overriding concern with the protection of women, which allowed these institutions to shelter, at the same time, unprotected honorable women, repentant women, and even women involved in criminal cases. Thus, women of many social backgrounds and ethnic groups lived under the same roof. The beaterio of Amparadas, founded in Lima in 1572, was originally a place for repentant prostitutes, but in time it began to accept economically needy women, changing in character and remaining a mixed institution throughout the colonial period. The *recogidas* or inmates of a shelter of Salta, known as the Bernardas, also mixed devout and repentant women. The most striking case of a change in character was that of the recogimiento of Jesús de la Penitencia, in Mexico City, also founded in 1572 for repentant women. It was put under the direction of a nun from the convent of La Concepción in order to help the inmates reform themselves, and attracted the patronage of several confraternities in the city. By the end of the century it had begun to admit women who sought to live as nuns, and who slowly came to make up the majority of interns. Finally, in 1667, it was converted into the convent of Nuestra Señora de Balvanera.

Yet another variation of the concept of protection for women was offered by orphanages established for the care of the orphaned descendants of conquistadores or settlers. In the seventeenth century these orphanages resembled recogimientos, but in the eighteenth century they became more like schools, stressing the educational training of the girls admitted. Some orphanages took in a number of girls as external students giving them education and shelter, and charging their parents a monthly fee. Thus, as time passed, they became known as "schools" instead of beneficent institutions. An excellent example of late eighteenth century orphanages was the school of Santa Teresa, in Córdoba, established by the Bishop of Tucumán, Fray José Antonio de San Alberto, in 1782. He endowed the school with church funds to cover the living expenses of orphan girls, and established that a maximum of 40 girls would be admitted. The outside pupils would pay for their education. Eventually, a day school was also maintained for girls of mixed racial descent. Inspired by this example, the cabildo of Catamarca was promoting the foundation of a home for orphans by 1809. Beaterios, recogimientos, and orphanages offered alternatives to life within convents. By not demanding dowries, beaterios and recogimientos served the needs of women of limited means; by foregoing the observance of formal vows, they became acceptable to women who, wishing to live in a religious environment, did not have a strong spiritual vocation entailing a complete commitment to religion.

Conclusion

The foundation of the most important cities in Spanish America took place at a time of rapid and far-reaching intellectual, religious, social, and economic changes in Europe, spurred in part by the discovery of America. The church, which played such an important role in the conquest and early settlement of the New World, was being challenged by significant schisms developing from within. In reaction, it initiated internal reforms in search of new religious answers and new modes of observance. Contemplative religious life for women was one of these reforms, and convents flourished in Spanish America as an essential part of the new civilization taking shape in the urban centers founded by conquistadores and settlers.

Contemplative religious houses turned women inward, away from the challenges of a world in transition. Convents created small, contained worlds where some women could be saved from the unexpected results of displacement within a new society and, at the same time, partake of the wave of intense religiosity sweeping through Spain, then the center of European counter-reformation. Despite the fact that convents and recogimientos were founded in the sixteenth century to serve the needs of unprotected women who found no secure niche in postconquest society, these institutions were not founded solely to serve as repositories for unwanted or excess women. The convents also represented a way of life and a system of beliefs, which held in part that women were naturally pious, as well as emotionally and physically in need of protection.

The convents were seen as rendering both material and spiritual services both to the community in general and to some women in particular. Those services may not have been considered as important as that of other urban institutions, such as the cabildos. However, they were important enough to make them desirable to many cities, which vied for the establishment of nunneries in their midst. A support network which involved all the other major urban institutions was activated with the foundation of each convent. The pledges given by lay and religious cabildos, audiencias, other religious institutions, and the general population to help sustain convents implied a permanent commitment inherited by successive generations, which, in general, did not forget their obligations. Their support, which did materialize despite lean years, could not have been elicited if the convents had been perceived as catering only to the needs of a small group of people. Whether this perception was a correct one is irrelevant. Convents were symbols of a particular aspect of worship and ritual in Roman Catholicism. They were part of the culture transplanted to the American continent by the Spaniards.

Did the church really respond through the convents to the special needs of part of the female population? The answer is not simple. Unquestionably, the convents gave women with religious vocations a channel for personal expression. They also provided shelter and comfort to others who were less motivated by religious ideals. It has been argued that nunneries also gave women an environment of their own, away from direct male authority, in which they could rule themselves, be creative in their own manner, develop their own personalities, and, to some extent, free themselves from some of the encumbrances which burdened the female sex in colonial Spanish American society. This picture is partially true, but requires some qualifications. Internal control of the convents rested in the hands of the nuns, and there is enough evidence to indicate that they were capable of exerting this control in personal, financial, and administrative matters. There was, however, an ultimate subordination to the male hierarchy which was both binding and unavoidable, especially in the spiritual sphere. Even the most personal literary expressions produced in the convents were the result of the urging of male spiritual directors, Sor Juana notwithstanding. There was a certain degree of freedom within the nunneries, to be sure, but never enough for these institutions to be regarded as genuine oases of female liberty. Their restrictions, however, were both understood and accepted, since the margin they allowed for personal fulfillment was broad enough to satisfy the women of the period.

When science produced the Enlightenment, and revolution and republicanism challenged established political orders, nunneries and the contemplative life they represented fell out of tune with new realities. Hence, their attraction diminished and fewer women chose to live in them. Education slowly displaced contemplation as a desirable alternative for women, and by the end of the nineteenth century relatively few were committing themselves to the religious life. Convent buildings and their churches remained as witnesses of a period when their walls defined the boundaries of a very special female world within Spanish American cities.

Notes

1. Rubén Vargas Ugarte, S.J., *El monasterio de La Concepción de la Ciudad de los Reyes* (Lima: Talleres Gráficos de la Editorial Lumen, 1942), 16.

2. Vargas Ugarte, *La provincia eclesiástica chilena* (Friburgo: Imprenta de la Casa Editorial Pontificia de B. Herder, 1895), 353; Cayetano Bruno, *Historia de la iglesia argentina*, 6 vols. (Buenos Aires: Editorial Don Bosco, 1970), 4: 458; Salvador Reynoso, *Fundación del convento de Capuchinas de la Villa de Lagos* (México: Editorial Jus, 1960), 13.

3. Asunción Lavrin, "La riqueza de los conventos de monjas en Nueva España. Estructura y evolución durante el siglo XVIII," *Cahiers des Ameriques Latines*, 8 (1975): 92–122.

For Further Reading

The ecclesiastical history of Spanish America has been dominated by the themes of the spiritual conquest, the conflict between church and state, and the history of several orders associated with the task of conversion or with successful economic enterprises. The historical literature on female convents, both in English and in Spanish, is relatively limited. Some general histories of the church and of religious orders have devoted some attention to female orders, but largely as an ancillary subject, related to and dependent on the history of the male ecclesiastical hierarchy. For these reasons, the most common subject of research and publication on nunneries has been their establishment, seen as yet another chapter in the process of expansion of the church.

General histories of the church offer reliable, though not extensive, information on the foundation of nunneries and on special events in their history. Among the best examples is Antonio de Egaña, S.J., *Historia de la iglesia en la América española. Desde el descubrimiento hasta comienzos del siglo XIX. Hemisferio Sur* (Madrid: Editorial Católica, 1965–66). The histories or chronicles written by the official historians of the regular orders also supply a considerable amount of information on foundations of convents and on their early development. They usually include brief biographical sketches of notable nuns or *beatas*. While the factual information on the foundations is straightforward and helpful, the biographies tend to be hagiographical in character, requiring a different kind of analysis to appreciate their value as an expression of religious mores. The following is a good example of contemporary chronicles: Fray Diego de Córdova Salinas, O.F.M., *Crónica franciscana de las provincias del Perú*, ed. Lino Canedo, O.F.M. (Washington, D.C.: Academy of American Franciscan History, 1957). In addition, local histories, whether lay or ecclesiastical, usually provide some information on nunneries, since they often are linked to notable families, local personalities, cabildos, or confraternities. One example of this kind of work is Manuel Antonio Bueno y Quijano, *Historia de la diocesis de Popayán* (Bogotá: Editorial ABC, 1945). Few studies, however, have delved into the social or economic linkages of the nunneries with their communities, or tried to assess the extent and meaning of such linkages within the larger context of the history of the church, the province, or the viceroyalty.

General studies of the history of nunneries in any city, let alone in any larger administrative division in Spanish America, are extremely rare. The one exception to this rule is Josefina Muriel, *Conventos de monjas en la Nueva España* (Mexico City: Editorial Santiago, 1946), which covers the history of the convents of Mexico City from the sixteenth through the nineteenth century. This work has a significant amount of information retrieved from archival sources, although the information is not methodically analyzed. It suffers from a certain degree of uncritical piety in the narrative; nonetheless, no other work has superseded it in terms of breadth of coverage. Less extensive in chronological coverage, but more systematical in the treatment of several topics, is Asunción Larvin, "Religious Life of Mexican Women in the XVII Century" (Ph.D. diss., Harvard University, 1963).

Monographs on the foundation of nunneries, especially those which include transcripts of original documents, are extremely helpful in the task of gauging the community's involvement with the religious institutions and learning about the regional or local socio-economic networks which supported them. For an example of this type of work, see Manuel del Socorro Rodríguez, *Fundación del monasterio de la Enseñanza* (Bogotá: Empresa Nacional de Publicaciones, Biblioteca de la Presidencia, No. 14, 1957). Another type of work, comprising historical chronicles of specific institutions, varies in the quality of the information supplied, but the monographic character of these chronicles allows the reader to follow the development of some nunneries beyond the first years of their lives. An example of this genre is Ricardo Mariategui Oliva, *La ciudad de Arequipa del siglo XVII en el monasterio de Santa Catalina* (Lima: n.p., 1952).

Studies of specific aspects of convent life are a recent trend in the historiography of female convents. They allow a greater depth in the coverage of certain aspects of convent history which were glossed over by older studies. Most of this new research focuses on New Spain, except for the recent doctoral dissertation by Donald L. Gibbs on the convents of Cuzco in the seventeenth century. See his "Cuzco, 1680–1710: An Andean City Seen Through Its Economic Activities" (Ph.D. diss., University of Texas, 1979). Other examples of this type of study are Josefina Muriel, *Las indias caciques de Corpus Christi* (Mexico City: Universidad Nacional Autónoma de México, 1963), which is a transcription of an anonymous collective biography of the first Indian nuns to profess in New Spain; Sister Ann Miriam Gallagher, "The Family Background of the Nuns of Two *Monasterios* in Colonial Mexico: Santa Clara de Querétaro, and Corpus Christi of Mexico City (1724–1822)" (Ph.D. diss.,

Catholic University of America, 1972). This work is the only extant systematic analysis of the social background of nuns, using archival sources not available to lay researchers.

Asunción Lavrin has written a number of monographs on Mexican nunneries, stressing their economic structure and certain aspects of their activities as intellectual and religious centers. See the following works by her: "Ecclesiastical Reform of Nunneries in New Spain in the Eighteenth Century," *The Americas* 22 (October 1965): 182–203; "The Role of the Nunneries in the Economy of New Spain in the Eighteenth Century," *Hispanic American Historical Review* 46 (November 1966): 371–93; "Values and Meaning of Monastic Life for Nuns in Colonial Mexico," *The Catholic Historical Review* 58 (October 1972): 367–87; "La riqueza de los conventos de monjas en Nueva España: Estructura y evolución en el siglo XVIII," *Cahiers des Amériques Latines* 8 (2o semestre 1973): 192–222; "El convento de Santa Clara de Querétaro: la administración de sus propiedades en el siglo XVIII," *Historia mexicana* 97 (julio–septiembre 1975): 76–117; "Women in Convents: Their Economic and Social Role in Colonial Mexico," in Berenice Carroll, ed., *Liberating Women's History* (Champaign, Ill.: University of Illinois Press, 1976): 250–77; "Women and Religion in Spanish America," in Rosemary Ruether and Rosemary Skinner, eds., *Women and Religion in America: A Documentary History* (San Francisco: Harper and Row, 1983); "Unlike Sor Juana? The Model Nun in the Religious Literature of Colonial Mexico," *University of Dayton Review* (in press).

Susan A. Soeiro has produced works on the role of one Bahian convent in colonial Brazilian society. See "A Baroque Nunnery: The Economic and Social Role of a Colonial Convent: Santa Clara do Desterro, Salvador, Bahia, 1677–1800" (Ph.D. diss., New York University, 1974); "The Social and Economic Role of the Convent: Women and Nuns in Colonial Bahia, 1677–1800," *Hispanic American Historical Review* 54:2 (May 1974): 209–32; "The Feminine Orders in Colonial Bahia, Brazil: Economic, Social and Demographic Implications, 1677–1800," in Asunción Lavrin, ed., *Latin American Women: Historical Perspectives* (Westport, Conn.: Greenwood Press, 1978): 198–218.

The role of nunneries as cultural centers remains to be investigated in full. Two types of works need to be considered for this task, those produced by the nuns themselves, and those written about the nuns, which tend to be biographical in nature. One of the best examples of the first type is Sor Francisca Josefa de la Concepción de Castillo, *Obras Completas*, 2 vols., ed. Darío Achury Valenzuela (Bogotá: Talleres Gráficos del Banco de la República, 1968). An example of the second type is Pedro Salmerón, *Vida de la venerable madre Isabela de la Encarnación, Carmelita Descalza* (Mexico City: Imprenta de Francisco Rodríguez Lupercio, 1675), available in microfilm at the Library of Congress.

The bibliography on Sor Juana Inés de la Cruz is extraordinarily extensive, but few titles are in English. The first biography in English was Franchon Royer, *The Tenth Muse: Sor Juana Inés de la Cruz* (Paterson, N.J.: St. Anthony Guild Press, 1952). Still among the best biographies in Spanish is Anita Arroyo, *Razón y pasión de Sor Juana* (Mexico City: Editorial Porrúa, 1952). The most recent comprehensive examination of this notable woman is Octavio Paz, *Sor Juana Inés de la Cruz o las trampas de la fé* (Barcelona: Seix-Barral, 1982). A brief study of the poet is available in Irving Leonard, *Baroque Times in Old Mexico: Seventeenth Century Persons, Places, and Practices* (Ann Arbor: University of Michigan Press, 1959). A recent translation of Sor Juana's best known essay on her life, the response to the Bishop of Puebla, has been penned by Margaret Sayers Peden, as *A Woman of Genius: The Intellectual Autobiography of Sor Juana Inés de la Cruz* (Salisbury, Conn.: Lime Rock Press, Inc., 1982). Sor Juana's works may be consulted in two collections: Sor Juana Inés de la Cruz, *Obras completas* (Mexico City: Editorial Porrúa, 1969), and *Obras selectas: Prólogo, selección y notas,* eds., Georgina Sabat de Rivers and Elias L. Rivers (Barcelona: Editorial Noguer, S.A., 1976).

The literature on *beaterios* and *recogimientos* is very scarce. Two useful titles are Josefina Muriel, *Los recogimientos de mujeres* (Mexico City: Universidad Nacional Autónoma de México, 1974), and Rodolfo Alanis Boyzo, "Fundación y establecimiento del beaterio del Carmen de la ciudad de Toluca," *Boletín del Archivo General del Estado de México* 2 (mayo–agosto 1979): 3–7.

SEVEN

Military

CHRISTON ARCHER

Introduction

Shortly after 8:00 P.M., June 23, 1802, a senior treasury official hurried through the busy streets of Mexico City on his way to an evening at the theater. Near the Lunetas bridge, he caught sight of a beggar woman whose miserable condition and pleas for alms aroused his compassion. He approached her and reached for his purse to give her a coin. Before he could complete the transaction, he was felled from behind by savage saber blows. Without offering a word of explanation, Luis Cortés, a grenadier of the infantry regiment of New Spain on sentinel duty at the Puerta del Vestuario, left the charitable official prostrate on the street with chest contusions and bruised lungs. Formal complaints to the officer of the guard brought the arrest of Cortés, but no further punishment for an assault that easily could have caused permanent injury or death. At 2:00 A.M., September 14, 1802, a patrol of the dragoon regiment of Mexico chanced upon a lightkeeper who had fallen asleep during his nightly rounds. The corporal in command dismounted and attacked the unsuspecting keeper, beating him severely, stealing his pike and hand light, and threatening him with worse treatment if he reported the incident. On similar occasions, soldiers on night patrols confiscated property from lightkeepers and extorted a real or two before they returned lights and other items. The city *alcaldes* (magistrates) demanded an end to abuses committed under "the cloak of authority" and suggested that some army officers must be involved in the criminal activities of the patrols.

Although these incidents were relatively minor, acts of gratuitous violence by soldiers against civilians were quite common in public parks, in the streets,

197

and even in the theaters. The viceroys of New Spain issued and reissued detailed instructions regarding misuse of arms and improper behavior of army personnel. Investigations revealed that sergeants and corporals commonly saber-whipped their soldiers to discipline them and to command obedience. In a number of cases deaths resulted from particularly severe beatings. Inured to violence, the soldiers comported themselves similarly in their relations with the civilian population. Assigned to traffic control duty, or to public parks and gathering places with instructions to keep away beggars, the barefoot, and naked or otherwise indecent persons, they abused the very people they were supposed to protect. In many instances, substitutes hired by urban militiamen to serve during active duty were drawn from vagabond and petty criminal elements.

These examples suggest an all too familiar relationship between an arbitrary and ill-disciplined military force used to police urban centers and the civilian sectors of the populace. One might anticipate similar incidents in many nations today where the military governs or where conditions demand the employment of soldiers in the civil sector. However, there was also a more positive side to the colonial military presence in Spanish America. Provincial militia officers received privileges under the *fuero militar* (corporate privileges granted to the military) that allowed them freedom from arrest and incarceration in the public jails and transferred their cases from the ordinary civil and criminal courts and other tribunals to the military jurisdiction. While many of the privileges were honorific, the army granted social status to creoles who hungered for official recognition. Impecunious Spanish-born officers employed their uniforms and status to meet and marry creole heiresses. Some became great land owners, miners, and merchants with business connections that propelled them into the colonial elites. Even artisans and common laborers manipulated their militia connections to tweak the authority of police officials and arbitrary governors. They wore a cockade on their hats or a militia badge to identify their special position, to evade the wrath of their bosses in the workplace, and to gain immunity during wild drinking sessions in the taverns and streets. Whether it was planned or not, the militia allowed such men to gain a certain confidence in themselves and to break out of tight social constraints. This was certainly true with the *pardos* and *morenos* (free *mulatos*, or persons of black and white ancestry and blacks) who lived in coastal towns and in many of the larger cities. Stained socially by their African blood, men of these sectors valued their militia connection, which brought recognition and blurred at least some racial discrimination.

The Military Before the Reform Era

We can identify a definite dividing line in the military history of Spanish America during the decade of the 1760s. Before this date, large military forces were not required to defend the various provinces or to maintain internal calm.

Afterward, the presence of external and internal dangers compelled the Spanish regime to transfer regular forces from Europe and to raise provincial regiments, battalions, and companies of infantry, cavalry, and dragoons throughout the American domain. Historians identify the British assault on Havana in 1762, as the single event that galvanized the Spanish imperial government into altering the old coastal defense system that hinged upon a few theoretically impregnable fortresses. By the time of the Seven Years' War (1756–63), Britain and France possessed the naval strength to dispatch forces from Europe and their Caribbean colonies that would serve as bases for major operations against Spanish America. In 1741, Admiral Edward Vernon had attempted a major attack against Cartagena that had failed, but Spanish weaknesses were evident. The shock of losing Havana and possibly all of the district of Cuba, which was known as the "key to the Caribbean," was enough to begin a series of military missions designed to implant armed forces headed by a few professional regular battalions and supported by more numerous provincial militia units.

In most Spanish American provinces, the military reforms began jurisdictional controversies and annoyed both the existing administrators and portions of the privileged elites. A much broader military presence expanded the number of people who could claim the fuero militar and thereby evade other legal tribunals. Because the militias drew manpower from a cross section of elite and nonelite sectors, almost every legal jurisdiction predicted erosion of its special areas of competence. Urban magistrates felt that they were losing control over the populace, officers of the *acordada* (a police force and summary court) resisted any diminution of their powers to detain vagrants, and other groups such as merchants, miners, and guilds acted to defend their own areas of legal privilege. Many in Spanish America viewed the army as a dangerous competitor that might dramatically alter the existing balance of powers and jurisdictions.

What had become of the Spanish *conquistadores* (conquerors) whose audacity and military exploits had dominated much of the sixteenth century? When we think of Spanish America, one of the first images that comes to mind is that of the armored conqueror who overthrew great Indian civilizations for riches, lands, honor, and souls to expand the crusading faith. As is so often the case, the images do not represent reality. While the conquest of the Americas was something of a military operation, the conquerors themselves were not generally soldiers of long professional training and experience. The "soldier-civilian contrast" we know today did not exist in sixteenth-century Spanish America. Men of the conquest generation gained most of their war experience in Indian fighting. Once the conquest was completed, some of these men became *encomenderos* (recipient of a grant of Indian labor and tribute) who left their retainers in the rural districts while they spent most of their time in Mexico City, Lima, and other growing urban centers. Although they were obliged to take up arms in case of renewed Indian violence and to control turbulence among Spaniards, the destruction of the major sedentary Indian governing elites left little spirit for resistance. Many of the new interior cities grew without walls and defensive fortifications designed to deter a major attacker.

Other first-generation conquerors were restless adventurers who were addicted to the will-o'-the-wisp pursuit of glory and riches. They settled temporarily in one city and then moved on to new exploits on the frontiers and in the civil wars that cursed the early history of the viceroyalty of Peru. Many of these transients became rootless vagabonds who caused nothing but trouble for the new urban regimes. They congregated in the larger centers to drink, attend cockfights, gamble at cards, fight, commit crimes, and generally disrupt the community. By the mid-sixteenth century, the *cabildo* (town council) of Mexico City deplored the activities of these men and the constant drain of urban residents out of the city to join any new venture that offered the prospect of glory and wealth.

While the interior cities required few troops other than police patrols and guards for public buildings and senior administrators, the situation was quite different on the coasts. As early at 1550, for example, French and English corsairs appeared off the port towns of Veracruz and Campeche. By the 1560s, they were able to mobilize sufficient force to attack the ports. In 1568, John Hawkins captured Veracruz, which was waiting for the inbound Spanish fleet. The failure of imperial Spain to achieve naval dominance in the Atlantic and Caribbean left no alternative to the adoption of a defensive approach based upon a few major ports. Well-known military engineers such as Juan Bautista Antonelli were sent to the Americas to oversee the construction of immensely strong defensive works in coastal cities. Havana, Veracruz, Campeche, Santo Domingo, San Juan, Nombre de Díos, Cartagena, Maracaibo, and other towns were fortified so that they could deter or resist enemy attackers. The Pacific ports were thought to be safe until 1578–79, when Sir Francis Drake rounded Cape Horn to raid Valparaiso, Callao, and many other communities in the provinces of Central America and New Spain. As was so often the case in the Caribbean, the port towns were caught by surprise; local commanders could not gather effective forces to protect against a comparatively small number of attackers. Once again, Spain had to face the prospect of building fortifications and organizing a defensive system for the vulnerable coastal towns. (See Figure 18.)

Even if the defenses were kept in a good state of repair, it was difficult to motivate and maintain vigilance among the small companies of garrison troops assigned to the coasts. Few men volunteered to serve in cities where the unhealthy climate and diseases such as yellow fever, malaria, and other tropical ailments stalked the unacclimatized. Although some of the ports were defended quite effectively—Havana for 200 years until its fall in 1762—a combination of disease, desertions, corruption, and laxity reduced the effectiveness of the fortifications. Through much of the seventeenth century, Dutch, English, and wild buccaneer bands overcame the apparent odds to capture, pillage, and burn coastal ports and to hold the inhabitants for ransom. In many cases, the massive walls, redoubts, and castles offered only a hollow illusion of strength.

With the exception of the frontiers, most Spanish American provinces lacked effective regular or militia forces. News of a coastal raid generally caused chaos in the interior as the authorities attempted to recruit and move men to reinforce garrisons that all too often proved empty of manpower. Sudden mobilizations of assorted merchants, artisans, untrained urban militiamen, *hacendados* (large landowners) and any other available men accomplished very little. Buccaneer raids were quick, devastating blows that left the relief forces little to do other than repossess the pillaged ruins of a coastal city. In 1683, for example, reports reached Mexico City of a corsair seige of Veracruz commanded by Nicolás Agrammont and Laurent de Graff (Lorencillo). Levies raised in Mexico City, Puebla, Orizaba, Jalapa, and Córdoba arrived at the port too late to engage the invaders. Indeed, the unruly men from the interior found themselves without adequate provisions and equipment. Exposed to the climate and tropical diseases endemic at Veracruz, many of the militiamen perished before they could be withdrawn and returned to their homes. Despite angry recriminations and attempts to locate negligent administrators responsible for the failure, temporary activity did not produce better trained militiamen or repaired fortifications. In 1697, the traveller Juan Gemelli Carreri found that the walls of Veracruz were covered with drifting sand to such an extent that a horseman could ride over them without difficulty.

The Urban Militias

Lacking an organized militia system during the seventeenth century, the Spanish regime encouraged the enlistment of urban militias composed of merchants, guildsmen, and racial groups such as the pardos and morenos who made up a fairly cohesive segment of the population. The mulatos played a significant role in coastal defense, where they successfully resisted tropical diseases and formed growing communities in many of the larger cities. While the merchants and artisans were willing to join militia units to protect their property, men of African ancestry gained social prestige, recognition, and other advantages. The right to wear uniforms and bear arms raised the mulatos above other racially mixed elements and linked them to the urban authorities.

In some coastal cities, the pardos and morenos enjoyed lengthy traditions of exchanging their militia service for recognition and status. As early as 1586, the Havana militias included blacks and mulatos, and by 1600, these men had formed their own *compañía de pardos libres* (company of free mulatos). The city of Santo Domingo, also on the forward defense lines against both European enemies and unofficial raiders, needed to utilize every ablebodied man who was willing to take up arms. Necessity forced even the most racist whites to accept the hardy mulatos, who fought with loyalty and tenacity on numerous occasions. By 1651, there were two organized pardo and moreno urban squadrons available for duty in Santo Domingo.

In Lima the first pardo militias were formed as early as 1615, and similar units were recruited in Mexico City and Puebla. Normally, these urban militias played a ceremonial role in honor guards for dignitaries and during holiday celebrations when they paraded and fired salutes. However, in times of crisis caused by food shortages, disputes within the city, or a threat from abroad, they served to bolster the regime and maintain order. While they achieved no real equality of opportunity with the urban whites, they were both needed and accepted. Lengthy traditions of militia service and heroic acts in defense of the Spanish sovereigns identified these men as trustworthy and deserving of recognition.

The importance of the urban militias became evident in 1692, when food shortages and rising prices in Mexico City turned plebeians and vagabonds against the wealthy residents. The few police officials and soldiers available were insufficient to control angry rioters who entered the markets to loot shops. The situation might have become uncontrollable had there not existed within the merchant guild a militia organization called the *tercio de infantería de comerciantes* (regiment of commerce). The merchants mobilized themselves and took the lead in crushing the tumultuous mobs. When news of the uproar in the capital reached Puebla, the city governors feared a general uprising. The alcaldes activated several militia companies of pardo and moreno artisans to guard public buildings and to assist urban police patrols. One of these trustworthy mulato companies was sent to Mexico City to help restore order and to protect the viceregal palace.

Realizing the need for urban militias, the crown expanded and formalized the existing units. The pardo and moreno companies received new regulations and an enhanced reputation for loyalty to the king. In the case of the merchant militias, a royal decree in 1693 altered what had been a loose organization by forming the urban regiment of commerce. While this granted certain prestige and recognition to the loyal business community of Mexico City, many merchants were unenthusiastic about the new honors. The *consulado* (merchant guild) of Mexico City had to vote an annual subsidy to cover militia expenses, and the merchants sent their young apprentices, clerks, and other employees to bear the burden of training, holiday reviews, and occasional tours of guard duty within the city.

During the eighteenth century defensive necessity in the frontline colonies demanded even greater use of the urban pardos and morenos. In the district of Cuba the crown legislated protective measures to prevent racial discrimination. By the 1760s, there were three full battalions of free black and mulato infantry—available for active service in the garrison and in regions of Louisiana, Florida, and elsewhere. In Caracas, Veracruz, Santo Domingo, and other cities where the defenses needed strengthening, the crown utilized the free blacks and mulatos. In 1794, King Charles IV awarded gold and silver medals to black and mulato officers who supported the Spanish cause in the war against France. In some cities, such as Havana, the employment of these sectors in the militias removed them from direct competition for jobs with the urban whites. There was some apprehension concerning the political power of black officers, and the authorities in Havana resisted schemes to resettle loyal pardo and moreno troops from Santo Domingo. Elsewhere, the introduction of militia reforms and the expansion of provincial forces led to efforts to demobilize existing urban pardo and moreno units. In these situations, the pardos made every effort to resist the regime and to generate imperial support for their continued service. They were all aware that militia uniforms and privileges enhanced their social status and reduced racial discrimination.

The problems of the private urban regiment foreshadowed in many respects those encountered by the regular army and militias after the reforms of the 1760s. There was a permanent dichotomy between military service and almost every other profession and trade practiced within the city. While few merchants objected to the idea of assisting the regime in the suppression of rioters, permanent organization of the regiment meant a continuing financial commitment and time devoted to training, assemblies, and duty. Most merchants and shopkeepers could not afford time away from their primary occupations. Further, they complained bitterly that their apprentices, assistants, and clerks lost their subordination and dedication to business after they returned from service in the regiment. Companionship with men from the lower classes and the social life of the soldier turned many youths into idlers who resisted the rigorous preparation of a business education.

To avoid these problems the wealthy merchants and shopkeepers accepted a lesser evil of hiring substitutes called *alquilones* who came from the lower classes and did not have careers to interrupt. By the second half of the eighteenth century, the urban regiment of commerce was composed of unsavory characters who were quite unlike the solid citizens who had defended Mexico City in 1692. With much greater demand for garrison troops during and after the Seven Years' War (1756–63) until the end of the colonial period, the alquilones found themselves guarding the royal palace, the treasury, jails, and other important offices. These untrustworthy elements used the militia regiment to prey upon and exploit the civilian populace of Mexico City.

The urban regiment continued to cause considerable strain within the city. Successful merchants hired alquilones, while the smaller shopkeepers and dealers who could least afford to pay were compelled to serve themselves. Many had to close their shops in order to fulfill their militia obligation. Even monthly inspections were disastrous to shopkeepers who remained open on holidays and lacked employees to handle their duties. To operate and supply their shops, they had to work very long hours. This meant trips to the baker for bread, to the pork butcher for lard, to the candlemaker for candles, and to other merchants who supplied wholesale stock. Just as important, the smaller shopkeepers had to be present to accept credit purchases and to hold pledged items until their customers could repay their bills. Many shopkeepers with capital of only 100 to 200 pesos went bankrupt and fled from their creditors—thereby turning over still more personnel in the urban regiment.

The strain upon the merchant militia became much greater between May 1794 and 1801, when the unit was mobilized and placed on permanent duty. The transfer of regular and militia units out of Mexico City to guard against invasion threats left severe shortages of manpower. As crisis overtook the Spanish empire, the regime overutilized a militia unit that was supported by private funding. The merchant militia required at least 175 men daily to guard public buildings and look after patrols. Lacking sufficient merchants to fill their needs, the officers recruited guildsmen and the noncommissioned officers hired alquilones from the lower classes. Some of these mercenary substitutes were able to command up to a *peso* (monetary unit) per day for their services—three times the daily pay of a regular soldier. When they grew weary of guard duties they deserted, selling their uniforms, arms, and equipment. Despite the disadvantages and the high costs, merchants preferred to pay substitutes rather than lose their employees. They resisted any effort by senior army commanders and the regimental officers to ban the hiring of alquilones.

If the merchants feared the threats of urban militia life for their young employees, they also were concerned by the possibility of losing jurisdictional control over a militia unit that they described as "an unjust asylum for delinquents." They opposed rising demands for annual contributions to support barracks, purchases of new weapons, and other expenses. Writing to Viceroy Martín de Mayorga in 1782, the consulado complained:[1]

> We resist and will continue to resist for as long as is necessary this effort to embezzle funds to foment libertinage by those who abuse the fuero militar, flee the punishment of the ordinary magistrates, and mock the law.

To the disgust of the professional businessmen of the city, a small group of marginal dealers within the merchant community found loopholes in the laws to evade both merchant and ordinary justice. Operators of rickety stands and shops hid behind the privileges of the merchant militia to falsify weights and measures, to sell prohibited alcoholic drinks and operate gambling dens, and to run illegal pawnshops that victimized the poor. Such individuals manipulated military justice and often managed to escape from the far more rigorous penalties of the merchant and civil jurisdictions. From the point of view of the leading businessmen, the army had no place in the mercantile occupation. Once shady characters claimed the fuero militar, they could manipulate jurisdictions so that they were confined in the comfort of their barracks rather than in the public jails. The regiment permitted some men to live in sinful liberty while they committed crimes and mocked the judicial system.

With mixed nocturnal patrols in Mexico City of alquilones, guildsmen, a few merchants and their employees, and others recruited with no questions asked, trouble could be anticipated for the general populace and for other legal jurisdictions. The cabildo complained bitterly about hiring criminals to guard the royal treasury, the acordada officers were not happy at seeing militiamen on duty who under other circumstances would have been arrested and held by their tribunal, and the provincial militia commanders of the local infantry regiment could not locate recruits. Men sought refuge in the urban regiment knowing that it could not serve outside of the city. Night patrols assigned to assist police officials engaged in boisterous behavior in taverns, brawled in the streets, molested women, and extorted money and food from vendors.

In one notorious incident, an entire patrol of the urban regiment disappeared into a brothel. On the 10:00 to 12:00 P.M. rounds, a detachment under Sergeant Silva, passing a house at the Callejón de las Ratas, was greeted by two women who provoked the militiamen, offered themselves, and then called out obscenities when the patrol did not stop. During the 2:00 to 4:00 A.M. rounds, however, the entire patrol stopped at the house and then forced their way inside. The stories of what happened next differed in detail, but a court-martial established the general picture. When the militiamen entered, someone blew out the candles and at least three men handled the women and threatened to sexually molest them. One of the prostitutes was in bed with a civilian, and some witnesses stated that another woman began to embrace one of the soldiers. In the uproar of the moment, the corporal shouted that the women were "grandísimas putas." They responded that they were being attacked by "cuckold soldiers." At that point, the members of the patrol beat a precipitous retreat and continued their normal duties. When it was discovered that some of the soldiers were alquilones, not only were they punished with confinement to barracks, but the merchants for whom they served were arrested and sentenced to fifteen days' imprisonment.

Incidents such as this illustrated the much larger problem of maintaining law and order in the Spanish American urban centers. Through its ordinary system of policing, the regime maintained only limited control over the populace. As they do today, the more dynamic centers such as Mexico City, Lima, and Buenos Aires drew population from the smaller towns and rural districts. The city appeared to promise opportunities for employment or survival based upon a variety of activities that went on outside of the law. Large numbers of vagabonds and criminals frequented the cockpits, gambling dens, and taverns—making law enforcement difficult for the *comisarios* (justices of the peace) and *cuadrilleros* (police patrols) assigned to keep order among the urban populace. In many cities, the high level of violent crime and lack of an effective police force caused the cabildos to request aid from the military. Where possible, the municipal governments drew upon the provincial militia regiments and battalions to create permanent police pickets that supported other law officers. To cover expenses, the city governments levied special taxes on imports of flour, wool, grain, wine, and other commodities.

Even before invasion threats by foreign enemies caused the regime to strengthen the army, it was obvious that internal changes of the eighteenth century made similar demands. The movement of population into the cities presented constant headaches for regulatory authorities. In larger cities such as Mexico City and Puebla, the lack of statistical information meant that the regime could not quantify the population adequately or even maintain an accurate idea of the size of communities. The new "hidden suburbs" lacked street names or numbered addresses; as Viceroy Conde de Revillagigedo pointed out, ". . . this provides the most secure asylum for criminals who commit the most grave criminal offenses."[2] Those who lived at a permanent domicile were counted by the census and became eligible to serve in the militia units. In many cities, efforts to quantify the population were blocked by the people, who believed that the only real purpose of a census was to obtain unwilling recruits for the army. Wives described themselves as widows or neglected to offer information about their sons, sisters left off their brothers, and entire families disappeared temporarily into the maze of uncontrolled streets. Others left the city until the census had been completed. Those who were recruited into the regular army or the militias used the same chaos in the cities to desert and to hide out with their friends and families. Lack of communication between army authorities and the *alcaldes de cuartel* (neighborhood police and judicial authorities) and acordada officers meant that many escapees were not apprehended.

The use of militia forces for police duty became more common in the latter decades of the eighteenth century. Urban growth was not accompanied by sufficient expansion of city budgets to permit adequate policing. In New Spain cities such as Guanajuato, Oaxaca, Puebla, and Guadalajara became notorious for robberies and assaults. In Guanajuato, where militiamen had aided in the suppression of mob violence in 1767, during the expulsion of the Jesuits, militia guards and roving patrols offered effective protection. The militiamen knew the hiding places used by criminals and could root them out quite quickly. Members of the provincial infantry battalion served on police duty for two months per year, with the costs paid by special taxes levied in the city. At any given time there were 63 militiamen available to guard public buildings or to assist in any other area of urban protection. In Guadalajara assaults upon wealthy residents and private dwellings became so frequent that the *alcaldes ordinarios* (city magistrate) and the *alguacil mayor* (chief constable) failed utterly in their efforts to curb violent crimes. Gangs of vagabonds loitered in the countryside just outside of the city until they felt confident enough to raid houses and to murder any unfortunate servant or owner who resisted.

To end what they viewed as a dangerous crime wave, the municipal authorities estimated that the city required at least two militia police patrols of 60 men. Some urban officials in Guadalajara and in other cities were less sanguine about the power of a few militiamen to prevent any further increase in the level of crime.

The Regular Army

Although some viceroys and captains-general introduced military reform programs prior to the Seven Years' War, there had been no substantial re-evaluation of imperial policy to meet the increasing dangers. The occupation of Havana by British forces in 1762 renewed debates in Spanish army circles about the advisability of arming large numbers of colonials and the relative merits of transferring peninsular units or recruiting regular and militia forces in the Americas. Most Spanish-born officers held a low opinion of Spanish Americans, believing that many of them were tainted by racial mixture, inherent laziness, and a lack of true devotion to the *patria* or homeland. From all regions, until independence was achieved, haughty peninsular officers in the army and civil bureaucracy wrote lengthy reports denigrating the *americanos* and sometimes proposing that European mercenaries of any nationality would offer better protection than units of colonial Venezuelans, Peruvians, Mexicans, or others. Not only were such attitudes narrow-minded in the extreme, but for political, economic, and social reasons they were completely unrealistic. No imperial minister seriously envisioned the enormous costs and drain of manpower that would be entailed in dispatching sufficient regular infantry and cavalry regiments to defend the Americas. Moreover, few regular officers wanted to accept transfers to colonial postings that stigmatized military careers. It was well known that officers disappeared into the Americas and were forgotten. This was not the best incentive for men who spent much of their careers grooming their *hojas de servicio* (service dossiers), competing to attain battlefield recognition, and attacking each other over small points related to army seniority that might give them an edge for promotion.

The attitudes of Spanish Americans toward the army tended to confirm some of the prejudices expressed by European officers. Regular army duty was viewed as similar to arrest for vagrancy and sentence to long imprisonment in the presidios or *obrajes* (textile workshops). Regular soldiers often served in the least hospitable climates on the coasts or frontiers, where life was harsh and often very short. As was the case in other eighteenth-century armies, civilians and army officers disagreed as to how to improve the military image and attract high-quality volunteers. The army needed to tap the young male population to fill its infantry regiments, but in the Americas the crown would not introduce a general system of conscription. Despite efforts to establish the regular army as an honorable career option, few Spanish Americans subscribed to this point of view. Disease, harsh discipline, low pay, and very high desertion rates made the regular forces unpopular with all segments of the population. Lacking volunteers, army recruiters focused their efforts in the urban centers where there were concentrations of young men who might not be needed in other essential pursuits. At certain times, cities such as Valladolid (Morelia) and Querétaro hosted as many as four *banderas de recluta* (recruiting teams). Recruiters from the four regular infantry regiments of the province of New Spain competed with others from the districts of Cuba and Louisiana for a very limited pool of manpower. They searched the cities for deserters, examined jail populations, and swept up any green youth who happened to imbibe too heavily in the taverns. At the same time, the regulars cast covetous glances at militia companies, and there were efforts to recruit from the militias into the regular forces. In instances where regular soldiers decoyed militiamen and employed tricks to entrap them, both the urban administrations and the militia officers resisted. Pressures upon artisans and laborers by regular recruiters caused considerable fear and unrest. Few men wanted to risk lengthy enlistments and the real possibility of death from tropical disease in some garrison far from home. Failing to fill their quotas, some regular officers threatened to apply pressure by transferring urban militiamen directly into the regular army.

Levies of vagabonds designed to purge the cities of unwanted elements and to dragoon regular army recruits produced less than satisfactory results. Although the civil authorities jailed loiterers, vagrants, and petty criminals of all kinds, major campaigns were organized from time to time under the 1775 *reglamento de levas* (code regulating conscription) or under often repeated legislation concerning nakedness in public places. While such efforts may have been more successful in a homogeneous society, the nature of the population in New Spain and in other provinces confused the situation. The first question was how to distinguish a vagabond from the common urban resident. Even army deserters evaded easy recognition because the operators of taverns and shops accepted military badges, uniforms, arms, and other equipment in exchange for civilian clothing and food. The underlying problem, however, was more complex. The levy swept up a cross section of the male population and caused the authorities numerous difficulties with regard to status and racial origins.

Many men who frequented cockpits, gambling dens, and taverns were totally unsuited for military service or could claim legitimate exemptions from duty. Those who were married with dependents, single with invalid or aged parents to support, physically disabled, or racially excluded from enlistment petitioned for immediate discharges. Others claimed exemptions based upon the position and privileges of their employers, and a large number swept up in raids on taverns were permanently besotted by alcohol. They were incapable of serving the king in any capacity, let alone in the army. Even if such individuals were found to be in contravention of the antinakedness laws, they might claim to support dependent wives and children. More confusing yet, Indians and others from the lower *castas* (persons of mixed racial ancestry) were supposed to be exempt from military service. By the end of the eighteenth century it was often impossible to make an accurate assessment of racial origins. Once detained by the army, it was a simple matter to claim Indian or some other ineligible status even if one's documentation was not in order. The mobility of the urban population was such that checks of birth registers could not be made easily. Moreover, even these documents were considered suspect.

The *tribunal del crimen* (criminal chamber of the high court) in Mexico City reported during 1801, that of 652 men apprehended in two levies, only 69 were declared suitable for regular army enlistment. Even to attain this low level of success, physicians relaxed normal military regulations on height, health, and other characteristics. When officers had an opportunity to examine these recruits, they shipped most off to serve in the navy. Other men appealed successfully for exemptions, which the tribunals were obligated to hear. Some suffered from physical disabilities at the time of their arrests and others fell ill in jail during the lengthy period needed to hear appeals. Examining the situation, some authorities questioned the expenditures needed to hold levies and argued that the real vagabonds slipped out of the city or went into hiding until it was safe to resume their normal activities.

If the levy caused concern among popular elements, most urban residents had little to fear if the law was followed and access to appeal allowed. Detention in the small hours of the morning or in a suspicious location such as a gambling den was only one aspect of evidence. If a detainee could obtain the testimony of three citizens of his behalf, that in itself was sufficient proof of innocence. It was thought to be rare that a man who held legitimate employment could not obtain this kind of support from his associates and family members. With care taken to prevent extortion, revenge, and illegal practices by urban magistrates, the levy was seen as a useful method of cleansing the cities of vagabonds, even if they had to be sent to work in the presidios rather than to serve the army.

Unfortunately, there were some urban officials who used their orders to round up vagabonds to extort money from innocent persons of the lower classes. During 1797, in Mexico City, José Antonio Alzate petitioned Viceroy Marqués de Branciforte to intervene in a situation of growing abuses. With general orders to detain suspected vagrants, police officials cast a wide net and apprehended anyone who appeared to be a possible candidate for military service. They detained their victims at bakeries and pork butcher shops, where they were given opportunities to pay bribes for immediate releases. Rather than searching the cockpits and taverns for candidates, these officials stationed themselves in the streets and even outside of churches where they were certain to locate young men. On July 27, 1797, for example, they arrested men leaving the Church of La Merced at 12:15 following the noon mass. Alzate blamed the *comisarios, alguaciles, cuadrilleros,* and some scribes for creating a situation of near chaos. Masters refused to send their servants into the streets on errands for fear that they would be swept up by the military patrols or the *vampiros de día.*

Alzate made specific charges against a number of urban officials who abused their posts to extort money from the laboring classes. He identified the alcalde de cuartel José Conejo as one of the worst offenders. According to Alzate, Conejo had dissipated his personal fortune of over 200,000 pesos in gambling before he took on employ as an *alcalde de barrio* (neighborhood police and judicial authority); his intentions from the beginning were to use the post to recover his financial position. Under the pretext of the levy, Conejo detained men and boys, planning to obtain money for their freedom. Small boys of 8, 10, or 12 years of age were taken into custody with the expectation that their parents would pay to obtain their releases. Some poor mothers contributed as little as a peso or even a few *reales* (one-eighth of a peso) if they had no other financial resources. Other offenders included Sergeant José Salazar and Corporal Manuel Cristalinas of the Provincial Regiment of Mexico, who held special commissions to detain vagabonds. Cristalinas was said to have collected a fortune from his activities so that he could ". . . gamble ounces of gold as if they were grains of sand."[3] In Alzate's opinion, criminals such as these deserved to be sentenced to row in the galleys. He noted that anyone who possessed money could evade both the levy and the regular army. Only the poorest residents actually ended up having to serve the king.

The Provincial Militias

Without a strong regular army, neither defense nor internal security could be adequately guaranteed. It was unrealistic to suppose that Spain could provide troops or sufficient funds to defend all of the American possessions. Although centralizing reformist viceroys such as the Conde de Revillagigedo in New Spain and many peninsular army commanders wanted to garrison the cities with regular army companies, shortages of troops and greater needs elsewhere prevented the implementation of any such plans. Revillagigedo did assign regular companies to police Guanajuato and Guadalajara, but he could not afford to leave these units in garrison duty. Despite the opposition of Bourbon centralists, the only solution was to seek some accommodation with the provincial elites that dominated the major urban centers. If regular troops could not be obtained and there were few privately funded units like the urban regiment of commerce in Mexico City, the only other answer lay in the provincial militia. To gain support from the elites meant that certain powers would have to be delegated and honors granted to those who lent their prestige and funds to the army. In New Spain, the urban cabildos were the obvious level of government to distribute honors and to mobilize sufficient manpower within the cities and their dependent districts. While no Bourbon army commander or administrator wanted to face a diminution of authority— especially if it meant an enhancement of powers wielded by the regionally-oriented, localistic, and creole-dominated urban governments—there was no other solution. From the 1760s forward in New Spain, the army had to delegate some of its prerogatives to the urban cabildos. It would not be until 1810, and the outbreak of the Hidalgo Revolt that army officers could reverse the loss of important urban civilian controls over the provincial militias.

In other provinces, and particularly in isolated locations distant from the restraints of *audiencias* (high courts) and viceroys, aggressive militia commanders were sometimes successful over the short term in shielding their men from the ordinary cabildo legal jurisdiction and against competing privileged sectors. In Popoyán in New Granada, for example, local militia officers alienated the cabildo by encroaching upon its urban prerogatives. The conflict marked an effort on the part of those in the community with social pretensions to break into the urban oligarchy. In such cases, the army became a focal point in existing regional and urban factional struggles. The Popoyán elite appealed to the imperial government for assistance, and was able to keep the matter entangled in confusion and disputation. If urban elites and other privileged jurisdictions such as the merchant guilds, mining tribunals, and the ecclesiastical sector could not maintain their legal position against the emerging militias, conflicts inevitably resulted. Similar struggles erupted in Peru, where Spanish-born officers mistrusted the creoles and wished to maintain strong peninsular domination over the provincial militias.

Most Spanish Americans, even those of the creole elites, did not volunteer for militia duty out of a patriotic love for the crown. Where there were no clear advantages, they resisted efforts to enlist them into provincial forces. Regular army officers commissioned to raise militias exercised great care when approaching cabildos to stress the direct benefits of a military presence, as well as the honor for the city. They were instructed to point out that once a militia battalion or regiment was in place, there would be much less crime and more security. As one officer noted, ". . . even the man who most abhors the soldier demands help when he finds himself among thieves."[4]

In New Spain more than in any other Spanish American province, the cabildos acquired considerable power over the selection process for militia commissions. Although officer candidates had to be approved by the army command and the crown, the financial implications generally meant that only the wealthiest residents applied for regimental commands and senior rank. Prospective militia commanders had to donate large amounts of money to uniform, to arm, and, where necessary, to mount their units. Denied the opportunity to occupy offices in many other jurisdictions, the wealthy creole miners, merchants, and landowners realized the social implications of holding militia commissions. Here was a way for the urban patricians to gain immediate recognition and added status. In many cities, they competed in their offers for donations to obtain regimental or battalion commands and the rank of colonel or lieutenant colonel. In exchange for their money, they received royal commissions, attractive uniforms, and the privileges of the fuero militar.

This was not to say that the elite sectors agreed completely that an enhanced military presence was a positive feature for their cities, or concurred on how to dispense the new source of patronage. As might be expected, members of the cabildos rewarded themselves, their relatives, and their friends before they handed out the chance for a commission to others who possessed equal wealth and status. In Guayaquil, for example, the great majority of militia officers were related directly to men who were or had been cabildo members. There was a close connection between the urban government and those who held militia commissions. In many other cities, however, the urban magnates were not convinced that the benefits to one segment of the elites were worth the cost elsewhere. They complained that the military jurisdiction threatened existing urban legal authorities by exempting a significant segment of the populace from the urban magistrates and police officials. In many provinces, the viceroys and senior army commanders encountered opposition from the cities that continued long after the introduction of the reformed military program.

In Popoyán in New Granada, local magistrates rejected the fuero militar and passed harsh sentences upon any plaintiff who claimed the protection of army legal jurisdiction. Moreover, men of the city elite protested against efforts to raise militia units that mixed members of the local nobility with others of lower social status and origins. In the city of Oaxaca in 1796, Lieutenant Colonel Pedro de Laguna experienced innumerable complications in fulfilling his viceregal orders to raise a provincial infantry battalion. While there were sufficient officer candidates, the five *regidores* (city councilmen) of the cabildo resisted the introduction of military privileges that might reduce the powers of the city government. They set the city alcaldes against the new militiamen and blocked the introduction of any special laws that might interfere with the urban interest. After numerous battles, Laguna asked Viceroy Branciforte to alter the composition of the cabildo in order to add new members who would not identify themselves with narrow local concerns.

Similar resistance to the potential centralizing influence of a provincial army presence could be found in many colonial Mexican cities. In 1780, Inspector General Pascual Cisneros described the cabildo of Querétaro as ". . . seditious in spirit and willful in its capricious opposition to the sovereign intentions."[5] The Querétaro militia commander Pedro Ruiz Dávalos condemned factions within the cabildo that opposed any suggestion of intervention in local affairs and passed salacious rumors that kept the whole city in a state of anxiety. Given that gossip, petty grievances, and smears against reputations abounded in almost all of the provincial cities, it is easy to understand the difficulties of the military and the regime. Ruiz Dávalos, like Laguna in Oaxaca, concluded that the only way to curb the intense localism of the cabildo was to add new members who would not identify themselves with the existing factions. Indeed, during his *visita general* (general inspection) to New Spain, José de Gálvez encountered similar problems with the urban governments of Mexico City, Puebla, and Valladolid. He appointed additional regidores who were willing to support his point of view on good government.

In their zeal to defend local urban prerogatives, the regidores and alcaldes could not avoid disputes with the military jurisdiction. The establishment of a militia battalion or regiment meant the institution of new taxes, the arrival of a regular army training cadre that brought with it the intrusion of central authority, and the poorly defined privileges for militiamen included in the fuero militar. In raising new battalions or regiments, large sums of money were collected and applied toward the purchase of arms, uniforms, and utensils. All of these elements threatened to alter existing relationships and to bring intervention from outside the city and region dominated by the cabildo. Taxes raised for militia support caused resentment from those who paid and temptations for those who managed the funds. The fuero militar threatened to reduce the powers of municipal magistrates over a large segment of the populace. Poor understanding and overzealousness on the part of regular officers assigned to the training cadres created acrimonious battles over what courts should have precedence in cases involving militiamen. The urban *justicias* (magistrates) could not accept the idea of a privileged military jurisdiction that encompassed the militiamen, their families, and their dependents, particularly since the part-time soldiers were of lower social and racial status.

Throughout Spanish America, the fuero militar created frictions and exposed old grievances. In Lima the merchant guild engaged in litigation with the army to prevent a loss of jurisdiction in cases involving merchant-militiamen. Wealthy merchants resented both the danger to their tribunals and the fact that less successful businessmen could gain militia commissions and thereby enhance their prestige. In Mexico City the officers and non-commissioned officers of the urban regiment of commerce often invoked race and purity in their efforts to promote the interests of their regiment. Unlike other militia units, the urban regiment claimed to enlist a majority of Spanish-born who were most loyal to the crown. The merchant-officers swore to guard Mexico City, to defend the viceroy, and to shed their last drops of blood for the royal cause. They neglected to mention that most merchants disliked militia duty so much that they hired substitutes to serve in their places.

As might be anticipated, the army commanders and viceroys felt that civilians—even those of the elites—lacked the professional skills to play any meaningful role in military affairs. Some officers challenged the rights of the cabildos and consulados to propose officer candidates or to administer militia support tax funds. In New Spain, Sub-Inspector General Pedro Gorostiza declared that the military ordinances were unclear on where powers lay in the question of militia officer appointments. In 1793, he sought to expand the prerogatives of his own office to nominate candidates for militia commissions. After inspecting the Provincial Regiment of Mexico, Gorostiza expressed disgust at its unmilitary state and went as far as to doubt its real existence. He told two militia captains that their service was unworthy of reward or attention and he underscored his opinion by issuing new regulations that lowered officers' salaries by a third and soldiers' pay by two pesos per month. Gorostiza made similar efforts to curtail the privileges of the consulado to nominate officers for the Urban Regiment of Commerce, and he prohibited the hiring of mercenary alquilones to replace merchants during mobilizations.

Viceroy Revillagigedo supported Gorostiza's offensive on behalf of the military jurisdiction, but he had to appeal to the imperial regime for a definitive ruling. In the interim, however, fears of war against France caused the imperial regime to transfer several regular regiments of the army of New Spain to guard Veracruz and overseas to protect Havana, Santo Domingo, and New Orleans. Revillagigedo convened a *cabildo extraordinario* (special town council meeting) in Mexico City in which he mobilized the provincial regiment for garrison duty and asked the cabildo to shoulder the financial burden—some 170,000 pesos per year—through donations and subscriptions. Already upset by the intervention in the process of officer selection and angry about salary reductions, the regimental captains formed a junta to demand full pay for officers and soldiers. Electing two delegates, the junta warned the viceroy that soldiers would desert if their families suffered hardships and their wives might be forced into prostitution. While the artisans who served in the militia regiment normally made adequate wages, they could not survive on the sums alloted by Gorostiza. The officers feared that ordinary citizens would turn to crime and that future recruitment into the regiment would be impossible. Once mobilized for guard duties and patrols, the militiamen did not have time to engage in their normal occupations. For those who attempted to do both jobs, the result was poor service and sometimes broken health.

Revillagigedo rejected this forceful opposition from militia officers in representation of their urban constituency. Gorostiza stated that a real and a half was sufficient daily pay for a soldier—any more was squandered on drink and entertainment. In his view, the officers had no reason for grievances because they were persons of high rank who served for honor and to prove their loyalty to the king. Instead of seeking higher pay from the treasury, Gorostiza believed that they should donate their salaries to the royal service. Revillagigedo took an even stronger position on the captains' petition, describing their actions as dangerously seditious behavior. He ordered the regular army major of the Provincial Regiment of Mexico to assemble the captains and to read them the army regulations on the subject. He condemned the militia captains for their ignorance of service and of the ordinances that governed the army. If the officers did not obey promptly and without further obstreperous behavior, he threatened to make an example of them that would be an object lesson to all.

While the replacement of Viceroy Revillagigedo and the death of Gorostiza defused the conflict, the Mexico City elite was not about to accept this sort of treatment. The bad-tempered outbursts insulted rather than corrected the creole officers and the urban politicians who helped to fund the regiment. Although members of the cabildo donated 100 pesos each, the voluntary subscriptions were not taken up. Instead of producing a fund of 170,000 pesos, the effort raised only 11,496 pesos. Officers and politicians felt embarrassed when the king wrote to thank the capital for its loyalty and devotion to the Spanish imperial cause. Viceroy Branciforte decided to have the royal treasury support the mobilized regiment rather than to press the matter further with the cabildo and the populace. The crown agreed, and at the same time reaffirmed the rights of the cabildo of Mexico City to propose candidates for militia commissions.

Confusion about the role of the cabildos in the officer selection process and in militia funding continued unabated. In New Spain, Viceroy Branciforte reversed Revillagigedo's policies to take advantage of the creole desire for recognition and privileges. Rather than disputing the role of the cabildos, Branciforte stimulated them to raise new units. He offered militia commissions and the fuero militar in exchange for donations to arm and equip the new battalions and regiments. While cities such as Oaxaca continued to resist the intrusion of the military jurisdiction, others managed to utilize militia police patrols and to take advantage of the army presence. Branciforte's approach acknowledged the urban elites and the capacity of the cabildos to generate support for the militias.

The cabildos in other provinces of Spanish America did not exercise the same powers of nomination within the militia structure. Regular army officers transferred to New Spain expressed surprise and revulsion at the idea that civilians should have any say in military affairs. Félix Calleja, the rising star of the Mexican army, argued on numerous occasions that groups of merchant politicians would debase military honor and position. This point of view notwithstanding, the crown and many other senior administrators in New Spain recognized the essential links between the cabildos and the militias.

Urban-Military Relations

For most urban dwellers, the expansion of the colonial army intruded upon such diverse areas as housing, food prices and availability of staples, and regulation of marketing. While the residents of major garrison towns and defended coastal cities were accustomed to dealing with the army, this was not the case elsewhere. The mobilizations and cantonments of large numbers of men in urban centers strained the local economies and the normal provisioning network. Both foreign invasion scares and major uprisings such as the Comunero Rebellion in New Granada and the Tupac Amaru Revolt in Peru strained urban resources as the army requisitioned supplies and property. Even a minor militia mobilization removed rural food producers, transporters, and sellers who carried fresh products for sale in the urban markets. When food prices rose, the army attempted to regulate the market place through the application of fixed price schedules and tight controls over distribution and sales. Army efforts to rent suitable housing for officers and buildings large enough to serve as barracks disrupted commerce and displaced wealthy residents. Especially in the smaller centers, the cabildos had to select officials to expropriate residences temporarily and to billet soldiers. As might be expected, there were numerous complaints about vandalism and willful damage done by soldiers to the windows, woodwork, fixtures, and even basic structures of buildings. Although some merchants and artisans made profits from supplying garrisons and cantonments, most lengthy mobilizations strained relationships between the cities and the army.

The regular army officers and non-commissioned officers assigned to train and administer militia units were a source of particular friction in the urban communities. Many of these soldiers were the discards of the Spanish army and the regular regiments—men whose careers had stagnated because of laziness, alcoholism, addiction to gambling, weak health, or a variety of other reasons. Stationed for decades in provincial cities away from the mainstream of their profession, they were often impecunious and bored with their existence. Some officers sought to marry into the local elite, using the prestige of their Iberian origins and rank to seek a wealthy heiress. While some men did achieve wealth and position in the provincial elites, others encountered opposition. At San Miguel in New Spain, Major Vicente Barros de Alemparte was arrested when he attempted to marry an aunt of his wealthy colonel. In many instances, a regular army major or lieutenant was left in de facto control of a militia regiment. The colonel, lieutenant colonel, captains, and lieutenants came from the local elites and did not want to be burdened with day-to-day administration. Left to their own resources, the regular officers and non-commissioned officers lost their military vocation and squandered militia funds. Most militia instructions attempted to circumvent these weaknesses by requiring the senior officers to oversee the activities of regular adjutants, sergeants, corporals, and drummers. The colonel and his regular army major were to ensure that their officers respected the judges and ministers of other privileged tribunals and jurisdictions.

In fact, however, hunger for position and recognition led many militia commanders into direct conflict with other authorities. Some colonels paraded their regiments at their own whim, employed honor guards, and showed up at official functions with large escorts that appeared to give them precedence over other officials in the city. In Puebla, Guanajuato, and Oaxaca, for example, militia commanders challenged the provincial intendants for preeminence within their jurisdiction. The Intendant of Guanajuato, Juan Antonio Riaño, held an army rank of lieutenant colonel. When local miner and merchant Antonio Pérez Gálvez paid thousands of pesos to attain the rank of colonel in the city militia, he claimed that his seniority made him *comandante de armas* (chief of the division) of Guanajuato. Although Pérez Gálvez was unsuccessful over the long run, the dispute dragged on for years to embitter relationships between the military and civil jurisdictions in the city of Guanajuato.

Conflicts between militia commanders and the provincial intendants eventually forced the viceroys to intervene. No viceroy could condone challenges to the powers of the intendant that would weaken central authority and the prestige of the regime. In 1789, when a supercilious militia lieutenant challenged the military preeminence of the intendant of Puebla, Manuel de Flon, Viceroy Revillagigedo left no doubt about his position. He argued that Puebla, as the second city of New Spain and a major supply base for the defense of Veracruz, could not afford any division in command between the civil and military authorities. The intendant had to assume absolute military control over the city and its "insolent and scandalous" plebeian sectors. Revillagigedo pointed to gang activities in Puebla during 1789, and 1790, that included a bold assault by a local outlaw against the acordada jail. To add support, the viceroy stationed in Puebla a regular dragoon regiment and six companies of infantry.

The power of the cities to resist military plans depended upon political acumen and the ability of the urban leaders to negotiate concessions regarding the size and type of militia units to be raised. City and town cabildos lacked the political strength to engage in direct confrontations with the army. At Zamora in New Spain, for example, efforts by the town cabildo to name totally unknown local citizens to senior militia posts were bound to fail. Acting as a viceregal commissioner assigned to raise militia units in 1795, Colonel Juan Velázquez found that the cabildo of Zamora passed over obvious candidates for senior posts in favor of local selections. In Velázquez's opinion, the municipal government had created total confusion in the town that had driven men to flee to the hills rather than accept the idea of enlistment. He reported, "This stormy cabildo commits errors that are the legitimate children of its ignorance."[6] Velázquez refused to admit that the cabildo wanted to appoint local residents rather than to accept army candidates who resided some distance from the town, but who were more wealthy and trustworthy in the eyes of the central administration. By refusing to make concessions and to accept a compromise solution, the Zamora cabildo convinced Velázquez that its plan was to "disturb good order" by placing unknown and untested residents in militia posts that they could not handle. In the end, Zamora yielded to viceregal pressures, but several other cabildos fought on for their own selections until they lost the privilege to make proposals of officer candidates.

As we have seen in other circumstances, not all Spanish Americans desired to obtain the benefits of a military career or part-time vocation. Brigadier Manuel de Pineda, inspector-general of military forces in Lima, found that most Peruvians exhibited antipathy rather than enthusiasm toward the army. Even if there was no shortage of candidates to become colonels and lieutenant colonels, the young men of the best families saw limited prestige in a lieutenancy or sublieutenancy. Few peninsular Spaniards were willing to assume a rank if they were to be made subservient to creoles, and most anticipated that the regime would reserve the highest posts and commands for its most loyal minority.

Not all wealthy men with pretensions toward army rank could expect to command a regiment or even a company of provincial militias. This made the political pressures within the cabildo quite difficult, and there were no easy solutions. Sometimes the municipal governors committed errors and insults because they nominated men who lived outside of the urban boundaries in subordinate towns, but still within the regimental or battalion jurisdictions. The cabildo of Guanajuato, for example, passed over volunteers and proposed men for lieutenancies who had not been consulted and who had no ambition to hold a royal commission. Miners and merchants might possess the wealth to become militia officers without wanting to accept a subaltern rank. Smelter operator Francisco de Septién petitioned the viceroy of New Spain to overturn a cabildo nomination that he be commissioned as a captain of grenadiers in the provincial battalion of Guanajuato. Because of Septién's wealth, the sub-inspector general of the army rejected the request, but named him to a less demanding post as captain of fusileers. To evade the recommendations of the Guanajuato cabildo, residents of the city, the surrounding towns, and the region claimed to be illiterate, lacking in sufficient wealth to serve as officers, in poor health, the sole support of large numbers of dependents, or overworked in other professions. Viceroy Branciforte dismissed most of the attempted renunciations, certain that most candidates simply wanted to escape from their patriotic duty.

For every man who wished to evade the honor of a militia commission, there were others who desired the social recognition of nomination. In Guanajuato José Antonio de Rivero complained that despite his background of militia service, willingness to donate 100 pesos per month when the militia was on active service, and offer to uniform and equip six soldiers, he had been passed over by the cabildo. He charged that the municipal government selected men of "no standing or experience" and acted maliciously in its preference for those who enjoyed special connections. Others wrote confidential letters to the viceroy condemning malcontents in the cabildo who stirred up "mortal rancor and hostilities," or belonged to factions that worked for their own interests. Anonymous letters were even more critical, and made personal attacks upon both the cabildos and the individuals selected for commissions. In one case, an unknown writer attacked the cabildo of Léon, near Guanajuato, for proposing Manuel García Parra, who made his living selling mescal and who was married to a mulata well known for her "indecorous tendencies."

Quite clearly, the possession of militia rank permitted the urban gentleman to show off and on some occasions to flaunt his fueros in the face of city constables and magistrates when he was caught at illegal gambling games or cockfights. While men of truly great wealth gained little monetary reward for taking on militia commands, the additional privileges, status, and recognition within their cities and provinces were more than sufficient reasons to seek senior posts. The captains and lieutenants were often merchants, shopkeepers, and landowners of quite modest resources who desired greater prestige and social position. In Oaxaca the intendant, Antonio de Mora y Peysal, complained that many of the militia officers in the city wore their uniforms and badges even when they were not on military duty. Some were to be found in full uniform in their shops during working days as they looked after small mercantile transactions. In some units the militia officers fought among themselves to exclude colleagues who were not considered socially acceptable. An officer's wife's *limpieza de sangre* (purity of blood) was sufficient cause for gossip and petty attacks designed to force the victim out of the militia. Even the most ridiculous and unsubstantiated rumors spread through the provincial cities, causing great strain and embarrassment.

For the common residents of the cities, the advantages of militia service were not at all evident. Unlike the soldiers of the urban regiment of Mexico and urban units elsewhere, provincial militia forces could be mobilized and marched to garrisons and cantonments far from their home jurisdictions. In the case of New Spain's militiamen, active service could mean being sent to the tropical coast to guard Veracruz, where yellow fever and other diseases killed a significant percentage of those who were unacclimatized. Some militiamen were transferred into regular infantry companies that were dispatched to defend the districts of Cuba, Florida, Louisiana, and Santo Domingo. Experience with tropical diseases or with duty overseas was sufficient deterrent for other men in New Spain who might have considered service in the provincial militias. Those who returned after years of duty overseas or deserted from Veracruz told tales that instilled truly antimilitary attitudes among the artisans and laborers of most cities.

Given these general attitudes and the resistance of Spanish Americans to the idea of traveling outside of their home provinces, the urban authorities experienced considerable opposition when they had to raise militia units or recruit replacements for forces already mobilized and on active duty. When Colonel Pedro de Laguna went to Oaxaca in 1796, to raise a provincial militia infantry battalion, he encountered opposition from both the potential recruits and the municipal authorities. As noted previously, the cabildo opposed mi-

220 / Christon Archer

litia interference in its sphere of influence and feared that the introduction of
the fuero militar would diminish the powers of the city government to control the populace. Because resistance to Laguna was impossible, the cabildo
feigned acquiescence and then did as little as possible to cooperate. Laguna
had to form the battalion from lists of guildsmen which were available in the
city. Many of the eligible young men escaped from Oaxaca and did not participate in the *sorteo* (lottery) to draft recruits into the battalion. Employers
and city officials conspired to aid the exodus of bachelors, who remained
out of the city until recruitment had been completed. As a result, Laguna
enlisted many married men who had dependents to support and others
who lacked the physical stature to serve in the army. Laguna believed that
the municipal government and the regular army major assigned to the
Oaxaca battalion could replace these men with bachelors once they returned
from hiding.

In fact, however, the cabildo did nothing to sort out errors in recruiting
and forgot all about the unsettling interference of Colonel Laguna. A few
months later, when the battalion was ordered to mobilize and march to serve
at the cantonment of Orizaba (near Veracruz), the army authorities were del-
uged by petitions requesting exemptions and releases. The battalion commander, Luis Ortiz de Zárate, complained that the cabildo produced no recruits
other than married men who had large families to support. On their part, the
municipal authorities reported that even rumors of mobilization caused tumults in the city. When orders arrived that the battalion would march on
August 1st, the cabildo and intendant agreed to surround the city with police officials in order to apprehend young men as they fled to safety. Despite
these efforts, the cabildo could not produce bachelors to replace married men.
Zárate ordered married militiamen to find their own replacements if they
wished to stay home. Representatives from the cabildo scoured the jails and
produced 38 men to fill 61 vacancies in the battalion. After these men were
examined for physical disabilities, stature, and exemptions, only 11 were declared suitable for duty. New efforts to turn up recruits produced only married men, Indian tributaries, and those who suffered physical ailments.

In the view of senior army commanders, the real blame and responsibility
for the poor efforts at Oaxaca lay with the opposition of the cabildo to the
military. They argued that Oaxaca, like many other major cities of New Spain,
was a gathering point for vagabonds and mobile laborers who were deleteri-
ous to the city although useful material for the army. Despite the existence of
this pool of available manpower, of 32 replacements sent by the cabildo to
reinforce the Oaxaca battalion at the cantonment, all but 5 were taken from
small villages in Oaxaca province and not from the city. Of the remaining 5
recruits, 1 turned out to be an Indian tributary who claimed total exemption
from military obligations. Viceroy Branciforte warned the municipal authorities of Oaxaca that they must terminate their resistance to the army. As a
result, the cabildo set aside the first three days of the New Year in 1798, to

scour the city for recruits. No one was permitted to leave the urban boundaries without permission from the intendant; the penalty for illegal flight was enlistment in the battalion plus a month in prison. When these measures failed to turn up men, the cabildo agreed once again to hold a lottery of the male population, promising to exercise "scrupulous formality" to prevent anyone from evading his duty to the crown.

Despite their difficulties with militia recruitment, the municipal leaders of Oaxaca had a lengthy connection with the local battalion. As early as 1777, José de Gálvez authorized a militia police detail in Oaxaca designed to assist the city law officers in their campaigns against vagabonds and the plebeian elements. Each of the three city magistrates received the aid of four soldiers who were to be relieved on a daily, weekly, or monthly basis. To pay for this force, Gálvez authorized a militia tax of 4 reales on each *carga* (300-325 pound load) of sugar and *tercio* (approximately 200 pound bale) of cacao entering the city.[7] In 1803, the militia detail was increased from one corporal and 12 soldiers to two corporals and 16 soldiers. These men were activated for three months of police duty and the obligation was to revolve through the militia battalion. By this time, the police detail had taken on additional tasks of guarding the jail, the treasury office, and the home of the provincial intendant. There were loud quarrels over honor guards and over how the militiamen should be employed. Some members of the cabildo felt that they had lost control over the police detail, and both the militia commander and the intendant bickered incessantly about minor questions.

While the sugar and cacao taxes produced sufficient revenues, the police detail remained a center of friction between authorities. Men of Oaxaca found police work particularly onerous, and they resisted any connection with the provincial battalion. As early as 1801, militiamen on urban patrols complained that they were too few in number to cover their duties. Some men had to serve on both the day and the night rounds. By 1806, the uniforms worn by the militiamen were in rags, their weapons were unserviceable, and it was impossible to replace men who had completed a tour of service. Even increases in salaries were not sufficient incentive to attract new replacements. At the termination of their active duty, militiamen discovered that their officers simply extended the length of police service. Of the 20 men available in 1806, all had been on duty for 2 years rather than 3 months. Others simply fled from the city rather than permitting themselves to fall into a similar trap. The exhausted militia policemen abandoned guardposts, slept while on duty, sold uniform components, and sometimes absented themselves without permission. Most tried to maintain their regular occupations and families. Militiamen such as Ceferino Corte, 1 of only 5 men left in his grenadier company, petitioned for relief from police duty. He claimed that the battalion was empty of manpower and unable even to replace the small police detail. In his own case, Corte had been forced to close his tailor shop and had lost all his regular customers. An inspection of the battalion strength underscored Corte's arguments. Only 30 men were listed on the battalion roster and 6 of these were fugitives.

Beginning in 1810, with the outbreak of the Spanish American Wars of Independence, the relationships between the cities and the military altered dramatically. Some units disintegrated and a few joined the insurgent cause, but most regular and militia forces remained for a time with the royalists. The lengthy mobilizations of provincial forces and, in many cases, their campaigns far from home jurisdictions altered the district urban and regional characteristics that were present in the eighteenth century. The cabildos and local officials lost patronage powers over officer appointments and promotions. No longer would the army take into account the civilian administrators or the special privileges and jurisdictions. Brigade commanders and other senior officers took control over promotions, special war taxation, forced loans, and confiscation and appropriation of property. Many of the provincial units that had been recruited in a major city and its environs became much more like regular battalions and regiments, which gathered manpower wherever they could rather than in a restricted population base. For the regular army officers who had felt constraints prior to 1810, the wars offered many opportunities. The cabildos, intendants and other officials complained bitterly about their loss of authority, but commanders responded that fighting capacity and intelligence were of more importance than social position. In San Luis Potosí in New Spain, for example, Brigade Commander Manuel María de Torres disregarded the cabildo entirely to appoint his own candidates for militia commissions. On one occasion in 1817, he scandalized the city by selecting José Joaquin Basave as an ensign. Basave was a well-known dice and card shark, lived with a fallen woman named doña Joaquina, and had faced previous criminal charges for concubinage and bigamy. While cabildo representations to Viceroy Juan Ruiz de Apodaca confirmed the theoretical powers of the city government in militia appointments, he ruled that the urgency of the times precluded normal constitutional procedures.

With the increase in military presence and power, soldiers who had exhibited violent tendencies toward civilians felt even less constrained in their activities. In 1815, the cabildo of Mexico City reported wanton attacks on the lives and properties of the populace. The lower classes were the main targets—especially the poor Indians who carried fruit, vegetables, and other food products into the city for sale. Those who put up resistance were beaten unmercifully within full view of witnesses. Even at midday, soldiers robbed urban residents who were going about their normal business. Some soldiers seemed to make a sport of robbing money and goods from shopkeepers and dealers who ran market stalls. Other troops became involved in drunken brawls between regiments in which arms were used and damage to civilian property was a common occurrence. On October 17, 1815, soldiers from one of the European regiments stationed in New Spain bayoneted a man twice and beat up his wife when the couple could not produce a light when they wanted to smoke. On the same day at Paseo Nuevo, where Manuel Fletes was removing spouts from the fountain, soldiers from the regiment of Zamora grew angry when he did not respond to their directions on how to do his job. They inflicted a vicious saber slashing upon him. Later, at Paseo de la Viga, these same troops ripped planks off fences and then used them to smack passers-by and to disrupt urban traffic.

Conclusions

From the beginnings of the militia reforms in the 1760s, the Spanish American cities had to deal with a growing army presence and role. The loosely organized urban militias had been sufficient to maintain domestic peace and to give at least some protection against intrusions that might move beyond the often ravaged coastal ports. After the conquest of Havana in 1762, Spain's enemies possessed the capacity to launch larger amphibious attacks and even invasion forces that might occupy whole provinces. Within the urban centers, the increasing numbers of regular and militia troops offered greater protection and obligations. The militias granted honors and social recognition to urban leaders who used their wealth and connections to obtain commands. Some racial groups, such as the pardos and morenos, gave their services as militiamen in order to win acceptance and recognition. Even if the regime intended no alterations in the balance between legal jurisdictions, the fuero militar opened loopholes and suggested that soldiers were to be separated from the ordinary courts.

Existing tribunals viewed the army with considerable apprehension and jealousy. While the cabildos of New Spain and some other provinces proposed officer candidates for royal commissions, no city government wanted to see the emergence of a powerful, privileged sector of soldiers who could flaunt the powers of the urban magistrates. Overbearing militiamen offended their social betters when they put on regimental cockades or badges and then went about drinking, fighting, gambling, and carousing under claimed immunities offered by the cloak of military protection. When detained by alcaldes, alguaciles, and other police officers, they demanded to be sent to their barracks for confinement rather than to the ordinary jails, and to the military authorities rather than to the ordinary magistrates.

These rather minor advantages of military service were not sufficient to blind most urban residents to the more negative aspects of army life. The lengthy wars of the late eighteenth century and the Napoleonic period generated invasion scares and an increasing demand for garrison troops. City artisans and laborers faced lengthy mobilizations and active duty at pay that was often a third of their regular earnings. These disruptions threatened family life and caused the loss of jobs and livelihood. Moreover, many men had to face service in distant coastal or overseas garrisons where different climates exposed them to the horrors of yellow fever, malaria, and other diseases. Many deserted, to become fugitives from the army who could not return home. Spanish Americans avoided voluntary enlistment in the regular regiments, which they considered suitable only for murderers, criminals, and vagabonds.

Although there were differences from one province to another, the degree of real social mobility granted by militia connections must be questioned. Many officers were creole merchants, businessmen, miners, hacendados, and others who enjoyed the privileges of other tribunals and who were important residents of their cities. They were well off, but they aspired to greater recognition from the regime. Their glittering uniforms and militia ranks gave them opportunities to meet intendants, bishops, and other civil and religious dignitaries. They marched during holiday inspections and fiesta parades that enhanced their desire for prestige and their thirst for official status. In wartime, however, these men faced duty away from their homes and business interests that rapidly eroded their martial ardor. For the common soldiers, these stresses offset all of the possible advantages. In most urban centers, the army became an unavoidable necessity that had to be tolerated. With the outbreak of the Wars of Independence, Spanish Americans faced a much greater expansion of military power and of the conflicts provoked by military service.

Notes

1. Consulado of Mexico to Mayorga, December 17, 1783, Archivo General de la Nación (Mexico City), Indiferente de Guerra (cited hereinafter as AGN:IG), vol. 122–A.

2. Revillagigedo to Antonio Valdés, no. 296, February 6, 1790, Archivo General de Simancas, Guerra Moderna, leg. 6959.

3. Alzate to Branciforte, October 16, 1796, AGN, Historia, vol. 44.

4. Nueva idea para formar Cuerpos Provinciales en el Reino. . . .," by Manuel Antonio de Mora, May 25, 1784, AGN:IG, vol. 14.

5. Pascual Cisneros to Mayorga, May 11, 1780, AGN:IG, vol. 104–B.

6. Juan Velázquez to Branciforte, January, 1795, AGN:IG, vol. 211–B.

7. Jose de Gálvez to Bucareli, March 19, 1777, AGN:IG, vol. 53–B.

Income of the Oaxaca Sugar and Cacao Taxes

1786	1,759 pesos
1788	1,918 pesos
1789	2,528 pesos
1790	2,299 pesos

The militia police detail cost 1,601 pesos in 1786. By 1807, there was a surplus of 3,163 pesos in the fund. See AGN:IG, vol. 126–B, and Reports to Iturrigaray, April 7, 1807, AGN:IG, vol. 53–B.

For Further Reading

Although most published works on the colonial army do not focus specifically upon the city, the majority refer to urban topics and deal with questions of interest. For the sixteenth century military men see James Lockhart, *Spanish Peru, 1532–1560: A Colonial Society* (Madison, Wis.: University of Wisconsin Press, 1968), and *Men of Cajamarca: A Social and Biographical Study of the First Conquerors of Peru* (Austin, Tex.: University of Texas Press, 1972). For detail on the role of the pardos and morenos in the early period, see Frederick P. Bowser, *The African Slave in Colonial Peru, 1524–1560* (Stanford: Stanford University Press, 1974), and J. I. Israel, *Race, Class and Politics in Colonial Mexico* (Oxford: Oxford University Press, 1975). Israel examines the frictions in Mexico City that required the presence of militia forces. For two studies on fortifications, see Guillermo Lohmann Villena, *Las defensas militares de Lima y Callao* (Seville: Escuela de Estudios Hispano-Americanos, 1964), and José Antonio Calderón Quijano, *Historia de las fortificaciones en Nueva España* (Seville: Escuela de Estudios Hispano-Americanos, 1953). While there are numerous studies on buccaneer raids upon Spanish American port cities, one of the best is Juan Juárez, *Pirates y corsarios en Veracruz y Campeche* (Seville: Escuela de Estudios Hispano-Americanos, 1972).

Beginning with the Seven Years' War and the initiation of the military reforms, the bibliography on the army is much stronger and more comprehensive. Two major, pioneering works treated aspects of military reform in New Spain, and more recent researchers have tested their conclusions in other Spanish American provinces as well as in Mexico. Lyle N. McAlister, *The "Fuero Militar" in New Spain, 1764–1800* (Gainesville, Fla.: University Presses of Florida, 1957) examines the impact of military privileges upon other jurisdictions and segments of the population. María del Carmen Velázquez, *El estado de guerra en Nueva España, 1760–1808* (Mexico City: El Colegio de México, 1950) surveys the broader administrative picture. More recently, Bibiano Torres Ramírez, *Alejandro O'Reilly en las Indias* (Seville: Escuela de Estudios Hispano-Americanos, 1969) examines the military reforms in Cuba. Excellent published documentation for the period may be found in Santiago Gerardo Suárez, *El ordenamiento militar de Indias* (Caracas: Biblioteca de la Academia Nacional de la Historia, 1971). This key source incorporates many documents from the reform era, including the famous Reglamento para las Milicias de Infantería y Caballería de las islas de Cuba, 1769, which influenced military formation throughout Spanish America. For numerous articles on military topics in Spanish and Portuguese America, see Academia Nacional de la Historia, Venezuela, *Memoria del tercer congreso venezolano de historia,* 3 vols. (Caracas: 1979).

For the late colonial period, there are three studies that detail aspects of military-urban relationships and offer detailed examination of the reform program in different provinces. Allan J. Kuethe, *Military and Society in New Granada, 1773–1808* (Gainesville, Fla.: University Presses of Florida, 1978) offers wideranging examples of urban-military rivalries and material on the pardo and moreno militias. Leon G. Campbell, *The Military and Society in Colonial Peru, 1750–1810* (Philadelphia: The American Philosophical Society, 1978) examines the question of military privilege in Peru and the involvement of the army in the rebellion of Tupac Amaru II. Christon I. Archer, *The Army in Bourbon Mexico, 1760–1810* (Albuquerque: University of New Mexico Press, 1977) deals with social themes and the relationship of the military to other sectors. For recent analysis, see Jorge I. Domínguez, *Insurrection or Loyalty: The Breakdown of the Spanish American Empire* (Cambridge: Harvard University Press, 1980), and Peggy K. Liss, *Atlantic Empires: The Network of Trade and Revolution, 1713–1826* (Baltimore: John Hopkins University Press, 1983). Useful documentation for the period may be found in Santiago Gerardo Suárez, *Las fuerzas armadas venezolanos en la colonia* (Caracas: Biblioteca de la Academia Nacional de la Historia, 1979).

EIGHT

Artisans

LYMAN JOHNSON

The European Background

At the time of the discovery and conquest of the New World, the artisan communities of Spain and Portugal had achieved a well-established place in urban society. In every major peninsular city, artisan trades were organized in self-governing guilds and *cofradías* (lay brotherhoods) with formal constitutions that regulated nearly every facet of individual and collective behavior, often in minute detail. Guilds were primarily economic institutions that established rules for the production and sale of goods. All matters related to recruitment, training and promotion, as well as working conditions and wages, were controlled by the guild. The cofradía, on the other hand, supervised religious activities and social welfare benefits.

The historical origins of these artisan organizations are obscure. Some historians have argued that the guild was a lineal descendant of an ancient Germanic social custom transmitted throughout Europe in the wake of the mass migrations that overwhelmed the late Roman Empire. Others have held that the self-regulating urban trades of the late Roman Empire were the organizational antecedents for later artisan craft development. The identification of the specific historical origins of the craft guild is not, however, a necessary precondition for understanding the corporate economic and social functions that evolved in the late medieval and early modern cities of Europe. The basic elements of the craft guild were found throughout a broad geographic area, and the guilds of Spain and Portugal were fundamentally similar to those of England, France, Italy, and Germany. We may speak with some confidence, then, of a widely dispersed European institution with only minor regional differences imposed by historical circumstances.

The authority of the craft guild originated in the delegation of regulative powers to master artisans by municipal authorities. The development of self-governing guilds and cofradías, therefore, was the direct outgrowth of increasing municipal authority and independence. Cities freed from feudal political authority provided the essential economic and social preconditions for the development of guilds, as well as their physical setting. In every city where guilds developed, the right to produce and sell manufactured goods was limited to guild members. The participants in each craft determined the criteria for guild membership, the requirements for promotion, the products that could be produced, prices, wages, and even, in some cases, the type and quality of clothing worn by the membership. The corporate ideal expressed through the guild was hostile to both competition and social differentiation, the dominant ideals of the later industrial era. Urban craft guilds worked effectively to inhibit innovations in technology and products because these kinds of changes would provoke competition and price cutting and would lead eventually to significant inequality of wealth among guild members. Guilds, then, were inherently conservative bodies dedicated to the preservation of inherited skills, standards, and the social status quo.

There was, however, an important hierarchical dimension of the European guild. Each trade was organized vertically in three ranks: masters, journeymen, and apprentices. Only master craftsmen could own shops and sell directly to the public. They were also the only members of the trade who could vote for and hold guild offices. Masters supervised the work of journeymen and apprentices and were solely responsible for promoting craftsmen from one level to the next. Guild constitutions prescribed a broad range of requirements for admission to the trade, admitting only Catholics and Spaniards, but individual masters were given discretion in the selection of their own apprentices.

Apprentices lived in their master's household, where they were initiated into the social and religious life of the craft as well as trained in job-related skills. Depending on the craft, apprentices graduated to journeyman status after two to six years, and thereafter operated as independent wage earners. Ideally, after an additional two- to four-year period, journeymen were eligible to be examined as masters. In order to become a master, however, a journeyman had to accumulate enough savings to pay the required examination fees, purchase tools and materials, and pay the rental on a shop, since masters were not allowed to accept employment as wage laborers.

As early as the fifteenth century a dangerously large proportion of journeymen in many trades were prevented from gaining the rank of master. Most of the obstacles that hindered the mobility of journeymen were imposed by powerful, wealthy master craftsmen who sought to enhance their own social status and earnings by reducing competition and creating a market monopoly for themselves. By imposing exorbitant examination fees and other financial requirements, they effectively closed the rank of master to all but a minority of journeymen—most commonly their own sons and nephews. This profit-maximizing self interest of individual masters led to increased inequality within artisan trades and undercut both the egalitarian ideology of the corporate tradition and the informal interpersonal bonds that served as the foundation of community life.

In European cities both guild regulations and municipal law operated to limit inequalities of wealth and power within skilled trades. However, it was the organization of the artisan workplace, with the master craftsman serving as both mentor and employer, and the social organization of the craft itself, with its emphasis on shared religious, ceremonial and social-welfare obligations, which provided European artisans with the strongest and most enduring sense of common purpose and worked most effectively to inhibit competitive tendencies. These organizational patterns, in turn, were reinforced by living arrangements and residential customs. Artisans in each craft tended to live and work in the same neighborhood, often on the same street. As a result they were in constant communication with each other both in and out of the workplace, frequenting the same commercial and recreational places, and even attending the same churches. Over time this communal style of life, lived in close proximity with workmates and competitors, produced a powerful secondary mechanism of intermarriage and *compadrazgo* (ritual co-parenthood) between participant artisan families.

The Conquest Period

The scant evidence available on the social origins of the conquerors and first settlers of colonial Latin America suggests that artisans were probably the largest single occupational group during this early period. The unsettled period of the Conquest provided a limited opportunity for a handful of ambitious and lucky artisans to demonstrate military and political abilities and to gain substantial material rewards. However, even during this period of exceptional social mobility artisans were unable to enter the highest levels of colonial society. Few artisans who participated in the Conquest had the military skills and experience that were prerequisites for leadership, and, more importantly, no Spanish noble, no matter how weak his claim to that status, would accept service as a subordinate to an artisan. There was a clear sense among the conquerors and early settlers that the social order of the Old World should not be challenged or threatened and that the basic Spanish class hierarchy should be reestablished in this new setting. Artisans were seen as valuable members of society, men with well-established and respected roles to play, but they were also seen generally as members of the lower orders without any claim to *hidalguía* (petty nobility).

In Peru artisans and other skilled workers constituted the largest occupational category among Pizarro's forces at Cajamarca, and many were rewarded with *encomiendas* (grants of Indians) and shares of the enormous booty seized after the defeat and capture of Atahualpa, the Inca ruler. The tailor Juan Chico was an example of this pattern. Born into an artisan family in Seville, Chico immigrated to the New World as a young man. As a reward for his participation in Pizarro's expedition, Chico received a small encomienda and later became one of the founders of the city of Lima. He lived in modest circumstances with an Indian mistress and apparently was involved in business dealings with another artisan veteran of the early military campaigns. He was killed in action during the Indian rebellion of 1536, and his estate was divided among his three *mestizo* (persons of Indian and white ancestry) children in Peru and his family in Spain.[1] Artisans like Chico who participated in the expeditions of Pizarro, Cortés, and the other Spanish leaders who located and defeated rich and populous Indian societies achieved substantial social mobility and lived out the remainder of their lives as marginal members of the new colonial elite. Their children, many of them mestizos, married into higher levels of colonial society and regularly claimed and used the honorific title of *don* or *doña* (gentleman or gentlewoman).

It would be an error, however, to see these cases as representative. Few of the hundreds of early military expeditions ended successfully, and it was more likely that artisan participants would die, often horrible deaths, chasing after elusive El Dorados. However, the artisans immigrating in the wake of these early adventures were seldom drawn directly into Indian wars and civil conflicts except as suppliers of arms, clothing, or other equipment. It was this second generation of Spanish immigrant artisans that transmitted European technology, European consumption patterns, and European corporate organization to the colonial cities of Spanish America.

The Establishment of Guilds

Spanish artisans in the New World moved quickly to organize their crafts and to seek a clear legal basis for the establishment of their traditional rights and privileges. The carpenters and masons of Lima, for example, elected guild officers and established an examination system in 1549. This was followed in 1560, by the creation of the cofradía of San José by another group of Lima artisans. In Mexico City the 1540s and 1550s witnessed substantial organizational efforts by artisans. Within 30 years of the Conquest, guilds were established by silkweavers, chain makers, cord makers, gilders, painters, and shoemakers. Even in secondary cities such as Guatemala City, shoemakers, blacksmiths, and smelters had organized themselves formally by 1548, and by 1580, at least seven additional artisan trades had created guilds.

These early efforts by artisans to gain legally enforceable guild powers were almost universally successful. The merchants, owners of large estates, and Spanish officials who dominated the municipal governments of the region accepted without question the ideal of social organization represented by guilds and cofradías, and actively sought the practical economic benefits that guilds seemed to offer. In some cases a *cabildo* or city council, initiated the effort to or ganize a guild in response to complaints of fraud or poor quality in a trade. This occurred, for example, in 1561, when the cabildo of Mexico City ordered the hatmakers to form a guild. This action was followed in 1592 by a city council initiative to create a guild of weavers. However, the evidence indicates clearly that the vast majority of guilds were organized by the artisans themselves.

Artisan guilds played a particularly significant role in the tumultuous years of the early colonial period, when the small European populations of the region were compelling a large, culturally diverse, and often hostile Indian population to accept a range of economic and political structures derived from European experience and practice. Craft guilds in New Spain and Peru functioned to organize and supervise large-scale Indian workforces in the early years, particularly in religious and municipal construction. In trades such as weaving, silver and goldsmithing, and apparel manufacture, where Indian craftsmen utilized distinct technologies to produce for Indian consumers, the early guild, with its traditional close supervision of production and training, was an effective vehicle for imposing European tastes and transmitting European technology.

In New Spain, Peru, and the other areas where Spaniards dominated urban-based, advanced Indian civilizations, the sixteenth century was a period of organizational and technological transition. This was particularly evident in artisanal manufacture. In these areas, Indian craftsmen, using indigenous materials and technologies, continued to service the needs of Indian consumers and, in many cases, competed directly with Spanish artisans. The evidence suggests that in New Spain many Indian crafts continued almost unchanged, except for the removal of explicit religious content, and were treated by Spanish political authorities as the equivalents of Spanish guilds. This was the case with the makers of feather robes, obsidian mirrors, cotton armor, and other traditional goods. More typically, however, Indians were drawn into European trades, learning new skills and mastering new technologies. Although white racism was a powerful force in colonial society, many of the early guilds permitted Indians to enter without restriction, and within a short period Indian master craftsmen were found among the painters, sculptors, silk weavers, glove makers, and many other artisan groups.

Guilds and Cofradías

Membership in a guild gave the individual artisan a recognized and respected place in urban society. It would not be an exaggeration, in fact, to say that this corporate identity often superseded such individual characteristics as ethnicity and even wealth. Guilds sometimes served as the basis for urban militia units, with guild officials serving as officers. Civic and religious participation in the colonial city tended to be organized and defined by an individual's corporate identity, and even the informal employment of leisure activities was likely to occur within the social boundaries of craft membership. Artisans helped organize and fund all of the numerous civic and religious processions and celebrations—sometimes including plays, fireworks, and music—that were so important to the residents of these preindustrial cities. Disputes over the costs of these public spectacles, however, could provoke bitter disputes within guilds and, on occasion, lead to law suits. Nevertheless, it is clear that the prominent participation in civic life by organized craftsmen helped to fix their place in the urban social structure. In some cases, artisans, particularly silversmiths, were actually given precedence over merchants and other wealthier groups in municipal celebrations.

The most important functions of the colonial craft guild, however, were associated with the actual production and sale of goods. Guild regulations stipulated the products that could be produced, the materials that could be used, and the price that could be charged. These requirements were enforced by elected officers who regularly inspected the shops of guild members. Failure to meet guild standards could result in fines, seizure of goods, and even the closure of a shop. In addition, guilds closely controlled recruitment, training, and employment practices. All apprenticeships were registered with guild officials who also fixed the length of the training period. Even the length of the work day and wage scales were set by the guild. In all cases where disputes arose between craftsmen, guild officers acted as mediators or, when necessary, as judges.

The cofradía organized the religious life of the artisan community. Typically, each craft formed a cofradía devoted to the veneration of a patron saint or saints. For silversmiths the patron was San Eloy, for tailors San Homobono, for dyers San Gabriel, for shoemakers San Crispián and San Crispiniano and so on. In a small number of cases, primarily in Mexico City, craftsmen in a single trade belonged to more than one cofradía. However, since cofradías, like guilds, were sustained by membership dues and fees, few artisan groups were wealthy enough to create more than a single religious brotherhood. Cofradía members maintained an altar devoted to the veneration of their patron saint in a parish church, provided compensation for a priest, and arranged and paid for the funeral services and burials of members. This final function was of real importance in the devout Catholic societies of Spanish and Portuguese America. It meant that every member, regardless of his material circumstances and social origins, was buried with great dignity and provided with memorial masses. Following funerals, cofradías even provided alms for beggars at the church door.

Cofradías also functioned as mutual benefit societies. Commonly, these lay brotherhoods provided small amounts of financial assistance for the widows and orphans of deceased members. Sick and disabled artisans could also expect regular, if limited, assistance for medical care and medicines. Guilds also contributed to this safety net of benefits. One of the most common provisions of guild regulations was the absolute prohibition of shops owned by anyone but documented master craftsmen. In virtually every surviving guild regulation, however, widows of masters were exempted from this prohibition. In most guilds, a journeyman who married the widow of a master was promoted preferentially to master, paying reduced examination fees, and often receiving exemption from some probationary service. From the perspective of the twentieth century, these benefits may appear meager indeed, but for the artisan of colonial Latin America they were powerful inducements to support and sustain these cooperative institutions. The alternative, experienced by the majority of unorganized urban workers in colonial Latin America who became ill or disabled, was impoverishment and the degradation of begging.

These features of artisan life were developed most completely and dispersed most widely in a handful of large colonial cities—Mexico City, Lima, Guatemala City, Puebla, and Potosí among others. In these places most artisan trades were formally organized in guilds and cofradías. But the majority of colonial Latin America's artisans lived and worked in smaller cities and towns where this formal institutional apparatus was much less developed. In fact, substantial and important colonial cities, like Buenos Aires and Bogotá, had no legally recognized guilds until the eighteenth century, and, in the case of Buenos Aires, these late developing guilds were weak and ineffective. Nevertheless, many essential features of the European artisanal tradition were practiced and defended in these smaller cities, despite the absence of legally sanctioned guilds.

In those cities where guilds were not formally organized, artisans maintained the basic hierarchical structure of the European craft tradition. Parents, guardians, or the state itself, in the case of orphans, regularly placed young boys as apprentices with master artisans. Formal contracts, registered with a notary, stipulated the obligations of both parties and set the length of service, as was the case where guilds existed. Although some journeymen and even some apprentices took advantage of the absence of enforceable guild regulations by opening shops without having passed through the traditional crucible of the examination process, it is striking that the examination system, with all its costs and rigors, remained a central feature of artisan life.

The survival of these two characteristics of the artisan tradition—apprenticeship and the examination system—provides a useful illustration of the essential social differences between artisanal and industrial manufacture. Unlike modern industrial workers, colonial artisans lived and worked in a world where prestige and status were primarily a function of recognized skills, not personal income. Artisans in each trade knew concretely the skills and abilities of their peers. Most, in fact, could identify the maker of a given product

234 / Lyman Johnson

without close examination. This is not to suggest that material success, wealth, was of no concern to colonial artisans. The history of the artisan class is filled with examples of clever and resourceful artisans who acquired substantial wealth. Nevertheless, demonstrated practical skill remained the central measure of a man's worth within the most meaningful social reference group, the craft itself. Artisans, therefore, strove willingly to meet the traditional standards of achievement developed in Europe, despite the absence of enforceable guild regulations in many cases.

The small scale of the colonial marketplace, the result primarily of great inequality of income, reinforced these culturally based tendencies. Particularly in the sixteenth century, urban artisans in Latin America served the needs of a small number of Europeans and a small, but growing, population of Europeanized Indians, mestizos and blacks. Although the size of the colonial market increased substantially during the colonial period, artisan manufacturers in the region seldom had access to the mass markets that are a necessary precondition for the specialization of task and economies of scale associated with the factory system. Small scale production for largely inelastic markets was an ideal economic environment for the development and maintenance of artisan production, since the individual master working with hand tools potentially could sustain the entire production process alone. Although most masters took on apprentices and hired journeymen, the master artisan rightfully saw his own skills, not his capital, organizational ability, or entrepreneurial sophistication, as his primary resource and most valuable asset.

Wealth and Social Status

The artisan guilds of Europe and colonial Latin America were organized in a hierarchical structure of presumed prestige and wealth. This order was largely based on the market value of the raw materials used in the product or process. Gold and silversmiths were generally viewed as the aristocrats of the artisan community and commonly had the right to carry swords. In Spain participation in these prestigious trades was not incompatable with the claim of *hidalgo* (gentleman) status. Others skilled at working with precious stones and metals—gem cutters, jewelers, and gilders, among others—also enjoyed high status and often high income. Among artisans in the textile trades, the largest group of skilled craftsmen, had a similar hierarchy. Craftsmen who worked with silk, both weavers and tailors, had more prestige and generally higher incomes than those men and women who worked with wool or linen.

This presumption of greater merit and wealth was recognized in the public parades and festivals that marked the numerous religious and secular holidays in European, and later colonial Latin American, cities. Traditionally, artisans in the precious metal crafts were given precedence, marching at the front of parades or being seated before the representatives of other less respected artisan groups. In the New World these social presumptions and hierarchical structures were put in place at the same time as the establishment of guilds. Because of the abundance of silver and gold in the American colonies, silversmiths and goldsmiths dominated both the secular and religious life of urban artisan communities. The excessive opulence of the costumes, fireworks, plays, and pageants of the silversmith guild of Mexico City and Lima were noted with wonder by European visitors. Even in smaller cities like Buenos Aires and Guatemala City where economic resources were less abundant, the members of these crafts felt compelled to imitate the style and level of public display and the lavish expenditure found in the wealthiest cities. The result of these competitive pressures was often lawsuits and sometimes violence when bills were called due.

It is not clear if this social hierarchy sustained by both custom and law reflected the actual distribution of wealth among artisan groups. Although we simply lack any systematic studies of wealth holding and income, the evidence that does exist suggests that the colonial economic reality was complex and unpredictable. Wage data from Buenos Aires, the only colonial city for which we have documentation, indicate that daily wages in the building trades were higher than those in more respected and prestigious trades. Journeymen in the shipbuilding trades, for example, were the highest paid workers in the city. This evidence suggests that market forces, rather than prestige or legal preferment, actually determined the income levels in the skilled trades. Probate records, especially the inventories of goods that were a standard part of the judicial supervision of inheritance, are in general agreement with the wage data. The estates of carpenters, blacksmiths, and other craftsmen in little-respected outdoor trades were often larger than those of silversmiths, tailors, and other artisans in the more prestigious indoor trades. This does not seem to have been the case in Mexico City and Lima where wealth was concentrated in the traditional elite trades. There may have been a connection between the political strength of guilds and the survival of the economic advantages of these traditional elite crafts. Guilds were strongest in the oldest viceregal capitals, those cities where the correlation of social prestige and actual economic advantage were most clear. In the smaller cities of the region, guilds seldom had formal legal sanction. It is in these cities that evidence of market factors disrupting the inherited hierarchical order is the most obvious.

Without strong guild controls, the economic success of skilled workers was determined largely by individual characteristics, such as skill, initiative, creativity, and access to capital, rather than by membership in a specific craft organization. Ambitious artisans formed speculative partnerships with other craftsmen or, commonly, with merchants to purchase raw materials, buy slaves, or pursue commercial ventures. The most successful and wealthiest artisans in colonial Latin America were those with the most diversified investments.

The essential precondition for this form of economic activity was access to investment capital, either in the form of personal savings or loans. In the competition for capital, Spanish-born artisans had an important advantage over their American-born competitors because they could rely on their personal connections with wealthy immigrants from their native cities. These old country loyalties and friendships were commonly noted in the contracts that formalized the limited partnerships and loan agreements that initiated artisan enterprise. (See Figure 18.)

Nevertheless, the vast majority of the region's artisans were poor. They did not suffer the terrible privations of urban unskilled workers, but the general income levels throughout the region were low. The most successful master craftsmen in colonial Latin America had incomes that were comparable with those earned by the lower level officials of the bureaucracy and military. Less successful masters and the vast majority of journeymen lived close to the subsistence level, earning relatively high wages during periods of peak demand and then surviving on their meager savings during periods of economic contraction. For workers in the outdoor trades, carpenters, masons, and others, there was an important seasonal character to their earnings. For these men and their families, the winter brought high food prices, reduced wages, and long periods of unemployment.

The reduced prestige and less predictable earnings of artisans in the colonial environment reduced the loyalty of artisans to their trades and promoted the open pursuit of social mobility. In Europe, the sons of master craftsmen commonly followed their fathers into the guild. In the cities of colonial Latin America, however, there was a clear tendency for the sons of the most successful artisans to seek careers in the professions, especially in the church and, in the eighteenth century, in the military. Intergenerational participation in artisan crafts was most visible among the less successful sectors of this class. The wealthiest members of the urban guilds sought to diversify their investments, to participate in wholesale trade, and to propel their children toward a life outside the artisan community. Poorer artisans, mostly the native-born or the nonwhite, struggled within the traditional structures of artisan production and left their children little more than the increasingly devalued legacy of the craft tradition and guild membership.

The Issue of Race

As noted previously, urban artisan trades in Latin America were also mechanisms of economic domination and cultural assimilation in the colonial period. In the years immediately following the Conquest, European artisans in the building trades trained and supervised masses of Indian laborers in both private and public sector construction. Even in the apparel trades, the manufacture of metal tools and weapons, and the production of luxury goods, Spanish artisans, along with a small number of immigrants from Italy, France, and the Low Countries, recruited and trained Indian apprentices, and, as a result, Indian masters became an important component in many trades. This process of integration was promoted and encouraged both by colonial municipalities seeking to expand the production of European goods and by imperial law which sought legal equality between Indians and Europeans.

By the end of the sixteenth century, the colonial racial situation had been transformed. Epidemic diseases took a frightful toll among Indian populations located near Spanish cities. Intermarriage, concubinage, and less formal arrangements between Spanish males and Indian females, produced a substantial and rapidly growing racially-mixed population within a generation. This racial class was not protected from formal discrimination by Spanish colonial law and quickly came to be treated by Spaniards as an inferior racial caste. As a result, in Meso-America and the Andean zone, mestizos came to constitute an urban under-class, culturally as well as racially separated from both Indian and European society. While early guild regulations in Mexico City, Puebla, and other cities permitted full participation by Indians, nearly every guild in Spanish America imposed discriminatory limits on the participation of mestizos. Some artisans barred mestizos completely from participation in their guilds. More commonly, however, European artisans prohibited mestizos from gaining the rank of master, thereby barring the members of this increasingly large and important racial group from any role in the political life of the guild and from independent ownership of shops.

In the cities of the Spanish Caribbean, in the tropical coastal zones surrounding this basin, and in regions with smaller, less urbanized Indian populations, such as southern South America and Brazil, colonial urban economies came to depend on the labor of black slaves at an early date. African slaves, their American-born offspring and the racially-mixed population of African descent (*mulatos*), were specifically excluded from the legal protections against discrimination afforded Indians. As a result, virtually every guild constitution produced in colonial Latin America contained discriminatory provisions that excluded blacks completely from participation in the craft or restricted them to lower craft ranks. Even in those trades where blacks were admitted freely, black artisans were subjected to a broad range of humiliating requirements that segregated them at meetings, placed them at the end of processions and parades, and even excluded them from cofradías. These forms of discrimination were rooted in the generally held racial attitudes of the European population of colonial Latin America and sustained by the concrete economic advantages that white artisans derived from restricting black competition in the marketplace.

In addition to the economic advantages associated with eliminating possible competition from black artisans and assuring high prices for their own products, white artisans sought also to achieve less tangible benefits of social status by maintaining a clear racial and cultural linkage between themselves and the exclusively European groups that controlled colonial society politically and economically. Immigrant white artisans realized, correctly, that the unrestricted racial integration of their social and economic organizations would lead to a general decline in the perceived social status of all craftsmen, since the society's elite would assume that work which could be done by presumed racial inferiors was itself unworthy of respect. In the fast growing cities of sixteenth- and seventeenth-century Latin America, where the status hierarchy was essentially the result of the Conquest and the slave trade, racial categories became shorthand mechanisms for allocating social status. European artisans, many of whom were quite poor, defended segregated guilds and cofradías as the most effective means of protecting their own status as full participants in urban life. Would it be possible for racially integrated crafts which included large numbers of slaves to maintain traditional corporate rights and practices within the colonial social order? The white leadership of the early guilds realized that the answer was no.

Yet, despite these powerful economic and social reasons for instituting a system of racial exclusion and discrimination, the artisan trades of colonial Latin America were integrated within a generation. Not only did Indians, blacks, and racially mixed groups enter artisan trades in large numbers, but members of these groups also succeeded in gaining the statutorily restricted rank of master. In many of the region's cities, in fact, nonwhite craftsmen represented a majority of the artisan work force by the middle of the eighteenth century. Even among master craftsmen the evidence suggests that nonwhites, with blacks being the largest group, came to constitute a substantial minority in most trades and a majority in some, the construction trades in particular.

It would be a gross misrepresentation of colonial social reality to suggest that these changes in the racial characteristics of artisan trades meant that racism and discrimination had been overcome. Race remained a volatile and divisive force in Latin American society throughout the colonial period and remains so today. White racism and repeated efforts by European artisans to impose and perpetuate racially discriminatory regulations, laws, and less formal arrangements provoked numerous conflicts with black craftsmen throughout the colonial period, and ended by undermining the basic institutional structures of class solidarity—guilds and cofradías. However, while the integration of industrial production and the development of a large class of free black craftsmen were successfully prevented in colonial North American cities by legal barriers, in Latin American cities the artisan crafts became the most accessible and dependable mechanism of social mobility for ambitious black families.

The development of a racially-mixed artisan class was the result of both market conditions and labor demands in the cities of colonial Latin America. Although thousands of Spanish and other European artisans immigrated to the Americas, the region experienced a chronic shortage of skilled labor through-out the colonial period. The inability of European immigrants to meet the demand for artisan-produced goods and services compelled the recruitment, training, and utilization of slave operatives. This process began early with the first skilled black slaves brought to the New World by the conquerors themselves. The Spanish crown and many of the religious orders drawn to the New World by the early evangelical effort contributed to the integration of the workforce by sending slave artisans to participate in the construction of churches, governmental buildings, and fortifications.

The role of black artisans in urban Peru during the early colonial period is known in some detail and is typical of Spanish America. Four of the six brick-layers hired to build the royal mint in Lima in 1569, were black, and the highest-paid bricklayer on this job was a slave. Black slaves were also used to construct many other early public works projects in Lima. In 1606, for ex-ample, the city purchased 18 slaves to help reconstruct a bridge destroyed by an earthquake. As early as 1543, the Spanish crown sent slaves from Spain to aid in the construction of Dominican monasteries.[2] The evidence suggests that in virtually every public and religious construction project in Peru dur-ing these early years, slaves, some of them skilled artisans sent directly from Spain, provided much of the labor.

In sixteenth-century Mexico black artisans played a similar role. As was true for Peru, virtually all of the early guild constitutions in New Spain ex-cluded both slaves and black freedmen from membership. Yet the evidence of black participation in all but a handful of artisan trades is overwhelming. Black slaves worked alongside white artisans in construction, weaving, and other apparel trades. Slaves also were commonly found in the metal-working trades, although silver and goldsmiths effectively maintained a color line. In some trades, including that of the tanners of Mexico City in 1565, for exam-ple, the level of black participation eventually compelled the reformulation of guild regulations to recognize legally the existence of black apprentices, journeymen, and even, masters.

Slave Artisans

Given the acute shortage of skilled free labor in these colonial cities, mar-ket conditions drove up labor costs, and the region experienced a chronic scarcity of artisan-produced goods and services. The use of slave labor, there-fore, proved to be a profitable expedient for meeting urban demand for labor at a price that these colonial societies could afford. Slaves, even skilled slaves sent from Spain, were comparatively inexpensive given their earning poten-tial in the labor-short New World. Scholars who recently examined the wages paid to skilled slaves and their initial purchase prices suggest that, on the average, the owners of slave artisans recovered their initial investments in less than two years. The purchase of a skilled slave from Spain or Portugal, or the purchase and training of a slave brought from Africa was an excellent investment. Within 50 years of the Conquest ownership of artisan slaves had become common among royal officials, churchmen, merchants, and, increasingly, among artisans themselves. By the middle of the seventeenth century a majority of the slaves working in the skilled trades in colonial Latin America were owned by white artisans.

Because of the small number of young European males resident in colonial cities, there was no prospect of attracting adequate numbers of free apprentices into artisan trades. European craftsmen turned quickly to the purchase and training of slave apprentices. A master artisan who purchased a slave was virtually assured of a profitable return on his investment unless death, incapacitation, or escape deprived him of the slave's labor. As was the case with free apprentices, master craftsmen earned as profit the difference between the cost of the slave's subsistence and the value of his production. As the slave's skills improved, the owner's profit increased as well. The artisan who owned a skilled slave was able further to capitalize his investment in the development of the slave's skills by offering him for sale. Since there was a constant market demand for skilled slaves in these colonial cities, many artisans found the training and sale of slaves a profitable supplement to their regular business activities. Analysis of the average prices paid for young, unskilled African slaves and for skilled slave artisans suggests that profits of 200 or 300 percent were not uncommon, even after the costs of the slave's maintenance were subtracted.

The use of slave labor also gave master artisans greater control of the workplace. Guilds established and enforced regulations that covered the wages, hours, and working conditions of free apprentices and journeymen. Slaves, on the other hand, were virtually unprotected by these regulations. Generally speaking, slaves worked longer hours at more arduous tasks for fewer material rewards than did free artisans. The result, of course, was greater profit for the artisan slave owner. However, the most important advantage of slave labor to the master artisan was its greater adaptability to new methods of organization. Both guild regulations and the self-interest of free journeymen operated to prevent the development of the factory system in colonial Latin America. The essential characteristics of the factory system—the subdivision and specialization of the production process—led inevitably to the deterioration of worker skills and the loss of independence and mobility. Free journeymen and apprentices naturally opposed these outcomes. By using slaves instead of free workers, some master artisans were able to introduce these unpopular characteristics of factory production and to profit from the lowered labor costs and increased productivity. As a result, the use of large slave work forces, organized on the factory model, became common in the traditional artisan trades of baking, textiles, metallurgy, and construction. In those trades, where slaves were used in large numbers, the number of free apprentices and journeymen declined precipitously, thus suggesting that, at least in some trades, slave labor was both productive and more cost-effective.

Black Freedmen in the Artisan Trades

The growth of a large class of free black artisans in colonial Latin America resulted in large part from the common practice of hiring out skilled slaves. Owners of slave artisans routinely hired out their slaves on a daily or longer-term basis. In many cases, owners allowed their slaves to seek employment on their own, requiring only that the slave turn over a fixed cash payment on a weekly or monthly basis. Regardless of the specifics of these labor practices, the result was that skilled slaves commonly earned cash wages, and, in many cases, accumulated savings. Spanish law and common colonial practice recognized the right of a slave to purchase his or her freedom—even providing a process of judicial arbitration to set a fair price when master and slave failed to reach agreement. Because of their greater earnings, slave artisans and their families were the most likely segment of the urban slave population to gain freedom through manumission.

The growth of a free black artisan class was also promoted by the clear tendency of black families, slave and free, to place their sons in artisan trades. For free black families confronting an enormous array of legal and informal discriminations, the skilled trades offered the highest wages and the most reliable employment opportunities, as well as the greatest prestige available to them. Since the professions, government service, and the church were racially restricted, the leadership of the colonial black community was provided by artisans. Because they feared that mixing with blacks would undermine their social status, white families were less likely to apprentice their sons as black participation in artisan trades increased. These fears, the natural result of the inherent racism of these colonial societies, operated to create even more opportunities for blacks in the skilled trades. As a result, by the end of the colonial period free blacks and other *castas* (persons of mixed racial ancestry) provided the largest single pool for artisan recruitment in most of the region's cities.

Free black artisans seldom held offices in guilds or in artisan cofradías, other than in racially segregated institutions. Although the surviving evidence has not been studied systematically, it also appears that free black artisans were generally poorer than their white competitors. A number of factors contributed to this inequality of wealth. Many black males in skilled trades were forced to commit a significant part of their savings to purchase freedom for themselves and their families. This expensive process decreased their capital and limited their ability to expand their businesses or pursue other investments. In addition, black artisans found it difficult to borrow money for expansion or diversification. For credit needs, white artisans could rely on kinsmen, personal contacts with other immigrants from their home communities, and other mechanisms denied to black competitors. Without access to credit, black artisans were restricted to small-scale, less profitable production. Finally, black artisans found it difficult to overcome the economic impact of white racism. In nearly every craft, wealthy consumers, particularly the immigrant-dominated elites of church, state, and commerce, preferred to trade with European artisans. Although some black artisans gained clients among the urban elite, this presumption of superior European skills drove black artisans toward the less profitable mass market and thereby limited their earnings.

Brazil

The Brazilian case was generally similar to that of Spanish America. There were, however, two differences in organization and recruitment that separated the Brazilian artisan trades from those found in the major cities of Spanish America. First, and most importantly, guilds were institutionally much weaker in the cities of colonial Brazil. There were fewer guilds and those guilds that were established in Rio de Janeiro, Recife, or Bahia lacked both the wealth and political power commonly found in Spanish colonial cities of comparable importance, such as Mexico City or Lima. Second, from the earliest years, there was a greater reliance on slave labor in the skilled trades of colonial Brazil. As was generally true in Spanish America, the wealthiest and most influential artisans in Brazil were immigrants from the European metropolis. However, there were proportionally fewer immigrant artisans in Brazil, and these white master craftsmen relied much more completely on slave labor than did their Spanish American contemporaries. The development of slave-based artisanal production was further promoted by the greater supply and lower prices of slaves in Brazil and by the absence of compatible artisan skills in the indigenous population.

Toward the end of the colonial period, free blacks began to replace slaves in the artisan workforce of most Brazilian cities. As was true in Spanish colonial cities, the growth of a free black artisanate was fueled by the high wages earned by skilled slaves and by the hiring out system. In fact, blacks predominated numerically in Brazil even in trades that legally were reserved for whites. As one royal judge in Pernambuco noted, "(there are an) excessive number of artisan goldsmiths and silversmiths who exist in Olinda, Recife and other places, the majority of them being mulatos and Negroes, and even some being slaves, which is against the law and results in great damage to the republic."[3] In Brazil, as in Spanish America, royal laws, discriminatory guild regulations, and white prejudices failed to prevent the racial integration of the artisan workforce. Inadequate levels of artisan immigration from Portugal resulted in unacceptable skilled labor costs, promoted the widespread use of slave labor, and led ultimately to the rise of a free black artisan class.

Women in Artisan Trades

There is abundant documentary evidence that women played an important role in the urban artisan industries of colonial Latin America. Indian women were actively involved in the production of textiles, ceramics, and other products before the Conquest and continued to dominate many of these fields throughout the colonial period, particularly in the Andean area. Certainly the production of rough quality, inexpensive cloth for the colonial mass market remained the domain of female weavers until the advent of cheap, machine-made textile imports from Europe in the nineteenth century. In sixteenth-century Mexico women organized and maintained guilds in a number of textile trades—silk weavers, cotton weavers, and wool weavers. Mexican women, mostly Indians and castas, also founded guilds in some food processing trades—sweet makers and pastry makers—and in apparel production—hat decorators, belt makers, and comb makers. This process of organization continued to the end of the colonial period, with women silk-spinners organizing their own guild in 1788, with 23 masters, 200 journeymen, and 21 apprentices. These guilds of female artisans were organizationally and functionally similar to male guilds in other trades, having both written constitutions and elected officers.

In New Spain, Central America, and Peru in the eighteenth century, textile production was dominated increasingly by *obrajes,* large-scale factories or workshops, owned by merchants or other capitalists. Obrajes utilized slaves, prisoners from local jails, and other bound workers, as well as traditional free female labor. Although the obrajes were largely unmechanized, they were nevertheless able to produce textiles more cheaply than their artisan competitors as a result of economies of scale and lower labor costs. Unable to compete successfully with the obrajes, the number of both male and female weavers in organized guilds declined steadily at the end of the colonial period.

There were also a small number of colonial artisan trades that admitted both men and women. Gender-integrated guilds were organized in pottery production, tobacco processing, and the production of some specialized footwear. Little is known about these guilds or the men and women who joined them, but adequate numbers of references to them have survived for colonial Mexico to suggest that this pattern was not uncommon. We can only wonder, however, whether female artisans in these trades held guild office, became masters, or owned their own shops.

Widows, wives, and daughters of male artisans commonly were involved in the production and sale of goods. Most artisan shops in colonial Latin America were small-scale affairs that barely produced enough income to maintain the artisan's family and to replace his materials and tools. Many master craftsmen were unable to bear the cost of an apprentice or hire journeymen on a regular basis. For them the labor of family members was often the difference between profit and loss. Wives and children helped prepare materials, waited on customers, and delivered finished goods. In some cases wives and daughters became skilled assistants, even though they had no direct link with a guild and received little recognition or compensation. Artisanal production, in this sense, was family production—the manufacturing equivalent of the family farm.

Widows of master artisans usually were permitted to continue their husband's business until they remarried or their male children reached majority. Commonly widows hired one or more journeymen to run their shop, although it was not uncommon for a widow to undertake direct supervision of both the production and sale of goods. If the widow of an artisan remarried, she lost this privilege unless her new husband was also a guild member. This was not a likely event since there were compelling reasons for remarrying within the trade. Given the severe poverty of this class, the husband's tools, materials, and customers were likely to be his only substantial material legacy. It made sense, therefore, to marry someone who would use these resources to earn an income. For a single or widowed journeyman, the widow of a master artisan was an attractive match, since she brought to the match her first husband's capital, tools, supplies, and preferential access to the guild's examination procedure as the equivalent of a dowry. These same factors influenced the selection of marriage partners for the daughters of artisans. Marriage to someone in her father's trade allowed the daughter of an artisan to maximize her share of her father's estate, while providing her husband with an ally in guild affairs and potential partner in business. In most cities of colonial Latin America, therefore, these marriage patterns produced tight-knit, interrelated artisan communities characterized by a close reciprocity between family life and economic activity.

Eighteenth-Century Social and Economic Change

Artisan corporations in colonial Latin America, with the exception of the guilds of Mexico City and Lima, failed to attain the political influence, wealth, and social status that were common in Europe. The relative institutional weakness of the colonial artisan class was the inevitable result of the structural weakness of the colonial marketplace. Every city in the region required a range of artisan-produced goods and services similar to that required in a contemporary European city of comparative size. Generally speaking, however, Latin American urban demand was shallow and unpredictable in comparison with European demand. The largest cities in the region, viceregal capitals and mining centers, had populations that were large enough and wealthy enough to provide artisans with a dependable, expansive marketplace during much of the colonial period. These are the cities where guilds and cofradías were most successful. In most of the other cities and towns of colonial Latin America, however, artisans primarily serviced the needs of a relatively small class of urban residents with disposable income beyond subsistence needs—colonial officials, churchmen, professionals, and landowners. The pervasive poverty of the urban masses and the slow rate of growth of the colonial economy were, therefore, major obstacles to the development of artisan production and artisan institutions during much of the colonial period.

These conditions changed significantly during the eighteenth century. Although confronted with short term contractions, the colonial economies of Latin America experienced sustained economic growth, beginning in the last decade of the seventeenth century and lasting until the trans-Atlantic trade disruptions provoked by European wars in 1796. A number of factors contributed to this economic resurgence: expanded colonial silver production, population growth (both by natural increase and by immigration), fiscal and administrative reform, and a dramatic increase in colonial spending on the part of the Spanish crown. Although colonial artisans were not the major beneficiaries of this economic expansion, the demand for artisan goods and services did increase throughout the region.

The improved economic conditions of the eighteenth century accelerated the process of structural change in artisan production. Because guilds were generally ineffective in maintaining internal discipline and work rules, many master artisans responded to growing consumer demands by using slaves and other nontraditional laborers. They became, in effect, obraje owners rather than artisan producers. The best known example of this tendency is textile production in Puebla and Querétaro. This process clearly undermined the traditional cooperative and egalitarian values of the artisan community and tended to devalue the skills of journeymen and apprentices.

In addition, many artisans began to cross traditional craft boundary lines in order to gain maximum benefits from changing consumption patterns. There were silversmiths who manufactured clocks, bakers who traded in imported textiles, carpenters who owned slaves producing boots for the Spanish military, and at least one tailor in Buenos Aires who raised mules for the mines of Upper Peru.

Generally speaking, the most successful artisans of the late colonial period were individuals who had put some distance between themselves and their trades. In the expanding late colonial marketplace, access to credit and a flexible, inexpensive labor force were more important predictors of material success than were the individual skills and corporate institutions associated with traditional artisan life.

One of the inevitable results of this process was the redefinition of social mobility and achievement among artisans. The idea of social mobility, although present, was not central to the corporate tradition. As colonial Latin America moved rapidly toward a class-based social order in the eighteenth century, successful artisans sought and in some cases achieved types of social recognition that would have been impossible in the old order. Wealthy artisans endowed charities, sought memberships, along with merchants and bureaucrats, in prestigious cofradías, and sent their sons into higher status careers in the military and the church. With the reorganization and expansion of colonial militias during the reign of Charles III, artisans were often successful in becoming officers, thereby gaining the *fuero militar* (corporate privileges granted to the military). Both the personal achievement of improved social status and the intergenerational achievement of familial social mobility through the education of children were accomplished, however, by the artisan and his family self-consciously separating themselves from the workshop and from the communal elements of artisan culture. One important consequence of this process was the decline of support for guilds and other traditional artisan institutions on the part of the wealthiest, most successful segment of the artisan community.

The rise of this small class of artisan-entrepreneurs occurred reciprocally with a decline in the status and economic well being of the majority of the region's artisans. In Buenos Aires, one of the most economically expansive cities in the late colonial period, the daily wages of most bricklayers and carpenters failed to keep pace with increased food and housing costs. As a result, artisans, including middle-aged journeymen, commonly lived in barracks-like apartments or in makeshift accommodations where they also worked. Relatively low wages and unstable working conditions affected both traditional marriage and family patterns. Many artisans deferred marriage until their mid- to late-twenties, while a substantial minority remained single. Another common response to limited opportunities was migration. In the colonial period it appears that both single and married artisans regularly moved from city to city seeking improved opportunities and better working conditions. Clearly the geographic mobility of the artisan workforce further undercut traditional class bonds—both personal and institutional—and reduced the shared experiences and communal consciousness that were the essential underpinnings of the corporate tradition.

The general weakness of the artisan sector in Spanish America provoked a number of reform efforts in the eighteenth century. In most cases these reform efforts were promoted by royal officials, although some city councils provided reform initiatives. These reform efforts were generally conservative in intent, seeking to create or reinvigorate artisan guilds. In Buenos Aires, a viceregal capital after 1776, Viceroy Vértiz ordered in 1780, that each craft organize a guild. As a result both the shoemakers and silversmiths organized guilds and submitted regulations for royal approval. Similar efforts occurred throughout Spain's American colonies. For example, José de Gálvez during his famous inspection visit to New Spain, ordered the bakers of Mexico City in 1773, to organize a guild in order to reduce fraud and improve bread quality. These efforts were seconded by local groups who sought to promote economic development. One of the most ambitious examples of this type of local initiative was the effort to reform and reorganize the guilds of the district of Guatemala by introducing new skills and new industries.

Nearly all these efforts to revitalize the guilds of Spanish American ended in failure. Racial and ethnic rivalries within the artisan class made it virtually impossible to gain internal agreement on either political or economic issues. Black artisans feared, with some justification, that proposals to improve standards and supervise business practices were, in fact, efforts to give white artisans effective control of the marketplace. Wealthy artisans who crossed successfully from one craft to another or operated obrajes using bound labor, were unenthusiastic about the development of more effective guilds that would restrict and control their activities and, as a result, withheld their support of guild reform.

Without a broad base of support in the artisan trades, the colonial reformers who sought to strengthen the guild system institutionally found it increasingly difficult to resist the arguments of a small but influential faction of Spanish and creole critics who argued for the complete abolition of guilds. These supporters of economic liberalism viewed guilds as obstacles to both individual freedom and work force productivity. Although the promoters of this ideology seldom dominated policy implementation during the colonial period, they did gain an occasional victory. In Buenos Aires in 1799, for example, the liberal-dominated city council refused to certify the constitution of the shoemakers' guild that had been created in response to the initiative of a reforming viceroy. In a pristine statement of liberal political economy, the city council condemned guilds as obstacles to personal freedom and economic development. By the end of the independence period in 1825, most efforts to reform and strengthen guilds had been abandoned in Latin America and most of the region's new republics abolished or restricted guilds.

Post-script

The nearly complete triumph of the supporters of economic liberalism after independence opened colonial Latin America to direct trade with the industrializing nations of Western Europe. Tariffs were generally reduced and exports were promoted. European machine-made imports, especially textiles, were often less expensive in Latin American cities than domestically produced artisan goods. Cheaper production costs that resulted from mechanization, reduced transportation costs, and reduced credit costs gave European goods insuperable advantages. The political decision to abolish guilds after independence was therefore little more than the recognition of this massive change in the Atlantic marketplace.

Unable to compete for the mass market or, increasingly, for the luxury goods market with European factories, Latin American artisans survived in the national period only in those industries that were naturally protected from import competition—construction, food processing, and repair and maintenance. The collapse of the artisan marketplace and the loss of the institutional basis for collective political and social action, the guild, accelerated the loss of social status and the decline in material well-being throughout Latin America. The rise of mechanized factories also contributed to the decline of craft guilds and the destruction of the artisan mode of production in Europe as well. However, the stronger institutional and social bases of the European artisan community provided working men and women with a better foundation for organization and resistence to factory discipline and devalued skills. As a result the European union movement grew directly out of the craft tradition, building on the militancy and class consciousness of the artisan workforce. In Latin America, the relatively weak artisan institutions of the colonial period provided an inadequate base for the effective organization of a modern working class consciousness. As a result, the union movement in Latin America is unconnected to the colonial artisan experience. Instead the effort to organize a union movement and the intellectual justification for this struggle flowed to Latin America from Europe with immigrants who arrived in the region after 1850.

Notes

1. James Lockhart, *The Men of Cajamarca: A Social and Biographical Study of the First Conquerors of Peru* (Austin, Tex.: University of Texas Press, 1972), 373–74.

2. Frederick Bowser, *The African Slave in Colonial Peru: 1524–1650* (Stanford: Stanford University Press, 1974), 127, 129, 130.

3. Herbert S. Klein, "Nineteenth-Century Brazil," in David W. Cohen and Jack P. Greene, eds., *Neither Slave Nor Free: The Freedmen of African Descent in the Slave Societies of the New World* (Baltimore: Johns Hopkins University Press, 1972), 309–34.

For Further Reading

Although there is a scarcity of materials in English on Latin American artisans, some work has begun to appear. Chapter VI of James Lockhart, *Spanish Peru, 1532–1560* (Madison, Wis.: University of Wisconsin Press, 1968) discusses artisans. See also Lyman L. Johnson, "The Artisans of Buenos Aires during the Viceroyalty, 1776–1810" (Ph.D. diss., University of Connecticut, 1974). For specific artisan groups, see Lyman L. Johnson, "The Silversmiths of Buenos Aires: A Case Study in the Failure of Corporate Social Organization," *Journal of Latin American Studies* 8:2 (November 1976): 181–213, and Lyman L. Johnson, "The Entrepreneurial Reorganization of an Artisan Trade: The Bakers of Buenos Aires, 1770–1820," *Americas* 32:2 (October 1980): 139–60.

One of the best discussions of black artisans is found in Frederick Bowser, *The African Slave in Colonial Peru, 1684–1750,* (Stanford: Stanford University Press, 1974). See also Lyman L. Johnson, "The Impact of Racial Discrimination on Black Artisans in Colonial Buenos Aires," *Social History* 6:3 (October 1981): 301–16. The best general study of the larger issues of racism and discrimination is Leslie B. Rout, Jr., *The African Experience in Spanish America* (Cambridge: At the University Press, 1976).

Among the work available in Spanish is Manuel Carrera Stampa, *Los gremios mexicanos* (Mexico City: Instituto Nacional de Antropología y Historia, 1954). The same author also has published "La mesa directiva del nobilisimo gremio de la platería de la ciudad de México," Instituto Nacional de Antropología y Historia, *Anales,* 3 (1947–48): 163. See also Richard Konetzke, "Las ordenanzas de gremios como documentos para la historia social de Hispano-américa durante la época colonial," *Revista Internacional de Sociología* 5:18 (April–June 1947): 430–31, and Raul Carranco y Trujillo, *Las ordenanzas de gremios de Nueva España,* (Mexico City: Crisol, 1932). More recent work includes Emilio Harth-Terré and Alberto Márquez-Abantó, "Perspectiva social y económica del artesano virreinal en Lima," *Revista del Archivo Nacional del Perú* 31 (1967): 357–59, and Hector Humberto Samayoa Guevara, "La reorganización gremial guatemalsense en la segunda mitad del siglo XVIII," *Antropología e historia de Guatemala* 12:1 (January 1960): 64–67. See also Julio Jiménez Rueda, "El certamen de los plateros en 1618 y las coplas satíricas que de él se derivaron," *Boletín del Archivo General de la Nación* (México) 16:3 (July–September 1945): 345–84.

A number of authors have published guild regulations. The following articles by Hector Humberto Samayoa Guevara represent the general case: "El gremio de plateros de la ciudad de Guatemala y sus ordenanzas (1524–1821)," *Antropología e Historia de Guatemala* 9:1 (January 1957): 19–37; "El gremio de salitreros de Antigua Guatemala," *Antropología e Historia de Guatemala* 7:1 (January 1955); 25–53; and "Los coheteros de Santiago de Guatemala," *Antropología e Historia de Guatemala* 6:2 (June 1954): 22–51. See also Ernesto Chinchilla Aguilar, "Ordenanzas de Escultura," *Antropología e Historia de Guatemala* 5:2 (January 1953): 29–52.

For an excellent short summary of the historical antecedents of Spanish guilds see Práxedes Zancada y Ruata, *Derecho Corporativo Español,* (Madrid: J. Ortiz, n.d.). A highly illuminating discussion of the differences between industrial and artisanal social organization is provided by E. P. Thompson, "Eighteenth-Century English Society: Class Struggle without Class?", *Social History* 3:2 (May 1978): 133–65. See also John Super, "Querétaro Obrajes: Industry and Society in Provincial Mexico, 1600–1810," *Hispanic American Historical Review* 56:2 (May 1976): 197–216; and Jan Bazant, "Evolución de la industria textil poblana (1554–1845)," *Historia mexicana* 13 (1964): 473–516.

Of additional interest are Lyman L. Johnson, "Francisco Baquero: Shoemaker and Organizer," in David G. Sweet and Gary B. Nash, eds., *Struggle and Survival in Colonial America* (Berkeley: University of California Press, 1981): 86–101; Humberto Triana y Antorveza, "El aprendizaje de los gremios neogranadinos," Banco de la Republica (Bogotá), *Boletín Cultural y Bibliográfico* 8:5 (1965): 735–43; and Humberto Triana y Antorveza, "La libertad laboral y la supresión de los gremios neogranadinos," Banco de la Republica (Bogotá), *Boletín Cultural y Bibliográfico* 8:7 (1965): 1015–24.

NINE

Suppliers, Sellers, Servants, and Slaves

MARY KARASCH

Introduction

Other essays in this collection examine the elites of colonial cities: bureaucrats and merchants, large landowners, military officers and priests. Those who did not occupy such positions, the majority of urban residents, had to find other niches in society where they could earn their livings and raise their families. The powerless, the poor, the enslaved, many females, and the majority of people of color, as well as their children, were coerced through economic necessity or slavery to supply, serve, and care for the elites of the colonial cities.

This chapter seeks to identify and describe the groups which fed, served, and slaved for the merchants and the bureaucrats. The focus is colonial Brazil, with an emphasis on the late eighteenth and early nineteenth centuries. Comparisons, or more often contrasts, to the urban centers of the Spanish Empire also will be included. Those who performed the occupations perceived as "vile" and appropriate to the poor and the enslaved varied over time and region, both in Brazil and Spanish America. The distinctions, as well as the commonalities, are important.

Essential to the well-being and comfort of the elites and to the physical upkeep of the cities themselves, the amorphous non-elites, usually perceived as a homogeneous mass in traditional studies, were actually quite diverse in income, legal status, color, and self-image. There is no simple way to classify the members of this group. Here they are described by the type of work that they performed, because all did, in fact, pursue what the elite deemed "lowly" occupations. But in another sense, it is misleading to use the term "lower

251

status" to describe these individuals because they did not necessarily share low incomes. True, they were often the poorest of the poor, who owned little if any property, but many still chose not to engage in criminal or vagrant behavior, and the prosperous market women and vendors of alcoholic drinks often outranked artisans in wealth. Using entrepreneurial skills, the most ambitious and skillful often parlayed a "vile" occupation, disdained by their Iberian rulers, into a wealth-producing service that permitted them to buy land and to raise their own, or at least their childrens', status.

The case of the market women is also revealing of the character of this group in another respect. In both traditional Indian and African societies women sold fruits and vegetables in the markets, and, not too surprisingly, the market women of colonial Latin America were of Indian and African origin; Iberian women rarely entered the markets. Why individuals of particular nationalities worked in certain non-elite occupations often was due to their cultural values and immigrant status. When they entered a colonial city, either through voluntary or involuntary migration, they pursued the activities familiar to them from their previous towns and villages. In their own terms, they engaged in status-productive occupations that gave them a strong sense of their own self-worth; only their rulers defined these occupations as "vile."

In addition to cultural values and income, another feature distinguishing members of the non-elites from one another was legal position. Members of this group might be free, freed, or enslaved persons. Freedpersons were originally slaves who, during their own lifetime, had bought their freedom or had been manumitted by their owners. Fewer in number than the slaves or the free, and primarily women (and children), freedpersons frequently engaged in the same occupations at which they had worked prior to manumission, such as street vending or washing clothes. Over time, in Brazil, a large free population of color emerged that could support itself in areas of the urban economy that were not restricted to slaves and their owners. The urban non-elites included the three different legal categories from the beginning of the colony. In sixteenth-century Brazil, the Portuguese founders of settlements brought with them Portuguese- or African-born slaves and freedpersons. From 1559, black slaves were transported directly from Africa. Although slave status is associated with blacks, Indians might also be slaves. In contrast to Spanish America where Indian slavery had been abolished in the sixteenth century, enslavement of natives continued to flourish in Brazil, although repeatedly outlawed by the Portuguese crown. Thus, in Brazil the category of slave encompassed the entire range of the color spectrum, including light-skinned persons who could "pass" as whites. From the sixteenth century self purchase and manumission transformed part of the slave population into an ethnically and racially diverse group of free people of color.

The racial origins of those who pursued non-elite occupations varied according to the region in which they lived. In the Spanish colonies they ranged the color continuum from Indians to *mestizos* (persons of Indian and white ancestry) and peninsular Spaniards and from newly imported Africans to *mulatos* (persons of black and white ancestry), as well as Indian and African mixtures (called *zambos, sambos,* or *coyotes*). In general, the urban non-elites in the highland areas of New Spain and Peru were Indian or mestizo. Minorities of blacks and mulatos resided in the mining towns or worked as servants in large inland cities, such as Mexico City. Cities on or near the coast, such as Veracruz, Portobelo, Caracas, Cartagena, Guayaquil, Lima, Valparaiso, Buenos Aires, and Montevideo tended to have greater numbers of blacks and mulatos in their non-elite populations. In Brazil, however, the coastal cities of São Luis, Recife, Bahia and Rio de Janeiro, were overwhelmingly black and *pardo* (mulato), while the mining towns of Ouro Prêto and Vila Boa de Goiás also had large numbers of blacks and pardos. Only in the Amazon region, São Paulo, and the far south did Indians, *caboclos* or *mamelucos* (Portuguese terms for mestizos), and *cafuzos* (Portuguese term for zambos) outnumber blacks and mulatos in non-elite occupations. Here the settlers were not prosperous enough to purchase large numbers of African slaves. By the early nineteenth century, the racially mixed population of Brazil had migrated into the major port cities and worked at diverse non-elite occupations beside recent immigrants from Portugal, the Azores, and Madeira. People of all colors and legal status labored at these occupations and intermarried. Whether Indians, blacks or mixtures, free, freed or slave, composed a particular work force usually depended on the demographic makeup of the population and the city's historical experience.

Urban non-elites were also heterogeneous in the types of work they performed. In general, we can group their diverse occupations into six categories: suppliers, transporters, food processors, sellers, servants, and municipal workers. They obviously labored at many other skilled and unskilled manual occupations not described here, but these major groupings demonstrate the striking variety of their tasks that were essential to the complex economic organization of the colonial cities. Although official correspondence often complained of their growing numbers and the alleged "threats" they posed to public order, they were neither vagrants nor parasites, but active participants in and contributors to the economy of each colonial city.

The relative numbers and significance of each category of workers to the economy is impossible to determine for colonial Brazil, since officials seldom recorded accurate censuses and almost always omitted occupations. What data exist for the late eighteenth century can merely point to the relative proportions between free and enslaved, and between whites, pardos and blacks. Earlier censuses are even more suspect. In the late eighteenth and early nineteenth centuries, the only possible estimate is that two-thirds to three-fourths of Brazil's coastal urban population comprised people of color, most of whom were descendants of Africans, i.e., blacks and pardos. Beyond such a generalization, historians must turn to other sources for the racial and occupational breakdown of a particular town or city, such as court records and notarial

Table 9.1 The Population of Late Colonial Brazilian Towns and Cities by Race

Town/City	Year	Free/Whites	Free/Freed Pardos	Persons Blacks	Slaves	Sum Total
Belem	1793	4,432	—	1,099[a]	3,051	8,573
Belem	1822	5,643	—	1,109[a]	5,719	12,471
São Luis	1810					20,500
Recife	1789					15,000
Recife	1810					5,441[b]
Recife	1810					22,350
Bahia	1700					40,000
Bahia	1775	12,720	4,207	3,630	14,696	35,253
Bahia	1807					51,000
Cachoeira	1800					10,000
Espírito Santo[c]	1800					19,000
Rio de Janeiro	1799	19,578	4,227	4,585	14,986	43,376
Rio de Janeiro	1821	43,139	—	—	36,182	79,321
Paraty	1790	3,961	300	103	2,308	6,672
Ouro Prêto	1804				2,740	8,785
Barbacena	1813					14,064
São João del Rei	1818					6,000
São João del Rei	1819					7,000
Vila Boa de Goiás	1804	1,222	2,811	1,012	4,432	9,477
São Paulo	1772				5,160	21,272
São Paulo	1798				6,075	21,304
Itú, S. Paulo	1813	3,090	436	162	3,653	7,341
Ilha de Santa Catarina[c]	1810				3,313	12,471
Rio Grande de São Pedro[c]	1780				5,102	17,923
Colônia do Sacramento	1777	324	77	23	(111?)	535

Notes to Table

[a] Includes blacks, Indians, and persons of mixed ancestry.

[b] Families.

[c] Includes rural and/or suburban inhabitants as well as the urban nucleus.

Sources for Table

Belem: Vicente Salles, *O negro no Pará sob o regime da escravidão* (Rio de Janeiro, Fundação Getúlio Vargas 1971), 69–71; São Luis: Dauril Alden, "Late-Colonial Brazil, 1750–1807 . . . Leslie Bethell, ed., *The Cambridge History of Latin America* (6 v., 1985–), 1:1 (in press); Recife: Gadiel Perruci, "A Cidade do Recife (1889–1930): O Crescimento Urbano, O Comércio e A Indústria," in vol. 1, *Anais do VII Simpósio Nacional dos Professores Universitários de História*, edited by Eurípedes Simões de Paula (São Paulo, 1974), no. 22, p. 585; Bahia: Stuart B. Schwartz, *Sovereignty and Society in Colonial Brazil* (Berkeley: University of California Press, 1973), 242; A. J. R. Russell-Wood, *The Black Man in Slavery and Freedom in Colonial Brazil* (New York: St. Martin's Press, 1982), 48–49, n. 58, p. 217; Patricia Aufderheide, "Upright Citizens in Criminal Records: Investigations in Cachoeira and Geremoabo, Brazil, 1780–1836," *The Americas* 38:2 (October 1981): 177; Espírito Santo: Caio Prado, Jr., *The Colonial Background of Modern Brazil*, translated by Suzette Macedo (Berkeley: University of California Press, 1969), 45; Rio: Maria Yedda Linhares and Maria Bárbara Lévy, "Aspectos da história demográfica e social do Rio de Janeiro (1808–1889)," in *L'Histoire Quantitative du Brésil de 1800 à 1930*, (Paris: Centre National de la Recherche Scientifique 1973), 129–130; James P. Kiernan, "The Manumission of Slaves in Colonial Brazil: Paraty, 1789–1822," (Ph.D. diss., New York University, 1976), 23–24; Ouro Prêto: Donald Ramos, "Vila Rica: Profile of a Colonial Brazilian Urban Center," *The Americas* 35:4 (April 1979): 497–98; Barbacena, Minas Gerais: Johann E. Pohl, *Viagem ao interior do Brasil*, translated by Teodoro Cabral, 2 vols. (Rio de Janeiro: Instituto Nacional do Livro, 1951), and Auguste de Saint-Hilaire, *Viagem pelo Distrito dos Diamantes e Litoral do Brasil*, translated by Leonam de Azeredo Pena (São Paulo: Companhia Editora Nacional 1941), Goiás: Luiz Antônio de Silva e Souza, *O Descobrimento da Capitania de Goyaz (Govêrno, População e Coisas mais Notáveis)* (1849); reprint ed., Goiânia, Universidad Federal de Goiás 1968), 51; Luiz Palacin, *Goiás 1722–1822* (Goiânia: Oriente, 1976), 104; São Paulo: Maria Luisa Marcilio, *La ville de São Paulo: peuplement et population, 1750– 1850* (Rouen: Université de Rouen 1968), 151; Itú: Eni de Mesquita, "Aspectos de uma Vila Paulista em 1813," in *A Cidade e a História*, 1:351–55; Ilha de Santa Catarina: Lawrence James Nielsen, *Escravidão em Santa Catarina*, unpublished paper, Universidade Federal de Santa Catarina, c. 1977–1978; Rudy Bauss, "Rio Grande do Sul in the Portuguese Empire: The Formative Years, 1777–1808," *The Americas* 39:4 (April 1983): 522; and Colônia: Dauril Alden, "The Population of Brazil in the Late Eighteenth Century: A Preliminary Study," *The Hispanic American Historical Review* 43:2 (May 1963): 187, 199.

registries, to document numbers for each occupation. Table 9.1 summarizes census data of the late eighteenth and early nineteenth centuries for selected Brazilian cities, while Table 9.2 provides an example of the type of data on occupation, civil status, race, and gender that may be compiled from archival sources. For the most part, however, exact figures for non-elite occupations by sex and race are elusive: moreover, racial categories are not consistently used from one census to another. In general, conclusions can be based only on literary rather than on statistical sources.

The more varied the functions of the colonial city, the more diverse the tasks of the non-elite workers. In the sixteenth and seventeenth centuries it was the major Spanish American cities, with their large populations and multiple administrative, commercial, and religious functions, that produced the full range of categories discussed here. By the late eighteenth century in Brazil, the city building of the mining boom in Minas Gerais and the transfer of the capital from Bahia to Rio de Janeiro had created a similar demand for a multifaceted urban work force. On the whole, however, most non-elites in colonial Brazil worked in small centers that performed one or two functions, such as the garrison town of Colônia do Sacramento or the port and fishing village of Paraty. Seldom did a city approach the size or complexity of Mexico City or Lima. Nonetheless, the variety of occupations exercised by non-elites in late colonial Brazil was genuinely impressive and illustrative of their significance to urban society.

Suppliers

The people identified here as suppliers provided the cities with food, fuel, and fodder. Living either in the city or in the countryside, they frequently moved between fields and markets, exemplifying the geographical mobility of some urban non-elites. Because they could not live in elite residential areas around the central square, they squatted on marginal lands or were segregated in Indian quarters removed from the center. The close proximity of their dwellings to the countryside, however, helped them gain their livelihood. They worked on small, specialized farms which encircled the cities of colonial Latin America and supplied them with fresh produce and small animals.

Brazilian cities were far less urbanized than those in Spanish America and only minimal barriers existed between city and farmlands. Tropical forests even edged the small farms and gardens near the cities, whereas in New Spain and Peru the Indians who had farmed nearby lands and supplied pre-Columbian cities for centuries continued to do so after the Conquest. Without such traditional urban-suburban ties in Brazil, sixteenth-century garrison dwellers had to leave the shelter of their fortifications to cultivate fields outside protected walls or to send their slaves to hunt, collect, and fish in the surround-

Table 9.2 Trades of Free Blacks and Pardos

Work Description	Total	Black	Pardo	African	Female	Born outside Paraty	Literate (sign name)	Freedpersons	(b)
Urban:									
Boat builder	1		1			1			
Butcher	1	1						1	
Carpenter	6	1	4 (a)	1		2	1	3	
Day laborer	7	3	4	1				4	
Foreman (work crew)	2		2					2	
Functionary of town council	2		2			1	2		
House builder	1		1						
Laundress	2		2		2			2	54 (46.2%)
Midwives	3	3			3			2	
Painter	1	1						1	
Seamstress	2		2		2			2	
Servant	3	1	2		2				
Shoemaker	12		12			2	1	3	
Shopkeeper	5	2	3		2	1	1	2	
Slaughter house worker	1	1						1	
Tailor	4	1	3					1	
Vegetable stall keeper	1	1		1				1	
Rural:									
"Bush Capitan" (slave catcher)	4	3		1				2	
Canoe builder	3	2	1					1	
Distiller	3		3						
Farmer/sharecropper	23	5	13	5	1		1	13	40 (34.1%)
Fisherman	3	1	2						
Sugar maker	2		2					1	
Wood cutter	2		2						
Transport:									
Mule driver	4	2	2			1			
Sailor	5	2	2	1		2			9 (7.7%)
Unknown	14	6	8		7			9	14 (12.0%)
	117	38 (32.5%)	71 (60.7%)	8 (6.8%)	20	10	5	51	117

[a]One carpenter described as "homen da terra"; was perhaps an Indian or mestizo.
[b]According to declaration; more freedom may have been undeclared.
Source: Court Records, Paraty (1789–1822), CUP. in James Kiernan, "The Manumission of Slaves in Colonial Brazil."

ing country. As the towns grew into cities, owners and their slaves moved on to suburban provision grounds (*chacaras* or *sítios*) and cultivated subsistence crops. Others remained in the cities and had their slaves and *agregados* (free servant, often a relative) raise fruits and vegetables in the backyard garden (*quintal*) attached to the house, or sent them to the chacaras to raise produce and small animals. Thus, slaves and agregados, while actually resident in a city, often worked as gardeners and caretakers of provision grounds. Larger chacaras raised commercial crops, such as *farinha* (manioc meal), corn, beans, tobacco, and small animals, employing a work force which labored at plantation-like activities in the shadows of the cities. By the late eighteenth century freedpersons and free people of color also raised and cared for "truck gardens" to supply Brazilian cities. They cultivated fruit trees, pineapples, vegetables, and flowers; while in the Amazon region collectors, especially Indians, entered the nearby forests to bring back tropical fruits, wild cacao, cinnamon, and Brazil nuts that they gathered from scattered trees. In some cases, the fruits and crops that slaves gathered or raised in the urban environs were used for the immediate consumption by the households to which they belonged, but in others the gardeners and gatherers raised or collected items for sale in the cities, either for their owners or on their own account.

While a number of agricultural slaves and workers resided in or near the cities, the frequent movement of plantation owners between their rural estates and their urban homes brought still more of these workers to town. The great *senhores de engenho* (lords of the sugar mills) usually resided on their estates near Bahia for at least part of each year, and administered their own estates. Because of their numerous ties and business responsibilities in Bahia, they often came to live in the upper city for part of the year. Not only did their favorite household slaves accompany them to their urban homes, but other plantation workers were used for the transport of their families to the cities. Upon arrival in the cities, these rural slaves often were set to similar occupations, such as gardening or porterage; upon the return of the family to their estate, their slaves went with them. Thus, some rural slaves moved between countryside and city as frequently as did their owners.

The care and feeding of animals was another full- or part-time occupation in the cities. Slaves raised cows, milked them, carried the milk in cans on their heads to the cities, and either sold the milk from cans in the streets or led the cows through the streets and milked them on the spot upon the request of their customers. In the northeast, the animal often raised for its milk, cheese, and hides was the goat—the "cow" of the poor. In general, most suppliers of fresh meat to the colonial cities were involved in the raising and care of small animals—goats, pigs, chickens, turkeys, and other fowl. They collected eggs, milked the goats, and slaughtered the animals for food. Because of the lower cost of these animals, many free people of color, Indians and freed persons cared for them on sítios as agregados in the environs of the cities. Large draft animals, however, were more likely to be under the care of slaves, owned by slave-holders who could afford teams of oxen and mules, or horses. Although most large animals were kept outside the city limits, some horses and mules were stabled in every city for use with the elegant carriages of the Portuguese nobility. Other small animals, such as dogs and cats, were cared for by the slaves of each household, who often had to share sleeping quarters with them on the ground floors of colonial houses.

Also involved in the supply of animal protein to the cities of Bahia and Rio were the herders. Throughout the colonial period, the cities depended on nearby farms, ranches, or plantations for fresh meat, obtained by slaughtering cattle and pigs driven to the cities. Cowboys drove cattle regularly to cattle fairs and then on to the licensed slaughterhouses of Bahia and other northeastern cities. In the eighteenth century an Italian Jesuit reported that 100 to 300 head of cattle arrived at Capoâme, eight leagues from Bahia, where merchants purchased them. Those who brought the cattle were whites, mulatos, blacks, and Indians. The city of Belem was supplied with cattle from Marajó island, where the Jesuits once had 50,000 head pastured in 1759. Those who brought cattle legally to Belem merchants in 1727 were 22 Indian herdsmen.[1] To the south, cattle from Minas and São Paulo were funneled regularly to Rio, as were pigs from Minas Gerais. In seventeenth-century Quito, however, the poor and widows petitioned and received licenses from the *cabildo* (town council) to supply the city with meat, and at least some women who raised cattle in the vicinity of Quito were involved in sending their cattle there. Although one suspects that poor men personally drove their own cattle to Quito, it is not known who brought the widows' cattle. But in colonial Brazil in general, a host of cowboys, herdsmen, and swineherders, who were Indians, slaves, freedmen, and free men of color, conducted animals to the cities for slaughter.

In the environs of the colonial Brazilian cities, where dense forests still existed, many animals were hunted by Indian and African slaves and retainers whose owners employed them as professional hunters. Either alone or with their masters, they pursued and captured monkeys, armadillos, lizards, birds, and small rodent-like animals. The further removed from Portuguese influence a city was, the more its inhabitants tended to supplement their diets with the delicacies of the forests: tapirs, lizards, monkeys, honey, and insects. Some blacks, trained from adolescence to hunt in the forests for their masters, returned to the cities with food for their owners' tables or to sell to the cooks of the rich households, who paid them for their armadillos and lizards. Once foreign naturalists arrived in Brazil, such slaves and freedmen went out and collected the specimens that ended up in European natural history collections. In effect, they were Brazil's first naturalists, who made important contributions to the collection and classification of Brazilian flora and fauna of the late eighteenth and nineteenth centuries.

Even more important than hunting, however, was fishing. Because Brazilian colonial cities were clustered along rivers or on the coast, the fruits of the fresh and salt water were sought by all. Slaves, freedmen, and free men of color, especially Indians and mestizos, went after fresh water fish and the turtles, octopus, sharks, and fish of the ocean. Some fished from shore with nets or poisoned the fish in the rivers in the Indian manner. Black and mulato freedmen of colonial Paraty generally used small nets, while others fished with spears or hooks and line from small canoes along the coast. They took their salted fish to town merchants to exchange for salt, line, and other equipment. Some of the fishermen did not own their nets, which belonged to merchants or urban residents to whom they delivered fresh fish. Slave owners in Paraty paid a mulato fisherman to make nets for their rural slaves so they could feed themselves. In the northeast, black fishermen took out *jangadas* (rafts with triangular sails) and went deep sea fishing in search of large salt water fish, including sharks, that were used for food and oil.

When whales played in the bays of Rio and Bahia and migrated along the coast of Brazil, whalers hunted down the giant mammals. Each morning near Bahia 40 to 50 launches put out in search of whales. Each long boat had 10 men, including 8 oarsmen, 1 patron, and 1 harpoonist.[2] Apparently, the crews were blacks and mulatos who were the property of the owner of the *armação,* where whales were processed for food and oil. Elsewhere in the south, free men were preferred as whalers because of the dangerous nature of the occupation. In the whole of Brazil, fishermen and whalers were probably the occupational group most responsible for the supply of fresh animal protein to the colonial cities.

Other sources of animal protein were far removed from the cities and had to be processed for preservation before shipment. In general, the methods of preservation used in the colonial period were salting and/or drying, and regions with access to animals or fish and salt developed industries to supply nearby cities. In the northeast, Ceará, Parnaíba, Piauí, and the Rio São Francisco region sent salted beef to Bahia, and in the far south Rio Grande de São Pedro developed its cattle industries to the point where it supplanted other regions in the trade of meat and cattle by-products. Additional beef by-products were exported into Brazil from the Río de la Plata region. By the late eighteenth century Bahia, Recife, and Rio regularly imported southern dried and salted beef, and people often preferred *carne sêca* to fresh beef for themselves or for their slaves, either because of lower cost or the lesser likelihood of disease. In the northeast and the far south, slaves and free men of color worked as cowboys on the large estates and as salted meat processors in or near coastal towns. Other slaves prepared hides, tallow, and leather for export to Rio or Bahia.

In Minas Gerais and São Paulo another important meat industry involved the processing of pork and preparation of the second meat staple of southern Brazil: *toucinho* (pork fat or bacon). Where dried or salted beef was unavailable, toucinho was often the only animal protein of slaves and the poor. The third important preserved protein product was salted fish, either prepared in

Brazil or imported from Portugal. Throughout the Amazon system and the coastal rivers of Brazil, including the São Francisco, Indians and free people of color often prepared salted fish for sale to nearby towns and cities. The Portuguese, however, seem to have preferred their imported Newfoundland codfish over all sources of animal protein. While their African and Indian slaves ate fresh fish or salted beef or pork, they dined on *bacalhau* supplied to them by Portuguese merchants.

Not only did the suppliers hunt and fish, but they also collected many of the natural resources around the colonial cities. They went into the nearby forests for the dyewoods that were exported from the port cities. Dyewoods had been sixteenth-century Brazil's first export, and they continued to be sold abroad even after sugar became the primary commodity. Most suppliers, however, simply collected wood for use in home fires or the making of charcoal. Wood gathering was among the most common occupations of household slaves and Indians throughout the colonial period. A close second to it was the gathering of *capim d'Angola,* a type of grass that served as animal fodder. Slaves collected the grass daily near Rio, where it grew wild, or cultivated it and carried it to the city on the backs of animals, on carts, in boats, or on their heads. They either sold it at the Praça do Capim in Rio de Janeiro, a market specializing in the sale of fodder, or peddled it from door to door. Finally, many Indian and African female slaves, especially old women, gathered herbs, spices, medicines, narcotics, plants, and insects for textile dyes and natural poisons, as well as greens and fruits for food that they found near the cities.

On the whole, the production and collection of animal protein, foodstuffs, and fuel occupied a substantial number of slaves, freedpersons, and free people of color who lived in or near colonial cities. They engaged in gardening, commercial agriculture, animal husbandry, and subsistence activities. The fact that the suppliers lived in a city or town did not mean they escaped the kinds of labor more typically associated with plantation slaves. In fact, they often had to perform the labor of both rural and urban workers: raise fruits and vegetables, care for such animals as chickens, pigs, and goats, and perform household services, while holding down another urban occupation.

Transporters

As urban populations grew in the last third of the eighteenth century, food had to be brought from even greater distances. The "food shed" of the major cities expanded. Thus, one of the most important occupations of non-elites in colonial cities was that of transportation—the movement of goods and people from one part of the city to another, or from the city to the countryside and back again. Sometimes they moved the goods by land porterage, especially to the mines, but they also journeyed by water. Not even women escaped the job of porterage on land, although they apparently were not used on water. Since an unwritten custom decreed that high status persons never carried anything nor walked for long distances, especially the ladies of the house, slaves had the burden of the porterage of goods and people in colonial Brazil. Before docks were constructed in nineteenth-century cities, all those who entered the port cities of Brazil were carried ashore on the shoulders of Indian or African slaves, who waded through the filthy waters to deposit them on land. Whatever they carried, whether a package of letters or an umbrella, had to be given to slave porters, or the newcomers risked the porters' revenge for depriving them of their rightful work.

Where Africans were available, owners tended to use them to carry heavy loads on their heads—in part because of African traditions of head porterage in the absence of large draft animals. At the time of independence, it was estimated that at least half of the porters in Rio were newly imported Africans, and they carried everything from bags of salt to pianos on their heads. While transporting furniture and other heavy loads, they worked in groups, with one of them serving as the leader. As they moved along, their captain danced and beat time with a gourd rattle or two pieces of iron and chanted an African song, after which the whole group joined in the chorus. This head porterage tradition, accompanied by vibrant music, was clearly distinct from Indian porterage customs in Brazil and Spanish America. Unless they adopted head porterage from their African colleagues, somber files of Indian men and women, both slave and free, bent forward under the heavy weights carried in baskets or bags attached to tumplines that crossed their foreheads.

Many of these porters worked in the busy ports of Brazil on the wharves and in the warehouses as stevedores. They were essential in unloading people and goods in all the coastal port cities of colonial Latin America, whether Cartagena, Havana, Buenos Aires, or Bahia. They unloaded the luxury imports of Asian textiles, Portuguese wines, and English manufactures and toted them on their heads and shoulders through customs and on to deposit in the warehouses of the city.

They also brought new Africans ashore for deposit in the slave markets of the coastal cities. Exports of sugar, tobacco, foodstuffs—in effect, all the products of Brazil—once again went on their heads and backs or were pulled and tugged on carts to the wharves. Especially large casks and loads were suspended from long cords attached to poles carried by four to six slave stevedores. Once at the shore or port area, the goods were stored in warehouses until ready to be taken to ships by slave boatmen or canoemen, who took the cargoes to the sailing ships anchored in the harbours. All that moved between ship and shore and in and out of warehouses in Brazilian colonial cities was portered by slaves, who appear to have had a monopoly on the dock activities.

Of all the porters, however, those with the most difficult tasks were those who worked in quarries, such as the one near Rio, and carried granite blocks on their heads, and those who worked in mining. In the city of Bahia one special assignment was the porterage of goods from the wharves of the lower city to the upper city, and thousands of slaves labored at that task at any one time. Another group of porters toted fragile items along the long and muddy roads from Bahia or Rio to the mines of Minas Gerais. Whenever draft animals were absent, costly, or unreliable, slaves carried the burden of porterage both within the cities and from the cities to the interior.

Slave porters also had to carry people. The mark of high status in colonial Brazil was the elegant sedan chair with curtains. Two pardo slaves in elegant liveries carried wealthy owners in gilded palanquins, known as *cadeirinhas* and *serpentinas*. In eighteenth-century Bahia their use was restricted to whites only; but in effect only the wealthiest whites could afford them because of the high cost of the chair and the two porters. Owners of low social status either walked or were toted about in simple hammocks, a method also used for transporting the bodies of the dead. When a poor person died, two slaves carried the body slung in a hammock tied on a pole to the gravesite.

The most common daily form of porterage in colonial Brazil was that of carrying water. Since most drinking water had to be brought from sources outside the household—fountains, wells, rivers, and streams—every household sent its women and/or slaves for its daily supply of water. Before 1808 in Rio, this was primarily the burden of slave women, who carried large water jars on their heads in the African manner. By the eighteenth century each large colonial city had ornate public water fountains, often carved by slave artists, or private wells controlled by owners who sold fresh water for a living. In Bahia there were many fountains and wells located throughout the city, but in Rio a viceroy had constructed an aqueduct to move water to the Carioca fountain in the center of the city. Previously, an army of slaves had been utilized to carry water from sources near Rio. In the seventeenth century, for example, the sole function of gangs of Indian slaves had been to carry water along a difficult trail from the Carioca river along Gloria hill to the port area of the city. The building of the aqueduct and canalization of the water supply eased this labor burden, but the city's urban and suburban growth resulted in houses being constructed further and further from the central fountains and added to the distance that slaves had to travel, unless there were alternative water sources. Because of the varying quality of the water supply in Salvador, owners also sent many slaves over long distances for the best water.

The porterage and disposal of a household's refuse was equally burdensome. In the colonial period squares, large fields, alleys, and streets, even in the center of the cities, were used as dumps. Upon the orders of their owners, slaves were sent out each day to dump the household's night soil, garbage, and dead animals. A few owners, wanting to avoid burial expenses, even had the bodies of dead slaves abandoned in the streets at night. Consequently, swarms of dogs, pigs, rats, and insects competed with vultures for the refuse, and carried diseases throughout the cities. In Bahia one of the most serious health problems involved the manner in which slaves from the upper city left refuse at the tops of the stairs leading to the lower city. Ordered by their owners to take it to the beaches of the waterfront, slaves walked only as far as they had to—to the top of the steps—and dumped the rubbish there or in nearby alleys. When the rains came, the night soil and garbage of the upper city washed into the lower city, imperiling the health of the people below. In most coastal cities, the beaches of the urban centers were also unhealthy, because slaves used them as dumps. The distasteful task of taking each day's refuse for disposal on the beaches or in the streets and squares usually was allotted to the family's single slave or to the lowest in status and value, such as old women or newly purchased Africans. Chained criminals carried the night soil and refuse from public buildings, prisons, and hospitals.

The incidence of head porterage and carrying of people reveal that Indian and African slaves frequently performed the functions of draft animals in colonial Brazil. But there were also slaves who worked beside and with animals in transporting people and goods. Within the cities, an elite group of elegantly liveried coachmen, footmen, and animal handlers directed or cared for the horses and mules that pulled the carriages, rode the animals to direct them, or stood behind the carriages as footmen. Less elegant animal handlers worked for businesses that provided a type of taxi service in nineteenth-century Rio. They served as the drivers for small carriages known as *seges* that waited for customers in the streets of Rio. When plantation families left the cities to travel to the country, they went in bullock carts conducted by their slaves. Similar carts were used to carry provisions to the city from the countryside. Either slaves transported slaughtered carcasses in the carts to Rio, or they accompanied herds of animals for delivery to the slaughterhouses of the city.

Because of the volume of goods that went by muleback in the colonial period, muleteers were essential to the long distance transportation of goods between colonial cities. Whatever did not go by water in coastal or riverine trade went on the back of a mule, the head of a slave, or the back of an Indian. The person in charge of a mule team was generally a free man or freedman, but the individual drivers were usually slaves, who walked beside the mules that carried plantation products to and from the cities. Newly purchased slaves being forwarded to the plantations often followed the mules with additional items loaded on their heads. If their owners accompanied the caravans, slaves carried them in hammocks slung on poles or walked beside the two mules that carried them in a hammock or a type of boxed sedan chair. Others walked behind owners who rode horses. When mules were not used, then most of the slaves, including the women, carried the provisions for the journey on their heads.

Black or Indian slaves or mules served to transport most items and people both in the cities and in the interior trade where navigable rivers did not exist. Except in the case of large mule teams, most of the burden of the transportation of owners on short trips to the rural areas fell on the urban slaves. who at a minimum had to carry the baggage for the trip and frequently had to carry the owner himself. Because of the shortage of draft animals in many parts of colonial Brazil, most black or Indian slaves had to engage in some form of porterage. Only high-status household slaves and personal servants escaped being beasts of burden at one time or another.

Boatmen

Similar to land porterage was the function of transporting goods and people by water, even in the cities. While cities in highland Spanish America were not situated on the ocean or along broad rivers, communication and transportation went by water in the coastal and riverine cities of Brazil. Only the interior mining towns did not use boatmen to a comparable extent. Because of the nature of Brazilian geography, the boatmen were proportionately more important to the supply of coastal and riverine cities than were the muleteers, who were essential to the supply of the interior mining towns of New Spain, Upper Peru, and Minas Gerais. Furthermore, Brazilian boatmen were as vital to intraurban trade and transport as were those of Venice or fifteenth-century Tenochtitlán and sixteenth-century Mexico City. Not only were they the urban "taxi drivers," but they were also the "truckers" who brought foodstuffs to the central markets. Two examples may suffice. When the Portuguese royal family established a residence in a suburb of Rio, they often prepared to commute by boat rather than by carriage from the central square. Along the coast to Paraty, the small towns and plantations that supplied Rio were linked by sea. In fact, a direct road between Paraty and Rio was not constructed until the 1970s. Because colonial Brazil did not inherit well-established highways such as those built by the Incas in the Andes, most transportation was waterborne, as in the period before 1500.

Canoes, longboats, rafts, small sloops and large sailing vessels traveled up and down the great rivers of Brazil, including the Amazon and Paraná systems, the São Francisco River, and especially the bays of Bahia and Rio, the canals and rivers of Recife, and the coast between the port cities. (See Figure 19.) One or two slaves, often Indians, would make and man the canoes that brought produce for sale in the cities, while others hired out their services to carry passengers ashore. Some poled large rafts loaded with logs or other objects, while black slave fishermen dared the waves of the Atlantic in small jangadas with lateen sails. While such individuals were usually trusted slaves, freedmen, or freemen of color, most slave boatmen and sailors worked under the supervision of owners or overseers as oarsmen and sailors. In the Amazon region, conscripted Indian crewmen manned the great sailing canoes of 40 oarsmen that brought the spices, fruits, woods, and slaves of the interior to Belem.

Slaves also worked as oarsmen on the small boats that moved between ship and shore in coastal ports like Bahia and Rio. Among the more common boats were the *faluas,* similar to those in Lisbon, which either had no masts at all or had two, each with a large sail and a covered stern to protect passengers from the sun. Four, six, or eight slave oarsmen, generally Africans in Rio, manned them under the orders of the Portuguese owner, who acted as steersman on the larger faluas. On smaller boats another slave often served as the captain. In nineteenth-century Rio the African oarsmen were all owned by the boat owner, although some were rented slaves.

A year after independence, Burford described a boat rowed by Africans, whose "tatooed and naked limbs are an extraordinary sight to Europeans; they rise at each stroke of the oar, and throw themselves backward into their seats, and invariably accompany their work with some wild national air."[3] The largest employer of slave oarsmen, however, was the royal family, which had elaborate royal barges (*galeotas*) with 10 to 20 oarsmen. In 1816, Ellis reported that Indians in Rio were employed "in rowing the royal barge and a few other boats."[4]

Other boatmen in the interior of Brazil ferried people and goods across large rivers at small towns and river crossings. In some cases owners set trusted slaves to working the ferries, but in others only poor whites, ex-slaves, or free men of color made their living in the ferry business. In Bahia the poor ferried passengers across the Paraguaçú River, but at other rivers there were black slaves and freedmen who used large rafts and small canoes. On long trips through the interior, where such services did not exist, slaves often carried their owners on their backs as they walked through the waters; while in the cities ambitious slaves earned extra money by carrying customers across waterlogged streets in the rainy season. Because of such traditions, it was natural for owners to set their slaves to work in rafts, boats, and canoes to transport people and baggage within the cities. Where cities were divided by water, as in Recife, slaves and freedmen provided a type of water-taxi service transporting passengers and baggage between cities and suburbs. In the Amazon region Indians labored in boats and canoes to carry people and goods to and from Belem.

Skilled boatmen, fishermen, canoemen, and oarsmen were vital to the local traffic that moved by water between sections of a city and its suburbs or between the towns along the coasts and the rivers. Brazilian and African sailors based in port cities also manned the ships that plied the coastal and international waters. Rented slaves, Portuguese seamen, and a motley mixture of free and freedmen of color worked as sailors, cooks, cabin boys, and barber-surgeons on the sailing ships of the colonial period. Even convicted criminals and *degredados* (banished persons) were recruited forcibly in Bahia to join the crew of a slaver bound for the Guinea coast or Angola. The indication from colonial records is that a shortage of seamen had led to the acceptance and even the forcible recruitment of those powerless to resist being sent to sea for long voyages throughout the Portuguese empire. Nevertheless, such recruits were essential to the continuing commerce between Brazilian coastal cities, the Spanish colonies to the south, Africa, Asia, and Portugal; and many African and Brazilian sailors made extensive voyages all over the empire, including Africa.

Food Processors

After importation by muleback or boat, the raw materials or living animals were deposited in the cities in warehouses or corrals. Other groups, especially women, then undertook the processing of the materials as foodstuffs. In tropical colonial Latin America, Indian women and slaves turned the raw manioc root into farinha, while in the highland areas they converted corn into corn meal. As staples in the cities, these were then sold to others who baked farinha and corn meal into manioc and corn breads, which were more likely to be the food of the poor than were wheat breads. In much of colonial Latin America, those who baked manioc, corn, or wheat breads, or corn tortillas in New Spain, were women who did so in their own ovens; but in the large urban centers such as Lima and Rio slaves were the bakers. In eighteenth-century Lima slaveowners who wanted to correct their disobedient slaves sent them to the bakers for punishments then regarded as more severe than those inflicted in the galleys. Thus, slaves in correction worked at kneading bread alongside the bakers' own slaves. In nineteenth-century Rio African male slaves were the bakers, who produced fine French breads and pastries in bakeries that employed 4 to 18 slaves. Most of the bakers were women in colonial Bahia and Ouro Prêto, while in Santiago and Potosí some of the bakers were black and Indian women. Slaves also processed cacao beans into excellent chocolate for the cakes and sweets of the city. Both in northern colonial South America and in Brazil black slaves were the chocolatiers. Where cacao was common, as in Central America, chocolate was part of the diet of the poor, often as a drink.

Slaves were also the alcoholic drink distillers and vendors. Since plantation and suburban slaves throughout the tropical regions in which sugar was grown had access to sugar cane, they simply cut it, removed the juice, and sold it as an unrefined sugar cane juice. Others processed it further into various qualities of rum, the most inexpensive of which was known as *cachaça* or *aguardente* in Brazil, or raw brandies that they or other slaves then bootlegged as illegal drinks to the urban poor. Taverns and *vendas* (market shops) in poor neighborhoods also sold or bartered cachaça for stolen goods, and the illegal rum trade often was linked with certain types of theft in early nineteenth-century

Rio. In the Andean region those who made and sold an alcoholic beverage distilled it from corn (*chicha*), and Indian women processed it along with their other household duties, weaving and farming. Indians also controlled the manufacture of the local alcoholic drink in New Spain, which was *pulque,* extracted and fermented from the maguey plant. In the late colonial period Indian women, especially widows, not only dispensed pulque from their houses or taverns, but also traveled from their villages to sell it in the streets of the cities. The expansion of the pulque trade even enabled some women to become the wealthiest persons in their own communities. Because of the mass market for cheap yet flavorful alcoholic beverages, making and vending them were among the more profitable occupations for women and slaves in colonial Latin America. They did not, however, bring high social status, for being involved in the vending of alcoholic beverages was sufficient to exclude one's daughter from becoming an Indian nun in New Spain.

Related in function to the food and drink processors were those who took animal by-products and converted them into useful items. Candlemakers formed tallow candles and soaps from animal by-products imported from the south and molded elegant candles for use in religious services and in homes from fine African wax. The chandlers also made ex-votos of wax to commemorate a saint's intervention on one's behalf. Others, with the skills of tanners, converted hides from the south or the *sertão* into leather products, such as bags for salt, saddles, and objects for use in animal husbandry.

Open air slaughterhouses on the sites of corrals employed many Indians and slaves, especially in regions devoted to cattle raising. In New Spain slaughtering animals apparently was done by poor Indians, and was considered to be such a "vile" occupation that it also disqualified one's daughter from becoming a nun in Mexico City. It is probably indicative of similar attitudes about slaughtering animals that the occupation was imposed on slaves in Brazil, who killed the animals that had been herded to the corrals and afterwards transported their carcasses to the butchershops.

In eighteenth-century Bahia 80 to 100 black men slaughtered cattle at the "corrals of the Council" near the fortress of the Barbalho, while in early nineteenth-century Rio slaves still butchered them near Santa Luzia beach in the center of the city. While the French artist Debret later painted this scene, an American doctor captured it in words: "If raw beef can be disgusting to the sight, it is when the blood is reeking down their bodies, and mingling itself with the smoking perspiration, excited by a heavy weight, a hot sun, and extraordinary exertion."[5] Another group of slaves worked in a separate area of the cities in the processing of pork. They also transported huge carcasses on their heads and shoulders to the shops that sold pork in Rio. In colonial Minas, the process for slaughtering pigs outside and transporting fresh pork into Ouro Prêto was so hazardous to health that the sale of fresh pork was prohibited in the city. The slaughterhouses of Rio also employed women. They worked as tripe makers under conditions that endangered their own health, as well as that of those who ate the meat, since they washed out intestines and prepared tripe on the same filthy beach in Rio where bad meat was dumped and flies abounded.

Another group of slaves labored in the factories that processed whale oil and meat in colonial Brazil. In Bahia a large settlement of people once lived near the fortress of São Lourenço and worked in the armação, where whale oil and related products were produced. In Rio the armações were located on the Rua da Misericórdia and across the bay in Praia Grande (now Niteroí). Other important factories were in the south in Santa Catarina.

Sellers

Once the commodities had been imported and the foodstuffs processed for the city, they were distributed and marketed by a variety of social groups. Although the Portuguese and Spanish merchants dominated the import-export networks and the interregional trade, Africans, Indians, and persons of mixed ancestry were important in the "other economy" of the cities, including the black market in contraband goods. While the Portuguese and Spaniards sat in their shops, stores, warehouses, and houses, the people of color worked the streets of the cities. The non-elites, especially African women in the port cities and Indians in highland New Spain and Peru, were prominent in the street trade and markets in the squares.

The poorest and those with the least capital, usually slaves and freedpersons, were those who engaged in peddling door-to-door through the streets of the city. (See Figure 20). Peddlers pursued their customers on a part- or full-time basis. Slaves, who had to work for their owners at other occupations, often devoted their free time on Sundays, holidays, or late evenings to the vending of foodstuffs or objects that they made, bought, or stole. Those who became successful at part-time peddling often were permitted to transfer their talents to a full-time occupation, while others worked for owners who had something to sell and wanted to live off their slaves' earnings. Other slaves merely served as the porters for immigrant Iberian peddlers, who went from door to door selling fine silverware and silks.

By the early nineteenth century in port cities like Cartagena, Havana, Rio, and Bahia, the majority of street peddlers were Africans, who called out their wares in rhythmic songs as they hawked them through the streets. They sold everything, including services. The only limitation on their activities was the size of the merchandise, which had to be carried or led from door to door. Balancing goods in baskets, on wooden trays, or in ceramic pots on their heads, slaves of both sexes hawked articles of clothing, books, copper pans and water pots, kitchen utensils, baskets, mats, candles, love potions, statues of saints, herbs and flowers, birds and animals, other slaves, and jewelry.

Some slaves specialized in a particular item, because they were employed by the person who made it, but it was also common for one slave to sell a varied selection of drygoods. In Bahia black women specialized in the purchase of contraband, black market textiles acquired from foreign ships or slavers newly arrived from West Africa. They then sold them throughout the city.

One of the most important peddling activities throughout colonial Latin America was the vending of fresh or prepared foodstuffs. While Iberian peddlers often competed with the drygoods businesses of creoles and Africans, they seem to have left the food business to other social groups. Africans and Indians, therefore, were the ones who carried vegetables and fruits, fowls and eggs, meat and fish pastries and sweets from door to door or sold them in the markets. Traditional divisions of labor by sex seem to have influenced who sold what in the markets. In Spain and Portugal, as well as in Santiago and Bahia, women sold fish and meat; but in Rio the licenses for peddlers reveal that men dominated the profession there. In Bahia, black slave women known as *ganhadeiras* bought fish, apparently at the fishing boats from black fishermen, and then resold it to other black women. Apparently, black women there followed the European tradition of women handling animal foods, while in Rio the African tradition predominated.

In many coastal cities, many women sold vegetables, fruits, and prepared foods. Not only did files of women bring in fresh produce from nearby chacaras and sítios, but they also sold it from door to door or to the market women for sale in the cities. Other women vendors who were skilled cooks took the foodstuffs and prepared foods for sale to the slaves and poor in open-air restaurants in the port areas and squares of the cities. In Brazil, many women who also had to labor as household servants, sold palm oil stew, fried fish, barbecued dried beef, coconut candies and sweets, and refreshing sweet and fruit drinks in the streets and markets. The role of people of color in the food business was repeated in many other urban centers. In Guatemala City, they sold corn, cheese, fish, salt, and vegetables. Fish from Lake Atitlán was sold door-to-door by Indians and mestizos.

Street peddlers who were successful then settled down in market produce stalls (*quitandas*) or vendas. Although both men and women worked as peddlers in the cities, it appears that the market stalls in which produce was sold in coastal port cities were owned by non-Iberian women. In the port cities the owners were usually African women, while in the Amazon and highland Spanish America they were Indian women. In the early nineteenth century the English artist Chamberlain plagiarized a Portuguese artist's depiction of the market women of Rio before independence. He depicted a prosperous black woman sitting in the shade under a woven mat and smoking a long stemmed pipe, while she negotiated with customers seeking to buy chickens, fruits, and vegetables. Apparently many freedwomen were the owners of market stalls, and their successful careers in the markets had even permitted them to purchase their freedom and own their own quitandas.

Another street trade in which some freedwomen and slaves engaged on a part- or full-time basis was prostitution. Since there were many frontier towns in colonial Latin America in which males outnumbered females, the demand for prostitutes led to the exploitation of slave women and boys. Those forced into prostitution by economic necessity or avaricious owners were usually women of color and, on the frontier, Indian women. However, in sixteenth-century Peru and eighteenth-century Bahia, white women also supported themselves by prostitution, and Vilhena inveighed against the number of lost and disgraced women.[6] More common, however, in the colonial period was the pattern in which slave owners, even from respectable families, as well as brothel owners and pimps, acquired slave women for their households and then sent them out at night on an *ao ganho* basis—that is, as blacks for hire who had to prostitute themselves in order to return the sum of money required by their owners. In many colonial cities slave prostitutes supported "respectable" households, and slave prostitution seems to have been a socially accepted and common aspect of slavery throughout the colonial period. Because of the money that could be earned in the trade, some slave women were able to buy their freedom, and another notable group of prostitutes were freedwomen, but it is uncertain at what point the latter obtained their freedom. The colonial sources are generally silent on male prostitution, but it must have been common, especially in cities in which women were scarce; and it was well established in coastal port cities of the early nineteenth century.

A final category of street vendors were the ambulatory barbers who peddled their services in the squares. Carrying their equipment with them, they practiced their medical and healing crafts, such as the application of leeches for bleeding; and they cut the hair of both sexes, even in African styles, and shaved the beards of men. In the colonial period it was the barbers who also acted as the surgeons of the cities—they pulled teeth, set fractures, and performed amputations. They were also the surgeons who accompanied slave ships to care for sick slaves during the voyage to America from Africa. Because of the shortage of trained persons with such skills, a few slaves and freedpersons were permitted to work as barber-surgeons in Rio, but most slave barbers only cut hair and applied leeches. In Bahia, between 1741 and 1749 all 38 barbers were of African descent—17 slaves and 21 free blacks or mulatos. A second sample taken between 1810 and 1822 reveals that 33 barbers included 20 slaves and 13 free persons of color.[7] Ladino Indians, however, were the ones who were the skilled bleeders in Quito.

Those who were successful in the street trades often left them to establish their own quitandas, *vendas*, taverns, and *lojas* (stores) in fixed locations. Itinerant Spanish *tratantes* or Portuguese *mascates* (peddlers) and African freedmen who had traveled from town to town or from town to plantation and farm as poor young men settled down in the cities as owners of permanent retail businesses when they were financially able to do so. Recent immigrant Spaniards turned to running *pulperías* (small groceries and bars) throughout Spanish America. In Caracas those who dealt in articles such as pottery, wines, tools, and cheese were unmarried Catalonians and Canarians. While the owners of retail stores were often Portuguese and Spanish immigrants, impoverished whites, especially new immigrants, found employment as their clerks and cashiers. In eighteenth-century Paraty and early nineteenth-century Rio, most clerks were Portuguese, with only a minority of pardos waiting on customers. In seventeenth-century Santiago the city council wanted to maintain the same racial order, preferring to grant licenses for pulperías to Spaniards, who were to employ whites as clerks and barkeepers, but in reality it gave eight women, including one black and an Indian, the right to run pulperías (out of 12 licenses granted). By the eighteenth century, however, pulpería licenses were given regularly to upper-class Hispanic widows in the province of Chile.

A similar pattern in which women received licenses for shops occurred in colonial Minas, where those who ran the shops were largely women, of all colors, and slaves. In 1734, 253 licenses were given for shops, of which 149, or almost 60 percent, were issued to women and another 82, or 32.4 percent, were alloted to slaves. Although women and slaves dominated the lowest ranks of the retail outlets, such as vendas and taverns, not one of them received a license for a store. By the late eighteenth century, slaves in Minas were still receiving licenses for shops. Of 71 licenses given to slaves between 1798 and 1806, 48 went to women and 23 to men.[8] Women and slaves undoubtedly received these licenses as a result of elite perceptions of those who sold groceries and liquor as lower in status, especially if they sold to the poor and enslaved. Such attitudes also would explain why blacks were permitted to own quitandas in nineteenth-century Rio and Bahia, while Indians controlled the produce business in highland Peru and New Spain. On the other hand, clerks who dealt with customers in larger stores were expected to be white or at least pardo. In sharp contrast to this Brazilian pattern, Indian women in the booming mining town of Potosí ran and may have owned stores that sold pastry, candy, silver items, groceries, bread, prepared food, and general articles of necessity. In other areas of colonial Latin America it was unheard of for an Indian or black woman to run such stores, especially selling silver. They usually were restricted to whites or at best to the racially mixed.

An unusual group that established shops in the cities of Bahia and Rio were the gypsies. Deported in large numbers to Brazil in the early eighteenth century, the gypsies established themselves in the Bairro da Palma in Bahia and on the Rua dos Ciganos and in the slave market of Rio. They took up the legal and illegal trade in horses and slaves, and openly dealt in stolen and purchased animals and slaves in their stores in the cities or surrepticiously transported them to interior plantations. In the police records of Rio they had the reputation of being "fences" or receivers of stolen goods, but apparently they were also important in the legal plantation trade in animals and slaves between coastal cities and the interior by the early nineteenth century. In the city of Rio some of the more prosperous gypsies were important wholesalers in the business of new slaves. They quartered them in their large houses in the Valongo market before sale to urban or rural slaveowners.

Servants

In modern societies sales occupations are distinct from household services and are performed by different individuals, but in colonial Latin America sales and services often were carried out by the same non-elite individuals. Taverns, shops, and "restaurants" often were established in a lean-to or front room of a colonial house, whose inhabitants cared for their customers as well as their own families. Thus, the *dona da casa* (lady of the house), often a widow, directed her slaves in waiting on customers and cooking and cleaning for her own household. If she had many slaves, she sent them into the streets as blacks for hire and street vendors. In São Paulo, where agregados were more numerous, whites and mestizos often performed the combined sales and service occupations.

In the largest households of colonial Brazil, including 60 to 70 *crias da casa* (slaves raised in the households), however, there was more labor specialization, the nature of which varied from city to city. In the Amazon, São Paulo, and the far south, household servants were more likely to be Indian and mestizo, while in Rio and Bahia, as well as in Mexico City, Lima, and the mining towns of Minas, they were more likely to be mulato or black and of slave status, in the homes of the wealthy. Agregados, often the relatives, although distant, of the senhores, whether recent rural migrants, as in the case of São Paulo, or freedpersons still attached to the household, also added to the court of the lord and lady of the house. The elite among the household servants were the elegantly dressed male and female personal servants of the couple. Among the slave women these were the ladies-in-waiting known as *mucamas* (or *mocambas*). Not infrequently of mixed ancestry, a mucama was often related to the family as the half-sister, child, or concubine of her owner. If her master were unmarried, she often served as his housekeeper or supervisor in charge of the other slaves, in which case she may have owed her senior position to the fact that she was his mistress or common-law wife. In other cases, mucamas were preferred as the wet nurses (*amas de leite*) for their owners' children. Not only did they nurse them, but they also reared the children as well. Owners who did not have a slave woman with milk who could nurse their children rented or borrowed a wet nurse from other masters. Because of their importance in the care and raising of their owners' children, nurses were often among the most esteemed of the household slaves. Another slave woman of status was the African midwife, who assisted the wives of slave-owners in childbirth.

While some mucamas spent all their time waiting on their ladies or caring for their children, others were the housekeepers and supervisors of the other slaves. They carried out the instructions of the lady of the house and supervised the daily household tasks, such as washing, sewing, mending, starching, and drying clothes. In a single person's house, they often undertook all the functions of the lady of the house, including the disciplining, instruction, and training of new slaves.

Next in status after the mucamas, housekeepers, and nurses were the slave children of the master, or at least the children raised in the household. Masters who recognized their children by their slave women often kept them within their households as their personal servants—but still enslaved. Women owners often gave preference to the children raised as crias in their households, and one of the most common reasons advanced for manumission in the colonial period was that the owner freed the slave because he or she was a cria raised in the household. While these slaves were children, they were raised together with their owners' children and served as their playmates and babysitters. As they grew up, however, the girls were trained in skilled household tasks as mucamas and the boys as pages and valets. Other male slaves of wealthy households occupied positions as coachmen, liveried footmen, stablemen, and sedan chair carriers. Their elaborate uniforms set them apart from other slaves. By the late 1820s in Rio, the privileged slaves who were coachmen were generally thought to be mulatos.

Slaves of both sexes worked as cooks and buyers in large households. Because of their culinary skills, African cooks were in particular demand in the port cities and mining towns of Brazil and were highly esteemed among the household slaves. Assisting each cook was a particularly trusted slave who went to the markets to purchase the foodstuffs needed by the household. After several years of service, a slave could sometimes rise to the esteemed position of buyer.

Throughout colonial Latin America household workers especially in demand were those who made clothing with skill and style. Work as weavers and seamstresses was among the most common occupations of non-elite women. Until English textiles made inroads into local textile production, women of all races commonly wove their own cloth for household consumption or for the interregional trade, while Indian men and women were coerced into laboring in *obrajes* (textile factories) in Spanish America. Although Indian women in highland Mesoamerica and the Andes continued to produce hand-woven textiles in Indian designs, in late colonial Brazil market preferences in the coastal cities for imported European and Asian textiles meant that women were more likely to be employed as seamstresses than as weavers. In the far interior, however, textile production remained alive in towns such as Vila Boa de Goiás. Whenever imported textiles were undesirable, unavailable, or costly, the women of the household obtained raw cotton, deseeded it with primitive wooden implements, spun it on small spinning wheels, and wove it into cloth on backstrap Indian or European trestle looms. The women who spun cotton in Rio using the rock and the spindle were women of color. In the northeast of Brazil, poor white women and women of color also made lace, for which they were famous throughout the country.

In general, the women of the house took the homemade or imported textiles and made them into items of clothing for the entire household, and most, if not all, female slaves were expected to do some sewing under the supervision of a mucama or their mistress. Although slave women did the plain sewing as a matter of course, some became such expert seamstresses that they duplicated imported European fashions for their mistresses or for sale in French dress shops in the early nineteenth century. Clothing for elite men in Rio, however, was made by male slaves employed by European tailors situated on the street of the tailors. One of the most common sights in colonial cities was that of the slave tailors seated at work on their owner's doorsteps. Other groups of slave craftsmen made all the other items of personal adornment: hats, shoes, canes, jewelry, neckcloths, and so forth.

Every household in the cities of Brazil had at least one slave, hired or owned, to do the laundry, starching, and ironing of the elegant dresses of the colonial period. In wealthy families, slaves specialized as laundrymen or women, starchers, or ironers, who worked under the supervision of a mucama. Laundry slaves usually had to work at a number of locations in the cities. Some cities with large fountains also had a sort of laundry tank where clothes were washed. At the foot of the aqueduct in Carioca Square in Rio was a large tank where slaves washed clothes by slamming them against nearby walls and spreading them on the ground to dry. By the nineteenth century it was so crowded that it usually was frequented by the slaves of the poor. Other laundry slaves washed clothes at the fountain in the Field of Saint Ann, which was the major laundry site of Rio. In the nineteenth century at least 200 men and women scrubbed clothes there in large wooden bowls sitting on top of water barrels. Afterwards they laid the clothing on the grass to dry. Other than the fountains, the most common laundry sites were the rivers of Brazil. All the major cities located along rivers, such as Santarem at the juncture of the Amazon and the Tapajós or those of the Rio São Francisco, had areas set aside for the women to do the laundry and grassy areas for the clothes to dry. In Rio the river was in the Laranjeiras valley. Slaves who washed clothes there in the nineteenth century also carried laundry into Rio in return for payment. Perhaps this was the area near Rio where some slave owners rented small farms and employed their black women as laundresses. Because doing laundry was so necessary and so profitable, nany slaves escaped slavery by using their laundry earnings to purchase their freedom and a notable group of laundrywomen in most colonial cities were freedwomen.

Ranked last among household servants were those assigned to the most menial household tasks and those farthest removed from the person of their owners. Most of these were African or Indian slaves. They were the people who did the work of cleaning, carrying water, waiting on tables, washing up, and emptying of refuse containers. Among those with the fewest skills were the old or the infirm, children, or new, unassimilated Africans or Indians, who shared no special relationship with their owners. They often had to scramble for places to sleep in the corridors or scavenge for food to survive. Infirm and old slaves unable to do even the most menial tasks were set in the streets to beg and forced to hand over a share of the small alms they received to their owners.

Municipal Workers

Urban non-elites were also important to the care of the colonial city itself. Municipal governments tended to use slaves, criminals, and Indians to build new buildings and streets or to refurbish old sections of the cities. They were especially important for all those tasks that required hard physical labor or gangs of workers. In general, the size of the work groups set out by city governments ranged from one or two dogcatchers to large gangs that paved streets. In Brazil, they comprised a mixed group of convict workers in chain gangs, slaves in correction upon the orders of their owners, Indian prisoners of war, rented Indians from nearby Jesuit mission villages, and slaves rented from urban owners. Together, the rented and the criminal workers constructed public buildings, such as jails, laid out and paved streets, repaired them as they disintegrated in the rains, erected public fountains and aqueducts, laid out canals, and filled in the swamps and lakes as the colonial cities grew in size during the eighteenth century.

One of their most difficult jobs was road construction, which in many cases involved swamp drainage and preparation of an elevated roadbed, and required gangs of slaves for moving earth. For these tasks the cities used chain gangs and rented slaves in Brazil and Indian forced labor in Peru. Apparently, the rented slaves were skilled stone layers, while the other groups provided the unskilled labor needed for moving dirt and preparing the streetbeds. Other convicts and slaves in correction worked in nearby quarries to supply the materials for roadbuilding.

The practice of renting slaves to Brazilian municipal governments was so common that slave owners even rented their slaves as lamplighters. One of the major changes in the atmosphere of colonial cities began in late eighteenth-century Rio when the viceroy, the Conde de Rezende, initiated the illumination of the city by whale oil lamps. From then on the once dark city of Rio, in which most activities had been restricted after sunset, was able to give security to the elites who ventured out to evening balls and to the theater and to ordinary people who frequented taverns. Ambitious slaves who wanted to earn extra money after their daily tasks were completed set up small stalls or trays of food beneath the lamps and hawked their wares to passers-by. But, most importantly, the whale oil lamps gave employment to a troop of black lamplighters who cared for them each day. Apparently, most were rented slaves until 1821, when free Africans were set to work on the lamps. For more than 50 years, then, the slave lamplighters of Rio and other Brazilian centers illuminated the cities with whale oil until they were converted to gas lighting in 1850.

Another public job in which slaves were employed was that of firefighter. In the colonial period, when destructive fires were common, slave owners sent out their slaves with water barrels and carts to put out fires. They literally manned "bucket brigades" to fight the fires. Other slaves were hired to catch and kill stray and rabid dogs and to clean the streets.

In addition to laboring for the government, slaves also worked for churches, convents, monasteries, and brotherhoods in the menial positions often associated with modern public hospitals and charitable organizations, or as the personal servants of nuns and monks. Owners who wanted to benefit a particular brotherhood, such as the santa casa da misericórdia of Bahia and Rio, donated one or more slaves to work for the santa casa in its hospital, foundling home, orphanage, retirement home, and other charitable activities. Fathers who provided dowries to daughters entering convents sent slaves to serve them in the convents. Donated slaves were often the barber-surgeons and bleeders, nurses, orderlies, and maintenance persons of the colonial hospitals. In Rio donated slaves appear to have been more widely used in these occupations at the santa casa da misericórdia than in colonial Bahia, where the nurses were illiterate whites because of racial barriers excluding persons of color from the more skilled jobs. At the foundling home and orphanage of the santa casa in Rio, slave women served as the wet nurses for abandoned children, raised them, and engaged in child care at the orphanage. In Bahia, however, the santa casa hired free women of color to work as wet nurses, and the children were sent to their homes for care. Because of the high mortality rate in the coastal cities, the patients and children who did not survive the contagious diseases that swept through colonial hospitals and homes were interred by slaves, who buried the dead in the graves of the santa casa. Except for the Catholic priest and the white brothers of the santa casa, much of the preparation, transportation and burial of the dead was done by slaves in Rio, or at least by people of color in Bahia. In nineteenth-century Rio slaves were even hired as professional mourners who dressed all in black and so earned the popular nickname of "crows."

Convicted slave criminals saw to the care and feeding of the prisoners and hospital patients in the colonial cities. Since the santa casa undertook to feed prisoners who were dependent for their survival on the charity of others, they had gangs of chained criminals transport food and water to the hospitals of the cities, as well as to the public prisons. Convicts were also the ones responsible for the punishment of slaves at the whipping posts in the public squares of the cities. They wielded the whips, giving 200 to 300 lashes to fugitive slaves and even more to convicted criminals. Female slave convicts whipped female slaves at the slave prison of the Calabouço in Rio. As late as the nineteenth century, slaveowners commonly hired others to punish their slaves for them. The city of Rio provided this service to slaveowners upon receipt of payment for 50 to 300 lashes, while private entrepreneurs hired out their services to discipline unruly slaves with more exotic tortures. In urban households, those responsible for the daily correction of slaves were the donas da casa, who had a reputation for brutality towards their slaves in Brazilian cities. At least by the early nineteenth century, it was true that Brazilian masters did not whip their slaves—such tasks were left to their wives, overseers, hired torturers, and the city government. Finally, those who carried out the ultimate punishment—execution on behalf of the government—were slave criminals who served as the hangmen at the public gallows.

Perhaps the only municipal service in which slaves did not engage in colonial cities was police work, but even then there were exceptions. Slaves often served as spies who kept the authorities informed on seditious and rebellious behavior in the slave quarters or on the part of their owners, who may have been engaged in smuggling gold and diamonds or counterfeiting coins. Rewarded with manumission for their services, they were often important in the control of criminal and/or rebellious activities in colonial Brazil. Other slaves, or, more often, ex-slaves, Indians, and free people of color, worked as slave hunters or their assistants and pursued fugitive slaves in the cities and countryside for a profitable bounty. The *capitão do mato* or *capitão do assalto* who led the expeditions that raided and destroyed *quilombos* (runaway slave communities) and returned runaways to slavery was most important in the process of slave control in colonial Brazil. As the man hunters of the period, they needed both police and forest skills in order to collect their bounties. For this reason, the bands that made up an expedition often were composed of ex-slaves and skilled Indian and Brazilian frontiersmen of color. Since skill was so often the determining factor in obtaining a license to hunt slaves, the licenses were given to men of all colors and civil statuses. Slaves and ex-slaves even participated in the area of slave control, although whites often headed expeditions.

In Brazil and along coastal Spanish America, owners also armed their slaves to defend themselves and their properties from enemies: hostile Indians, European invaders such as the Dutch and the French, and armed bands of escaped slaves. However, many slaves who worked in defense of Brazil did so on the supply lines and in the fortifications of the cities. They worked as the personal servants and porters of the militia, infantry, and artillery officers based in the port cities of Salvador and Rio. When their owners went on campaign against hostile forces, they carried their guns and umbrellas and served as their officers' beasts of burden. Gangs of slaves also were set to build the sizeable and numerous fortifications that defended the capitals of Bahia and Rio, as well as most other important colonial cities such as Cartagena. Slaves who fought for Brazil often did so as a reserve force, but as freedmen they joined the colonial black and pardo regiments popularly known as the *Henriques* and the *terços dos pardos* and defended the country from its enemies. In particular, they rendered valuable service in the ouster of the Dutch from Brazil in the seventeenth century. By the late eighteenth century Bahia could count on 575 men in the *regimento de artilharia auxiliar dos pardos* (the mulattos' auxiliary artillery regiment) and 603 in the *terço de Henrique Dias* of the blacks (named for the black hero in the war against the Dutch). Furthermore, the city had 6,000 *negros captivos armados* (armed black captives) as a reserve force.[9]

What was unique in Brazilian colonial cities, possibly because of Portuguese familiarity with the custom of Muslim soldier-slaves in North and West Africa, was the practice of giving the defense of its colonial cities in part to its slaves. Actually, one compelling reason for this was the refusal of white men to serve in any capacity as ordinary soldiers in the colonial armies. Throughout the colonial period such attitudes had led to the forcible recruitment of men from as far as the Madeira islands and the Azores and as near as the streets of Bahia or Rio. Although white men of high status in the landed elite served as colonels in the militia regiments, none but the powerless and the poor of any color served as common soldiers for the Portuguese. In Bahia the targets for forcible conscription were artisans, tavernkeepers, peddlers, and vagrants. Since the defense of Brazil in any position below officer rank was regarded as appropriate to men of low status, including ex-slaves, the nature of status and rank in Brazilian colonial society thus permitted and even required owners to arm their slaves. Other slave societies never dared to entrust such an important and potentially dangerous function to slaves and ex-slaves.

Conclusions

Why Brazilian or Spanish American colonial society ascribed particular occupations to urban non-elites tells us much about the functions of colonial cities as well as elite values. Since colonial cities were largely commercial-bureaucratic centers, mining and garrison towns on the frontier, or agricultural processing centers, persons of high status pursued occupations linked to international trade, ownership of land, secular or religious bureaucracies, or the military and militias. Most others became the servants or wives of those who fulfilled these primary functions. Since colonial elites tended to restrict the primary occupations to their own kind—that is, to Iberians or creole whites—these occupations also were racially defined, although light-skinned persons of African or Indian descent had made inroads into them by the early nineteenth century. The majority of women were excluded. Nuns and other women within the elite might assume important financial and commercial roles, but the middle or lower status women who had to support themselves by their own work, could find occupations only outside the profitable and influential ones pursued by white elite males.

Their occupations thus reinforced their non-elite status. To be a supplier, transporter, food or liquor processor, seller, servant, or slave was to be of low caste and status. When color and female gender were added to status criteria, an individual was ranked even lower in colonial society. These free, freed, and enslaved individuals of all colors who engaged in lowly urban occupations, were disparaged even though their jobs were both economically viable and significant to the overall development of late eighteenth-and early nineteenth-century cities. In spite of their low social status, however, they and their descendants contributed significantly to the urban economy in transportation, manufacturing, the retail trades, and sales and services. They provided not only labor, but also capital from their pulperías and vendas, as well as managerial skills acquired over decades of supervising the work of other urban laborers. They are the forgotten men and women of colonial Latin American history, whose true contributions to urban history have only begun to be appreciated.

Notes

1. Luiz dos Santos Vilhena, *Recopilação de noticias soteropolitanas e brasilicas,* ed. Braz do Amaral (Bahia: Imprensa Official do Estado, 1921–22), 1: 51, 161–62: Andre João Antonil, *Cultura e opulencia do Brasil por suas drogas, e minas,. . . .* (Lisbon, 1711: facsimile edition, Recife: Indústria Gráfica Brasileira, 1969), 188–89; and Sue Ellen Anderson Gross, "The Economic Life of the Estado do Maranhão e Grão Pará, 1686–1751" (Ph.D. diss., Tulane University, 1969), 32–34.

2. Louis F. de Tollenare, *Notes dominicales prises pendant un voyage en Portugal et au Brésil en 1816, 1817 et 1818,* edited by Léon Bourdon (Paris: Presses Universitaires de France, 1971–73), 3: 683, 702–05, 765.

3. Robert Burford, *Description of a View of the City of St. Sebastian, and the Bay of Rio Janeiro. . . .* (London: J. and C. Adlard, Bartholomew Close, 1828), 10.

4. Henry Ellis, *Journal of the Proceedings of the Late Embassy to China. . . .* (London: John Murray, 1817), 7.

5. Gustavus R. B. Horner, *Medical Topography of Brazil. . . .* (Philadelphia: Lindsay and Blakiston, 1845), 67.

6. Vilhena, *Recopilação,* 140.

7. A. J. R. Russell-Wood, *The Black Man in Slavery and Freedom in Colonial Brazil* (New York: St. Martins Press, 1982), 57.

8. Donald Ramos, "A Social History of Ouro Prêto: Stresses of Dynamic Urbanization in Colonial Brazil, 1695–1726," (Ph.D. diss., University of Florida, 1972), 182–84 (he does not identify who the other 22 people were who received shop licenses) and 233 (4 percent of freedmen and 7 percent of freedwomen owned shops in 1804): and Larry J. Neilson, "Of Gentry, Peasants, and Slaves: Rural Society in Sabará and Its Hinterland, 1780–1930," (Ph.D. diss., University of California, Davis, 1975) 198 (for identities of some slaves given shop licenses, 1798–1806).

9. Vilhena, *Recopilação*, 1: 46, 247, 253–70; 2: 823–25: and Tollenare, *Notes*, 2: 450–58 (for black and mulato regiments in Recife).

Suggestions for Further Reading

Sources on urban non-elites are fragmentary and scattered. The following suggestions for further reading are limited, therefore, to the more significant studies and do not include many lesser works that also were used to write this chapter. Additional documentation may be found in Mary Karasch, "From Porterage to Proprietorship: African Occupations in Rio de Janeiro, 1808–1850," in Stanley L. Engerman and Eugene D. Genovese, eds., *Race and Slavery in the Western Hemisphere: Quantitative Studies* (New Jersey: Princeton University Press, 1975): 369–93; "Rio de Janeiro: From Colonial Town to Imperial Capital, 1808–1850," (Dordrecht: Martinus Nijhoff Publishers, 1985); and *Slave Life in Rio de Janeiro, 1808–1850* (New Jersey: Princeton University Press, in press).

Students should begin their own research with two bibliographies: Robert Conrad, *Brazilian Slavery: An Annotated Research Bibliography* (Boston: G. K. Hall & Co., 1977); and John D. Smith, ed., *Black Slavery in the Americas: An Interdisciplinary Bibliography, 1865–1980,* 2 vols. (Westport, Conn.: Greenwood Press, 1982). Paulo Berger, *Bibliografia do Rio de Janeiro de viajantes e autores estrangeiros, 1531–1900* (Rio de Janeiro: Livraria São José, 1964) is indispensable for the travel literature on Brazil. See also such dissertations as Rae Jean Dell Flory, "Bahian Society in the Mid-Colonial Period: The Sugar Planters, Tobacco Growers, Merchants, and Artisans of Salvador and the Reconcavo, 1680–1725" (Ph.D. diss., University of Texas, 1978); Larry J. Neilson, "Of Gentry, Peasants, and Slaves: Rural Society in Sabará and its Hinterland, 1780–1930," (Ph.D. diss., University of California, Davis, 1975); Donald Ramos, "A Social History of Ouro Prêto: Stresses of Dynamic Urbanization in Colonial Brazil, 1695–1726," (Ph.D. diss., University of Florida, 1972); and Sue Ellen Anderson Gross, "The Economic Life of the Estado do Maranhão e Grão Pará, 1686–1751," (Ph.D. diss., Tulane University, 1969).

General histories that include material on Brazilian urban non-elites are Caio Prado, Jr., *The Colonial Background of Modern Brazil*, trans. Suzette Macedo (Berkeley: University of California Press, 1969); A. J. R. Russell-Wood, *Fidalgos and Philanthropists: The Santa Casa da Misericórdia of Bahia, 1550–1755* (Berkeley: University of California Press, 1968); C. R. Boxer, *The Golden Age of Brazil, 1695–1750* (Berkeley: University of California Press, 1969); Stuart B. Schwartz, *Sovereignty and Society in Colonial Brazil* (Berkeley: University of California Press, 1973); Dauril Alden, *Royal Government in Colonial Brazil* (Berkeley: University of California Press, 1968); and Dauril Alden, "The Population of Brazil in the Late Eighteenth Century: A Preliminary Survey," *The Hispanic American Historical Review* 43:2 (May 1963): 173–205. Essential for Indian labor use and slavery is John Hemming, *Red Gold: The Conquest of the Brazilian Indians, 1500–1760* (Cambridge: Harvard University Press, 1978).

A general urban history of Brazil remains to be written in English, and most recent histories of individual cities are still in Portuguese. A recent history of Salvador in the nineteenth century is Katia M. de Queirós Mattoso, *Bahia: a cidade do Salvador e seu mercado no século XIX* (São Paulo: Hucitec, 1978). Numerous articles on Brazilian cities appear in Euripedes Simões de Paula, ed., *A Cidade e a História*, vol. 1, *Anais do VII Simpósio Nacional dos Professores Universitários de História* (São Paulo: N. P., 1974). Excellent occupational data form part of Eulalia Maria Lahmeyer Lobo, *História do Rio de Janeiro (Do Capital Comercial ao Capital Industrial e Financeiro*, 2 vols. (Rio de Janeiro: IBMEC, 1978). Fundamental to any histories of Rio are Vivaldo Coaracy, *Memórias da Cidade do Rio de Janeiro*, 3 vols. (Rio de Janeiro, Livararia José Olympio, 1965); and the older but detailed works of Noronha Santos, such as *As Freguesias do Rio Antigo vistas por Noronha Santos*, edited, with a bibliography of his works, by Paulo Berger (Rio de Janeiro: O Cruzeiro, 1965). A rare study in English translation is the romantic Luiz Edmundo, *Rio in the Time of the Viceroys*, trans. Dorothea H. Momsen (Rio de Janeiro: n.p., 1936). For Vila Rica see Donald Ramos, "Marriage and the Family in Colonial Vila Rica," *Hispanic American Historical Review* 55:2 (May 1975): 200–225; and "Vila Rica: Profile of a Colonial Brazilian Urban Center, *The Americas* 35:4 (April 1979): 495–526. Essential to the demographic history of São Paulo is Maria Luiza Marcilio, *La ville de São Paulo: Peuplement et population 1750–1850* (Rouen: Université de Rouen, 1972); while an introduction in English is Richard M. Morse, *From Community to Metropolis: A Biography of São Paulo, Brazil* (Gainesville, Fla.: University Presses of Florida, 1958). Specific occupational data are also available in Elizabeth A. Kuznesof, "Household Composition and Economy in an Urbanizing Community: São Paulo, 1765 to 1836," (Ph.D. diss., University of California at Berkeley, 1976), and "Household composition and Headship as Related to Changes in Modes of Production: São Paulo,

1765–1836," *Comparative Studies in Society and History* 22:1 (January 1980): 78–108.

Travelers are an indispensable source of information on non-elites in the coastal and mining cities. For Hispanic America, a useful introduction is Jorge Juan and Antonio de Ulloa, *A Voyage to South America* (Tempe, Ariz.: Arizona State University, 1975). Rich sources on colonial Brazil are Andre João Antonil, *Cultura e opulencia do Brasil por suas drogas, e minas, . . .* (Lisbon, 1711; facsimile edition, Recife: Indústria Gráfica Brasileira, 1969); Luiz dos Santos Vilhena, *Recopilação de noticias soteropolitanas e brasilicas*, ed. Braz do Amaral, 2 vols. (Bahia: Imprensa Official do Estado, 1921–22). Early nineteenth-century travelers providing accurate material on northeastern slavery are Henry Koster, *Travels in Brazil*, 2nd ed., 2 vols. (London: Longman, Hurst, Rees, Orme, and Brown, 1817); and Louis F. de Tollenare, *Notes dominicales prises pendant un voyage en Portugal et au Brésil en 1816, 1817 et 1818*, ed. Leon Bourdon, 3 vols. (Paris: Presses Universitaires de France, 1971–1973).

The best depiction of slaves in Rio and their occupations is Jean B. Debret, *Viagem Pitoresca e Histórica ao Brasil*, 2 tomos, trans. and ed. Sérgio Milliet (São Paulo: Livraria Martins Editôra, 1954). Fine illustrations of black women at work are to be found in Jean B. Debret, *Viagem Pitoresca e Histórica ao Brasil: Aquarelas e Desenhos que não Foram Reproduzidos na Edição de Firmin Didot—1834* (Paris: n.p., 1954). Other travelers include John Barrow, *Voyage to Cochinchina in the Years 1792 and 1793 . . . (London: T. Cadell and W. Davies, 1806): Sir George Staunton, An Authentic Account of an Embassy from the King of Great Britain to the Emperor of China . . . , vol. 1* (London: W. Bulmer and Co., 1797); John Luccock, *Notes on Rio de Janeiro and the Southern Parts of Brazil . . .* (London: Samuel Leigh, 1820); Maria Graham, *Journal of a Voyage to Brazil and Residence There . . .* (London: Longman, Hurst, Rees, Orme, Brown, and Green, 1824); Sir Henry Chamberlain, *Views and Costumes of the City and Neighborhood of Rio de Janeiro, Brazil* (London: Howlett and Brimmer, 1822); João Maurício Rugendas, *Viagam Pitoresca Através do Brasil*, trans. Sérgio Milliet (São Paulo: Livraria Martins, 1967); and L. J. dos Santos Marrocos, "Cartas [1811–1821] de Luiz Joaquim dos Santos Marrocos," in *Anais da Biblioteca Nacional do Rio de Janeiro* 56 (1934): 5–459.

Travelers who also visited the mining regions include J. B. von Spix and Carl F. P. von Martius, *Travels in Brazil, in the Years 1817–1820*, 2 vols. (London: Longman, Hurst, Rees, Orme, Brown, and Green, 1824); Johann E. Pohl, *Viagem no interior do Brasil . . .*, 2 vols. trans. by Teodoro Cabral (Rio de Janeiro: Instituto Nacional de Livro, 1951); and Auguste de Saint Hilaire, *Voyages dans les provinces de Rio de Janeiro et Minas Geraes*, 2 vols. (Paris: Grimbert et Dorez, 1830).

Most histories of Brazilian slavery ignore the colonial period or urban slaves and are not available in English translation. The exception is Gilberto Freyre, such as *The Masters and the Slaves*, trans. Samuel Putnam (New York: Alfred

A. Knopf, 1946). Representative of a new generation of research on slavery are Jacob Gorender, *O Escravismo Colonial* (São Paulo: Editora Atica, 1978); Katia M. de Queirós Mattoso, *Être Esclave au Brésil XVI-XIX* (Paris: Hachette, 1979); Vicente Salles, *O negro no Pará sob o regime da escravidão* (Rio de Janeiro: Fundação Getúlio Vargas, 1971): Robert E. Conrad, *Children of God's Fire: A Documentary History of Black Slavery in Brazil* (Princeton, N.J.: Princeton University Press, 1983); and A. J. R. Russell-Wood, *The Black Man in Slavery and Freedom in Colonial Brazil* (New York: St. Martin's Press, 1982), which also examines the role of free and freedpersons of color. On the emergence of freedpersons, and *agregados,* see Stuart B. Schwartz, "The Manumission of Slaves in Colonial Brazil: Bahia, 1684–1745," *The Hispanic American Historical Review* 54:4 (November 1974): 601–35; Herbert S. Klein, "The Colored Freedmen in Brazilian Slave Society," *Journal of Social History 3* (Fall 1969): 30–52; and Maria Sylvia de Carvalho Franco, *Homens Livres na Ordem Escravocrata* (São Paulo: Editora Atica, 1976). A survey of the literature on manumission in Brazil is in James P. Kiernan, "The Manumission of Slaves in Colonial Brazil: Paraty, 1789–1822," (Ph.D. diss., New York University, 1976), which also has excellent occupational data by color and sex.

Sources on urban non-elites for Hispanic America are more numerous than those for Brazil. A few are listed here, and additional references should be sought in the suggested readings in other chapters. Of particular use are David G. Sweet and Gary B. Nash, eds., *Struggle and Survival in Colonial America* (Berkeley: University of California Press, 1981); Asuncíon Lavrin, ed., *Latin American Women: Historical Perspectives* (Westport, Conn.: Greenwood Press, 1978). A model of the types of census data available in Hispanic America is Patricia Seed, "Social Dimensions of Race: Mexico City, 1753," *Hispanic American Historical Review* 62:4 (November 1982): 569–606. A typical source for provisioners is Quito's *Libros de Cabildo, 1610–1616,* Vol. 26 (Quito: Publicaciones del Archivo Municipal, 1955). Recommended as a study on retailers is Jay Kinsbruner, "The Pulperos of Caracas and San Juan during the First Half of the Nineteenth Century," *Latin American Research Review* 8:1 (1978): 65–85. Some useful details on occupations of non-white women in Chile are found in Della M. Flusche and Eugene H. Korth, *Forgotten Females: Women of African and Indian Descent in Colonial Chile, 1535–1800* (Detroit: B. Ethridge Books, 1983).

TEN

The Underclass

GABRIEL HASLIP-VIERA

Introduction

The activities of mendicants, vagabonds, and the idle poor were of great concern to government officials in many cities and towns of colonial Latin America. Traveling through Cartagena on a scientific expedition in the mideighteenth century, Jorge Juan and Antonio de Ulloa observed that the churches and public thoroughfares of that city were filled with pathetic groups of beggars and vagrants. Further to the north, in Mexico City, the viceroy, Marqués de Croix, denounced the increased number of persons "who sustain themselves without a trade," "become brigands, and finish their lives on the scaffold."[1] Similar complaints also were expressed by observers and colonial officials in the Viceroyalty of Brazil. In Bahia, Rio de Janeiro, and other cities, drunken brawls, robbery, and knife attacks by the poor were said to be commonplace. Luis dos Santos Vilhena, a critic of eighteenth-century Bahian society, noted that a large segment of the population of that city was criminally inclined and "accustomed to hunger," partly as a result of "their lack of training" and partly because of "their pride and lethargy."[2]

Sixteenth Century Background

Although the problems of unemployment and poverty, and their potential for crime and social disorder, were quite serious in the eighteenth century, they were neither new nor unique to this period. Soon after the conquest in

285

New Spain and Peru, and soon after the first settlements were established in Brazil, observers and colonial officials began to notice a rise in the number of "idlers," beggars, vagabonds, and criminals. Initially, this underclass was composed of uprooted Indians, escaped African slaves, and Spanish or Portuguese fortune seekers who sank into a life of poverty or crime because of the economic and social uncertainties of the post-Conquest period. These original groups, however, were soon to be augmented by persons of mixed race, such as *mestizos* (Indian and white ancestry) and *mulatos* (black and white ancestry), who failed to find a place for themselves in the new colonial environment because of their vague legal and social status. Many of these individuals wandered through the countryside in an often desperate search for charity or economic opportunity. Others became highwaymen or bandits, attacking travelers and pack trains on the major roads between the mining camps, the cities, and the port towns. A considerable number remained in or came to the major cities, where they became the nucleus of an increasingly troublesome underclass.

In Mexico City the devastation which accompanied the Conquest resulted in the uprooting of thousands of Indians, many of whom were to become beggars, vagrants, alcoholics, and criminals. In an effort to maintain order, the Spaniards reorganized the city creating segregated areas of settlement for the Spanish and Indian populations. In the center of the city, the colonial authorities marked off an area called the *traza* which was to be the zone of settlement for the Spaniards and their African slaves. Several districts or *barrios* were then established for the Indian population in the areas that surrounded the traza. The colonial authorities tried to enforce this pattern of residential segregation during the sixteenth and seventeenth centuries, but they were unable to do so because of economic considerations and the rise of the racially mixed population. Escaped slaves and impoverished Spaniards began to wander into the Indian barrios soon after the city was rebuilt. By the 1550s and 1560s, groups of mestizos and mulatos were found in both Spanish and Indian sections of the city. Exploitation, economic crisis, epidemics, and floods also displaced thousands of Indians in the outer barrios during the late sixteenth and early seventeenth centuries. Many of these Indians wandered into the Spanish zone of settlement where they found temporary employment as wage laborers or as lower-status artisans. A considerable number, however, joined the ranks of the emerging underclass, which by this time was found in all sections of the city.

The underclass in Mexico City continued to grow during the sixteenth and seventeenth centuries. This growth came about as a result of rigid social stratification, limited economic opportunities, and continuous rural to urban population movement. Throughout this period, impoverished migrants came to Mexico City from the countryside or from other cities in search of employment and improved living conditions. The displaced peasants were generally Indian farmers, forced off their lands by the encroaching *haciendas* (large estates) or they were agricultural day laborers who were refused employment on the haciendas when the crops failed because of drought or frost. Those who came to Mexico City were inclined to settle with relatives or friends in the outlying shanty towns where ethnic Indians and other poor people were concentrated. Others joined the ranks of the transient population, moving from district to district in search of odd jobs or handouts. At certain times of the year, Mexico City also witnessed the arrival of another temporary migratory population of day laborers who were half rural and half urban. Working their small plots of land in neighboring villages, or working in the haciendas of the surrounding valley during the planting and harvest season, they would move into the city, swelling the ranks of the floating population to work or to peddle goods during the leaner months of the year. The men would come in search of occasional employment as vendors, porters, construction workers, and day laborers and often would be followed by their wives and children, who worked in the homes of the affluent as domestics or assisted their husbands or parents by selling foodstuffs or trinkets in the streets. One priest commented that the residents of the neighboring village of Tlalnepantla were compelled to peddle firewood and charcoal in Mexico City because agriculture failed to provide sufficient support.

With the exception of a few fortunate Spaniards and creoles, most of the migrants who remained in Mexico City on a permanent basis joined the ranks of the laboring poor or the underclass. Economic opportunity was already limited by the existence of a small Spanish and creole upper stratum which controlled or monopolized commerce, manufacturing, the professions, the higher-status trades, and all appointments to administrative positions and the clergy. In such an environment, there was little hope of achieving upward economic and social mobility. As a result, the vast majority of the urban poor desperately tried to subsist on the meager incomes which they earned as servants, wage laborers, street vendors, or artisans in the lower-status trades. Many of these individuals were unable to maintain a minimum standard of living even under these circumstances. This was especially true during the final decades of the colonial regime, when the economic status of the urban poor deteriorated because of a steady increase in unemployment and cost of living. Thus, many persons within this group fell into the ranks of the underclass by becoming beggars, alcoholics, vagrants, prostitutes, and thieves.

The Size and Composition of the Urban Underclass

The size of the urban underclass in colonial Latin America cannot be determined with any degree of accuracy because of the limitations in the census data. In general, a significant number of the urban poor were not included in the census enumerations of the colonial period. As a rule, lawbreakers, beggars, and the unemployed made a conscious effort to avoid the census takers. They feared, often correctly, that enumeration would lead to confinement or to some future obligation, such as the payment of taxes, involuntary work drafts, or conscription into the army. Fortunately, there are other records which provide us with some rudimentary information on the size and composition of the underclass. These include institutional reports, police records, and the written accounts of colonial officials, foreign visitors, and the more affluent or educated residents of the major cities. From these records, we learn that the size and the importance of the underclass varied from one locality to another and that these differences were based on the economic and social conditions which existed in each region at a particular time. For example, unemployment and crime were relatively predictable in those urban centers which were economically more stable, such as Cuzco, Guatemala City, and Querétaro. The opposite, however, was true of the port cities, the mining towns, and the more complex economic and administrative centers, such as Bahia, Potosí, Lima, and Mexico City. These urban centers were affected by the boom-and-bust cycles of a market economy to a much greater degree, and, as a result, they were particularly susceptible to the problems of unemployment, underemployment, mendicity, and crime.

There was a substantial underclass in the Upper Peru mining center of Potosí during its boom-and-bust cycle between 1545 and 1700. Colonial officials in the early seventeenth century complained that the city was infested with gamblers, prostitutes, and thieves. One Dominican friar, Rodrigo de Loaysa, described Potosí as a "sinkhole of iniquity." Nevertheless, it now appears that Mexico City consistently had the largest underclass in colonial Latin America. This was a direct result of Mexico City's greater size, its economic and social complexity, and its importance as an administrative center for the Spanish Empire. According to Alexander Von Humboldt, the Mexico City underclass numbered anywhere from 20,000 to 30,000 persons, or from 15 to 22 percent of the total population of 137,000, in the 1790s. We can assume that these figures are rather conservative because other visitors and residents provided estimates which were much higher. For example, Hipólito Villarroel, a prosecutor in the *acordada* (police force and summary court), gave an estimate of 40,000 for the urban underclass in 1787; however, the scientist José Antonio Alzate and others speculated that even this figure was much too low. There is no doubt that the size of the urban underclass varied from time to time. As a rule, economic and social factors, such as lower food prices or the establishment of a public works program, reduced the size of the underclass. Crop failures, rural to urban migration, and difficulties in certain sectors of the urban economy, however, usually resulted in a significant increase.

Although the size of Mexico City's underclass cannot be determined with any degree of certainty, the census data, the police records, and various institutional reports provide us with some information on the social characteristics of the destitute poor. The figures in Table 10.1, for example, clearly

Table 10.1   The Ethnic Composition of Persons Arrested by the Mexico City Municipal Authorities in 1796 and of Persons Confined to the Hospicio de Pobres in 1811

	Defined as Caucasian	Defined as Indian	Defined as Mestizo	Defined as Mulato	
Persons Arrested, 1796	33%	37%	24%	6%	N = 489
Inmates of the Hospicio de Pobres, 1811	55%	22%	17%	6%	N = 353
Population of Mexico City, 1790–1804	50%	24%	19%	7%	N = 104,760*

*This figure does not include the clergy, members of the religious orders, or the military.
Sources: Archivo Judicial del Tribunal Superior de Justicia, México, Libro de Reos, 1795–1796, fols. 46–128. Archivo General del la Nación, México, Padrones, 1811, vol. 72, fols. 38v–58. Alexander Von Humboldt, *Political Essay on the Kingdom of New Spain,* trans. John Black, 3rd ed., 4 vols. (London: Longman, Hurst, Rees, Orme and Brown, 1822), 293.

demonstrate that the underclass was composed of all the major identifiable racial groupings in Mexico City at that time. Nevertheless, the data also show that in certain social environments there were important differences in their relative representation. These differences were the result of specific insitutional procedures, prevailing public opinion, and the relative status enjoyed by each racial group in colonial society. For example, the non-white population was expected to commit most of the crimes in Mexico City, a belief that was reflected in the police procedures of the colonial period. Indians and mestizos, as a result, were arrested and confined in disproportionately greater numbers than were Caucasians. Likewise, a greater concern was shown for the well-being of impoverished Spaniards and creoles because of their higher status in colonial society. As a result, there was a disproportionately greater number of Caucasians listed as inmates in the *hospicio de pobres,* or royal poorhouse, and a disproportionately smaller group of Indians and mestizos. (The percentage of mulatos, however, is lower than it should be, considering that they also were expected to commit more crimes.)

The importance of migration from the countryside and from the other urban centers to the growth to the underclass in Mexico City is shown by the figures which appear in Table 10.2. Persons born outside of Mexico City accounted for 34 percent of the inmates in the hospicio de pobres and 46 percent of the persons arrested by the municipal authorities. Although a comparison

Table 10.2 The Geographic Origin of Persons Arrested by The Mexico City Municipal Authorities in 1796, and of Persons Confined to the Hospicio de Pobres in 1811

Geographic Origin	Arrest Records, 1796		Hospicio de Pobres, 1811	
	No.	*Percent*	*No.*	*Percent*
Mexico City	254	54%	252	66%
Valley and Province	216	46%	128	34%
Total	470	100%	380	100%

Source: Archivo Judicial del Tribunal Superior de Justicia, México, Libro de Reos, Alcalde ordinario más antiguo, 1795–1796, fols. 46–128. Archivo General de la Nación, Mexico, Padrones, vol. 72, fols. 38v–58.

cannot be made with the overall migrant population, it is again interesting to note the difference between these two figures. The smaller proportion of migrants in the inmate population of the hospicio de pobres was probably the result of procedural policies which favored residents born in Mexico City over migrants. Likewise, the disproportionately greater number of migrants arrested by the municipal authorities was the result of police procedures and the widespread belief that migrants were responsible for the majority of day-to-day crimes.

The precarious economic condition of the laboring poor and their close relationship to the urban underclass is clearly demonstrated by the figures in Table 10.3. Sixty-one percent of the inmates in the hospicio de pobres and 84 percent of the persons arrested by the municipal authorities were listed as being employed at one time or another in the lower-status trades. The figure for the hospicio de pobres is, of course, lower because of the substantial number of inmates (28 percent) who were blind, deaf, lame, or otherwise incapacitated. Nevertheless, the figures in both sets of records for persons employed in shoemaking, textiles, and construction are significant in their own right. Recent evidence indicates that a disproportionate number of persons employed in these trades fell into the ranks of the underclass during the late colonial period because of increased unemployment, underemployment, and deteriorating living conditions. As a result, carpenters, masons, shoemakers, tailors, and persons employed in the woolens industry, such as carders, spinners, and weavers accounted for 38 percent of the inmates in the hospicio de pobres, and 27 percent of the persons arrested by the municipal authorities.

Residency Patterns and Conditions of Life

As a rule, the urban underclass in colonial Latin America was a highly mobile group. In Mexico City the poor were inclined to move from one district to another in search of employment, shelter, or charity. If they could

Table 10.3 Occupational Status of Persons Arrested by the Mexico City Municipal Authorities in 1796, and of Persons to the Hospicio de Probres in 1811

Occupation*	Arrest Records–1796		Hospicio de Pobres–1811	
	No.	*Percent*	*No.*	*Percent*
Upper and Middle Strata				
Merchants	2		0	
Agents and Brokers	4		1	
Cashiers	3		0	
Vendors	10		6	
Barbers	5		2	
Scribes	3		3	
Others	10		1	
Total	37	12%	13	8%
High-Status Artisans, etc.				
Coachmakers	1		1	
Goldworkers	2		1	
Silversmiths	4		2	
Others	5		0	
Total	12	4%	4	3%
Low-Status Artisans, etc.				
Bakers	15		1	
Carders (wool)	0		9	
Carpenters	14		2	
Cooks	2		5	
Ironsmiths	8		1	
Masons	19		4	
Muleteers	7		1	
Porters	7		2	
Servants	22		2	
Shoemakers	11		7	
Spinners (wool)	4		10	
Tailors	25		14	
Tobacco Workers	11		1	
Weavers (wool)	8		15	
Others	105		26	
Total	258	84%	100	61%
The Dependent Population				
Blind	0		16	
Deaf	0		7	
Demented	0		3	
Epileptic	0		6	
Lame	0		11	
Simpleminded	0		3	
Total	0	0%	46	28%
Grand Total	307	100%	163	100%

*Occupations were listed for males only.

Source: Archivo Judicial del Tribunal Superior de Justicia, México, Libro de Reos, Alcalde ordinario mas antiguo, 1795–1796, fols. 46–128. Archivo General de la Nación, Mexico, Padrones, vol. 72, fols. 38v–58.

afford it, they would rent rooms in the many multiple family dwellings *(casas de vecindad)* which were concentrated in the center of the city. It was more common, however, to find the underclass living in the open, on park benches, inside the corridors of public buildings, or with friends or relatives in the many shanty towns which were located in the peripheral areas of the city.

In general, observers and colonial officials agreed that the urban environment in the outer districts was in total chaos. Streets and alleyways were said to be crooked and ill-defined. Most of the dwellings, whether they were shanties or multiple family dwellings, were described as being in need of constant repair. Potable water, drainage, and sanitation were said to be lacking, and observers noted that the maze of streets and alleyways was filled with rubbish, stagnant puddles, manure, and other debris. It was also noted that these places were frequented by groups of unsupervised, dirty, and semi-nude children, and that there was an unhealthy mixture of mud, filth, and wandering animals, which served as a breeding ground for disease and other disorders.

Although the majority of the poor lived in the outer barrios, a considerable number also were found in the center of Mexico City. Many of these individuals erected hovels or shanties which were placed against the walls of churches, monasteries, and public buildings, yet, it appears that the majority were forced to live, out of necessity, in the open, exposed to the elements. In his description of the underclass, Alexander Von Humboldt noted that thousands of "these dregs of people" slept on the cold ground, or in the corner of some building with nothing more than the "same flannel covering which they wore during the day."[3]

As a largely transient group, the urban poor spent a considerable amount of their time in search of employment and other sources of income. In mining centers, such as Potosí, Zacatecas, Guanajuato, and Ouro Prêto the destitute and the not-so-destitute found occasional employment in the extraction of silver and other precious metals. In 1792, at least 55 percent of the adult male population of Guanajuato was employed in the silver mining industry, while only 18.9 percent of the population was employed in the service or artisan sectors.[4] By contrast, the textile industry provided the major employment in manufacturing centers such as Quito, Querétaro, and Puebla. Working under the most abominable conditions imaginable, the urban poor were abused, exploited, and frequently imprisoned in textile workshops or *obrajes* for long periods of time.

In late colonial Mexico City employment for the underclass usually meant odd jobs or temporary work as street vendors, wage laborers, servants, messengers, and porters. (See Figure 21.) A considerable number also were employed in the bakeries, slaughterhouses, artisan shops, and manufacturing establishments as semi-skilled and unskilled artisans and laborers. Six to seven thousand were employed by the royal tobacco factory, which was the largest manufacturing enterprise in late eighteenth century New Spain, but here again the rule was temporary employment in menial, low-paying jobs.

In general, the work day for those who found employment was long and arduous, and the remuneration for this drudgery was often insufficient to support the average family. In the artisan shops and the manufacturing establishments, the work day lasted from sunrise to sunset, or anywhere from 10 to 14 hours, depending on the season. There were usually two 30 to 40-minute rest periods each day for meals, but there was often night work as well, even though this practice was illegal in most of the trades. The arrival of Sunday and the many religious and festive days brought some relief from the day-to-day routine of the workshops, but this leisure time had little meaning for the urban poor. More often than not, the holidays provided the underclass with an opportunity to perform odd jobs or sell trinkets in an often desperate effort to increase their meager incomes.

In Mexico City destitute peddlers sold everthing imaginable, from images of the Virgin of Guadalupe to old clothes and used household goods. One visitor to the city commented that the streets and plazas were full of the "barefoot who sell old shoes" and "the naked who sell old clothing."[5] Some of the peddlers sold their goods independently, while others were contracted by wholesalers and retailers. Scavengers or junk dealers regularly purchased old ironware for resale to wholesalers, and bakers contracted traveling vendors to sell baskets of unsold bread, or *pan duro,* in the streets and plazas of the city. With some luck and hard work, it was possible for some peddlers to rise above the level of the underclass, but such opportunities were extremely rare for those who worked as laborers in the manufacturing establishments.

As a rule, the position of the workers in the artisan shops and manufacturing enterprises was very tenuous. Disagreements and conflicts over contractual arrangements, productivity, wages, working hours, and the quality of craftsmanship resulted in corporal punishment, imprisonment, or sudden dismissals for most workers. At times there were strikes, although these events usually took place in the larger manufacturing enterprises. For example, in 1784, the workers in the bakehouse of Basilio Badamler went on strike to protest the "horrible working conditions" that they had endure. At one point, there was a "riot" in the workshop that involved the eventual intervention of the police and resulted in a comprehensive investigation by a committee composed of several inspectors from the bakers' guild. The tranquility of the royal tobacco factory and its employees also was disturbed by strikes and protests during the years 1780, 1782, and 1794. The most serious disturbance involved 1,400 men and women who marched on the viceregal palace on the morning of January 13, 1794, to protest the tobacco monopoly's decision to change a contractual arrangement in which the employees were permitted to take home part of their work in preparation for the tasks which had to be completed the following day.

Although the laborers employed in the workshops were at times prone to rebelliousness, they were considered less troublesome than the domestics and the other persons who provided essential services. For example, day laborers were accused of extracting excessive fees or tips from their contractors, and observers noted that porters were inclined to drop their loads at inopportune moments in order to gamble and get drunk. Hipólito Villarroel, who was particularly disdainful of servants and day laborers, complained that they were licentious, ill-mannered, and inefficient, and that those employed as servants were inclined suddenly to run away from their employers with stolen jewelry, silverware, and other valuables which they sold in the streets and plazas or in the *baratillo* or thieves' market.

The ill repute of servants, wage laborers, and the urban poor as a class was directly related to low wages, the high cost of living, and the erratic or seasonal nature of employment. In Mexico City the income for most employed persons within the lower stratum, was barely adequate to support an entire family during normal periods and quite insufficient during periods of economic crisis. Day laborers regularly earned wages of between two and three *reales* (monetary unit) a day. Servants received eight reales per month for spending money, in addition to their clothing, meals, and lodging, while water carriers were paid one-half real for four round trips from a water fountain to the streets being served.

A comparison of wages, income, and the cost of living for late colonial Mexico City clearly demonstrates the precarious economic condition of the urban poor. Table 10.4 provides a list of typical daily wages for construction and tobacco workers at various times between the years 1698 and 1804. Although the figures are fragmentary in nature and do not allow for detailed analysis, they indicate that urban wage scales remained relatively stable for the entire eighteenth century. It is also evident that the skilled and semiskilled workers received substantially higher wages than the unskilled workers. For example, skilled carpenters, masons, and "masters of the table" earned between 4 and 8 reales a day, whereas "packers," "sealers," and other unskilled laborers were only paid from two to three reales a day. Daily wages, however, are not a good measure of real income for the poor in late colonial Mexico City. As previously indicated, the urban poor had a difficult time securing steady employment because of the competition for jobs in manufacturing and the services. Thus we have the example of Antonio Mendoza, an employee of the royal tobacco factory, who earned 2½ reales a day wrapping cigars, but who only worked 12½ days during the month of March, 1798, for a monthly income of 31 reales or a mere 46 pesos a year.

At various times during the late eighteenth century, the administrators of a number of institutions calculated the cost of supporting an individual on a daily basis. Between the years 1769 and 1805, this cost was estimated conservatively at between ¾ and 1½ reales a day, or between 34 and 69 pesos a year. Calculated for the average lower-class family in late colonial Mexico City (consisting of 3.8 persons), the yearly cost of support came to between 129 and 262 pesos, which meant that a single wage earner in this family needed an average daily income of between 2.8 and 5.7 reales a day for every

Table 10.4 Daily Wage Scales for Construction Workers and Employees of the Royal Tobacco Factory, Mexico City, 1698–1804

	1698	1699	1775	1776	1777	1778	1779	1788	1790	1794	1795	1797	1798	1804
Construction														
Overseers	8r	8r							5r	6r	6r			
Carpenters				6r						4-5r			7r	7r
Masons				5-6r					6r	4-6r	4-6r			
Journeymen	6r	6r	4r	4r					4r					
Day Laborers	3r	3r	3r	3r					2½r	2r	2r	3r	3r	3r
Tobacco Factory														
Masters							8r	8r		8r			8r	
Wrappers						4r	4-5r	4-5r		4½-6½r			4½-6½r	
Recounters						3¼r	3-4r	3-4r		3½-5½r			3½-4½r	
Workmen			3-5r		3-5r		4r			2-4r				
Packers								4r		4r			4-6r	
Sealers								2½-7½r		3½r			3½-4r	
Moisteners													3-4r	
Shouters							2r	2-2½r		2-2½r			2-2½r	
Keepers of the Latrine								3¼r		3¼r			3¼r	

r = reales

Source: Archivo General de la Nación, México, Acordada, vol. 4, fols. 168–173; Ibid., vol. 5, fols. 172–178, 187–188, 192–192v; Ibid., vol. 26, fols. 270–273v; AGN, Criminal, vol. 58, exp. 14, fol. 205; AGN, Tabaco, vol. 84 (no fols.); Archivo Histórico del Ayuntamiento de la Ciudad de México, Cárceles en general, vol. 495, exp. 2, fols. 8–13v; AHA, Juntas de Policía, 1790, vol. 449, exp. 34, fols. 1–1v; AHA, Panaderías y pulperías, vol. 3453, exp. 60, fol. 1; D. Lorne McWatters, "The Royal Tobacco Monopoly in Bourbon Mexico," (Ph.D. diss., University of Florida, 1979).

295

day of the year.[6] As indicators of the cost of living in late colonial Mexico City, these figures demonstrate why the urban poor had to search continuously for work, charity, and other sources of income. As a rule, entire families had to work, with the men, women, and children alternately employed as day laborers, street peddlers, and servants. Observers noted that many women and children were employed in the manufacturing establishments of Mexico City, along with their husbands or fathers. In particular, they found occasional or regular employment in the hatmaking, clothing, and textile industries, or in the royal tobacco factory, which became a principal employer of women and children in the late colonial period.

Visitors to Bahia, Buenos Aires, Havana, Lima, Mexico City, and other colonial urban centers were always impressed by the high cost of living and the general poverty of the urban underclass. In Mexico City the cost of food was the heaviest burden, and the poor normally were compelled to pay more for poorer quality food than the affluent because they frequently were forced to make their purchases on a day-to-day basis and in the most minute of quantities. Generally, the poor were affected by the tiniest variation in food prices, and, unfortunately, food prices were inclined to fluctuate in a cyclical manner because the large landowners and speculators manipulated the supply and price of maize and other staples in order to maximize their profits. For example, the price of maize was at its lowest immediately after the harvest in October, and was highest during the months that preceded the harvest. This meant that the urban poor ate best during the fall and most poorly during the summer.

Concrete examples demonstrate this further. In 1777, the cost of maize went from 9 reales a *fanega* (about 1.5 bushels) in October to 7 reales a fanega in December; however, by the following May, the price had risen to between 10 and 12 reales a fanega. Nevertheless, the year 1777 was a year of relative agricultural abundance and low prices. During the many years that were characterized by inflation, economic crisis, and severe food shortages, many of the poor had to endure the real spectre of hunger and starvation. For example, between June and September of 1786, the infamous "Year of Hunger," the price of maize reached an incredible 48 reales a fanega. At the same time, the rapid rise in maize prices also affected the cost of other basic foodstuffs and necessities. Observers noted, as a result, that ½ a real purchased only 14½ ounces of bread; chickens were priced at 8 reales; and each egg was valued at ½ a real, which was one-quarter to one-sixth of the average daily wage for unskilled laborers at that time.[7]

In an effort to reduce the cost of nutrition, the poor of Mexico City were compelled to purchase and consume leftovers. Those persons who were fortunate enough to find employment as servants in the homes of the wealthy could obtain their leftovers from their employers. But the poor usually were forced to purchase inferior quality maize, pan duro, and other leftovers that were sold regularly in the streets and plazas of Mexico City. The itinerant street peddlers, many of them servants, sold leftovers which had been given to them or had been purchased in bakehouses, butcher shops, and other food-processing establishments. This food was frequently inedible or close to being so, but the poor were compelled to scavenge or purchase these scraps for lack of a better alternative. For the Indians, mestizos, and mulatos resident in Mexico City, and for the considerable number of poor Spaniards and creoles as well, the basic diet consisted of maize, bread, *chiles* (hot peppers), and beans, along with an occasional portion of meat or fowl. Bread apparently was consumed by everyone in Mexico City during the eighteenth century, regardless of class or ethnic classification. Von Humboldt asserted that maize and bread were consumed in equal quantities, that the overall consumption of bread was high, and that the per capita consumption of bread in Mexico City was equal to that in the great European cities.

Fresh water was brought to Mexico City by two aqueducts that originated at some distance to the west. The water was redistributed through a system of 28 public water fountains and 505 private ones which were appropriated by the wealthy for their homes and enterprises. The water was not entirely pure, but it was a potable supply. Those who lived in the center of the city had no difficulty in obtaining their water, but the residents of the poorer, outer barrios suffered because most of the public water fountains were located in the center of the city at a considerable distance. Admittedly, an alternative source of water was available under the ground at a depth of only four feet, but this was not a potable supply. As a result, many families in the outer barrios were required to purchase their water from water carriers who were inclined to charge high fees, especially during periods of water scarcity. In addition to water, large quantities of wine, brandy, and other liquors were consumed by the poor of Mexico City. The favorite intoxicant was *pulque*, which was fermented juice derived from the maguey plant. Observers commented that the poor consumed large or excessive quantities of the beverage. Alexander Von Humboldt asserted that "44,000,000 bottles" of pulque were consumed annually in Mexico City. If the consumption of pulque was indeed as high as observers claimed, this was probably due in part to the fact that pulque had real nutritional value.

In general, the high cost of food compelled many of the urban poor to get along without many of the other basic necessities of life. Although rents were generally low throughout the eighteenth century, and Mexico City had an excess of rental space, many of the poor could not afford to rent shelter or rooms anywhere in the city. Thus, many families lived in the streets, where they erected shanties and other temporary structures. Many of the families or persons who rented space in small houses or multiple-family dwellings were frequently delinquent in their payments. Landlords complained constantly that the poor would not pay their rent, or that they would suddenly abandon their lodgings when the rent came due. It appears that many multiple-family dwellings in the center of the city were plagued by a constant turnover of

298 / Gabriel Haslip-Viera

tenants. Account records demonstrate that there was a continuous procession of tenants who would rent rooms for three or four months and then suddenly leave without paying what they owed.

Living conditions in the multiple-family dwellings were difficult. The ground floor rooms, which were rented by the poor, were cold, dark, damp, and lacking in ventilation. Observers noted that most rooms lacked privies and frequently became flooded during the rainy season. Yet, if living conditions in the multiple-family dwellings were considered harsh, they were even more deplorable in the hovels and shanties where most of the urban poor were concentrated. Constructed of adobe, wood scraps, and other suitable materials, the shanties, called *jacales*, were prone to collapse during the most minor of earth tremors, or were swept away by the flood waters which periodically inundated the city, leaving thousands of persons homeless.

Flooding became a serious problem during the early seventeenth century because of the denuding of forests and other environmental changes in the surrounding valley. Entire sections of the city became uninhabitable for long periods of time, resulting in a desperate effort to divert the floodwaters away from the lakes which were situated to the north and east. Thousands of persons, mostly Indians, but also including a number of non-Indian convicts and vagrants, were recruited from the city and the surrounding countryside in the effort to control the floodwaters but flooding continued to be a serious problem for the remainder of the colonial period.

With the exception of a few meager household goods, furniture for the urban poor was practically nonexistent. As a largely transient group, the underclass had very little in the way of personal possessions. Most of the furnishings, when they existed, included two or three wooden benches, a few earthenware or metal pots for cooking, *metates y manos* for grinding corn, *petates* or straw mats to sleep on, and a few woolen blankets which also served as clothing during the winter months.

Clothing was another expense and a special problem for the urban underclass in colonial Latin America. In Mexico City the viceroy, Conde de Revillagigedo, estimated the total cost of the most basic wardrobe to be 24½ pesos for men and 12 pesos for women in 1790. Although several observers considered this to be an inflated estimate, there was universal agreement that clothing was prohibitively expensive. The cloth manufactured by New Spain's textile industry was generally high in price and inferior in quality. The same was true for all manufactured attire, such as shoes, hats, bonnets, and gloves. The poor, as a result, were compelled to purchase or "rent" used clothing from peddlers and shopkeepers, if they could afford it.

The rental and sale of used clothing was an important component of the petty commerce of Mexico City. Peddlers regularly bought used garments from the affluent or purchased the clothing of deceased persons. Observers commented that the city hospitals and asylums were frequented by peddlers eager to obtain the clothing of deceased or incurably ill patients. They also pointed out that the theft of clothing from freshly dug gravesites was not an uncommon occurrence. Those who could not afford clothing of any kind became thieves or scavengers of rags and other remnants. Visitors were constantly shocked by the many "dirty," "indecently clothed" and "naked" individuals seen in the streets and plazas of the city. In 1777, the Mexico City merchant's guild estimated that perhaps three-quarters of the population was ill-dressed or "practically naked." The Conde de Revillagigedo, who as viceroy was particularly infuriated by this problem, complained that the poor were generally "unwashed" and that they normally wore "dirty," "odorous rags and blankets" which were utilized as "clothing or as beds to sleep on."[8]

In all the urban centers of colonial Latin America, the lack of clothing and the inadequacy or the absence of other basic necessities contributed significantly to the poor health of the impoverished masses. Yellow fever and other tropical diseases were the major concern in the coastal cities of Bahia, Havana, and Cartagena, while smallpox, typhus, typhoid fever, and a number of respiratory ailments were the major preoccupation in high-altitude urban centers, such as Mexico City, Cuzco, and Quito.

In Mexico City the poor normally were afflicted with a variety of respiratory ailments, especially during the summer rainy season and the periods of cold weather which suddenly gripped the city between October and December. These illnesses, as well as the ailments which arose from polluted water, malnutrition, unwholesome food, lack of clothing, improper shelter, and poor sanitation, frequently resulted in death and contributed to the high level of infant mortality. Yet the impact of these ailments on the urban population was not as great as that of periodic epidemics of smallpox, typhus, and typhoid fever which resulted in sudden death for thousands and a temporary but drastic decline in the urban population (see Table 10.5). The spread of contagious disease and the mortality rates that were associated with these epidemics provoked morbid fears and near panic among the urban poor. Much of this fear resulted from the primitive state of medical care in the eighteenth century. Medical care generally consisted of purgatives, bloodletting, and other "remedies" which were totally ineffective against the major epidemic diseases. The poor, as a result, were fearful of internment in hospitals and had little confidence in doctors and the medical profession in general. The Indians, in particular, were distrustful of the medical profession. They much preferred the popular medicines and religious rituals that were administered by *curanderos* or herbal folk doctors, a perfectly understandable preference when one considers that the popular medicines were generally less painful, less expensive, less dangerous, and certainly just as effective. When the authorities and the medical establishment tried to implement emergency measures to hospitalize, quarantine, or otherwise treat the victims of epidemic disease, the resistance of the poor was universal. The sick were concealed by relatives and friends, the dead were carried away and buried in secrecy, and parents fled to

Table 10.5 Estimated Number of Deaths as Result of Epidemics in
Mexico City, 1697–1813

Year	Type of Epidemic	Estimated Number of Deaths	Population Estimates for Mexico City
1697			100,000
1736–39	Typhus (*Matalzahuatl*)	40,000	
1761–62	Typhus and Smallpox	25,000	
1772–73	Typhus	13,000*	112,462
1779–80	Smallpox and Measles	18,000	
1790–93			112,926–130,602
1797–98	Smallpox	7,143	
1804			137,000
1811			168,000
1813	"Fevers"	20,385	123,907

*This figure constitutes a partial estimate of the total deaths.
Source: Enrique Florescano, *Precios del maíz y crisis agrícolas en México, 1708–1810* (Mexico City: El Colegio de México, 1969), 164; Juan Francisco Gemilli Carreri, *Viaje a la Nueva España: México a fines del siglo XVII*, 2 vols. (Mexico City: Ediciones Libro-Mex, 1955), 1:45; Charles Gibson, *The Aztecs under Spanish Rule* (Stanford: Stanford University Press, 1964), 450–51; Alexander Von Humboldt, *Political Essay on the Kingdom of New Spain*, trans. John Black, 3rd ed., 4 vols. (London: Longman, Hurst, Rees, Orme, and Brown 1822), 2:61–67; 291–98; Timothy E. Anna, *The Fall of Royal Government in Mexico City* (Lincoln, Neb.: University of Nebraska Press, 1978), 4–5.

the countryside with their sick children in an effort to avoid the authorities and internment in the hospitals.

Crime, Social Disorder and Rebellion: The Response of the Underclass

The resistance of the urban underclass to hospitals and physicians was one expression of their collective sense of fear, alienation, and resentment. In many urban centers, the same structural barriers which prevented upward economic and social mobility conspired to produce a considerable amount of crime and social disorder. In addition to the problems of mendicity, vagabondage, and occasional strikes by workers, the civic pride of observers and colonial officials constantly was offended by reports of theft, assault, murder, and other crimes. (See Figure 22.) In the late 1730s, Jorge Juan and Antonio de Ulloa noted that "the common people and the Indians" of Quito were "greatly addicted to theft" and that they were "very artful and dextrous" in these endeavors, a fact which also was recognized in other parts of colonial Latin

America. In the early 1760s, the Peruvian viceroy Manuel Amat y Junient was thoroughly scandalized by the fact that the right of ecclesiastical sanctuary was abused by lawbreakers who used the monasteries, convents, and churches of Lima as a base of operations for their assaults and burglaries.

Colonial officials in Brazil also complained of the abuse of ecclesiastical sanctuary. However, it appears that interpersonal violence, especially violence motivated by economic gain, was the major concern in the urban centers of Bahia and Rio de Janiero. In Rio one visitor noted the ease with which "ruffians" could be hired to settle some vendetta. The visitor also observed that Rio was particularly dangerous because there was "no place in the world where people would commit murder at so cheap a rate."[9]

In Mexico City observers and colonial officials began to complain about thefts, assaults, murders, prostitution, vagrancy, and excessive drinking by the Indian population in the latter part of the sixteenth century; however, the problem of crime and social disorder was to become much worse during the late seventeenth and early eighteenth centuries. The viceroys and the magistrates of that period observed that houses were burglarized with great frequency, that affluent subjects were deprived unexpectedly of their purses, and that individuals were suddenly and violently assaulted for no apparent reason. Individual acts of theft and violence were sometimes transformed into the collective activities of organized groups. More often than not, the urban underclass participated in rebellions or uprisings that were initiated by mine workers, artisans, middle class interests or elite groups involved in political disputes. Examples of such rebellions included the uprising of mestizos in Potosí (1586), the War of the *Mascates* (peddlers) in Recife (1710), and the Comunero revolt in New Granada (1781). Twice during the seventeenth century there were major riots or uprisings of the poor in Mexico City which caused widespread looting and devastation. The first uprising, which took place in 1624, was brought about by an irreconcilable political dispute between a reformist viceroy, the Marqués de Gelves, and the local elite, led by the archbishop, Juan Pérez de la Serna and the magistrates of the *audiencia* or high court of appeals. However, this rebellion should be differentiated from the 1692 uprising, which was brought about by inflation and food shortages and thus constitutes a true people's revolt.

During the winter and spring of 1691-92, heavy rains, flooding, and the destruction of crops by an infestation of mildew and worms forced food prices to rise sharply and brought hunger and starvation to many parts of New Spain. In Mexico City the people were forced to compete for ever-dwindling supplies of maize, wheat, vegetables, and other foodstuffs. By early June, hungry mobs had gathered in front of the *alhondiga,* or public granary, to demand free grain as the price of maize rose to an astronomical 48 reales a fanega. Fist fights and other incidents broke out as officials tried to contain the desperate crowd. On the morning of June 6, 1692, an Indian woman was killed in the courtyard of the alhondiga during an altercation, and this brought an angry crowd of Indians to the viceregal palace to protest high prices, food short-ages, mistreatment and bad government. With the viceroy and the archbishop perhaps unwisely absent, the protest soon degenerated into a riot. Groups of mestizos, mulatos, and poor creoles joined the Indians in an attack on the inadequately defended viceregal palace. Several rioters set the building on fire, and the conflagration soon attracted other groups from the surrounding barrios. The crowd, now estimated at 10,000 persons, attacked and set fire to the town hall, the alhondiga, the residence of the Cortés family, and the collection of shops and stalls which were concentrated in the *Parian* or major marketplace. The attack on the Parian had a profound effect on the nature of the uprising, which soon dissipated into looting and squabbles over stolen food, clothing, and other merchandise. At about this point, the archbishop and the viceroy organized members of the clergy and the militia to put down the rebellion through a combination of persuasion and force. Nevertheless, the tranquility of the city was not restored for several days, and although casualties were never counted, it was believed that scores of people had been killed and many more injured.

Although mining centers, port towns, and large administrative centers, such as Bahia, Potosí, and Mexico City, appear to have had a disproportion-ately high level of crime and social disorder, all the urban centers of colonial Latin America were afflicted by these problems to some degree because of their unequal social structures and their limited capacity to permit upward economic and social mobility. Urban vagrants, prostitutes, thieves, and riot-ers were inclined to exhibit the same behavior patterns. Thus, the response to crime and social disorder on the part of the authorities was uniformly applied to all the urban centers, regardless of size or social complexity, even though it developed from a particular concern for the troublesome conditions which prevailed in the larger, more unstable urban centers.

Poor Relief and Social Control: The Response of the Elite

In response to the challenge of unemployment, vagrancy, and crime, offi-cials throughout colonial Latin America initiated policies and established in-stitutions which were designed to provide limited relief through charity, to maintain public order, and to preserve existing social relationships. Begin-ning in the sixteenth century, the royal governors and the municipal authori-ties established public granaries and issued decrees against speculators and middlemen in an effort to insure that everyone had fair access to the basic necessities of life. Public granaries were established in Mexico City in 1578, in Zacatecas in 1623, and in Oaxaca in 1690. Encouraged by the usefulness of these institutions, the Spanish crown ordered the establishment of grana-ries throughout the Empire by the end of the seventeenth century.

Colonial officials also sponsored the establishment of new towns and cities in an effort to promote trade and provide employment for the idle poor. In sixteenth-century New Spain, these included Puebla, Querétaro, Celaya, and León. In eighteenth century Brazil they included Colônia do Sacramento, Santa Catarina, and Pôrto Seguro. However, it appears that the new settlements had little impact on the growing number of destitute and dependent people. Rather a determined effort to establish agencies and institutions responsible for the administration of poor relief was required. As a result, wealthy individuals and an increasing number of churches, monasteries, convents, and hospitals began to provide charity and shelter to the indigent and the dependent soon after the establishment of the first settlements. In Mexico City seven hospitals were established between 1521 and 1590. Hernán Cortés endowed one of these, the Hospital de la Concepción, for indigent sufferers, soon after the Conquest. The other cities of Spanish and Portuguese America also experienced charitable generosity of a similar nature throughout the sixteenth century. In Bahia the first hospitals were established soon after the city's founding in 1549, but there, the hospitals and asylums came to be administered by a special lay brotherhood called the *santa casa da misericórdia,* which became a unique feature of charitable activity in Portuguese America.

It should be remembered that the poor were an important factor in the religious life of the affluent in both the Spanish and the Portuguese Empires. As a result, the social significance of private charity cannot be underestimated. According to traditional Catholic doctrine, all Christians labored under the obligation to dispense charity in proportion to their means, first as a tribute to the spiritual significance of the poor, and second as a necessary instrument for the attainment of eternal salvation. Spiritual advantages thus could be obtained through almsgiving because charity diminished the penalties imposed by sin. As one of the religious manuals explained it, "the man who is pious and charitable with the poor of Christ, altough he be guilty of many offenses, appears as a saint because, according to Saint Peter, charity covers a multitude of sins."[10]

In addition to the measures taken to alleviate the condition of the poor, the sixteenth century alos witnessed the establishment of courts, law enforcement agencies, and other security forces which were needed to maintain public order in the urban centers of colonial Latin America. The public tranquility was preserved by a combination of groups which included the military, the church, the courts, and the police. The military was divided into two sectors: a company of soldiers which guarded the viceregal palace and a citizen militia composed of voluntary units which represented the various corporate guilds. Their capacity as instruments of social control, however, was limited. From the early sixteenth to the middle of the eighteenth century, the palace guard and the militia functioned as a reserve force. They were called into action when they needed to put down riots and civil disturbances, but they rarely were employed in the day-to-day effort to control crime and social disorder. Given the weakness of the military forces during this period, the church became an important instrument of social control. Through its legal institutions, such as the Inquisition and the *juzgado eclesiástico* (church court), and through the moral authority of its clergymen, the church provided assistance to the civil authorities and often played a crucial role in the effort to supress riots and civil disorders.

Although the participation of the church and the military forces was essential to the maintenance of public tranquility, the courts and the law enforcement agencies had primary responsibility for the control of day-to-day crimes and social disorders. In the viceregal capitals of Spanish America there were three separate jurisdictions: the viceregal audiencia, which functioned as a court of appeals and sometimes also of first instance; the Municipal Court, which had the primary role in the fight against crime and social disorder; and Indian courts which had local jurisdiction over the designated Indian barrios of the city. During the sixteenth and seventeenth centuries, all of these jurisdictions had their own magistrates, prosecuting attorneys, and constables; however, the audiencia was recognized as the supreme tribunal because it reviewed all the major civil and criminal cases on appeal.

As the overall population of the urban centers increased during the late seventeenth and early eighteenth centuries, it became increasingly apparent that the existing institutions were incapable of dealing with the rising tide of impoverished idlers, vagabonds, and criminals. In Mexico City the church, the military, the law enforcement agencies, and the public granaries had failed completely to prevent the 1692 uprising. As a result, observers and colonial officials began to call for the implementation of new measures to maintain order and insure the public tranquility. Influenced by the ideas of the eighteenth-century Enlightenment, the Spanish and Portuguese governments centralized the administration of poor relief, increased the size of the military, expanded the judiciary and law enforcement agencies, and developed colonization schemes and other incentives to promote economic development and reduce unemployment. The two governments also adopted the new Enlightenment attitudes toward the indigent and the dependent. These attitudes were critical of the allegedly "wasteful" and "indiscriminate" charity which traditionally was given to the poor by affluent laymen and clergymen. As a result, a new system of poor relief was developed which limited the distribution of alms to the "deserving poor," advocated the establishment of institutions to confine the indigent and the truly needy, and imposed severe restrictions on the activities of beggars and vagrants.

In the viceroyalty of Brazil the new Enlightenment policies led to programs designed to promote employment. Incentives were established to increase the number of cochineal, hemp, indigo, rice, tobacco, and wheat enterprises in the second half of the eighteenth century. In 1768, the Marqués de Lavradio sponsored the establishment of a sailcloth factory in Bahia as part of the effort. Lavradio and other Brazilian viceroys also implemented programs designed to improve the administration of justice. These included the establishment in Rio de Janeiro of a second high court or *relação* in 1751; restrictions on the right to ecclesiastical asylum in churches, monasteries, and convents; and the shipment of vagrants and criminals to Colônia do Sacramento, Santa Catarina, and other colonies in the frontier areas of the viceroyalty.

In Mexico City the implementation of the new Enlightenment policies began in earnest with the arrival of the viceroy, Marqués de Croix, in 1766. A series of decrees issued between September, 1766, and February, 1767, required all able-bodied persons to demonstrate that they were gainfully employed within 30 days. All persons who failed to demonstrate gainful employment within the designated time period were to be arrested by law enforcement officers for subsequent placement in the army or on government-sponsored public works projects where they would serve as convict laborers. These decrees soon were followed by others which established programs for the employment of beggars, vagrants, and the idle poor. In Mexico City there was an increase in the number of public works projects after 1766. New roads were built, bridges and aqueducts were repaired, city streets were cleaned and paved, and many vagrants were sentenced to work as convict laborers in the frontier fortifications of the viceroyalty. In 1769, the crown established the royal tobacco factory in Mexico City as part of an effort to provide increased employment possibilities for the urban poor. During the final decades of the colonial regime, the tobacco factory employed thousands of men, women, and children, alleviating to some extent the problem of chronic unemployment and underemployment within the city. The success and the profitability of the tobacco factory encouraged colonial officials and the crown to sponsor the development of other state enterprises; however, most of these later efforts met with little success.

The measures which were implemented to employ beggars, vagrants, and the idle poor soon were supplemented by the establishment of institutions designed to house the indigent, the dependent, and recalcitrant vagrants. In 1774, Viceroy Antonio Maria Bucareli prohibited the solicitation of alms in the city streets and ordered all beggars to present themselves at the newly established hospicio de pobres. According to the guidelines that were established for its administration, the primary goals of the hospicio were the "care of the aged, the infirm and the needy . . . who wander about begging" and the assurance of the eternal salvation of those persons who were inclined towards "idleness, lack of discipline and bad habits."[11] To insure this goal, the hospicio contained an infirmary and employed a staff of physicians; however, in subsequent years, critics complained that treatment and rehabilitation in the hospicio were indifferent and that it had become merely a jail for idlers and criminals.

In addition to the hospicio de pobres, the crown established or took over the administration of other institutions, such as the *hospital general de San Andrés*, which was built on Jesuit property, and the *hospital del Divino Salvador*, an asylum for insane women, which was seized from the Jesuits in 1767. In 1772, a royal orphanage or *casa de niños expositos* was established in Mexico City under the sponsorship of Archbishop Francisco Lorenzana. The problem of orphans was sufficiently serious, however, that the hospitals and the hospicio also contained facilities for the care of foundlings. The problem of orphans, as well as complaints about widespread fornication, adultery, and concubinage, also resulted in the creation of a special facility for illegitimate births. This facility, called the *departamento de partos ocultos,* was founded by Archbishop Lorenzana in 1774, and was located in a building that was contiguous to the hospicio de pobres. Here, women could give birth to their illegitimate children in complete secrecy, with minimal risk and without impairing the honor of their families. They were obliged only, in the event of death during childbirth, to give their names to a priest, who recorded the event in a secret register. The secrecy of the illegitimate births was further insured by the option given to the women of keeping their faces covered during the entire proceedings; however, only Spanish and creole women (presumably poor) were allowed to use this facility. Apparently, the traditional code of family honor was considered more important for these groups than for Indians, mestizos, mulatos, and blacks.

The royal pawn shop or *monte de piedad,* was another institution which provided assistance to the poor of Mexico City in the late colonial period. Founded as a major philanthropic effort by the great mining entrepreneur, Pedro Romero de Terreros, the first Conde de Regla, the monte de piedad was created to deal with the abuses of the urban poor by moneylenders and shopkeepers with regard to the pawning of goods. Throughout the colonial period, and especially during periods of economic crisis, the poor of Mexico City were compelled to pawn their clothing and their other meager possessions for food and other basic necessities. Because of their desperation, however, the poor were almost always defrauded in these transactions. After repeated complaints, the Marqués de Croix issued a series of decrees (1768-1769) which were aimed at curtailing the most flagrant of these abuses. This was followed by the establishment of the monte de piedad in 1775, which gave the indigent poor an alternative to the moneylenders and shopkeepers for the first time. In accordance with a model already established in Spain, the poor could pawn their possessions in return for a small, interest-free loan. They then could redeem their pledges within a specified period of time or automatically would forfeit their goods to the monte de piedad, for eventual resale to the public. The importance of the monte de piedad must not be underestimated because it lowered the cost of credit significantly. But access to the institution was limited in later years because of the need to establish stringent rules regarding the acceptance of stolen property.

In addition to economic development programs and reforms in administration of poor relief, the colonial authorities also instituted measures to improve the maintenance of public order. These included new criminal statutes, restrictions on the right to ecclesiastical sanctuary, and an increase in the size of the judiciary. They also included the establishment of a permanent military garrison, the expansion of law enforcement agencies, the division of the city into police precincts, the placement of street lights in the public thoroughfares, and the establishment of a special correctional facility for wayward women called the *recogimiento de Santa María Magdalena*. The division of the city into police precincts in 1784, undoubtedly led the viceroy, Conde de Revillagigedo, to consider a number of proposals to straighten streets, tear down shanty towns, and reorganize the outer barrios. He also probably considered a number of proposals which advocated the construction of a wall around Mexico City. In 1787, the acerbic Hipólito Villarroel enthusiastically proposed the construction of a wall to "secure the King's revenue from smugglers and contrabandists" and to "cleanse this city of the many useless and licentious persons . . . who have no destiny, nor fixed occupation from which they can support themselves."[12] These ambitious plans, however, were never brought to fruition because of their massive scale and great cost.

Conclusions

Overall, the policies and programs of the late colonial period were successful from the standpoint of social control because they enabled the upper strata to maintain the public peace and preserve existing social relationships more effectively. It is true that crime and social disorder continued to plague the urban centers for the remainder of the colonial period; however, it is also true that the activities of the underclass were controlled to such an extent that the established social structure never was seriously threatened. In fact, there is reason to believe that a significant amount of crime and social disorder actually was tolerated by colonial officials. Persons employed in poor houses, orphanages, courts, law enforcement agencies, and other institutions of social control were not too anxious to reduce the level of crime and social disorder either because they were corrupt or because their jobs and livelihood would be jeopardized. As a result, an equilibrium was established between social order and social disorder. The urban elites may have had the capacity to reduce the level of crime and social disorder to a significant degree, but were unwilling to do so because certain constituencies within the upper strata benefitted from low-level disfunctioning in various ways. It is clear, for example, that there was a relationship between the prosecution of certain crimes and the labor needs of entrepreneurs and government. In Mexico City there was a dramatic increase in the number of persons arrested for vagrancy and public drunkenness during the second half of the eighteenth century because laborers were needed on public works projects or because soldiers were needed to fill the ranks of the expanded army. Widespread theft and corruption among colonial officials was another important factor in the relative toleration of certain crimes. Constables, lawyers, jail keepers, and the administrators of various institutions periodically were arrested and accused of offenses. These crimes included bribery, theft, burglary, smuggling, the sale of prohibited liquors, and even the stealing of food destined for the inmates and prisoners in the jails and charitable insitutions of the city.

In this and in many other respects, Mexico City was comparable to the other urban centers of colonial Latin America. Most of these urban centers were similar in their social and political configurations. All of them possessed a rigidly unequal social structure based on race and economic status. All were afflicted by the problems associated with a large and impoverished under-class. Poor diet, ill health, and horrendous living and working conditions were characteristic problems for this group, as were unemployment, vagran-cy, and crime. The differences that distinguished one urban center from anoth-er were differences in degree, due to size, function, demography, or geography. For example, in Buenos Aires, Cartagena, Havana, Lima, and Bahia, black and mulato slaves and freedmen accounted for a substantially greater proportion of the underclass than they did in Mexico City, Quito, and Cuzco.

In all urban centers the elites developed mechanisms and institutions designed to maintain public order and ameliorate the problems of the poor. Orphan-ages, poorhouses, public works projects, economic development programs, and law enforcement agencies were established or expanded when they were need-ed. Although they apparently failed to reduce the size of the underclass, or to change the conditions which produced it, they were effective from the stand-point of social control because they maintained the status quo. The urban elites were thus able to uphold the existing pattern of economic and social relationships and to continue to dominate the urban political system without too much difficulty for the remainder of the colonial period.

Notes

1. Jorge Juan and Antonio de Ulloa, *A Voyage to South America*, trans. John Adams (New York: Alfred A. Knopf, 1964), 32–33. *Instrucción del Virrey Mar-qués de Croix que deja a su sucesor Antonio María Bucareli* (Mexico City: Editori-al Jus, 1960), 84.

2. A. J. R. Russell-Wood, *Fidalgos and Philanthropists: The Santa Case da Misericordia of Bahia, 1550–1755* (Berkeley: University of California Press, 1968), 282.

3. Alexander Von Humboldt, *Political Essay on the Kingdom of New Spain*, trans. John Black, 3rd ed., 4 vols. (London: Longman, Hurst, Rees, Orme and Brown, 1822), 1:235.

4. D. A. Brading, *Miners and Merchants in Bourbon Mexico, 1763–1810* (Cambridge: At the University Press, 1971), 250.

5. Francisco de Ajofrin, *Diario de viaje que por order de la sagrada congregación de propaganda fide hizo a la América septentrional en el siglo XVIII,* 2 vols. (Madrid: Archivo Documental Español, 1958), 1:81.

6. According to Timothy E. Anna, "a decent living" in late colonial Mexico City was possible on "an income of 300 pesos a year." See Anna, *The Fall of Royal Government in Mexico City* (Lincoln, Neb.: University of Nebraska Press, 1978), 16, 231.

7. Enrique Florescano, *Precios del maíz y crisis agrícolas en México, 1708–1810* (Mexico City: El Colegio de México, 1969), 145, 174–77, 219–22 and passim.

8. Conde de Revilla-Gigedo, *Informe sobre las misiones e instrucción reservada al Marqués de Branciforte* (Mexico City: Editorial Jus, 1966), 167–69.

9. Dauril Alden, *Royal Government in Colonial Brazil, with Special Reference to the Administration of the Marquis de Lavradio, 1769–1779* (Berkeley: University of California Press, 1968), 50, fn. 95.

10. William J. Callahan, "The Problem of Confinement: An Aspect of Poor Relief in Eighteenth-Century Spain, *"Hispanic American Historical Review,"* 51:1 (February 1971): 3.

11. Archivo General de la Nación, México, Ramo de Bandos, vol. 10, no. 18.

12. Hipólito Villarroel, *México por dentro y fuera bajo el gobierno de los virreyes, o sea enfermedades políticas que padece la capital de esta Nueva España en casí todos los cuerpos de que se compone y remedios que se le deben aplicar para su curación si se quiere que sea util al rey y al público.* (Mexico City: Imprenta del C. Alejandro Valdés, 1831), 110–11.

For Further Reading

Studies which deal specifically with the urban underclass in colonial Latin America are few in number, tend to focus on Mexico, mix urban and rural populations, and are inclined to combine the study of the underclass with the study of the laboring poor. They also emphasize the issues of poor relief, and maintenance of public order, and they are inclined to focus on the fears or the concerns of colonial officials and elites. Published monographs which are generally accessible to the interested reader include William B. Taylor, *Drinking, Homicide and Rebellion in Colonial Mexican Villages* (Stanford: Stanford University Press, 1979); Colin M. MacLachlan, *Criminal Justice in Eighteenth Century Mexico: A Study of the Tribunal of the Acordada* (Berkeley: University of California Press, 1974); Norman F Martin, *Los vagabundos en la Nueva España: siglo XVI* (Mexico City: Editorial Jus, 1957); Josefina Muriel, *Los recogimientos de mujeres: respuesta a una problemática social novohispana* (Mexico City: Universidad Nacional Autónoma de México, 1974); and Ruth Pike, *Penal Servitude in Early Modern Spain* (Madison, Wis: University of Wisconsin Press, 1983). Other studies which deal with the urban underclass, at least in part, include Michael C. Scardaville, "Alcohol Abuse and Tavern Reform in Late Colonial Mexico City," *Hispanic American Historical Review* 60:4 (November 1980): 643–76; María Justina Sarabia Viejo, *El juego de gallos en la Nueva España* (Seville: Escuela de Estudios Hispano-Americanos, 1972); Norman F. Martin, "La desnudez en la Nueva España del siglo XVIII," *Anuario de Estudios Americanos* 29 (1972): 261–94; Mario Góngora, "Vagabundaje y sociedad fronteriza en Chile: siglos XVI a XVIII," Publicación No. 2, *Cuadernos del Centro de Estudios Socio-Económicos* (Santiago: Facultad de Ciencias Económicas, Universidad de Chile, 1966); Chester L. Guthrie, "Riots in Seventeenth Century Mexico City," in Adele Ogden and Engel Sluiter, eds., *Greater America: Essays in Honor of Herbert Eugene Bolton* (Berkeley: University of California Press, 1945); Rosa Feijóo, "El tumulto de 1692," *Historia mexicana* 14:2 (April–June 1965): 656–97; and Gabriel Haslip-Viera, "Crime and the Administration of Justice in Colonial Mexico City, 1696–1810" (Ph.D. diss., Columbia University, 1980).

For a discussion of the urban underclass, the laboring poor, and their relationship to urban elites in a rebellious environment, see John Leddy Phelan, *The People and the King: The Comunero Revolution in Columbia, 1781* (Madison, Wis.: University of Wisconsin Press, 1978); and Barry Danks Noblet, "Revolts of 1766 and 1767 in the Mining Communities of New Spain" (Ph.D. diss., University of Colorado at Boulder, 1979). For a discussion of urban social structure with reference to the urban underclass and the laboring poor, see Lewis Hanke, *The Imperial City of Potosí: An Unwritten Chapter in the History of Spanish America* (The Hague: Martinus Nijhoff, 1956); Charles Gibson, *The Aztecs Under Spanish Rule* (Stanford: Stanford University Press, 1964); Elsa Cecilia Frost, Michael C. Meyer, and Josefina Zoraida Vazquez, eds., *Labor and Laborers through Mexican History* (Tucson and Mexico City: El Colegio de México and University of Arizona Press, 1979); Mario Góngora, "Urban Stratification in Colonial Chile," *Hispanic American Historical Review* 55:3 (August 1975): 421–48; Patricia Seed, "The Social Dimensions of Race: Mexico City, 1753," *Hispanic American Historical Review* 62:4 (November 1982): 569–606; Alejandra Moreno Toscano, ed., *Ciudad de México: ensayo de construcción de una historia* (Mexico City: Instituto Nacional de Antropología e Historia, 1978); and Manuel Carerra Stampa, *Los gremios mexicanos* (Mexico City: Ibero-Americana de Publicaciones, 1954). Reference to the urban underclass also is made in Donald B. Cooper, *Epidemic Disease in Mexico City, 1761–1813* (Austin, Tex.: University of Texas Press, 1963); Christon I. Archer, *The Army in Bourbon Mexico, 1760–1810* (Albuquerque: University of New Mexico Press, 1977); Dauril Alden, *Royal Government in Colonial Brazil, with Special Reference to the Administration of the Marquis de Lavradio, Viceroy, 1769–1779* (Berkeley: University of California Press, 1968); C. R. Boxer, *Portuguese Society in the Tropics: The Municipal Councils of Goa, Macao, Bahia and Luanda, 1510–1800* (Madison, Wis.: University of Wisconsin Press, 1965); Enrique Florescano, *Precios del maíz y crisis agrícolas en México, 1708–1810* (Mexico City: El Colegio de México, 1969); and José Jesús Hernández Palomo, *El aguardiente de caña en México, 1724–1810* (Seville: Escuela de Estudios Hispano-Americanos, 1974).

In addition to published monographs and essays, descriptions of the urban underclass and the laboring poor also are found in the writings of travelers, colonial officials and other interested observers. These accounts include Alexander Von Humboldt, *Political Essay on the Kingdom of New Spain*, trans. John Black, 4 vols. (London: Longman, Hurst, Rees, Orme and Brown, 1822); Hipólito Villarroel, *México por dentro y fuera bajo el gobierno de los vireyes, o sea enfermedades políticas que padece la capital de esta Nueva España en casi todos los cuerpos de que se compone y remedios que se le deben aplicar para su curación si se quiere que sea útil al rey y al público* (Mexico City: Imprenta del C. Alejandro Valdes, 1831); "Informe sobre pulquerías y tabernas, el año de 1784," *Boletín del Archivo General de la Nación (México)* 18 (1947): 187–236; Luiz dos Santos Vilhena, *Recopilaçao de noticias soteropolitanas e brasilicas contidas em XX cartas*, ed. Braz do Amaral, 2 vols. (Bahia: Imprenta oficial do Estado, 1921–22); Guillermo Lohmann Villena, *Las relaciones de los vireyes del Perú* (Seville: Escuela de Estudios Hispano-Americanos, 1959); *Memoria de gobierno de Manuel Amat y Junient, Virrey del Perú* (Seville: Escuela de Estudios Hispano-Americanos, 1947); Bartolomé Arzans de Orzua y Vela, *Historia de la villa imperial de Potosí*, 3 vols. (Providence, Rhode Island: Brown University Press, 1965); and Jorge Juan and Antonio de Ulloa, *A Voyage to South America*, trans. John Adams (New York: Alfred A. Knopf, 1964).

In addition to material on the urban underclass and the laboring poor, there is also a literature on poor relief in colonial Latin America. Published monographs and articles include Woodrow Borah, "Social Welfare and Social Obligation in New Spain: A Tentative Assessment," XXXVI Congreso Internacional de Americanistas, *Actas y Memorias* 4 (1966): 45–57; A.J.R. Russell-Wood, *Fidalgos and Philanthropists: The Santa Casa de Misericordia de Bahia, 1550–1755* (Berkeley: University of California Press, 1968); William J. Callahan, "The Problem of Confinement: An Aspect of Poor Relief in Eighteenth Century Spain," *Hispanic American Historical Review* 51:1 *(February 1971): 1–24;* Jean Sarrailh, *La España ilustrada de la segunda mitad del siglo XVIII* (Mexico City: Fondo de Cultura Económica, 1957); Julia Herraez de Escariche, *Beneficencia de España en Indias* (Seville: Escuela de Estudios Hispano-mericanos, 1949); Frederick B. Pike, "Public Work and Social Welfare in Colonial Spanish American Towns," *The Americas* 13:4 (April 1957): 361–75; Germán Somolinos D'Ardois, *Historia de la psiquiatria en México* (Mexico City: Sep Setentas, 1976); Edith B. Couturier, "The Philanthropic Activities of Pedro Romero de Terreros: First Count of Regla, 1753–1781," *The Americas* 32:1 (July 1975): 13–30; Josefina Muriel, *Hospitales de la Nueva España:*

ELEVEN

Conclusion

LOUISA S. HOBERMAN

The urban history of Latin America has a long, respectable lineage. Colonial urban history began, in fact, at the outset of the colony itself, when, in the sixteenth century, official historians were appointed to write accounts of the cities which had been established in such numbers throughout the continent. The early interest in urban history led to the preservation of valuable documents and to a rich literature on the history of the Latin American city. Reflecting, to some degree, the concerns of the colonial practitioners, however, urban history has traditionally emphasized town founding, municipal government, and public works, topics which contribute to our knowledge of urban evolution but which are far from completing it.

Unlike urban history, social history is a relative newcomer to the discipline. Gaining momentum in the 1960s, social history sought to redress the conventional focus on laws, institutions, and impersonal economic forces. Social historians analyzed the characteristics of the diverse groups into which society was organized and determined their relationship to one another. The result of this innovative shift in perspective has been a fruitful proliferation of case studies of a variety of significant groups and regions in Latin America.

In bringing together urban history and social history, this volume has attempted to enrich both approaches. The essays broaden our concept of urban history by demonstrating the importance of social groups to an understanding of the development of cities in Latin America. By synthesizing the wide-ranging findings of the new social history and by comparing groups in the same physical setting, the essays make the conclusions of the social historians more accessible and more easily integrated with other approaches to history.

313

The fusion of urban and social history highlights a number of controversies which have fueled much scholarly activity in the past 15 or 20 years. For social historians, one such debate concerns the basis for social stratification in colonial Latin America. They agree that colonial society was hierarchical rather than egalitarian in character, but they disagree about the principles on which the hierarchy rested. To what extent were social divisions determined by race, as opposed to class? What combination of attributes defined a person's class? Another major issue involves the proper scope of the social historian's research. Since the whole of colonial society is too broad a subject for one scholar to encompass, a choice of smaller units must be made. But what is the appropriate sphere of study: the family, the neighborhood, the city, the region? Whichever unit is chosen influences the kind of conclusions the study will reach. A philosophical debate exists as well, although it is rarely made explicit. Was the social system characterized by conflict, by equilibrium, or by positive mediation among its component parts? Some historians make clear which of these assumptions they are working from, but others do not, and may be unaware of them themselves.

For urban historians, there is much discussion about which elements of the city are most germane to understanding its evolution. Some scholars view the city as a cultural artifact. They trace changes in the view of the city held by its residents at different times and show how these changes shaped urban life. Other historians see the city primarily as a response to changing circumstances that are demographic, economic, or political, perhaps, but not cultural in character. For them, the cultural dimension is, at best, secondary.

The city has long been recognized as a unique physical environment. Its dense and diverse population requires housing, transportation, public services, and recreational facilities on a scale not to be found outside the city. Urban functions, or what rural critics have called urban pretensions, have produced a distinctive layout of streets and plazas, as well as imposing civic and religious architecture. The question is: how are the physical and social dimensions to be integrated in a mutually satisfactory manner? Unfortunately, scholars of the physical aspect of the city—architects, geographers, and urban planners—and scholars of its social structure and politics have tended to go separate ways.

A final controversy involves the relationship of the city to other types of settlement. Cities were never isolated centers of population. They interacted with their surrounding countryside, with distant cities, and with outlying provinces. How should these ties be characterized? Some scholars believe that the colonial Latin American city was parasitic, draining human and productive resources from its hinterland. Others view the economic, judicial, and cultural functions of the urban centers as positive, contributing to the development of the regions in which they were located. Which interpretation is more accurate, and for which times and places?

The essays included here illuminate one or another of these debates. Some confirm commonly held opinions about the colonial Latin American city, while others challenge them or suggest new questions to be posed. Given the body of research which now exists in urban and social history, it is possible to synthesize its conclusions and take a fresh look at the major controversies from the standpoint of the new knowledge.

The colonial system of social stratification was hierarchical. Great inequality of wealth and status was taken for granted and justified, at least by the elite, as divinely ordained and socially useful. The groups at the poles of the social axis, the *hacendados* and *fazendeiros* (owners of large rural estates), on the one hand, and the underclass, on the other, clearly delineate the extremes which were represented in colonial society. Even in the provinces, hacendados owned property worth an average of 30,000 *pesos,* while the lowest stratum had no property at all, except for a few benches, pots, and blankets. The landed elite wore the finest silks and velvets imported from Europe and the Far East, but the underclass bought or rented second-hand clothing or scavenged rags from the streets. A fundamental cleavage existed between the "haves," those who owned property or the means of production, and the "have-nots," those who owned nothing but their labor, a cleavage symbolized by the groups at either end of the social spectrum. Some historians consider the dramatic division between the elite and the non-elite to be the most significant fact about colonial society. But much of the current research in social history is concerned with the intermediate groups and with how they held together the two social extremes. This research tries to distinguish one intermediate group from another, to show how movement up and down the social scale occurred, and to analyze how groups were linked with one another rather than how they were separated. Both approaches are valid, but one stresses dichotomy while the other takes note of plurality.

Social divisions rested on a number of factors: wealth, occupation, residence, race, title, and public office. The relative importance of race in determining social position in colonial Latin America has generated a great deal of controversy. The debate is important because of the larger implications of a race-based, as opposed to a class-based, society. If stratification were primarily racial, then colonial Latin America would have approached a closed, static society, resistent to new influences. Its transition to a class-stratified era would have been more wrenching and less complete. If class, a mixture of income, occupation, and other variables, were the primary determinant of stratification, however, then colonial society would have been more open and flexible, capable of accommodating, or even generating, the changes that eventually would lead to a modern, industrial society.

In the debate race refers to social as well as physical attributes. In colonial Latin America race was defined as a combination of appearance (and presumed biological inheritance), occupation, family ties, and status. Persons were legally classified by race and received privileges or were penalized according to their racial classification. At the time of the Conquest race did determine, in the vast majority of cases, whether a person was to be among the rulers or the ruled. Whites constituted the former, Indians and blacks the latter. The political division had an economic counterpart. The Indians were the tribute payers, laborers, and producers of food. Blacks were skilled and unskilled workers and servants. The whites owned the estates, plantations, and mines, and held the high public offices.

The controversy arises with respect to the years after the Conquest—the major part of the colonial period. Once the Spaniards and Portuguese were settled in America, some historians have asserted, race became a less important determinant of status than other factors, such as occupation. Most markedly in the late eighteenth century the bases for social stratification changed under the impact of the commercialization of agriculture and ranching, a mining boom, freer trade, and the Bourbon political reforms. The alleged shift was reflected in marriage patterns, with more partners marrying out of their racial group than previously suspected, a trend which indicated the decreasing importance of the racial variable. Similarly, the correlation between race and type of work became weaker. Persons of different races were found in a broad range of occupations. Thus, according to this interpretation, if late colonial society were divided into the five occupational categories of elite, professionals (including shopkeepers), high-status artisans, low-status artisans, and servants/peons, the elite was still dominated by persons classified as white, that is, by Spanish-born peninsulars and by American-born creoles. However, the creoles, contrary to what would be expected from the Conquest period cluster of whites in high-status occupations, were also found in artisan and servant/peon categories.[1] For a group which disdained manual labor, the percentage of creoles found in the artisan category was surprisingly high. In mid-eighteenth century Mexico City, it was 41 percent. In late-eighteenth century Oaxaca, it was 72 percent. For early nineteenth-century Buenos Aires, it was considerably lower but still significant: 24 percent of the white male population were artisans.[2]

Other historians take a different stance. They agree that race was by no means the exclusive determinant of social position for most of the colonial period, but assert that it was still the principal influence. The spread of the creoles among all occupational groups was therefore atypical. For the non-white groups, the Indians, *mestizos* (persons of Indian and white ancestry), *mulatos* (persons of black and white ancestry), and blacks, the vast majority were still skilled or unskilled manual workers or servants. The lower-status racial groups were identified with the lower-status occupations in the late colony just as they had been in the Conquest period. Even among creoles the race-occupation correlation of the early sixteenth century persisted, for while more creoles were found in the artisan category than in any other, the next largest number were concentrated in the higher-status professional category.[3] To put it another way, if the observed distribution of racial groups across the occupational structure is compared with the distribution that would be expected from the percentage of the total population comprised by the racial groups, creoles are overrepresented in the professional and artisan categories.[4]

What light does the urban society described in this book cast on the debate about the importance of race? The picture is complicated and richly textured. There was definitely a racial barrier confronting non-whites seeking to enter certain high-status occupations. Ganster states that clergymen were supposed to be, and usually were, white. Non-whites might enter minor orders or act as servants in monasteries, but they were rarely full-fledged, ordained priests. Where they were, exceptional circumstances, such as residence in an isolated region, were present. Lavrin, by the same token, notes that convents received girls of various economic standings but that they were, in most cases, white. Two Indian convents finally were founded in the eighteenth century, and there were some mestiza admissions, but these were the exceptions that proved the rule. Again, non-whites were members only of the lower-status religious or social institutions for women, such as *beaterios* (homes for pious lay women) and *recogimientos* (shelters for women). Burkholder does not even discuss the race issue, implying that it was not an issue for upper-level bureaucrats. Rather, he focuses on the proportions of creoles as opposed to peninsulars in the bureaucracy, a division within the white elite. In the military officers were supposed to be white, and Archer notes that objections were raised when the wife of a militia officer was of mixed ancestry. Other prerequisites to entering the clergy or the bureaucracy, such as education or wealth, were also important. But these might be met by a fellowship which allowed the "noble but poor" to study or by an endowment from a benefactor which enabled the monk or nun to profess. Or educational requirements could be downplayed, as when *audiencia* (high court) posts were bought by persons not qualified to hold them. Racial requirements, however, were not ignored, except in unusual circumstances. The *cédulas de gracias al sacar* (royal licenses changing a persons's racial or civil status) that could be purchased in the late eighteenth century did allow a minority of persons of color to become legally white. But this "escape hatch" simply reinforced the importance of whiteness as a prerequisite for entering the elite.

The situation of the artisans, a middle group, presents an interesting contrast to that of the elite. Artisans were racially mixed. Some guilds prohibited mestizos and blacks from becoming masters; others excluded them from membership entirely. The official restrictions, however, were evaded, and by the mid-eighteenth century a substantial minority of masters were non-white. Indians had always been allowed to enter guilds, which were an important acculturative institution for the Indian craftsman. Despite this heterogeneity, however, Johnson points out that free black artisans were generally poorer than white artisans and that racial divisions undermined the corporate unity of the guilds.

The lower-status occupations of selling, serving, and carrying were, of course, always open to non-whites. People of color were supposed to be the hewers of wood and drawers of water. However, there are two surprising features of the social system at this level. Whites were to be found in even the lowest social categories. Karasch points out that even in Brazil, where there were few whites compared to people of color, there were whites among the food suppliers, boatmen, peddlers, servants in hospitals, lacemakers, and prostitutes. The model of the white who never performed manual labor was an elite concept, contradicted by reality as circumstances mandated. The presence of white prostitutes and whites in service might possibly have been linked with the decline of the sugar economy in northeast Brazil, while the existence of white boatmen was the result of a labor shortage on the frontier. As Haslip-Viera points out, 33 percent of the people arrested by the police of Mexico City in the late eighteenth century were white, as were 55 percent of the inmates of the charity hospital in the early nineteenth century. Thus, scholars who emphasize the presence of whites at all levels of the social spectrum have made an important discovery. However, these essays also suggest that while during their lifetimes whites might move down the social scale to fill low-status occupations, or might be born into society at that level, people of color did not move up the scale with the same frequency. It was particularly difficult to move from plebean to gentlemanly status—that is, to overcome the main cleavage in colonial society. The essays, therefore, do not prove whether race or class was the principal determinant of social position. But they do make a strong case for the importance of race, especially for non-whites.

There were hierarchies within social groups as well as between them. Sometimes the internal stratification was linked to race. Karasch's description of the divisions among slaves in a Brazilian household, for example, indicates that the most prestigious jobs were those that brought the slave in closer proximity to the white members, such as the activities of personal servants, nursemaids, and housekeepers. The least prestigious tasks, such as the disposing of garbage, were those farthest removed from the white sphere of action. Such jobs were reserved for old and ill slaves, children, and new arrivals. In other instances, divisions within a social group had been established previously in Europe with no relation to race, but they became identified with racial divisions in the New World. The distinction between major and minor orders within the clergy, between officers and enlisted men in the military, and between masters and journeymen in the guilds was strengthened by the tendency for whites to occupy the higher positions and people of color to occupy the lower. But other types of stratification were not influenced directly by race. The state imposed distinctions among civil bureaucrats, for example, when it set different terms of appointment, levels of education, and salaries for the audiencia ministers, treasury officials, and *corregidores* (district governors). Comparable divisions existed in the army.

One of the best publicized distinctions in urban colonial society was that between creoles and *peninsulares* (persons born in Spain or Portugal), a distinction that held the most significance for the elite. The split was political in origin but it had racial overtones, because peninsular disdain for creoles was based partly on the perception that creoles were tainted by race mixture. Until recently, it was thought that peninsulars had dominated the civil and ecclesiastical bureaucracies. The revolutions for independence were believed to be, in part, a creole effort to gain access to government posts. These essays show that the exclusion of creoles was limited to specific time periods and types of office. Within the church, creoles outnumbered peninsulars in the secular clergy as early as the later sixteenth century, except in the positions of bishop and archbishop. In the regular clergy, peninsulars also became a minority, but because of the *alternativa* (rotation in clerical office) they held proportionately more than their share of offices in the orders. Rivalry between the two groups was intense within the regular clergy. For the civil bureaucracy, the pace of creole entry accelerated, especially between 1606 and 1750. At the end of the eighteenth century the government succeeded in limiting creole participation, which did contribute to American grievances against Spain and Portugal. In both bureaucracies there were specific conditions, such as the royal need for funds in the case of the civil bureaucrats, which permitted creole penetration.

Far less well-known, but quite important, were distinctions of ethnic origin within the non-elite groups. The essays allow a few glimpses of such distinctions. Among peddlers in Brazil, all groups sold European drygoods, but only Africans and Indians sold food. In New Spain as well as Brazil, gypsies were noted dealers in animals and slaves, some of them stolen. Seasonal or daily migrants to the city also should be considered a type of subgroup within the non-elites. As Haslip-Viera indicates, such persons were perceived by the authorities as less deserving of charity than persons with a permanent residence in the city.

Finally, sex differentiation further divided colonial society. The essays offer a fresh perspective on the roles of women in the city. Until recently, elite women were seen primarily as devout nonentities, philanthropists with few other significant economic or social functions, or as a small number of exceptional nuns. Non-elite women, it was assumed, worked at manual tasks, but little attention was paid to specialization of activity. Here it is seen that whether speaking of the roles of hacendados, merchants, or bureaucrats, women were crucial to consolidating and transmitting economic enterprises and maintaining social networks. As marital partners, in-laws, and godmothers, women possesed property and contacts which made association with them a source both of well-being and mobility. Lavrin reveals the cultural contribution of the nuns as a group. Whether women in such roles are seen simply as instruments of their male counterparts or as independent initiators of their behavior depends on the point of view of the historian.

The farther down the social scale women were, the more frequently they worked. For the artisans, Johnson shows how women and children were essential assistants in the production and sale of goods. Widows sometimes managed their husband's businesses until they remarried or their children were grown. There were even guilds founded and administered by women. Karasch describes the commercial activities of women, first as peddlers, then as stall or shop owners. In Minas, the majority of shop owners were black freedwomen and slaves. Cultural traditions sometimes influenced sex specialization. Following European practice, women were fishmongers in Bahia: following African custom, fishmongers in Rio were men. Another specialty of both Indian and African women slaves was collecting herbs and spices outside the cities. In late colonial New Spain, women were an important segment of the labor force, both in established forms of production, such as *obrajes* (textile workshops), and in new forms, such as the tobacco factory. Such work foreshadowed their future role as cheap wage laborers in industry.

The colonial period was, on the whole, a time of urban demographic growth. One reason for this was that people perceived cities as places of increased opportunity and migrated to them. To what extent was the perception borne out by experience? In a stratified society opportunities for upward mobility would, of course, be limited. Yet, the essays show that improvement of an individual's social standing was possible at all levels of society. Improvement meant different things, and occurred with varying frequency, however, at each level. For the chronically unemployed member of the urban underclass, upward mobility meant obtaining a steady job as a porter, peddler, or textile worker. For the slave prostitute or laundrywoman, it entailed earning enough money to buy her freedom, to change her legal status without necessarily changing her occupation. Movement from slave to free status also might occur through manumission. Black artisans, household servants, and police spies gained freedom in this way. Peddlers throughout colonial Latin America seem to have been one of the more upwardly mobile lower-status groups, progressing from walking the streets to buying a market stall. (See Figure 23.) *Pardo* (mulatto) and *moreno* (black) militiamen gained the *fuero militar* (code of military privileges) and higher social standing in becoming soldiers, though only at the cost of risking their lives or health.

In the high- and middle-status occupations, channels of professional mobility were institutionalized. Artisans advanced from apprentices to journeymen and then to masters, who owned their own stores and employed other men or women. Priests were tonsured, obtained their university degrees, were ordained, and were appointed to a benefice. Within the civil bureaucracy, a future corregidor might start as a *teniente* (lieutenant), receive a full appointment in a remote province, and ultimately reach a major city. Other groups had a more informal *asenso* (promotion system). Among merchants, immigrant nephews or youths from the same region in Spain or Portugal began as apprentices in the businesses of wholesalers. At some unpredictable but definite point, they joined their patrons as partners. Among hacendados the progress sometimes was from administration of a large estate to ownership. A person also might begin as a small rancher, gradually acquire agricultural land, and eventually end up as a sugar planter.

Opportunities for advancement among merchants and artisans are of special interest, because these were the two "middle" groups. Generally, the merchants were on the lower fringe of the elite, while artisans in the high-status trades were at the top of the non-elite. More evidence is needed to reach definitive conclusions. But Lugar and Ramírez point to an increasing social acceptance of merchants in the late eighteenth century. Johnson notes, however, that artisans could not enter the highest levels of society in the sixteenth century, and implies that this was still true for artisans as a group in the late eighteenth century.

Downward mobility was an important, if neglected, aspect of social stratification. The risks inherent in agriculture and trade resulted in a loss of status for particular hacendados or merchants. The limited number of bureaucratic posts kept high status aspirants on the sidelines as supernumeraries, waiting for an office to become vacant. The right of an officeholder to name his successor led to nepotism and restricted the entry of capable lower-status outsiders who sought to rise through a bureaucratic appointment. Certain groups experienced collective downward mobility, such as early sixteenth-century *encomenderos* (holders of grants of Indian tributaries) and the late-eighteenth century artisans. Social slippage was endemic to the laboring poor, whom seasonal employment and low wages periodically pushed into the ranks of the criminal and out-of-work.

There was also a degree of lateral mobility, or movement between occupations of similar social status. Among elites, encomenderos acted informally as merchants, as Lugar indicates. Hacendados also might be priests or civil bureaucrats. Domestic workers doubled as prostitutes. Slaves in charge of caring for animals or gathering fodder also acted as peddlers. The servant who also pilfered and sold his or her master's goods conforms to an elite stereotype which had some basis in reality.

Thus far, social stratification has been discussed in terms of horizontal distinctions, or distinctions which cut across society—race, occupation, property, and sex as linked to the other variables. If all distinctions within colonial society had been horizontal, however, it would have been highly fragmented and disparate—hardly a society at all. A significant component of the colonial order was institutions which integrated the horizontal groups. Corporations performed this function to some extent, as did family and godparent networks.

Corporations were organizations which represented individuals engaged in a particular form of activity: ecclesiastical, mercantile, artesanal. The corporations had internal and external duties. They regulated the behavior of their members, saw that they performed the services or produced the goods expected, contributed to their physical and spiritual well-being, and settled their legal disputes with one another. Such groups as the monastic orders, the *consulado* (merchant guild), and the artisan guilds held elections of officers, and, theoretically at least, were responsible for the welfare of all their members. These organizations also defended their group interests against the claims of other corporations, of the government, and of the unincorporated lower-status groups. Thus, corporations mediated between their membership and society at large.

Family and godparent ties meshed with corporate ties. While family structure varied considerably among social groups, the ideal consisted of a nuclear unit flanked by blood relatives, relatives by marriage, and godparent ties. The family was a vertical institution insofar as it brought together three or four generations and, through marriage or godparenthood, could unite different social classes. As Ramírez indicates, hacendados served as *compadres* (godfathers) of Indian children and as benefactors of their own landless, often needy, distant relations. Lugar shows that, through marriage, merchants, especially in the late eighteenth century, established upward links to the landed and mining elites. Of course, marriage also promoted lateral ties between members of society of equal status. These ties were economic as well as social. For merchants, risky and delicate transactions were entrusted more readily to a family member. Hacendados dowered their relatives and served as their sponsors in expectation of professional or political assistance. Like members of corporations, family members were bound by a combination of affection, self-interest, and common values.

Family and corporate groups exist in all societies but they are most prominent in a particular type of culture. The degree to which colonial Latin America conformed to this type, and the significance of such conformity, has been the subject of much debate. The model of society thought to have existed in the colonial period is sometimes called corporate or organic; it is contrasted with societies which are individualistic, competitive, and conflictive. Each model is identified with a prominent philosopher, the first with St. Thomas Aquinas, the second with John Locke. For Aquinas, the ideal society consisted of complementary subgroups, each performing a function essential to the general good and each related to the others in an hierarchical fashion. Balance and stability were valued over competition and change. Social peace took priority over social improvement. In this scheme there was to be no strong central government. Rather, the executive power delegated many of its duties to the corporations and family. The harmony sought in society as a whole was to exist within the subgroups as well. People, it was believed, should view themselves more as members of a group than as individuals, and, consequently, should cooperate to benefit their group.

Cities were to be the focal point of a corporate society, for it was here that activity was specialized sufficiently to permit functional organizations to exist. But in colonial Latin America cities were also the locus of the highest levels of central government. The viceroy, high courts, and treasury officers were, in theory, above the corporations and allowed to direct their activity. While cities were the places in which corporate impact on social structure was most pronounced, they were also the places where it met its greatest challenge. The particularism and personalism of the corporate groups clashed with the universalism and legalism of the state.

The balanced and orderly society envisioned in social thought and religion found some resonance in colonial urban life, but not to the degree, nor necessarily for the reasons, that its exponents prescribed. The rarity of collective, organized violence on the part of large groups does apear to corroborate the Thomistic model of harmony. The riot of 1692 in Mexico City is noteworthy for its exceptional character. Historians have commented frequently on the impressive stability of the colonial period, compared with the revolts of the nineteenth century and the revolutions of the twentieth century. For a society born of Conquest and enslavement, with no effective army until the late eighteenth century, the infrequency of large scale upheavals is quite striking. The equilibrium derived, to some degree, from the integration of non-elites into post-Conquest society through the church and through artisan guilds. As parishioners, sacristans, and servants, and as members of brotherhoods or recogimientos, the lower strata were drawn into rewarding contact with the elite. Within the household or fictive kin group, individuals might find a place denied to them outside. The slave *crias* (persons reared in another's house) of Brazilian households, as well as the racially mixed *huérfanas* (orphans) of Spanish American ones, sometimes received special treatment.

The absence of large-scale conflict cannot be attributed solely to successful integrative institutions, however. Elites relied on coercion, such as jails and forced labor, and on exile, to maintain their control. As Haslip-Viera describes, these procedures were systematized in the late eighteenth century, at the same time that social welfare institutions were expanded. Alienation, apathy, and the daily struggle to survive prevented the poor and people of color from launching a collective assault on the elites. City residents reduced to wearing clothing stolen from corpses and eating scraps and leftovers were not in a position to challenge the social order. In any case, the failure of any collective attack to materialize within the cities had as its counterpart endemic individual acts of violence and theft. As Archer shows, some of these assaults were perpetrated by the militias and regular troops, the very groups intended to prevent them. When civilians were beaten for failing to produce a cigarette light for a soldier, the prevalence of individualistic violence seems obvious.

With regard to relations within corporate and family groups, the performance of the harmonizing institutions seems also to have been mixed. The internal histories of monastic bodies suggest a reasonably orderly regulation of day-to-day affairs, punctuated regularly by intense battles between factions over particular issues. Lavrin describes the miniwar between the Clare nuns of Santiago and their Franciscan superiors. Ganster, too, stresses the quarrels that divided the monasteries and cathedral chapters. If this occurred within the bosom of the institution dedicated to the peaceful resolution of differences, what could be expected of corporations lacking an otherworldly outlook? Within the family, dispositions of wills and court divorce records testify, as might be expected, both to harmonious and conflictive family relations. The fact that wife-beating was the most common cause for womens' petitions for ecclesiastical divorce indicates the price that was paid, in some cases, for family life.[5]

Whatever the degree of conflict, group identity in colonial Latin America was very strong. Institutions composed of professionals, such as audiencia ministers, had a strong sense of esprit de corps. They were conscious of their distinct dress, training, and group purpose. Many bureaucrats did view office as a public trust, though others saw it as a means of self-enrichment. Artisans felt loyalty to their crafts. Nuns, as the only group of educated women in the colony, shared intellectual activities and read a common body of literature, as did the higher levels of the male religious. The brotherhoods and Third Orders were typically centers of collective feeling. In Bahia the Third Order of St. Dominic had a large representation of merchants and merchant clerks. While a sense of belonging is more difficult to document than racial exclusion or violence, there is no doubt that positive group identity formed an important part of colonial society. Families viewed themselves as a unit to which loyalty and service was owed. The achievement of one member affected the status of the rest, and the same was true of disgrace.

Corporate and family loyalties did not supplant individual striving, however. A tension existed between the two which was characteristic of this epoch. Masters exploited their journeymen workers. Merchants made fortunes at the expense of their fellows. Competition was not exalted as a virtue, but it was accepted as a fact of life. The law sanctioned the upward mobility of persons, as opposed to that of groups. Individual slaves could purchase their freedom, merchants could buy public office, and hacendados could receive titles.

The task of government was to oversee the activities of the corporations and resolve disputes between them. Public officials had a dual identity. They were members of corporate groups (audiencia, *cabildo* or city council) but they were also above them in a supervisory role. The civil government checked the clergy and exercised more control over less powerful corporations. The extent and nature of state power constitute a longstanding controversy in Latin American history. The Spaniards and Portuguese were the first nations to fashion an overseas imperial government. Their system was complex, sophisticated, and resilient. Some historians view the Iberians' state as an independent actor in colonial society, guided by a particular political philosophy and represented by men who, in many instances, brought order and justice to the colony.

Other historians see the state primarily as a captive of elite groups and a mere reflection of their selfish interests. Informal networks and personal contacts, they assert, were much more important than training, experience, or ideals in the operation of government. As the ties between public officials, and hacendados or merchants, indicate, the representatives of the state might be deeply enmeshed in the corporations they were supposed to regulate. In such circumstances the government could not function independently of local elites. But these important public official-local elite alliances do not completely account for the relations between state and corporations in urban society. During certain periods the state aggressively challenged some entrenched corporate groups. In late eighteenth century Spanish America, for example, the Bourbon government curtailed the authority of the church and some artisan guilds, while it promoted new corporations that, to some extent, supplanted them. The *tribunal de minería* (mining guild), the regional consulados, and, especially, the army fall in this category. When Archer describes the cabildos' resistance to the introduction of the military jurisdiction, he illustrates the clash between old and new corporate bodies. State policy might also change the internal character of corporate groups, as when the audiencias were again staffed with peninsular-born judges.

Urban social structure shaped and reflected the physical format of the city. There was a symbiotic relationship between the distribution of status and wealth among persons and the allocation and utilization of urban spaces. The location, design, and condition of homes, shops, churches, parks, markets, and public buildings provided the physical expression of the society they served. (See Figure 24.)

A fundamental distinction with regard to the appropriation of urban space was the division between public and private areas. The plaza at the entrance to the parish church or to a civic building was the place where all city residents mingled. Parks, like the Alameda in Mexico City, the Plaza Central in Buenos Aires, or the Jardim Público in Bahia, were the scene of wide-ranging physical contact, as were the interiors of churches, the markets, and the streets. The more public the area, however, the more it was used by lower strata individuals. In Brazil, for example, the Portuguese merchants sat in their shops and houses, while the Africans and Indians sold wares in the streets. For the unemployed, the public way had to double as a "private" space, as when this impoverished group slept on doorsteps or erected flimsy shelters against monastery walls. Likewise, the more private the space, the fewer and the higher-status were those individuals who had access to it. The *tertulias* or afternoon gatherings held in mansion drawing rooms were attended by a select group of professionals and socialites. The viceregal or episcopal audience, carried on in an elegantly appointed chamber, was a one-to-one conversation. A more extreme example of contact within private space was the exchange between the discalced nun and her visitor conducted through a curtain in the *locutorio* (room in the convent for receiving visitors).

Close physical proximity is synonymous with urban life, since the city is, by definition, a place where population density has reached a high level. In the sixteenth century the city founders had attempted to reduce spontaneous contact between persons of different races and occupations by designating areas of the city for habitation only by certain groups. As the essays indicate, they succeeded in one respect but failed in another. The urban elites, not to be equated with all urban whites, did remain in the center of town which originally had been set aside for them. Burkholder notes that high public officials often lived in, or within walking distance of, the public buildings in the heart of the city where they conducted their business. Ramírez describes the imposing mansions of the hacendados that were clustered around the main square, even in provincial towns where standards might be expected to be more relaxed. The initial scheme of residential segregation failed, however, to keep the non-elites out of the *traza* (central section of the city) and to restrict all whites to the central parishes. Laborers, especially, those whose services were needed daily—water carriers and porters as well as artisans, peddlers, keepers of animals, and of course, criminals and people looking for work—made their living from contact with the elite. The quest for segregation was not avid enough, nor the state machinery developed enough, to prevent these groups from moving into the central neighborhoods. Moreover, some members of the elite derived income from housing lower-status persons as tenants in the smaller rooms of their mansions or in nearby tenements. Finally, of course, the reliance on live-in Indian, racially mixed, or black servants made strict racial segregation impossible to accomplish even at the beginning of the colonial period. Despite the efforts of the legislators, the inner city was the setting of frequent and close contact among persons of diverse racial and occupational identities. However, according to plan, the periphery of the city, which included the truck farms and small grazing areas, was, until the nineteenth century, chiefly the domain of the non-elites. The upper strata only stayed in their suburban vacation homes during the summer season.

The colonial city was also distinctive in the proximity of work, living, and selling activity. As exemplified in the case of artisans, productive, domestic, and commercial functions occupied the same space. While some merchants and tradesmen were concentrated on a particular street and others dispersed in different neighborhoods, all were involved in multifunctional use of urban space. In this respect, the notion that the city was the locus of closely integrated relationships is confirmed.

Within the neighborhoods stood the households, groups of persons occupying a delimited space and linked by family or other ties. For the elite, the colonial household conformed to the pattern of a large diverse, social unit, long associated with Latin America. The middle and lower groups did not, however, fit the stereotype. In mid-eighteenth century Mexico City the mean size of upper-status households was 6.6 persons, while for lower-dependent households (the lowest status category), it was 3.4 persons. In late eighteenth-century Buenos Aires the average number of persons in elite households was 6.8, but for the non-elites it was only 5.6.[6] The larger households of the elites reflected the presence of more servants, retainers, and assistants. Elite households also might have more children. The households of laborers and the unemployed more often included people who had neither family nor servant relationships but were living together out of economic need.

Even elite groups which theoretically could not form biological nuclear families, clerics and nuns, duplicated the classic upper-strata households in other respects. Well-to-do priests would buy a *casa principal* or mansion and bring relatives, slaves, and younger clerics to live with them. Nuns had lay sisters and servants in their suites and received frequent visits from family members. The lay people and servants of the clerical household were comparable to the distant relations and domestics of the secular household. As in other elite households, convents had as their largest group of inhabitants persons who were not nuns, that is, not members of the nuclear "family." For the lower social groups, the same conditions that made it difficult to live in a house militated against the establishing of the classic household. Higher mortality rates from the epidemics, which took their worst toll among the malnourished and ill-clothed, also reduced the total number of inhabitants in their dwellings as well as the proportion of children.

In the late eighteenth century changes began to appear which later would alter urban spatial structure. In Mexico City planners wanted to extend the straight streets of the traza into the peripheral neighborhoods to permit "enumeration of blocks and houses, better government, and easier administration of last rites,"[7] a typical trilogy of motives for the Bourbon reformer. The government sought to open up the enclosed blocks of the ecclesiastical establishments in the center of town. The desire to systematize urban layout had its counterpart in the trend towards the separation of productive activity from residential or commercial activity. In Mexico City, for example, bread began to be sold not only at the bakeries where it was made but at designated retail outlets distant from the bakeries themselves. The rationalization and differentiation of functions associated with the modern era began in Latin America in the late colonial period.

The diverse activities of family, neighborhood, occupational and racial groups also reveal another facet of urban life. Few inhabitants were exclusively urbanites. Ties of different kinds bound them to the smaller centers and to the countryside. According to one school of thought, such ties were exploitative. Hamlets were dominated by villages, villages by provincial towns, and the towns, by the major cities, in a network which extended across the ocean to the imperial capitals of Lisbon and Madrid. The products of the haciendas, plantations, and mines, according to this viewpoint, were channeled to the cities, whose residents profited from their sale out of proportion to their own contributions. The most talented inhabitants were drawn off to the major centers, deepening the backwardness of the countryside. To what extent does the experience of urban social groups described in the volume substantiate this interpretation? While conclusions based on a study chiefly concerned with the internal life of the city must be tentative, the essays do suggest a more complex, multidimensional relationship than the interpretation permits. City and surrounding environment were engaged in an ongoing exchange, which certainly contained many elements of exploitation but also included a degree of reciprocity. Many urban residents moved back and forth between one setting and the other. Well-to-do hacendados and fazendeiros, with their city and country houses, bridged the two settings most comfortably, but their dual role as urbanites and country-dwellers was shared by other social groups. Suppliers of food, animals, and fodder, were daily or weekly visitors to the city. Junior merchants and peddlers, muledrivers and boatmen, students, public officials and clerics, all moved in and out in seasonal or career rhythms.

Indisputably, the city benefitted form the accumulation of wealth produced in the countryside. But urban centers were also magnets for rural migrants fleeing famine or unemployment. The migrants might constitute a burden on, rather than a contribution to, the urban economy, while their exodus might relieve the countryside of surplus labor. Moreover, the city periodically contributed some of its best educated or wealthiest residents to the hinterland. Urban elites preferred urban residence, but they did not necessarily attain their goal. Of the upper class youths who received their higher education in the cities, some married and remained there, while others left for the countryside, particularly in the early phase of their careers. Burkholder notes the *limeños* or natives of Lima who served as corregidores in various provinces. City born merchants often spent years of apprenticeship traveling around the countryside, acquainting themselves with rural markets. Most clergymen hoped to obtain a position in the city, but, as Ganster shows, these hopes were not always realized. Once the sale of office in the civil bureaucracy interrupted the promotion pattern which enabled officials to move from the country to the city, some of the educated elite were forced to remain in the less desirable regions. The city, therefore, did not simply draw off population from the countryside; it also sent some of its most enterprising residents to the rural areas.

The concept of the city as parasite, which has generated heated controversy, may have outlived its usefulness as a heuristic model, but it has contributed to an awareness of the importance of studying urban-rural relationships. The essays in this volume can serve as a point of departure for investigations of this subject. The essays also offer an introduction to the occupational and racial structure of different cities. Statistics on the demographic profile of cities prior to the mid-eighteenth century are rare, so authors writing about the earlier colonial period have drawn on such non-quantitative sources as notarial and Inquisition records. Future historians must refine the methodology of collecting and interpreting this data. For the later colonial period, religious and civil censuses are available and models for their analysis have been formed, but more such studies are needed before generalizations can be made with confidence.[8]

Within the city, the extent of social mobility, both upwards and down, is an area where additional research could be very revealing. The experience of immigrant merchant and artisan families over two or three generations is of special interest because these groups occasionally bridged the great social division between *gente decente* (gentlefolk) and *gente plebea* (common folk). Both birthplace and occupation were influential in determining whether a person could move from commoner to gentleman status. The self-perception of social groups is also a significant but still neglected area. Were the elites correct when they looked about them and saw a society organized by racial criteria? To what extent did the middle and lower strata share elite definitions of themselves as inferiors? The attitudes of groups toward their place in society is an intriguing subject which progress in other aspects of social history now makes it possible to consider.

The spatial dimension of social structure is a topic of much current interest which calls for integration with the traditional historiographical approaches. The location of buildings, markets, and parks reveals a great deal about urban society. The study of such structures allows the historian to ground a past society in its physical setting and to trace the natural connection between people and the place they inhabit. But a focus on urban space will not relieve the historian of the task of relating his or her findings to larger questions, which go beyond location theory and address economic and institutional relationships in their fullest dimension.

Chronologically, it is imperative that the period between 1550 and 1750, following city founding and preceding Bourbon and Pombaline reforms, receive more attention. Too often conclusions based on late eighteenth century materials are projected backwards in time to an era when the city may have been quite different. The traditional city of the early and middle colony requires more precise definition. Due to the abundance of statistical and other sources, much more is known about late colonial urban centers. For these cities it is now possible to relate such knowledge to key questions about the nature and pace of change at the end of the premodern age.

In conclusion, the field of colonial urban history has benefitted from the recent contributions both of social historians and of students of twentieth century cities. The traditional emphases of urban history—town founding, municipal government, architecture, and civic improvements—can now be fused in an interesting and novel fashion with such topics as informal political networks, social structure, and urban-rural relationships. The city has always been the meeting ground for diverse groups and ideas. The same now can be said for the history of the Latin American city.

Notes

1. John K. Chance and William B. Taylor, "Estate and Class in a Colonial City: Oaxaca in 1792," *Comparative Studies in Society and History* 19:4 (October 1977): 466, 475.

2. Patricia Seed, "Social Dimensions of Race: Mexico City, 1753," *Hispanic American Historical Review* 62:4 (November 1982): 580; Chance and Taylor, "Oaxaca in 1792," 475; César García Belsunce et al., *Buenos Aires: Su Gente (1800–1830),* vol. 1 (Buenos Aires; Emecé, 1976), anéjo 2.

3. Seed, Mexico City, 1753," 580, 582–83: Chance and Taylor, "Oaxaca in 1792," 475.

4. Robert McCaa et al., "Race and Class in Colonial Latin America: A Critique," *Comparative Studies in Society and History* 21:3 (July 1979): 431–32.

5. Sylvia Arrom, *La mujer mexicana ante el divorcio eclesiástico, 1800–1857* (Mexico City: SepSetentas), 28.

6. Dennis Nodin Valdés, "Beyond the Occupational Hierarchy: Household and Social Order in Mexico City, 1753," (Paper delivered at the Annual Meeting of the American Historical Association, Los Angeles, December 28, 1981), 3; Lyman Johnson and Susan Socolow, "Population and Space in Eighteenth Century Buenos Aires," in David J. Robinson, ed., *Social Fabric and Spatial Structure in Colonial Latin America* (Ann Arbor, Mich.: University Microfilms International, 1949), 365–66.

7. Alejandra Moreno Toscano, ed., *Ciudad de México: Ensayo de Construcción de una Historia* (Mexico City: Instituto Nacional de Antropología e Historia, 1978), 177.

8. Woodrow Borah, "Trends in Recent Studies of Colonial Latin American Cities," *Hispanic American Historical Review* 64:3 (August 1984): 553.

For Further Reading

For a good introduction to the history of colonial society, see James Lockhart, "The Social History of Colonial Spanish America," *Latin American Research Review* 7:1 (Spring 1972): 6–45. Other influential discussions of social structure are Lyle McAlister, "Social Structure and Social Change in New Spain," Howard Cline, ed., *Latin America: Essays on its History and Teaching,* (Austin, Tex.: University of Texas Press, 1973), and Mario Góngora, "Urban Social Stratification in Colonial Chile," *Hispanic American Historical Review* 55:3 (August 1975): 421–48. Magnus Mörner, *Estratificación social hispano-americana durante el período colonial* (Stockholm: Institute of Latin American Studies, 1980) reviews some of the debates in the field. Patricia Seed, "Social Dimensions of Race: Mexico City, 1753," *Hispanic American Historical Review* 62:4 (November 1982): 569–606; David Brading, *Miners and Merchants in Bourbon Mexico, 1780–1810* (Cambridge: At the University Press, 1971); César Garcia Belsunce et al., *Buenos Aires: Su Gente (1800–30)*, vol. 1 (Buenos Aires: Emecé, 1976); and Donald Ramos, "Vila Rica: Profile of a Colonial Brazilian Urban Center," *The Americas* 35:4 (April 1979): 495–526, use censuses to describe the social structure of the city. The growth of the field of social history has produced many monographs on urban and rural groups, too numerous to mention here. For an interesting collection of case studies, see David G. Sweet and Gary B. Nash, eds., *Struggle and Survival in Colonial America* (Berkeley: University of California Press, 1981).

Among Richard Morse's many writings on urban history, his "A Prolegomenon to Latin American Urban History," *Hispanic American Historical Review* 52:3 (August 1972): 359–94, is an unusual analysis of the cultural background of the Latin American city. Woodrow Borah, "Trends in Recent Studies of Colonial Latin American Cities," *Hispanic American Historical Review* 64:3 (August 1984), 535–54, brings reviews of research in this field up to date and offers a large bibliography. An approach which draws on location theory is David J. Robinson, ed., *Social Fabric and Spatial Structure in Colonial Latin America* (Ann Arbor, Mich.: University Microfilms International, 1979). Alejandra Moreno Toscano, ed., *Ciudad de México: ensayo de construcción de una historia* (Mexico City: Instituto Nacional de Antropología e Historia, 1978) includes excellent studies of the distribution of urban property and of social relations. For examples of ongoing work on Argentine, Mexican, and Venezuelan cities, see "Research in Progress on Urban History," *Latin American Research Review* 10:2 (Summer 1975): 117–31; Elizabeth Kuznesof, "Brazilian Urban History: An Evaluation," in *Latin American Research Review* 17:1 (Spring 1975): 263–75, gives an informative review of recent studies in that area. It is helpful to learn what students of modern Latin American cities consider important. For a good introduction to themes in contemporary research, see Jorge Enrique Hardoy and Carlos Tobar, eds., *La urbanización en América Latina* (Buenos Aires: Editorial del Instituto, 1969); and Manuel Castells, comp., *Estructura de clases y política urbana en América Latina* (Buenos Aires: Editorial S. I. A. P., 1974). In the *Journal of Urban History* 2:3 (May 1976), an interview with Richard Morse offers an interesting account of the evolution of the field of urban history and of the views of one of its notable practitioners.

Glossary

accesoria	small single room facing street; outbuilding
acordada	police force and summary court
agregado	a free (i.e., non-slave) servant, often a relative, living and belonging to a household
aguardiente (or aguardente)	literally firewater; brandy or spirits
alameda	tree-lined avenue or fashionable public walk
alcabala	excise or sales tax
alcalde	city councilman and magistrate
alcalde de barrio	a magistrate with policing powers for a neighborhood or urban district
alcalde de cuartel	see *alcalde de barrio*
alcalde del crimen	criminal judge of the audiencia
alcalde mayor	justice of the peace; governor and magistrate of a district.
alcalde ordinario	see *alcalde*
alcaldía mayor	district governed by an *alcalde mayor*
alférez (or alférez real)	royal standard bearer, member of the town council
alhóndiga	public granary
alguacil mayor	chief constable
alquilón	substitute paid to serve military duty
alternativa	a system of rotation in clerical office between Spanish- and American-born

ama de leite	wet nurse
antiguos ricos	literary, the old wealthy
ao gando	for profit
armação	
(pl. *armações*)	warehouse and processing plant for whale products
asenso	system of orderly promotion within the ecclesastical or civil bureaucracy
asiento	slave trade contract, usually a monopoly
audiencia	high court of Spanish America; also the territorial unit served by that court
auto-da-fé	public sentencing and punishment of persons convicted by the Inquisition
avería	tax on commerce, originally the maintain the fleet system
aviador	supplier of capital and goods for a mining or commercial venture
ayuntamiento	see *cabildo*
bacalhau	salted cod
bachiller	recipient of a first university degree
banda de recluta	military recruiting squad
baratillo	second-hand market; thieves' market
barrio	neighborhood or urban district
batallón de milicias	
urbanas del cuerpo de comercio	urban merchant militia unit
beata	a pious lay woman
beaterio	a home for pious lay women
caballero	member of a military order
cabildo	town council in Spanish America; ecclesiastical council
cabildo extraordinario	special town council meeting called in emergencies
caboclo	Brazilian of mixed white and Indian ancestry
cachaca	brandy
cacique cacica)	Indian of noble lineage
cadeirinha	palanquin chair
cafuzo	Brazilian of Indian and black ancestry
caja real	central royal treasury office
caja	branch treasury office
câmara	see *senado da câmara*
capellanía	endowed chantry fund
capim d'Angola	grass for animal fodder
capitão do assalto	leader of a slaving party

capitão do mato	catcher of runaway slaves
capitão mor	civil and military leader
carga	load of approximately 300 to 325 pounds
carne seca	jerked beef
carrera de Indias	Spanish fleet trade to the Indies
casa de contratación	Seville Board of Trade
casa de India	Lisbon Board of Trade for Africa and India
casa de niños expósitos	orphanage
casa poblada	inhabited or settled household
casa principal	principal family home; urban mansion
casa de vecindad	multiple family dwelling; colonial apartment house
castas	persons of mixed racial ancestry; caste
cédula	royal decree
cédula de gracias al sacar	royal license changing an individual's racial or civil status
censo	redeemable mortgage which pays a fixed annuity
chacra	
(or *chacara*)	small agricultural plot, usually on the outskirts of a city
chicha	alcoholic beverage made of fermented corn
chile	hot pepper
cofradía	lay confraternity or religious brotherhood
colegio	secondary school
comandante de armas	chief of a military division; often highest ranking local military officer
comendador	person who receives title of nobility
comerciante	import-export merchant
comisario	justice of the peace
comisario volante	commercial traveler
compadrazgo	ritual co-parenthood
compadre	godfather, ritual kinman
compañía	partnership or company
compañía de pardos libres	company of free mulattos
composición (de tierra)	payment to the crown to regularize land deeds
conde	count
congrua	
(or *congrua vida*)	guaranteed lifetime means of support for a clergyman
conquistador	conqueror of Spanish America
consulado	merchant guild
contador	comptroller of a government agency; accountant; auditor
contador mayor	chief accountant of the *tribunal de cuentas*

coro	choir-loft
corregidor	district governor and magistrate
corregimiento	district administered by a *corregidor*
correo mayor	postal agency; also postmaster general
coyote	person of Indian and black ancestry
cria	
(or *cria da casa*)	a slave or poor person, sometimes an illegitimate child, brought up in another person's home
criollo	a white person of American birth; a creole
cruzado	monetary unit in Brazil
cuadrillero	police patrol member
cuarto	small single room
curaca	Indian chieftain
curandero	herbal folk doctor
degredado	banished person
departamento de partos ocultos	hospital for "hidden," i.e., illegitimate, births
depósito	a fixed-term loan
diezmo	tithe
doblón	monetary unit
don	term of address used to denote a Spanish gentleman
doña	term of address used to denote a Spanish gentlewoman
doña de casa (or *dona da casa*)	female head of household
donatário	proprietary lord of a Brazilian province with extensive judicial and military powers
duque	duke
encomendero	holder of an *encomienda* grant
encomienda	grant giving the recipient permission to use Indian labor and receive tribute
entretenido	aspirant to a bureaucratic post; bureaucratic apprentice
escribanía	office of a notary public
escribano	notary public
escribano mayor	chief government notary
escudo	monetary unit
español	a person of Spanish birth or descent; a white
estancia	cattle ranch
europeo	one born in Europe, usually a Spaniard
factor	business manager in a government agency
falúa	small sailing barge
familiar	a lay representative of the Inquisition
fanega	dry measure of about 1.5 bushels
fanegada	unit of land measurement of about 7.16 acres

farinha	manioc meal
fazendeiro	large landowners
feitoria	temporary trading station along the coast of Brazil or Africa
fiscal	crown attorney
fora da cidade	outside of the city limits
fray	monk, religious brother
fuero	a set of legal privileges granted to certain groups
fuero eclesiástico	code of corporate privileges granted to churchmen
fuero militar	code of corporate privileges granted to the military
futura	right to a future appointment
gachupín	one born in Spain
galeota	large sailing barge
ganhadeira	black slave woman engaged in petty vending
gente de razón	literary, "people of reason"; white people
gente decente	refined people; those of the upper class; gentlefolk
gente plebea	common folk
gobernación	district or province
gobernador	governor and magistrate of a large district; sometimes a military commander also
habilitador	see *aviador*
habitante	inhabitant or resident
hacendado	owner of a large estate
hacienda	royal treasury; also a large landed estate
hacienda y trapiche	sugar estate with some lands reserved for grazing cattle
hermandad de la caridad	Brotherhood of Chairty
hidalgo	gentlemen; petty noble
hidalguía	petty nobility
hijo de provincia	a person born in Spain but reared and educated in the New World
hoja de servicio	service dossier
hombres nuevos	literally, new men; the new wealthy
homens bons	gentlemen
hospicio de pobres	poorhouse
huérfano (or *huérfana*)	orphan
intendente	provincial governor
irmandade	religious brotherhood in Brazil
jacal	shanty dwelling
jangada	triangular-sailed raft

juiz ordinário	city councilman and magistrate, in Brazil
junta do comércio	Lisbon Board of Trade
justicias	magistrates
juzgade de capellanías	Chantry Court
juzgado de la cruzada	Court of the Bulls of Crusade
juzgado de obras pías	Court of Chairtable Foundations
juzgado de testamentos	Probate Court
juzgado eclesiástico	Church Court
lépero	leper; criminal; member of a mob
licenciado	licentiate, a university degree after *bachiller*; the recipient of that degree
limeño	one born in Lima, Peru
limpieza de sangre	literary purity of blood; legal proof of old Christian lineage
locutorio	place in the convent for receiving visits
loja	store
mameluco	Brazilian of white and Indian ancestry
marqués	marquis
mascate	peddler
matlazahuatl	typhus (New Spain)
mayorazgo	entiled estate
mayordomo	manager; foreman
mercader	wholesale merchant until the eighteenth century; retail merchant thereafter
mercador de sobrado	member of the merchant elite of Bahia; literally a townhouse merchant
merced	a royal grant or gift
mesa de inspeção	Brazilian board of commodity inspection
mestizo	
(or *mestiço*)	person of Indian and white ancestry
metate y mano	grinding stones similar to a mortar and pestle
mita	system of forced Indian labor
mitayo	Indian draft laborer
mocamba	personal household servant
monja capellán	unendowed nun
monte de piedad	government sponsored pawn shop
moreno	a black, usually free
mucama	personal household servant
mulato	person of black and white ancestry
negros captivos armados	armed black captives
obraje	large workshop or factory usually engaged in weaving cloth
oficial real	government official; senior bureaucrat
oficio vendible y renunciable	public office which could be sold or transferred to a third party

oidor	judge on the high court
operario	laborer
oposición	formal competition for a clerical or university post
pan duro	stale bread
pardo	a mulatto, usually free; any person of color
the Parián	major Mexico City market
patio	central courtyard in a house
patria	motherland
patronato real	royal patronage; crown control of the church
peninsular	a person born on the Iberian Peninsula, i.e., Spain or Portugal
peruleiro	Portuguese merchant resident in Spanish America (often involved in smuggling)
peso escudo	monetary unit
peso fuerte	monetary unit
peso	monetary unit
petate	straw mat
plaza mayor	central square of a city
poncho	cloak or blanket
populacho	mob
porteño	a person born in Buenos Aires
portería	entry room in a convent
presidio	garrisoned frontier fortress
pretendiente	officeseeker
procurador geral	attorney-general of a Brazilian town council
propios y arbitrios	municipal income, consisting of rent for public lands and local taxes
pulpería	small grocery and bar
pulque	intoxicating beverage made from fermented maguey cactus juice
quilombo	runaway slave community
quintal	backyard
quitanda	market stall
radicado	non-native born permanent resident of a city
real	one-eighth of a *peso real*
real audiencia	high court of Spanish America
recogida	an inmate of a shelter for women
regidor	city councilman; alderman; member of the cabildo
regimento de artilharia auxiliar dos pardos	auxiliary artillery regiment of mulattos
regimiento	military regiment
regimento dos homens	

uteis do estado	tradesmen's militia unit of Bahia
reglamento de levas	code regulating military conscription
relação	Brazilian high court of appeals
relator	officer of the court
renta	source of revenue
repartimiento	system of Indian draft labor
repartimiento (*de bienes* or *de comercio*)	forced distribution and sale of goods to Indian communities
sacristán	sexton
sambo	person of Indian and black ancestry
sangre limpia	see *limpieza de sangre*
santa casa da misericórdia	House of Charity
sege	small carriage
senado da câmara	town council in Brazil
senhor	gentleman
senhor de engenho	lord of the sugar mill
serpentina	palanquin chair
sertão	arid backland of northeastern Brazil
sesmaria	immense tract of land granted to the first settlers by the Portuguese Crown
síndico	syndic, treasurer of a lay brotherhood
sitio	small country farm often producing foodstuffs for the city
sorteo	lottery
subdelegación	district or province under the eighteenth-century Intendency system
teniente	lieutenant; assistant
teniente de cura	assistant parish priest
tercio	bale weighing approximately 200 pounds
tercio de infantería de comerciantes	merchants' regiment
terço de Henrique Dias	Henrique Dias regiment
terços dos pardos	mulattos regiment
tertulia	afternoon gathering of friends
tesorero	treasurer of a government agency
título de suficiencia de lengua	priestly ordination stressing knowledge of an Indian language
tonsura	tonsure, clipping the back of the hair, a rite associated with entering the ecclesiastical state
toucinho	pork fat
tratante	petty merchant in regional trade; traveling merchant
traza	large plot of land; central zone of the city
tribunal de cuentas	royal accounting office; Tribunal of Accounts

tribunal de mineria	mining court and guild
tribunal del crimen	criminal chamber of the high court
vampiro de día	military levy patrol
vecino	property-owning permanent resident of a city
venda	shop
vereador	town councilman in Brazil
vicariato	vicarship
vida común	communal religious life
villa	Spanish town
virreina	viceroy's wife
visita general	general inspection
vivienda	apartment
yerba mate	Paraguayan herb tea
zambo	see *sambo*

Notes on Authors

Editors

Louisa S. Hoberman   (Ph.D., Columbia University) is an Assistant Professor at George Mason University. She is the author of a number of articles on colonial Mexican history, including studies on the bureaucracy, technology, and political theory. She is currently continuing her study of Mexican merchants in the seventeenth century and is beginning research on technology and urbanization in late eighteenth century Mexico.

Susan M. Socolow   (Ph.D., Columbia University) is an Associate Professor at Emory University. She is the author of *The Merchants of Viceregal Buenos Aires: Family and Commerce,* and a number of articles on aspects of colonial Argentina, including demography, women and crime, and independence. Her current research is on the bureaucracy of colonial Argentina.

Contributors

Christon I. Archer   (Ph.D., State University of New York, Stony Brook), has written extensively about the military in eighteenth century Mexico, Spanish-Indian relations along the Northwest American coast, and hospitals and disease. His publications include *The Army in Bourbon Mexico, 1760-1810.* Professor of History at the University of Calgary, he is continuing his study of Spanish-Indian relations and of the Royalist Army of New Spain during the Independence Period.

Mark A Burkholder (Ph.D., Duke University) has written extensively about the Spanish imperial bureaucracy. His books include *Politics of a Colonial Career: José Baquijano and the Audiencia of Lima* and *From Impotence to Authority: The Spanish Crown and the American Audiencias, 1687-1808* (co-author, D. S. Chandler). Professor of History at the University of Missouri-St. Louis, he is currently studying the Spanish courts in the eighteenth century.

Paul B. Ganster (Ph.D., University of California at Los Angeles), is Director of the Institute for Regional Studies of the Californias at San Diego State University. The author of several articles on the clergy and colonial society, he has also co-edited *Environmental and Bioresource Issues of the United States-Mexico Borderlands* (with Hartmut Walter).

Gabriel Haslip-Viera (Ph.D., Columbia University) is an authority on the criminality of the urban poor in colonial Mexico. His publications include "Criminal Justice and the Poor in Late Colonial Mexico City" in Ronald Spores and Ross Hassig, eds., *Five Centuries of Law and Politics in Central Mexico*. An Assistant Professor at the City College of New York, he is now doing research on Hispanics in New York.

Lyman L. Johnson (Ph.D. University of Connecticut) is an Associate Professor at the University of North Carolina at Charlotte. He has published a number of articles on artisans and slavery in eighteenth and nineteenth century Buenos Aires.

Mary Karasch (Ph.D. University of Wisconsin) is noted for her work on Africans and the slave trade in nineteenth century Brazil. Her publications include *Slave Life and Culture in Rio de Janeiro, 1808-1850* and a chapter in S. Engerman and E. Genovese, eds., *Race and Slavery in the Western Hemisphere*. An Associate Professor at Oakland University, she is now studying the social history of Goiás in the nineteenth century.

Asunción Lavrin (Ph.D., Harvard University) is an Associate Professor at Howard University. She has written several articles on women religious in colonial Mexico and on women in Latin American society. She is the editor of *Latin American Women: Historical Perspectives* and is currently researching feminism in Latin America.

Catherine Lugar (Ph.D., State University of New York, Stony Brook) has done extensive research on Portuguese and Brazilian merchants in the Atlantic trade. Her publications include "The Portuguese Tobacco Trade and Tobacco Growers of Bahia in the Late Colonial Period," in Dauril Alden and Warren Dean, eds., *Essays Concerning the Socio-economic History of Brazil* *and Portuguese India.* An Assistant Professor at the University of Connecticut, she is now researching the participation of women in Catholic Action groups in twentieth century Brazil.

Susan Ramírez (Ph.D., University of Wisconsin) is noted for her research on colonial landowners. Her publications include *Provincial Patriarchs: Land Tenure and the Economics of Power in Colonial Peru.* An Associate Professor at DePaul University, her current research is on the history of Indian societies in northern Peru.

Index

agriculture: commercial crops, 257, 260;
encomienda, 21, 36; food processing, 266–68;
landowner control of, 24; marketing, 268–71;
meat sources, 257–60; reforms, 37
animals: for food, 257–60; for transportation,
263
armed forces: the conquistadores, 199; economics
and, 216; merchant militia, 202–4, 214;
police, 206, 221, 277, 303–7; provincial
militia, 210–21; public violence, 197, 301;
recruiting for, 207–9, 211–15, 217; regular
army, 207–9; status, 216–21; urban militia,
201–6, 215; Wars of Independence, 222. *See
also* military, the
artisans: as businessmen, 245–47; economic
reform and, 244–48; guilds and cofradías,
227, 230–33; non-guild groups, 233; Indians
as, 231, 243; marriage, 244; military and,
246; race, 236–43; slaves as, 239; freedmen
as, 241; ranking of, 228; status, 234–36;
women as, 243
audiencias, 79, 88

barber-surgeons, 270
beaterios, 188
boatmen, 264
brotherhoods, 67, 141, 227
bureaucrats: audiencias, 79, 88; education for,
89, 92, 95; marriage, 97, 99; military and,
92, 100; offices of empire, 79, 81; sales of
offices, 82–94; opportunities for, 98;
patronage and, 82; provincial administration,
86–88; race, 89; reforms, 91; status, 77,
94–100; treasuries, 84–86; viceroyalties, 79,
92, 93. *See also* municipalities
business: artisans in, 245–47; centralization of
trade, 58, 61, 62; comerciante, 47;
consulados, 53; guilds and cofradías, 227,
230–33; landowners in, 22, 39; nuns in, 182;
obrajes, 243; priests in, 159; sales of
bureaucratic offices, 82–94; seaports, 48, 71;
sellers, 268–72; shopkeepers, 270–71;
suppliers, 52, 255–60. *See also* economics

Catholic church, the: charity, 67, 303; clergy,
138, 141; cofradías, 67, 232; crime and, 301;
landownership and, 31, 33, 159, 182; nuns,
166, 175; organization, 140–42; patronage,
140; race, 144, 147, 151; reforms, 148, 166,
184; Third Orders, 67. *See also* churchmen *and*
nunneries
churchmen: career patterns, 154–58; the clerical
state, 142–43; cofradías, 67, 232; congruas,
146; education, 144; factions, 149; family,
150, 160; Indians as, 146; ordination,
143–47; as patrons for nunneries, 171; parish

347